Archaeology
and the
New Testament

Archaeology

and the

New
Testament

John McRay

BAKER BOOK HOUSE
Grand Rapids, Michigan 49516

Fifth printing, April 2003

Printed in the United States of America

Library of Congress Cataloging-in-Publication Data

McRay, John.
    Archaeology and the New Testament / by John McRay
       p. cm.
    Includes bibliographical references and index.
    ISBN 0-8010-6267-5
    1. Bible. N.T.—Antiquities. 2. Mediterranean Region—Antiquities. 3. Christian
Antiquities—Mediterranean Region. I. Title.
    BS2406.5.M37 1990
    225.9'3—dc20   91-11663
                                                        CIP

Unless otherwise noted, all Scripture references are taken from the Revised Standard
Version of the Bible, copyright 1946, 1952, 1971, and 1973 by the Division of Christian
Education of the National Council of the Churches of Christ in the United States of
America. Other versions cited include the King James Version (KJV), the New American
Standard Bible (NASB), and the New English Bible (NEB).

Designated photographs are used by permission from the National Geographic Society
and the Holy Shroud Guild. All other photographs are by the author. Adapted
diagrams are used courtesy of the Israel Exploration Society in Jerusalem and the
American School of Classical Studies at Athens.

The research for and writing of this volume were funded in part by grants from the G.
W. Aldeen Fund; the Alumni Association, Wheaton College; William J. Wilson, Jr.,
Nashville, Tennessee, and Mr. and Mrs. Charles McRay, Fort Smith, Arkansas.

For information about academic books, resources for
Christian leaders, and all new releases available from
Baker Book House, visit our web site:
            http://www.bakerbooks.com

To my wife,
Annette,
with whom I have shared the hilltops

Contents

List of Illustrations

Diagrams

Maps

Foreword

To the Christian who takes biblical faith seriously, "the Word became flesh and dwelt among us" (John 1:14) not only in God's incarnated Son, Jesus Christ, but also in the pages of what we have come to call the Holy Bible. As with the historical Jesus, his New Testament is nearly two thousand years old. The latter survives in documents that go back in many cases to within a few generations of the autographs. But they are still in a language that is quite foreign to most of us and written by and to people whose geographical, historical, and sociological context was quite different from our own. How then can we put ourselves back into the time, place, and circumstances that enable us to more fully understand the New Testament and more accurately interpret it for our time?

Enter the pertinent discoveries of archaeology. The results of the archaeological fieldwork carried out in the lands bordering the Mediterranean Sea in the last two hundred years, but especially since World War II, have probably done more than any other discipline to make the New Testament "live" for twentieth-century Christians.

During my graduate school days I was digging at a spring in the small West Bank village of Khirbet el-Kom. I happened upon a Hellenistic-age dwelling whose foundations and floors were perfectly preserved. On the floor of one of the rooms lay a cache of ostraca (broken pieces of pottery used for writing) belonging to a peddler. How did I know? Because one of the ostraca contained a bilingual (Edomite and Greek) transaction between an Edomite named Qos-yada' and a Greek named Nikeratos. Nikeratos borrowed 32 drachma from Qos-yada', who was called a *kapelos*. That is a *hapex legomenon* in the New Testament, a Greek word which appears only once. Found in 2 Corinthians 2:17, the King James Version of the Bible translates *kapelos* as "corrupt," while several modern versions translate it as "peddle." The word is well-known, however, in Greek literature, inscriptions and papyri, where it is normally translated "retailer," "shopkeeper," "peddler" or "huckster." Inasmuch as nowhere in the group of ostraca I found was there a commodity mentioned, but rather money was being given and received, probably as loans, I suggested that the technical definition of a *kapelos* must be broadened to incorporate moneylending. So you see that even chance archaeological finds can help lexicographers more carefully define the semantic range of words used in the original languages of the Bible.

What my find did for 2 Corinthians 2:17, John McRay's book does for the whole New Testament. He has marshaled archaeological evidence that will help a student of the New Testament to better understand, and thus accurately apply, its message. The book you hold is detailed, comprehensive, authoritative, and up-to-date. Because of the rapid pace of discovery, it is the nature of books on archaeology that they are always out-of-date. So whatever source you have used, you need this book—not only to learn of the latest finds and their significance, but just as important, to be attuned to concerns current in approaches to the study of the Bible. In my estimation, no one is better qualified to do this than John McRay. For years he has personally been involved in significant field research and publication. He has an enviable reputation as a teacher and lecturer, now connected with Wheaton College—an institution known for biblical archaeology. This volume profits from Professor McRay's personal photographs and acquaintance with the lands of the New Testament. And he has used all the best original and secondary sources at his disposal. His footnotes offer a gold mine for further research and study.

The Preface tells you succinctly what to expect, as well as what not to expect, from this book. John McRay is a trustworthy guide through the dynamic relationship of archaeology and the New Testament. Perusing this book will send you back to the New Testament afresh with new ability to hear its message.

Lawrence T. Geraty
President and Professor of Archaeology
Atlantic Union College
South Lancaster, Massachusetts

Summer, 1991
In celebration of the centenary
of the birth of William Foxwell Albright,
the "Father of Biblical Archaeology"

Preface

It may seem unnecessary to add to the virtual avalanche of books and periodicals on archaeology and the Bible issuing from modern presses. The justification for this work is in the scope of its contents. For my own classes in archaeology and the New Testament I have searched without success for a text that would include both up-to-date site information and also important information about the overall archaeological enterprise—the methodology of excavation, the nature of period cultural institutions, the contributions of archaeology to our understanding of the transmission of the New Testament text, and the primary sources that allow the reader to expand understanding of special interests.

It is evident that a book with such goals will not be able to include all sites mentioned in the New Testament, and my intent is not to produce an encyclopedia of archaeological sites. Even sites where considerable archaeological work has been conducted, such as Cyrene, in North Africa, must be omitted because they are mentioned infrequently or are comparatively less important to the task of illustrating and understanding the message of the New Testament. Neither is it my intention to attempt to "prove" the truth of the New Testament or to solve complex problems arising from the study of the New Testament text and the practice of modern field archaeology. I hope, rather, to provide information that will enable others to better understand and apply biblical teaching.

The study of archaeology has moved in the late twentieth century from a preoccupation with chronology and architecture to a sociological concern. Where appropriate, I have addressed the new concerns regarding what excavated remains may tell us of how ancient people lived and interacted with their environment. However, my aim is to provide material useful to others in their own study of ancient culture, so I have avoided embarking on sociological analyses myself. That would require another volume. Consequently, little space is given to the analysis of pottery, coins, and other cultural artifacts. This is readily available in standard works on everyday life in Bible times.

In these pages we invite readers to step inside the current study of archaeology as it relates to the New Testament period. It is for those who wish a convenient, one-volume introduction to the field. If it stimulates its readers to further research, reflection, and respect for the New Testament as the historical revelation of the Word of God, it will have fulfilled its author's hopes.

A book that has resulted from more than twenty years of research and four years of writing owes a debt to many people. Chief among these is my wife, Annette, who has shared these years with me as a traveling companion, fellow "digger," cherished advisor, diligent scholar, and patient proofreader. Without her, the book would never have been completed.

The research required has been expensive, requiring frequent travel through the Mediterranean and Middle East countries. Among those who have made substantial financial contributions to these travels, I want to thank William J. Wilson, Jr., of Nashville, Tennessee, who contributed much and often to my work and made possible my acceptance of an appointment to the W. F. Albright Institute of Archaeological Research, Jerusalem, in 1972–73.

The simultaneous appointments my wife and I shared in 1988 at the American School of Classical Studies in Athens, Greece, during my sabbatical were made possible by the kindness of Wheaton College and its Alumni Association. Research done in Italy and Israel in 1987 was made possible by a financial grant from the G. W. Aldeen Memorial Fund at Wheaton College.

Deep appreciation is also expressed to Charles and Linda McRay of Fort Smith, Arkansas, whose unsolicited generosity made possible the extension of the sabbatical into the summer, including considerable travel in the Greek islands and a month's residence on the Island of Santorini, where the chapter on Greece was written.

My indebtedness reaches back to 1967 when L. T. and Betty Moss of Little Rock, Arkansas, graciously sent me on my first study trip to Israel and the Middle East, shortly after the Six-Day War.

Unless otherwise noted, photographs, maps, and diagrams are mine. Maps and diagrams were initially put on computer from my drawings by Janet Seaberg, secretarial coordinator of the graduate school division of the Biblical, Theological, and Archaeological Studies Department of Wheaton College. My graduate assistant, Robert Gladstone, diligently worked on the input of data into the computer and assisted with proofreading.

I am especially grateful for my appointments to the W. F. Albright Institute of Archaeological Research in Jerusalem, and the American School of Classical Studies in Athens, which provided access to their extensive libraries, as well as to museums and archaeological sites of Israel and Greece. My service on the boards of trustees for the Albright Institute, the American Schools of Oriental Research, and the Near East Archaeological Society have facilitated my access to materials and people which have contributed to the effectiveness of my research. Working as an archaeological consultant to the art department of *National Geographic Magazine* has provided many opportunities to enrich the research on this book. Prompt response to my requests for ancient road maps of Israel and Asia Minor is but one example of the magazine's gracious assistance. Frequent consultations with Robert Teringo and Karen Gibbs of *National Geographic* contributed to important aspects of this work, as have lengthy conversations with Richard Batey of Rhodes University in Memphis, Tennessee.

Leslie Shear of Princeton University and John Camp of the American School of Classical Studies in Athens, directors of the excavation of the agora in Athens, and Charles Williams, II, director of the excavations of Corinth, also gave valuable comments and help during my tenure at the American School. I am grateful for the privilege of having worked as a supervisor on excavations in Israel at Caesarea Maritima under the direction of Robert J. Bull, at Sepphoris under the direction of James Strange, at Herodium under the direction of Ehud Netzer, and briefly at Shechem with William Dever.

This book is the product of relationships and experiences shared with all of these people and many others over many years in a field of study and a part of the world we all love and about which we are deeply concerned.

John McRay
Wheaton College
Wheaton, Illinois

Introduction
The Role and Method
of Archaeological Excavation

The Role of Archaeology in New Testament Studies

We begin our exploration by noting some of the invaluable contributions that archaeological investigations have made to the study of the New Testament. First, archaeology has enlightened our understanding of the geographical setting in which some biblical events occurred. For example, consider the enigmatic statements in the Gospels that when Jesus was going into Jericho (Luke 18:35), and when he was coming out of Jericho (Mark 10:46), he healed blind Bartimaeus. Excavations there have shown that Jericho, like such other sites as Beersheba, flourished in different periods of history and that its center varied by as much as several miles. The palace complex of Herod the Great was south of the Old Testament site, and the New Testament city is yet to be found. Jesus may have been going out of one area of Jericho into another when he healed Bartimaeus.

Similarly, the place where Jesus, having encountered a demoniac who lived among the tombs, cast the demons into a herd of swine which ran into the Sea of Galilee and drowned, is said in variant readings to have been Gergesa, Gerasa, and Gadara (Matt. 8:28–34; Mark 5:1–13; Luke 8:26–39). Excavations have been done at Gerasa (modern Jerash in Jordan) and at Gadara (modern Umm Qeis in Jordan), revealing remains of cities from the Roman period. However, both are miles from the Sea of Galilee so the swine could not have run off a cliff into the sea from these locations. The solution to the problem, however, may have come to light in 1970, when a road was being constructed on the east side of the sea. The discovery of a Byzantine church built over an earlier burial vault indicates a settlement of long standing. Since the Byzantines were wont to mark the sites of Christian traditions by constructing churches, and since this is the only recorded visit of Jesus to the "other side of the sea," it is most likely that the site of this Byzantine church, modern Kursi, was ancient Gergesa. It is the only place on the entire east coast where a cliff comes out to the sea and tombs have been found in the adjacent hills.

Second, archaeological excavation has contributed to our understanding of the religious milieu of the New Testament world. The extensive Gnostic library that was found at Nag Hammadi in Egypt in 1945 has provided us with new information regarding heresy in the early church and about the nature of the canon of the New Testament at this time.[1] The discovery of scores of pseudepigraphical and apocryphal books testifies to extensive literary activity in this part of the Christian world in the second century A.D. And then in 1947 and the years immediately thereafter, a similar cache of documents, which shed a great deal of light on the nature of Jewish sectarianism in Palestine at the time of Christ, was found in eleven caves near Qumran on the northwest shore of the Dead Sea. These documents have been influential in the current reassessment of Jewish religion during the time between the Old Testament and the New. Any notion of a monolithic Judaism during this period has been decisively dispelled. We now see Palestine as a veritable crucible of religious ideas and philosophies about everything from the Law to the Messiah. However, comparatively little light has been shed on the New Testament itself, except for the background of the ministry of John the Baptist.

Third, the results of archaeological excavations help to constrain the imaginations of scholars who would mythologize the New Testament. Finds inevitably keep returning biblical studies to the realm of history and historical geography. The discoveries at Qumran have shown that the "dualism" (e.g., between light and darkness) in the writings of John goes back to the first century B.C., rather than to the second century A.D. The mythological presuppositions of Rudolf Bultmann regarding the Gospel of John are no longer so compelling. Discoveries of the Well of Jacob (John 4:12), the Pool of Bethesda (5:2), the Pool of Siloam (9:7), the probable location of the Gabbatha or stone pavement near the Jaffa Gate where Jesus appeared before Pilate (19:13), and the name of Pilate himself on a stone in the Roman theater at Caesarea,[2] have lent historical credibility to the text of John. The name of Erastus (Rom. 16:23) has turned up on an inscription in the stone pavement near the large theater in Corinth. Gallio (Acts 18:12) left an inscription bearing his name in Delphi, and reference to Claudius's expulsion of the Jews from Rome (Acts 18:2) appears in the *Teaching of Addai*,[3] Orosius's *Seven Books of History Against the Pagans*,[4] and Suetonius's *Lives of the Caesars*.[5] Even the name of Quirinius (Luke 2:2) has turned up recently on a coin.[6] These are but a few of the examples that could be produced which put New Testament contexts squarely in the stream of history and geography.

Finally, archaeological excavation often recovers the evidence necessary for reconstructing the biblical text. The most recent and perhaps most important examples are the Egyptian papyri (Colt, Oxyrhynchus, John Rylands, Chester Beatty, Bodmer, etc.). These portions of the New Testament text, written in Greek and dating from the late first to the mid-third century, have radically altered our understanding of the Greek text (see chap. 11).

The Limitations of Archaeology as Proof

While archaeology has made enormous contributions, it cannot prove the New Testament to be either theologically inspired or historically accurate. Those who make such demands from the discipline are going beyond the purpose of excavation and inadvertently betray the uncertainty of their own approach to religion. The New Testament does not need external confirmation of its theological truths and its historical references in order to achieve the purpose for which it was written and canonized—the production of faith in the hearts of its readers (John 20:30–31). Seldom does a discovery bear so directly on a written text that it may be said to confirm (or refute) that text.

We are reminded of Heinrich Schliemann, whose search for Troy was driven by a passion to demonstrate the historical accuracy of Homer's *Iliad*. This same passion led him to erroneously exclaim that he had gazed on the face of Agamemnon when he found a gold mask at Mycenae. Schliemann did find Troy; he did not, however, prove the *Iliad* to be true, but only accurate in a particular geographical reference. The identification and excavation of such New Testament sites as Corinth, Philippi, Thessalonica, Ephesus, Caesarea, Capernaum, Jericho, and Samaria have greatly illuminated our understanding of historical settings for events described in the text, but they have not proven the New Testament to be correct. Proving that Mecca and Medina existed in the sixth and seventh centuries in western Arabia does not prove that Mohammed lived there or that the Koran is true.

The historical references in the New Testament, which some seek to verify through archaeological excavation, are sometimes forced into molds they were never intended to occupy.[7] Its authors never intended to write history in the way Collingwood, Toynbee, Churchill, and Durant wrote it, nor for that matter, in the way Thucydides, Herodotus, and Tacitus wrote it. While all history is written from a historian's point of view, and none can be considered unbiased, it was never the purpose of the writers of the New Testament to fill the role of historian.[8] Even Luke, who did careful research before writing (1:1–4), wrote more as a theologian than a historian.[9] Yet Sir William Ramsay was as intrigued with proving Luke's historical trustworthiness as Schliemann was with Homer's, and spent many years in the Mediterranean world in an effort to vindicate the accuracy of Luke-Acts as history and geography.[10]

Biblical Archaeology

When we speak of "biblical archaeology," we must be aware of the limitations inherent in the use of the term, especially vis-à-vis the New Testament. The New Testament covers only about fifty years, as opposed to about fifteen hundred in the Old Testament. Further, the New Testament is largely limited to the immediate Mediterranean world; the Old Testament, by contrast, covers the whole of the Middle East.

We must also bear in mind that "biblical archaeology" does not have reference to an independent discipline nor to a methodology peculiar to the Bible. Like classical archaeology, biblical archaeology exists not as a separate discipline, but as a field of inquiry within the general discipline of archaeology. To dig Corinth to ascertain information about its relation to the New Testament is as legitimate an enterprise as to excavate the site to determine its relation to the Peloponnesian wars in classical history. To refer to such an excavation as either biblical or classical is to describe the field of inquiry rather than the general discipline or the methodology.

The Technology of Excavation

The methods now used in archaeological excavations to retrieve the past are as different from those that were used fifty years ago as modern automobiles are from the Model-T Ford built in 1903. There is constant change, usually for the better, in the maturing discipline of scientific excavation.[11] Subsurface

Richard Batey reads a printout from subsurface interface radar at Sepphoris (Copyright, National Geographic Society).

interface radar, for example, was introduced at Sepphoris by Richard Batey and was used also at Lahav in southwest Judea.[12]

Both ground and aerial photogrammetry are now being used to produce extremely accurate three-dimensional drawings of balks (vertical walls of soil left around an excavation plot), tomb façades, and other structures as well as to create more accurate maps. Magnetometers and resistivity-measuring instruments locate underground discontinuities in much the same way as does subsurface radar. Infrared photography is used to locate stones beneath the ground (stones and the soil around them give off different amounts of heat). It is also used to enhance the study of faded frescos and similar projects. Where economics allow, laser-guided and computerized transits have replaced the old models, thus providing faster, more accurate surveys.

Small computers and microfiche systems are being used in some excavations to record data and bring compact but thorough libraries into the field.[13] Neutron-activation analysis determines the origin of the clay used in pottery. Thin-section and petrographic analyses of the temper and content of the clay enable us to pinpoint the geographic distribution of the wares more effectively.

It is customary to find a number of specialists on any excavation. Physical anthropologists process human and animal bones to discover details like age and sex. Paleoethnobotanists compare the carbonized remains of ancient plants that have been found by a new technique of flotation with modern plants that grow in the area around the dig. Pollen samples, climatic conditions, the effect of grain on the teeth of ancient people, and similar data come within the scope of such specialists. Cultural anthropologists study the social milieu, the horizontal perspective, and provide valuable insights into the historical or vertical relationships between the strata of ancient mounds. The "new archaeology," which has reached the Mediterranean world from New World archaeology in America is largely responsible for the gradual change in the methodology of excavation. Numismatists read the inscriptions on coins and thus provide more-precise dating than is presently available through ceramic typology. Carbon 14 is used, though with decreasing frequency and correspondingly less confidence, to provide dates for organic material, while potassium-argon dating is used for the much older inorganic materials. It is probably self-evident that today's archaeologist does not need to be a master of all these scientific processes. Indeed one cannot be.

Much of this technology is available only after the dig is over and the materials have been brought to laboratories where analyses can be made. Some of the techniques, for example, ground photogrammetry, are so expensive as to be prohibitive. Accordingly, a number of field archaeologists, recognizing that there is an obligation to dig sites and strata that justify the time and expense, are urging more focus on excavations.[14] It should be remembered that only about two hundred of the approximately five thousand sites in the Holy Land have been excavated.[15] As of 1985, about ten thousand sites in Mesopotamia were officially listed as possibilities for excavation.[16] Some compromise must be reached between the desire to retrieve every bit of available information a site can produce and the pragmatic realization that such thoroughness means few sites will ever be excavated. There are only so much time and money available!

The Basic Method of Excavation

Methods vary to some degree from site to site according to the archaeological period. However, there is a basic scenario that characterizes most excavations: choosing and locating the site, making a survey of the surrounding area, excavating a part of the site, and dating and publishing the material.

Choosing and Locating the Site

The first step involves choosing a site for excavation. In some cases, once the site has been decided, it may be necessary to search for and identify its precise location. Today's methods, involving great expense for equipment, labor, and publication, demand the selection of a site (or portion thereof) that can be successfully dug *and* published. Some sites, because of their very size and importance, are the objects of ongoing problem solving digs—Rome, Athens, Corinth, Ephesus, and Jerusalem are examples.

In ancient times the choice of a site upon which to build a city was governed largely by pragmatic concerns:

1. A strategic, readily defensible location was crucial; this usually meant trying to build on a natural hill.
2. Easy access to a defensible water supply was important for daily life and particularly in time of siege. Water is not found on the tops of hills, so a vertical shaft sometimes had to be cut to create a reservoir deep down at the bottom. Then a tunnel dug horizontally brought water from an underground spring outside the city wall to the reservoir. The best-known examples of this are at Megiddo, Hazor, Gezer, and Jerusalem. By Roman times, when the New Testament was written, the legions had secured the *Pax Romana* in the Mediterranean world, and such secret water systems were no longer needed. Water was now brought openly from source to city on huge, well-constructed aqueducts for which the Romans became famous.
3. Close proximity to major roads was important for commercially oriented cities. The Via Maris (the Way of the Sea) and the King's Highway in Palestine were dotted with cities, and every pass into the Jezreel Valley in Galilee had a settlement at the entrance (e.g., Legio, Scythopolis). When the major roads or caravan routes changed, the results were often disastrous for a city, as when the trade routes shifted to the north through Palmyra, turning Petra, south of the Dead Sea, into a ghost town inhabited only by local bedouin.
4. The need for food necessitated the location of a town either near a major road system, so that food could be transported to the site, or in close proximity to good agricultural land, where the food could be grown and animals raised.

If the location of a particular site is already known, the problems of the selection stage are minimized. There has never been any doubt about the location of Athens or Jerusalem. However, if an archaeologist wants to dig a site mentioned in the Bible but not yet identified in the land, diligent attention must be given to three factors:

1. *Geographical.* Where is the site located in extant literature? Does the topography offer corroboration?

2. *Linguistic.* An analysis of the name of the site has to be made. The name *Sychar* is preserved in the name *'Askar,* and that of Nain in modern Nein. Jerash is ancient Gerasa, while Lod is New Testament Lydda. And modern Saffuriyeh clearly preserves the name of Sepphoris.

3. *Archaeological.* Is there any evidence, such as portions of structures visible above ground, that a site actually existed in the area during the period under consideration?

Surveying the Site

Once a site has been selected for excavation, a thorough survey of the surrounding territory puts the site in its proper geographical and historical setting. It has now become standard practice to map the general area around an excavation,[17] including a survey of structures and artifacts. There is some disagreement as to whether extensive or intensive surveys are better.[18]

In addition to looking for potsherds on the site, archaeologists must take into account nearby water sources, roads, agricultural conditions including crop cultivation and animal husbandry, the defensive capabilities of the site, economic resources such as deposits of metal ore, and the general cultural environment prevalent in the region. Aerial photography, ground photography, underwater photography where appropriate (such as at Caesarea Maritima), underground interface radar, and proton magnetometers are only a few of the techniques and devices now being used in such surveys.

Excavating the Site

Heinrich Schliemann discovered that a large truncated cone of earth at Troy was actually buried cities that had been destroyed and rebuilt so many times that an artificial mound had been created. The reasons that led ancient settlers to establish a city on a particular site also led to repeated resettlements after the site was destroyed. In course of time, the various strata produced by multiple rebuildings formed a mound. Since Schliemann's work at Troy, efforts have been made to identify such mounds, which number more than ten thousand in the Levant and Mesopotamia, and several thousand in Turkey and Greece. They are called tells. Evidence that this phenomenon was unknown for centuries can be found in the King James Version of the Bible, which translates Joshua 11:13 "But as for the cities that stood still in their strength, Israel burned none of them." We now know that the Hebrew word translated "strength" (*tēl*) means "mound"; later versions such as the New Revised Standard translate more accurately: "But Israel burned none of the towns that stood on mounds."

The height of mounds at sites such as Tel Beth-Shan witness a long, cyclical history of occupation, destruction or abandonment, and rebuilding.

The discovery of the reason for the rise of tells was of tremendous importance for field archaeology, prompting the development of a methodology of excavation based on analysis of the stratigraphy of a site. There are a number of fundamental presuppositions of stratigraphical digging:

1. The latest strata are at the top and the earliest at the bottom, so that one digs history backwards, beginning with the present and ending with the earliest occupation of the site.
2. All available evidence that can be obtained from each stratum within reason (recognizing constraints of time and money) must be carefully recorded and analyzed.
3. Only representative portions of a site should be excavated; and, therefore, a careful selection should be made. Removal of an entire stratum would prevent later investigation and application of new techniques. Almost all the older excavations have been redone in recent years.
4. The strata are not uniform, like layers of a cake, but vary in depth from place to place on a tell. Thus, transitions from stratum to stratum, and from phase to phase within a stratum, must be carefully identified, examined, and dated. Differences of opinion exist as to the accuracy of each of the various methods used for dating. Kathleen Kenyon criticized the tendency among American and Israeli archaeologists to date a structure from the material found on the floor rather than the material beneath the floor, under the walls, and in the trenches beside the walls.[19]

5. Ceramic typology helps to establish the chronology of the strata, since the forms of ceramic vessels changed from time to time in the same way that automobile models have changed. In addition to changes in style there are also discernible differences in the content of the clay and the method of firing.

One of the best examples of a New Testament city located on a large tell is Sebaste (Samaria). It was rebuilt over the ruins of several previous periods. One of the largest excavations ever undertaken in Israel was done here; but, fortunately, the mound was much too large to dismantle, and only selected areas were dug. Sebaste provides an interesting example of stratigraphic excavation, which was recently discussed in an excellent article by Gus Van Beek of the Smithsonian.[20]

It should not be assumed, however, that stratigraphy is to be found only in tells. There are many multilayered sites in the Mediterranean world which are not elevated. Among low-level settlements are Rome, Ostia, Pompeii, Herculaneum, Corinth, Philippi, Ephesus, Sardis, Pergamum, Hierapolis, Capernaum, Caesarea, Magdala, Chorazin, Gerasa, and Baalbek.[21] Although they do not stand on tells, most of these sites are stratified, to some extent at least. Caesarea Maritima, which stands virtually at sea level, contains Hellenistic, Roman, Byzantine, Arabic, and Crusader levels. The reason most of these sites never developed into tells is probably that they had room to expand hori-

Figure 1
Stratigraphy of a Tell

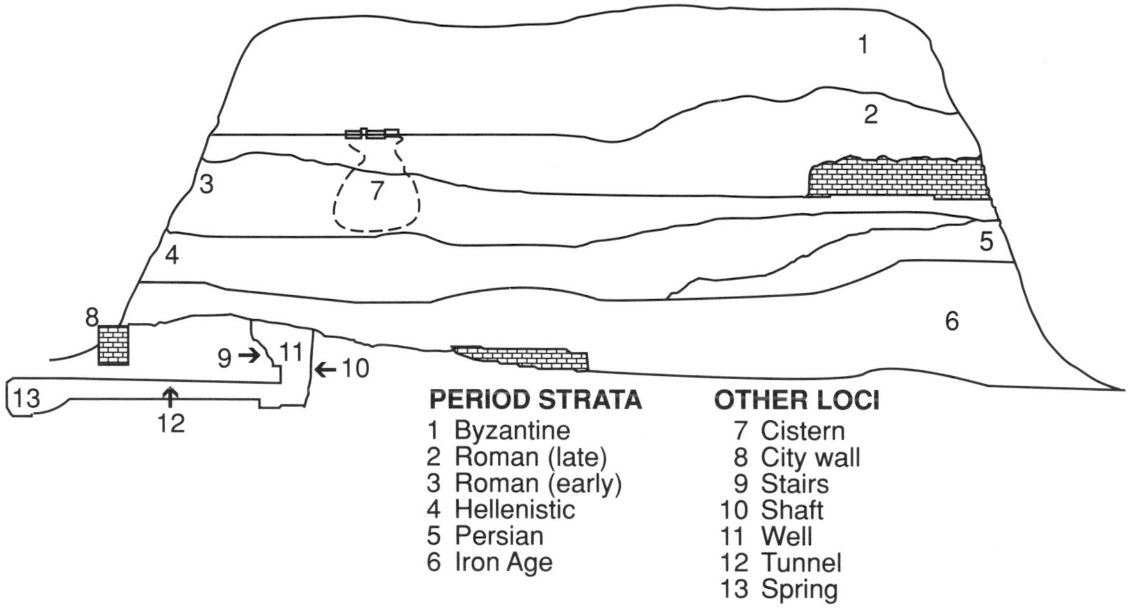

PERIOD STRATA	OTHER LOCI
1 Byzantine	7 Cistern
2 Roman (late)	8 City wall
3 Roman (early)	9 Stairs
4 Hellenistic	10 Shaft
5 Persian	11 Well
6 Iron Age	12 Tunnel
	13 Spring

A small table holds most of the equipment needed by this worker. Behind him is the balk.

zontally without serious problems. My examination of more than twenty-five manuals on archaeology revealed no mention of low-level sites in the discussions of stratigraphical methods. In the one hundred years since Schliemann we have gone from perceiving a tell as an enigmatic oddity to presupposing tells whenever we discuss stratigraphical archaeology. It is ironic that we now have to provide some explanation as to why a site never became a tell.

Excavation areas are normally laid out in squares 5 meters long, though at times large sites like the 8000 acres of Caesarea necessitate the use of 10-meter squares. A transit is used to superimpose a grid that lays the site out like a checkerboard. Maximum control is achieved by numbering each of the squares and leaving a meter-wide balk between them. Strings are used to delineate the limits of the square and normally are triangulated at the corners to make them secure. The number of squares is determined by the number of volunteers and qualified supervisory staff.

The Kenyon-Wheeler method, as this way of excavating is known, digs probe trenches (usually 1 meter by 3 meters or so) to reach bedrock rapidly and thereby get a preliminary readout on

A square is laid out at
Caesarea Maritima.

the various strata that will be dug in the larger square. The face of
the balks then becomes the means of reading the chronological
history of the site. Sometimes the most important find of the
season lies partially embedded in a balk. Although balks should
not be disturbed unnecessarily, it should be remembered that
the balks exist for the sake of the dig; the dig does not exist for
the sake of the balks.[22] They are important—but not sacrosanct.

Digging proceeds as fast as circumstances allow. Burials and
especially important loci (three-dimensional features in a square)
slow the process of excavation.[23] Heavy equipment, such as front-
loaders, backhoes, and bulldozers, is rarely used unless irrele-
vant overburden or previously dug debris needs to be moved.
The most common tools used in digging are a simple 5- or 6-
inch garden trowel and a small pick (patish).

Since excavation is, by its very nature, systematic destruction,
it is extremely important to keep careful records of everything
that is done. From these records is written the history of the site
months or years after the dig is finished and exact recall of what
took place is impossible. Careful records are kept in the field by
supervisors, which then are turned over to the dig director for
use in research and publication.

In addition to official photos—both color slides format and
black-and-write prints—excavations use self-developing-film
cameras for quick shots of artifacts or loci that will be disturbed
before the official photos can be made. Elevations are constantly
recorded and samples of soil are classified by the Munsell color

chart. All balks are eventually drawn to scale (1:25) for publication. A final drawing of the square will usually be done by a professional draftsman; for greater accuracy deep squares may be divided into meter sections.

Ingenuity is sometimes required for producing aerial photos of the squares. For example, a huge collapsible tripod was devised for shooting aerials at Caesarea Maritima. It resembles a giant praying mantis and is built of aluminum for durability and light weight. A camera with a motor drive is drawn by pulley to an arm projecting from the tripod about 30 feet above the square. There the camera fits into a saddle and is operated from the ground by compressing air through a plastic hose.

Photogrammetry, a newcomer to field archaeology, is being used at Sepphoris and Caesarea Maritima in Israel, and at Tell Qarqur in northeast Syria, among others.

> It measures an artifact or site in three dimensions. . . . To use the system, one selects eight control points on the artifact or site and measures them relative to one reference point. These figures are the basis for generating all three dimensional data. . . . Next, the photographer takes two overlapping color slides. . . . The measurements are fed to a computer and the slides go into a stereo plotter. The computer can then provide exact measurements of any dimension on the photo. Using the stereo plotter, one can make a line drawing on the computer screen of any part of the photogrammetric image.[24]

Charts with pertinent information about every coin found are drawn up, and burial records are kept for every skeleton. These records include detailed information about the skeleton's position *in situ*, photos, soil samples, observations on age and sex derived from the teeth and pelvis respectively, and anything else that might be helpful.[25] In many excavations conducted by Americans it is commonplace to use the Wentworth scale to classify rocks and stones by size: a granule is 2–4 millimeters in diameter, a pebble 4–64 millimeters, a cobble 64–256 millimeters, and a boulder is more than 256 millimeters in diameter.

It becomes evident, even after such a cursory presentation, that the process has become highly scientific, extremely time-consuming, and frustratingly tedious. The question can legitimately be raised as to whether more information is being gathered than will ever be useful and whether it justifies the time and expense involved. Going for the heart of the site relatively directly and quickly, Israeli digs tend, on the whole, to be less tedious than American ones. Whether this is a better technique is arguable. Perhaps a compromise between the two approaches would be worth pursuing. All agree that accuracy, thoroughness, and caution must not be sacrificed, but there is also a growing awareness that these ideals must be blended responsibly with constraints of time and money. Only so much can be expected of the discipline. We must keep in view that its contribution to our understanding of ancient culture consists in lending support to other well-established disciplines such as history, literature, science, art, and language. Archaeology simply cannot stand alone, unattached to other arts and sciences.

Dating the Material

Stratigraphical excavation moves in progressive order from the latest occupational levels to the earliest. It is necessary to put excavated material into its proper chronological framework if we are to determine the historical/sociological contexts to which it belongs. Relative chronology is established by the sequential relationship of the strata—layer one is later than layer two, which is later than layer three, and so on. Absolute dating is possible only when there is a literary history bearing on the materials discovered in an excavation, when date-bearing coins are found in sealed loci, or when dated inscriptions in stone or mosaic are unearthed.[26] Many methods of dating material, some of them old and some new, are available to most excavations. These methods, which are discussed in the manuals on excavation, vary in their applicability, depending on the type of archaeology being done. Some are of especial benefit in current Middle Eastern archaeology.

The most important method of dating strata in Middle Eastern excavations is ceramic typology.[27] While excavating Egyptian tombs dated by inscriptions, Sir Flinders Petrie found that certain forms of clay pottery seemed to be characteristic of certain periods of time. Later, while excavating Tell el-Hesi in southern Palestine, he observed that each stratum had unique pottery; some of it he was able to correlate with his work in Egypt. He recorded the pottery and observed the differentiating characteristics from stratum to stratum. In 1890 he published his method of dating by stratigraphy and typology of pottery. William F. Albright, working at Tell Beit Mirsim (also in southern Palestine) from 1926 to 1932, refined, confirmed, and greatly expanded Petrie's pioneering work.[28] From that time the establishment of a dependable ceramic typology that would form the basis of stratigraphic chronology in Palestine has been a major concern of every archaeologist.

Israel and surrounding countries have rarely been a prosperous part of the world. Few expensive works of art and architecture have been found there, nor are inscriptions common. The discovery that a stratified site could be dated with a relative degree of accuracy by common, inexpensive pottery was a major breakthrough in efforts to produce an archaeological history of the area. The importance of the discovery is seen in the abundance of such pottery at every ancient site. People made it from the clay around them and rarely carried much of it with them when they moved. It was more easily replaced than transported. So it was left behind; being fired clay, it was virtually indestructible. It only remained for someone to develop a way to use this abundant and permanent cultural deposit to reconstruct the past. Many decades later we are still expanding and refining the work of Petrie and Albright.[29]

The most interesting examples of demonstrable changes in ceramic typology are the household oil lamps of Palestine.[30] The earliest datable lamps (Bronze Age or possibly Chalcolithic) were shaped somewhat like a dish, with pinched spouts for pouring out the oil. A radical change occurred in the Hellenistic period (332–63 B.C.) when lamps with almost completely closed tops and elongated tubelike spouts began to appear. The reason for this is not yet evident. Interestingly, among the remains of sites occupied by Jewish zealots midway in this period are lamps which are open at the top like those of the Iron Age but much smaller. They come from the Maccabean period of the second century and are called slipper lamps because of their shape. They

Styling indicates the period type for pottery: top row, from left, Hellenistic, Maccabean, Herodian; bottom row, from left, Late Roman, Early Byzantine, Late Byzantine.

seem to reflect a cultural reaction against Hellenism and a return to (or continuation of) the pre-Hellenistic way of life.

Nevertheless, the Greco-Roman influence prevailed, and during the Roman period (63 B.C.–A.D. 324) lamps were generally round with closed tops which contained holes of various sizes; they were much like Hellenistic lamps but without the lengthy spouts. Lamps of the Roman period were made in molds cut from soft stone; they usually consisted of two parts—top and bottom— which were stuck together. During the early Roman period (63 B.C.–A.D. 70) a type of lamp appeared which probably originated in the reign of Herod the Great (37–4 B.C.) and is, accordingly, designated as Herodian. Lamps of this type were made in three sections—top, bottom, and spout. The spout was unusual, resembling a spatula. These may be the lamps referred to in the parable of the wise and foolish virgins in the twenty-fifth chapter of Matthew. Nahman Avigad has called the Herodian designation into question, however, arguing that his work on the Western Hill of Jerusalem has not supported a date earlier than the first century A.D. for these lamps.[31] His call for a reconsideration of the evidence may be warranted, but his argument from silence is hardly compelling.

The Byzantine period (A.D. 324–640) saw the continuation of Roman lamps, with the spouts now made as a part of the body. Sometimes these lamps were decorated with crosses or Greek inscriptions referring to Christ as the "Light of the world." In such cases the Byzantine (Greek Christian) influence is clearly present. Ornamentation of both Roman and Byzantine lamps became more pervasive as the economy became more affluent. We assume, of course, that poor people purchased the cheaper, plainer products.

The potters of antiquity were careful imitators but reluctant innovators. They tended to make what they were familiar with and what could be produced and sold the quickest. The daily life of the average peasant gave little encouragement to creativity in producing the utensils necessary for the home, although such creativity did manifest itself on occasion—perhaps out of sheer boredom with the customary or perhaps in an effort to produce something unique that would sell better. At any rate style did seem to change from period to period, slowly but decisively, and we are now able to observe those changes in style and from them establish a chronology.[32] The methodology is not exact, but within reasonable limitations it does provide a workable typology upon which to construct a fairly reliable chronology.[33]

A more accurate but often unusable technique for dating archaeological finds is numismatics, the study of coins.[34] Coins were not manufactured before the eighth century B.C., and are thus of limited help in dating materials from the Old Testament period. By the late fifth century B.C. coins were minted in Egypt, Palestine, Syria, Anatolia (Turkey), Persia, and Mesopotamia. Important mints were located in Jerusalem, Damascus, Babylon, Tyre, Sidon, Byblos, Aradus, Persepolis, and Samaria.[35] Some minting was also done in Caesarea, Ascalon, Tiberias, and Bethzur. For the New Testament period, coins are of paramount importance. The date of production and the name of the ruler or official who authorized it were inscribed on many coins. This provides a basis for absolute dating of the material associated with them. A floor, for example, with coins sealed under it cannot have been laid before the date the coins were minted. The occupational level above the floor must, therefore, be later than the date of the coins.

The limitation of this dating technique lies in the scarcity of coins in ancient ruins. Unlike cheap pottery, coins were not intentionally discarded, and hoards are rarely found.[36] However, one coin found in the right place may well prove invaluable. Only one is needed to establish a *terminus a quo* for an archaeological context.

Gold, silver, copper, and bronze coins found from the New Testament period have been found. Gold was, of course, relatively scarce. Silver coins were abundant, the denarius being the most common silver coin in the Roman Empire and the most frequently mentioned in the New Testament (sixteen times). In size and appearance it resembled an American dime, but it had far more buying power. It represented a day's wage in New Testament times. Most of the coins that have been found in excavations are bronze. These were of lesser value and thus more plentiful and more widely circulated. They were also more likely to be carelessly lost.

Another means of dating used in modern excavations is Radio Carbon 14.[37] This method was developed in World War II in connection with the production of the atomic bomb and for a while seemed to offer good possibilities of dating organic material within two hundred years. Normal carbon has an atomic weight of 12. Carbon 14 is a radioactive (i.e., unstable) isotope produced in the upper atmosphere by the bombardment of nitrogen atoms by cosmic rays. Both varieties combine with oxygen to form carbon dioxide and spread evenly through the air. This process is constant, so all living creatures that participate in respiratory exchange with the atmosphere (animals and plants taking in oxygen) have an identical ratio of carbon 14 to carbon 12 in their tissues. When respiration ceases, the radioactive carbon 14 decays at a constant and measurable rate, since the organism no longer ingests carbon 14 from the atmosphere. Because we know that it takes approximately 5,730 years for the amount of carbon 14 to drop to half of its former level, it is possible, by measuring the amount of carbon 14 remaining in a sample of wood, bone, or shell, to determine how long ago the organism died.

Unfortunately, several recent discoveries combine to indicate that carbon 14 is not as valuable as was once hoped: (1) radioactive carbon atoms may not have existed in the earth's atmosphere before 2000 B.C.; (2) the natural concentration of carbon 14 in the atmosphere has varied in certain periods, and (3) there is a high probability of sample contamination. Nevertheless, carbon 14 is still being used in conjunction with other determinants such as stratigraphical evidence, statistical analysis, dendrochronology, and established historical chronology to provide information on the dates of ancient cultures.[38] Most recently it was used in an attempt to date the controversial Shroud of Turin (see pp. 217–21).

Several other modern techniques hold out some prospect for help in dating but at present are suffering growing pains.[39] Archaeomagnetism is a process that measures the amount of magnetism in a ceramic vessel that has been remagnetized by the earth's magnetic field after having been completely demagnetized when it was fired in a kiln. It is theoretically possible to determine the date of the demagnetization by measuring the direction and intensity of the remagnetization.

Thermoluminescence is a technique that measures the amount of energy given off in the form of light when a ceramic vessel is reheated after having been fired sometime in the past.[40] The amount of time since the firing is determined by the amount of light emitted by reheating. However, a number of relevant variables have been found to inhibit the production of reliable dates, so the method is not yet dependable.

Dendrochronology (tree-ring dating) is of little value in most areas of the Middle East because most ancient remains are in the form of stone rather than wood. This technique, which is proving valuable in parts of the United States and Europe, offers little promise in lands of the Bible. Palynology, the study of pollen, may prove more promising.[41]

Many other modern methods of dating such as potassium-argon, fission track, fluorine and nitrogen analysis, trace-metal analysis, and obsidian dating are of only marginal value in most excavations. Stratigraphical analysis and ceramic typology supported by coins, glass typology,[42] architectural analysis, and historical documents remain for the present the most important means of dating Mediterranean and Middle Eastern excavations.[43]

Comparatively little benefit is derived from excavations that expend enormous quantities of time, money, and energy in the process of removing dirt, but never publish the results of their work. This amounts to little more than a legal brutalizing of a site. Time, money, and energy must also be budgeted for final publication.[44] This is, after all, the ultimate contribution of archaeology to society.

PART 1

The Architecture
of New Testament Times

City Layouts and Civic Structures

City Layouts

The Hellenistic City

The most significant structures and cultural institutions of the Roman period were to be found in the Greco-Roman city. The Romans shared the Greek view that government of provinces was best performed through cities, so their first task in newly conquered provinces was the creation of new cities, as well as the renovation of existing ones.[1] There were about one thousand cities in the Roman Empire; most of those that relate to the New Testament had been Greek cities prior to their Romanization.[2] Plutarch tells us that Alexander the Great had built seventy cities, most of them built according to orthodox Greek colonial planning.[3] That is to say, they had typical Hellenistic features.

The Hellenistic city conformed to a standard type, consisting of a network of uniform, rectangular blocks, half as wide as they were long, and orthogonal. At least one open space was reserved for an *agora* (ἀγορά, "marketplace") and public buildings. One or more of the longitudinal streets (and sometimes one or more of the transverse streets) were wider than the rest, such as the "street called Straight" in Damascus (Acts 9:11) and the axial avenues of Antioch.

Dura-Europos (ca. 300 B.C.–A.D. 250) is a prime example of the Hellenistic plan. City blocks 100 by 200 feet were laid out on a grid of nine longitudinal and twelve transverse streets. The streets were all 18 feet wide except one longitudinal avenue which was 36 feet wide, and two transverse avenues (the fourth and the eighth) which were 24 feet wide. Space was left between these two larger transverse avenues for the agora and various public buildings.

This geometric style of formal city planning, rooted in Persian times (sixth century B.C.) but popularized by Hippodamos of Miletus in the fifth century B.C., influenced the western part of the empire as well, being especially evident in the city of Paestum (Poseidonia) in southern Italy. It had three long avenues and at least thirty-two cross streets with open spaces for an agora and public buildings in the center of town.

The Roman City

The great achievements of Roman town planning were continuations of these Greek accomplishments. Both cosmetic and pragmatic differences inevitably arose because of topographical conditions, social and political requirements, and inclination and taste. Religious superstition was a factor in locating, founding, and dedicating every new Roman city.[4] Although the elongated blocks were reused when the Romans renovated Hellenistic cities, the norm of newly constructed cities was the square, a circumstance due primarily to the work of Roman land surveyors, who customarily laid out the region before a town was built.[5] In such cases one of their lines became the central axis for the city. Herodotus attributed the creation of the science of geometry to these land surveyors (The word *geometry*—γεωμετρέω—is Greek, meaning literally "to measure or survey the earth."). According to Polybius, the internal dispositions of Roman military camps in the second century B.C. resembled cities, a factor due in part no doubt to surveyors.[6]

The normal practice among Roman city engineers was to lay out squares, although variations did occur as a result of topography or reutilization of the Hellenistic rectangles.[7] The squares usually measured 2400 Roman feet to a side, the theoretical equivalent of one hundred small areas which were known as "centuries" (*centuriae*); the process was called "centuriation." The city was normally oriented to the points of the compass, with a central north-south street called the *cardo maximus* ("main street") and a central east-west street called the *decumanus maximus*. Attention was given to compass orientation, Vitruvius wrote, because of pragmatic concerns, such as avoiding the blasts of cold wind down the streets.[8] The width of the average street in Jerusalem during the Roman-Byzantine period was about 18 feet, while the cardo maximus was four times that (72 feet). The streets of Samaria, Gerasa (Jerash), and Palmyra also measure 18 feet in width.[9] This checkerboard layout naturally served to emphasize the main intersection of the town and contributed to a tendency among Romans toward centralization and axial planning which was not characteristic of Greek cities, whose buildings were situated with a view to beauty and accessibility.[10]

Eventually the major arteries were ornately decorated with colonnades in one of the Greek orders (Doric, Ionic, Corinthian, or Composite). The earliest example of this trend was the colonnade built by Herod the Great in Antioch of Syria.[11] For the next three hundred years such streets were characteristically, and almost exclusively, found in the eastern part of the empire, for example, at Gerasa, Caesarea Maritima, Jerusalem, Samaria, Damascus, Tyre, Ephesus, Hierapolis (Pamukkale), and Sardis. Inscriptions in Sardis indicate that its colonnaded main avenue was begun under Tiberius and finished under Claudius.[12]

Because of the might of the Roman legions, defense played little part in the location and layout of cities. Very few walls were

The *Cardo Maximus* in Jerash, Jordan.

built around Roman cities in the empire. A more important matter was communication, which necessitated locating cities on natural harbors along trade routes and at river crossings. Fertile soil in the immediate vicinity was also important. Water could be brought by aqueduct from great distances.

Another pragmatic element involved in the planning and operation of cities was the political expediency of providing for the masses' various comforts which were enjoyed only by the rich in most ancient societies, for example, entertainment in the theater. Moreover, it was felt that every urban citizen should be able to benefit from well-maintained public buildings, streets, and water systems, and accessible marketplaces. This was at least the theoretical goal, even if every citizen was not able to share fully in all municipal benefits, especially those pertaining to education and health.

Civic Structures

Fora

The heart of every Greco-Roman city was the agora, which the Romans called the *forum*. This was a large open area reserved for public functions. An intriguing variation here is that while Greek city blocks were rectangular, the agora was square; on the other hand, while Roman city blocks were square, the forum was rectangular. There were exceptions, of course, due to topographical considerations (Gerasa had an oval-shaped forum), but square agoras and rectangular fora were the ideal. Generally, the forum or the agora lay in the center of town and was paved with large rectangular or square limestones, such as can still be seen at Philippi. The open forum was surrounded by a colonnaded portico which was covered and contained shops. Such colonnades are well preserved today in Ephesus and Athens, and some of the shops are still standing at Ephesus, Corinth, and Rome.

Sometimes a *cryptoporticus* (underground vaulted corridor) was built beneath the colonnaded portico of a forum, such as the one at Thessalonica, which could be used as a thoroughfare. A large vaulted basement with shops opening to an outside street was built under the north portico in Smyrna's forum.

In some cities, like Ephesus and Smyrna, there were both a commercial forum and a state forum. The former functioned as a marketplace and the latter as a kind of civic center for the conducting of municipal and state business. This was essentially the case in Corinth (see p. 324). In Athens the old Greek agora became a seldom visited repository of monuments and statues,

while the adjacent Roman forum was the site of the commercial activities of the city (see pp. 302–304).

Philippi's Roman forum was placed in the center of the city, typical of agoras and fora.

Basilicas and Bouleteria

Eventually, large cities such as Rome outgrew the forum and had to construct additional conveniently located buildings to serve particular purposes. We find in Pompeii and Corinth a building which specialized in food (a *macellum*). Many cities also built a *basilica* (βασιλική, "royal house") near the forum. This was a colonnaded building used as a covered marketplace in which people could conduct their business out of the weather. Official functions of government were also conducted there, and a tribunal (*bema*) was frequently built nearby, where magistrates sat to perform duties that were primarily judicial in nature (for a discussion of the tribunal at Corinth see pp. 333–335).

The basic design of the basilica—a long rectangular building with a central nave and side aisles—is found in the architecture of both Jewish synagogues and Christian churches in the fourth century and later. Whether it was copied intentionally is a matter of debate. The style of the structure accommodated large crowds under one roof and was therefore of pragmatic value to both Judaism and Christianity. Unlike Roman civic basilicas, Christian basilicas had only one entrance, on a narrow side of the building,

41

and there was often an annex in the form of an additional room or apse (semicircular projection) on the east end. In almost all Christian basilicas yet found in the Middle East which have one, the apse faces the east, perhaps because of the symbolic connection between the resurrection morning and the rising sun. Excellent examples of this type of building in Israel are the Church of the Nativity in Bethlehem and synagogues in Hammath-Tiberias, and Beth Alfa. Another example is Sardis in Asia Minor. The Sardis synagogue was originally a civic basilica. Constructed as a part of a gymnasium and lying adjacent to a row of shops, it was subsequently turned over to the Jewish community to be used as a place of worship.[13]

Another type of building constructed near the forum was the *bouletērion* (βουλευτήριον, "senate chamber"; Lat., *curia*). The one in Corinth, built in the civic area of the south part of the forum, is reasonably well preserved, but the best-preserved and best-known one is in the Forum of Rome. It was here that Julius Caesar was assassinated. The bouleterion should be taller and statelier than the basilicas, Vitruvius wrote, because of the eminence of the assemblies which met there. The bouleterion symbolized the rule of Rome in the provinces. Its members, as well as other local magistrates who held office by Rome's permission, found it expedient to express appreciation by donating some work of art or architecture to the city. A well-preserved first-century inscription in a stone pavement beside the theater at Corinth asserts that Erastus "laid the pavement at his own expense in appreciation for being elected treasurer of the city" (see Rom. 16:23 and pp. 331–333). The Babbius monumental fountain in Corinth is probably another example (see p. 332)

Water Installations

Greek Baths

Bathhouses were among the most characteristic institutions of urban life in the Roman Empire.[14] They became the most frequented centers of social life, eventually surpassing the forum in popularity. The earliest known Roman baths are the Stabian Baths in Pompeii, which were built in the early first century B.C.

However, the Greeks had already built bathhouses much earlier. For centuries both sexes had bathed in cold water, purely for the sake of cleanliness rather than indulgence. Ancient Greeks were always bathed at birth, marriage, and death. It was said that these were the only three times in life when the Illyrians were bathed! In Homer's day, frequent indulgence in a warm bath was considered a sign of luxury and effeminacy.[15] Socrates and Demosthenes expressed a similar opinion in later times, when bathing was done before the major meal of the day. Ancient

Greek vases depict people standing beside a basin (λουτήρ or λουτήριον; Lat., *labrum*) and pouring water over themselves from a pitcher (ὑδρία). Shower baths and pools (κολυμβήθραι) for both men and women are also portrayed on these vases.[16]

Roman Baths

In time, almost every Roman city in the empire had one or more bathhouses. The first one in Rome was built by Marcus Agrippa, the general and deputy of Augustus, in the Campus Martius near the Pantheon. In 33 B.C. a survey showed at least 170 baths in Rome.[17] By the fourth century A.D. there were almost a thousand![18] In the first century A.D. these facilities were cramped, claustrophobic, and not well lit. Eventually, however, they were constructed with sufficient windows and doorways to correct these problems.

By combining the bathhouse with the *gymnasium* (γυμνάσιον), which was an educational and cultural establishment as well as athletic center, Roman bathhouses represented a step beyond the Greek. The Roman complexes were larger and more appealing social centers.[19] Simple Greek baths (βαλανεῖον; Lat., *balneum*) became, in the hands of Roman engineers, magnificent facilities called *thermae* (from θέρμαι, "hot springs"). They were surrounded with stores for the shoppers, libraries for the scholars, *palestrae* (exercise yards) for the athletic types, and *exedrae* (semicircular or rectangular recesses) in which rhetoricians pontificated, poets recited, and philosophers lectured. Porticos, vestibules, shaded

Entrance to the Roman bathhouse at Herculaneum.

walks, and gardens were not uncommon, rounding out a facility not unlike some modern-day clubs.

One of the reasons for the widespread appeal of the bathhouse was that it made personal hygiene and recreation accessible to even the very poor. What had once belonged to only the wealthy could now be found throughout the city. The price of a bath in New Testament times was a Roman *quadrans*. To appreciate the reasonableness of this price, one need only recall the story of the poor widow who cast into the temple treasury all she had—two mites (λεπτά) which make a farthing (κοδράντης = the Roman quadrans) (Mark 12:42 KJV). The baths offered the Romans "a microcosm of many of the things that make life attractive."[20] They became so much a symbol of first-century luxury that Caligula (of all people!) made it a capital offense to indulge in the luxury of bathing on any religious holiday.

Although baths were usually open from sunrise till sunset, most people bathed between midday and evening, a practice which appealed to both the urbanite and the farmer.[21] Furthermore, whereas most Greek cities had been content with one or two fountains located at natural springs, the commissioning of the first aqueduct in Rome in 312 B.C. eventually led to a situation in which bathhouses were available in every part of a city.

While the construction of the baths followed no uniform pattern, they all contained essentially the same components. Even the earliest ones, for example, the Stabian Baths and the Forum Baths in Pompeii, and the Forum Baths in Herculaneum, in-

The hot room or *caldarium* of a bathhouse in Salamis, Cyprus.

Figure 2
Schematic of Stabian Baths

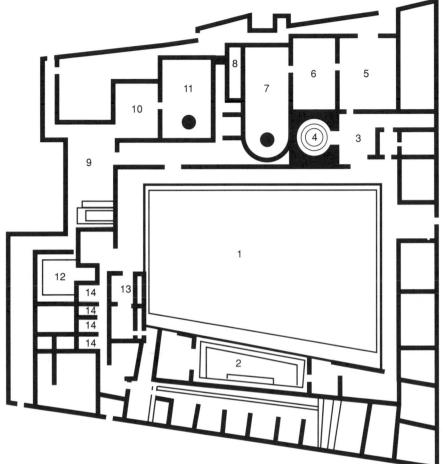

1 Palestra
2 Natatio
3 Entrance hall
4 Frigidarium
5 Apodyterium
6 Tepidarium
7 Caldarium
8 Furnaces
9 Women's apodyterium
10 Women's tepidarium
11 Women's caldarium
12 Latrine
13 Bath supervisor's office
14 Individual "hip bath" cubicles

cluded separate facilities for men and women.[22] Each facility contained a dressing room (*apodyterium*) where the bathers undressed and stored their garments in bins, usually above benches.

Then there was a series of rooms, each one progressively hotter because it was closer to the furnace. The first room was the cold room (*frigidarium*), which contained a cold-water pool large enough to accommodate several people. In very large complexes, the pool was so big that it could not be roofed, as was the case in Bath, England (first century A.D.). Next was the warm room (*tepidarium*), which was provided with benches and only slightly heated. In larger baths, such as the Caracalla and Diocletian baths in Rome, these rooms were enormous, resembling the nave in a basilica. Finally, there was the hot room (*caldarium*). In baths large enough to accommodate both sexes, the furnace was located between the men's and women's hot rooms.[23]

Apodyterium with niches in the wall to hold the clothing of bathers at the Stabian baths.

The floor of the caldarium (and the tepidarium sometimes) was supported by rows of small columns or pillars (*pilae*) about 2 feet high, although their height varied depending on the size of the room. The pillars were composed of an average of ten tile bricks (*besales*), each about 8 inches square, and were situated 16 inches apart. On top of the pillars were placed 2-feet-square tile bricks (*tegulae bipedales*), whose corners rested on the centers of the pillars. Vitruvius does not mention a common practice in Britain of placing an additional 1-foot-square cap over the 8-inch-square pillars in order to better support the larger *tegulae*.[24] The elaborate floor system (*suspensura*), placed over the pillars, was usually rather thick, consisting of brick and cement topped by a mosaic or similar surface.

Hot air from the furnace was channeled between the pillars. The heat was then quickly and effectively conducted through the bricks to the floor above, which sometimes reached such a high temperature that slippers were required. Tile flues built into the walls were another means of circulating heat. Examples have been found in excavations at Salamis on Cyprus and Ostia near Rome, where a central heating system seems to have been used for some of the buildings. This technique of utilizing hollow floors and tile flues (*hypocaust*) to heat a building seems also to have been used in coastal cities such as Caesarea Maritima to keep library documents free of humidity.

The caldarium contained a large basin which was kept filled with hot water and hung from the ceiling on an adjustable chain for regulation of the temperature and moisture content in the room.[25] The basins were sometimes made of marble, for example those in the Forum Baths at Pompeii, or even of silver.[26] In the less prosperous provinces of the empire, such as the eastern Mediterranean, the basins were made of bronze or even plastered stone. Some caldaria also had a basin filled with cold water at one end and an *alveus* ("quadrangular tub") at the other end. Bathers could sit in the tub and have a pitcher of cold water brought to pour on their sweating brow. Or they could sprinkle themselves with hot water and scrape their skin with a strigil to clear away the perspiration.

Vitruvius mentions three large bronze tanks that were set above the furnace and held water to be used in each of the three rooms.[27] The one nearest the furnace had hot water and fed the caldarium. It was supplied by the next tank, where warm water was kept for the tepidarium (although many tepidaria did not use water). The second tank was fed by the cold tank, which supplied the frigidarium. A noteworthy example of such a system was found in the excavations of the Forum Baths in Pompeii.[28]

The particular ritual of bathing differed from place to place and, undoubtedly, from person to person. It has been argued that the baths in Palestine were unique in design and "represent an independent Hellenistic bathing tradition, an attested counterpart to the Italian."[29] Wherever in the empire the complexes were small and the facilities limited, the bathing procedure was probably as follows: the bathers undressed in the apodyterium, storing their clothing in a bin, and then went to the frigidarium for a refreshing plunge. The next move was to the tepidarium, where the body temperature would be moderated, and then on to the caldarium for sweating. The bathers then returned to the apodyterium to dry off.

Many of the larger bathhouses, such as the Suburban Baths of Herculaneum or the Forum and Stabian baths at Pompeii, had additional facilities, for example, *palestrae* and *sudatoria* or *laconica* (dry, hot-air rooms that induced sweating; cf. Turkish baths), and consequently followed a slightly different ritual. Males and females who were going to participate in the games and wrestling matches in the palestra were first rubbed with oil and wax, which made the skin more supple, and then received a massage. After the matches were over, the participants went to the baths and entered one of the sudatoria which flanked the caldarium in order to induce further sweating. Then it was on to the caldarium where the bathers would sprinkle hot water from the labrum basin on their skin and scrape the oil and perspiration from their body with a strigil. After this ritual of cleaning and drying was completed, the bather went to the tepidarium to cool off gradually while engaging in social conversation in what was usually the most ornately decorated room of the baths. Then, after a plunge in the frigidarium, the bather dressed in the apodyterium. These were the basic steps recommended by Pliny.[30]

Mixed bathing, not forbidden until the time of Hadrian,

inevitably resulted in scandal, especially since some women, prior to bathing, participated in the games and the preliminary rubdowns with olive oil (applied by men).[31] Rather than using the bathing places intended exclusively for women, which provided no opportunity for participation in the sports, many women compromised their reputation and bathed with the men.[32] Women of respectability did not engage in the practice, and eventually the Christian emperor Justinian recognized it as grounds for divorce.

Miqwaot

Miqwaot (sing., *miqweh*) are Jewish ritual baths. In the Mediterranean world they are found in private homes as well as in various public establishments. These larger bathhouses are especially abundant in the land of Israel, which "challenges Italy as the most fruitful area for the study of late Hellenistic baths."[33] They appear to have first been built in Judea in the Herodian period.[34] Herod the Great built at least ten spacious baths in his various palace-fortresses, which have now been excavated. These include Masada, Herodium, Herodian Jericho, Cypros, and Macherus. Although the baths reflect various features of indigenous architecture and may have been built "according to Palestinian principles of construction and design,"[35] they nevertheless clearly reflect the basic pattern of Roman bathhouses all over the Mediterranean world, that is, caldarium, tepidarium, frigidarium, and apodyterium.

A *miqweh* at Jericho fulfilled the Jewish need for ritual cleanliness.

Jewish ritual baths were constructed differently from Roman bathhouses. Directions for the construction and use of miqwaot are given in detail in the Mishnah, which specifies that the pool must be large enough to contain approximately 60 gallons of water (40 seahs) and deep enough to allow the total immersion of the body (5 feet). The pool must either contain "living" (i.e. running) water or have such water funneled into it from natural sources. The water cannot be hand-drawn.[36] Early Jewish Christian immersions (baptisms) emulated this Jewish practice of using running water.[37] The miqwaot of Qumran were designed to accommodate the need for running water and also provided partitioned stairways to prevent an exiting bather from being defiled by touching an impure person just descending into the bath. Such divided stairways have also been found in private homes of the wealthy in Jerusalem.[38] Although many ritual baths have been found which consist of only one pool (in Jerusalem, Sepphoris, and Herodium), it seems that the second-century trend toward three basins or pools was already present in the first century in both Masada and Jerusalem.

Aqueducts

Although most Greek cities had one or more large public fountains fed by local springs, a few of them did build aqueducts. Greek aqueducts were usually rectangular channels cut into rock or made of solid masonry. They followed the winding terrain where possible, going subterranean through tunnels when necessary. Herodotus described the construction of a remarkable aqueduct on the island of Samos about 540 B.C.: it "is a tunnel nearly a mile long, 8 feet wide and 8 feet high, driven clean through the base of a hill 900 feet in height. The whole length of it carries a second cutting 30 feet deep and 3 broad, along which water from an abundant source is led through pipes into the town."[39]

Even though aqueducts were not built in Rome until the late fourth century B.C., it was the Romans who made the aqueduct an essential part of everyday life in the ancient world. The first in Rome was commissioned in 312 B.C. by Appius Claudius Caecus.[40] When the empire replaced the republic, about the time of the birth of Christ, the need for water rapidly expanded with the rise in population and the increased construction of private and public baths. By the beginning of the second century A.D. there were nine aqueducts in Rome which supplied the city with an estimated 332,306,624 gallons of water a day.[41] Four of these had been constructed in the time of the republic and five under the empire. The Claudian aqueducts were the keystone of the water system in the New Testament period, dwarfing the others in both capacity and height.[42] The Anio Novus, extending for 59 miles, was the longest of the Roman

Aqueduct serving
Antioch's water system.

aqueducts. In addition to the aqueducts built by Caligula and Claudius,[43] Nero seems to have had a part in improving Rome's water system as well.[44]

Aqueducts built in the provincial cities followed the same principles as those of the capital. A magnificent aqueduct which spanned 30 miles and reached a height of 165 feet was built for the city of Nîmes (in southern France).[45] An aqueduct built by Herod the Great at Caesarea Maritima is still standing over several of its original 13 miles. The cement-enclosed upper portion, which rose on a series of small arches wherever the ground level fell, contained a water channel made of ceramic pipe (see pp. 142–143).

The water was normally delivered to a *castellum divisorium,* a reservoir with settling basins and a system of sluices for further distribution throughout the city. One of the best preserved is in Segovia, Spain. Secondary water towers were built (as at Pompeii) to insure adequate local supply. Many public facilities were dependent upon the water thus provided; for instance, public lavatories, bakeries, fountains which were the immediate source of water for the ordinary urban citizen, and even brothels. Private citizens paid a tax for the water they channeled from the public system. By the fourth century there were 1352 sites at which water was available in Rome.[46]

Drainage Systems

By the time of the beginning of the empire, in the first century B.C., the Romans had already developed and widely established a system of covered drains beneath the center of their paved streets. The sewers at Caesarea Maritima were so constructed that the northeasterly flowing currents would flush them into the sea at high tide. The sewers (*cloacae*) of Rome were so large that in places a wagon loaded with hay could drive through them easily. Marcus Agrippa, who greatly expanded and improved them, traveled their entire length by boat. Seven channels diverted the overflow of the aqueducts into the sewers. The Cloaca Maxima (the central collector for all the others from the forum to the foot of the Aventine Hill) may still be seen today with its semicircular arch, 16 feet in diameter, opening into the Tiber River at the Ponte Rotto.

Theaters

Greek Theaters

The theater was one of the most important and impressive institutions in urban life during the New Testament period. Our knowledge of the ancient theaters of Greece and Rome is largely dependent upon archaeological evidence in the form of preserved theaters and, for the period prior to the late fourth century B.C., vase paintings. The literary evidence is quite sparse. Although long lists of plays performed in the Greek theaters are preserved, only a few of the plays themselves have survived in toto: seven by Aeschylus, seven by Sophocles, eighteen by Euripides, eleven by Aristophanes, and one by Menander. Having originated in the context of the evolution of religious drama, theaters eventually served many functions in the ancient city. The history and development of theater in the ancient world is reflected in the changing patterns of construction evident in the many surviving structures.

The oldest theater in Greece, the Dionysus Theater in Athens, was located at the foot of the Acropolis. Originally consisting of only a dancing floor and an altar, it was provided with wooden benches probably by the beginning of the sixth century. During the time of Alexander the Great, it was rebuilt in stone by the Attic statesman Lycurgus (ca. 330 B.C.). Greek drama had reached its zenith by the fifth century B.C., so the oldest surviving theaters were built or renovated a century after the composition of the plays that were performed in them. It seems that the cessation of creative writing after the fifth century was compensated for by concentration on modifications in the physical facilities.[47]

Greek drama developed, as did almost everything in ancient civilization, in the context of religion. Greek theaters, unlike the later Roman ones, were traditionally constructed in conjunction with temples and sacred precincts. The Pergamum theater, for instance, partly overlapped a terrace connecting the forum with the Temple of Dionysus. Theatrical performances actually originated at festivals conducted in honor of the god Dionysus. Songs by a chorus of dancing peasants dressed as animals, maenads, or satyrs became the fundamental component of Greek theatrical performance.[48]

Three types of drama developed from this beginning: tragedy, comedy, and satyr plays, each requiring its own distinctive scenery.[49] All the tragedies dealt with religious concerns and were performed around an altar of Dionysus (θυμέλη) which was built on the dancing floor. Aeschylus (525–456 B.C.) used drama to articulate the rules of conduct between humans and the gods; Sophocles (496–406) wrote of learning wisdom through suffering; and Euripides (485–406) dealt with psychological makeup and reactions to stressful situations. The deaths of Sophocles and Euripides in the same year effectively ended creative tragic drama, and the medium succumbed to external forces that altered both the function and construction of ancient theaters.

Greek theaters basically consisted of three components: the *orchēstra* (ὀρχήστρα, "space for the chorus to dance"), the *theatron* (θεάτρον, "place for spectators"), and the *skēnē* (σχηνή, "stage" or "scene building").[50] The orchestra (from ὀρχεῖσθαι, "to dance") was a circular area in which the dancers performed. An example can be seen in the well-preserved fourth-century theater at Epidaurus, which measures almost 400 feet in diameter. Aristotle attributed the origin of tragedy to the lead singers of the "circular dance" (κύκλιος χορός).[51] A decline in the activity and status of these singers by the fourth century, brought on by greater involvement of the actors, eventuated in the virtual abandonment of the orchestra in favor of an elevated stage.

The theatron (perhaps from θεᾶσθαι, "to look at") surrounded approximately two-thirds of the orchestra. Spectators originally looked down on the performance from the bare hillside. But by the fourth century the hillside was lined with wooden or stone seats. This seating area was effectively partitioned into two or more sections by horizontal passageways or gangways (διαζώματα) providing easier entrance and exit for the enormous crowds. Theaters were usually large enough to handle virtually the whole population of a city. The one at Ephesus, for example, would seat more than twenty thousand. The Dionysus Theater in Athens would seat about fifteen thousand.[52] The horizontal sections, in turn, were divided into wedge-shaped sections (κέκριδες) by narrow vertical stairways. As early as the fourth century special seats of honor were built among the first few rows. These seats were called *thronoi* (θρόνοι) or *cathedrae* (καθέδραι). Sixty

The fourth-century Greek theater at Epidaurus measures 400 feet in diameter.

of them may still be seen in the Dionysus Theater in Athens; fourteen were found in place.

In archaic times, only one actor appeared in a performance. He "answered" or "reported to" the chorus on the orchestra (the Greek word for "actor," ὑποκριτής [hypocrite], literally means "one who answers"). Aeschylus introduced a second actor and Sophocles a third, thus reducing the importance of the chorus. When actors became supreme they were elevated to a height of 10 or 12 feet to give them greater prominence.[53] This meant that the simple tent or wooden house that originally stood behind the orchestra as a dressing room for the actors was replaced by a wooden stage-building (skene), and eventually by one made of stone. Between the stage (προσκήνιον) and the seats, a passageway (πάροδος) on either side allowed entrance to the orchestra from the street for both the spectators and the chorus. With the decrease in activity by the chorus, part of the orchestra was eventually used for portable seating.

In the classical period the stage was enhanced by the addition of portable wooden or cloth backdrops. These were simply placed on the stage and then removed as necessary. Eventually, flat panels which portrayed architecture in perspective were attached to the wooden stage building itself. These were called σκηνογραφία ("stage paintings"). Similarly, in the Hellenistic period (ca. 300–100 B.C.) paintings of architectural scenes were attached to the walls of the stone stage-building. Soon thereafter, elaborate backdrops having two or three stories and three doors opening to the stage were constructed (e.g. the Dionysus Theater

Figure 3
Greek and Roman Theaters

1 Theatron
2 Kekrides
3 Orchestra
4 Diadzoma
5 Parodos
6 Proskenion
7 Ramp
8 Skene
9 Paraskenion

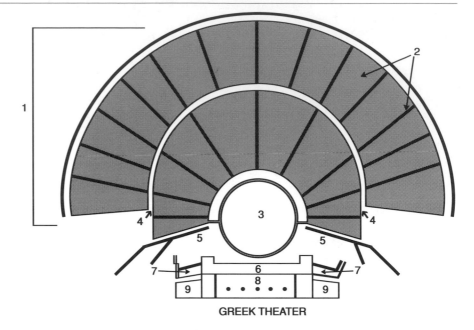

GREEK THEATER

10 Cavea
11 Orchestra
12 Scaenae Frons
13 Parados
14 Pulpitum

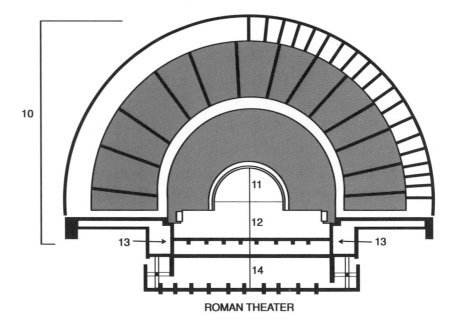

ROMAN THEATER

in Athens, and theaters at Priene in Asia Minor and Segesta, Sicily).

It was probably comedy rather than tragedy that stimulated most of the developments in staging. This was because tragedies had been performed in religious contexts and were largely restricted to sets depicting a temple or palace, whereas most comedies required backdrops representing houses or a street (satyr plays demanded a cave or forest). More secular in tone than tragedies, comedies reflected more the world of ordinary people and were thus more amenable to change. In the Hellenistic period, with the removal of the action from the orchestra to the newly built stages, both the choruses and the gods as dramatic characters disappeared from theatrical productions. Theater architecture lost most of its early religious characteristics and became quite secular.[54]

The stage was sometimes augmented by wings on either side called *paraskenia*. These wings made the stage about twice the width of the diameter of the orchestra. Another innovation in the stone theater was the enhancement of the acoustics by the addition of bronze vases which served as reverberators.[55] Scientifically placed throughout the theater, they amplified the voices from the stage. Earthenware vases used apparently for this purpose have been found in excavated theaters, but as yet no bronze ones have appeared.

Roman Theaters

The construction of theaters in Rome was relatively late, a factor due in part to the bad reputation that the medium had acquired in the eyes of many leading conservative citizens. This reputation reflected the fact that Roman theatrical performances were from the beginning connected to the games (*ludi*) and other spectacular events that took place at state religious festivals, for example, chariot races, gladiatorial combats, animal hunts or men fighting with animals, boxing and wrestling matches, and specialty acts.[56] Conservative Romans viewed the acting profession with disfavor; by the time of the empire it had degenerated to the point of being the exclusive province of slaves.[57] All of the actors in ancient theater, Greek and Roman, were males; even the female roles were played by males.

The first Roman theaters were temporary structures made of wood and pulled down when the event was over. Some of them had every quality of grand style except permanence. An attempt had been made in the second century B.C. to build a stone theater in Rome, but the senate was persuaded to have it torn down before it was completed.[58] Not surprisingly, therefore, the first stone theater was not built in Rome, but in Pompeii, where around 75 B.C. Roman colonists who had been separated from the influence of the conservative senate for only five years constructed a small theater that would seat about 1500. The first stone theater in Rome was dedicated by Pompey in 55 B.C. Within forty years two more had been built, one by Lucius Cornelius Balbus and the other by the emperor Augustus with a seating capacity of 29,500.[59]

Roman theater at
Amman, Jordan.

Provincial towns had enjoyed Greek theaters, of course, for a
very long time. The Roman-type theater was only a modification
of the Greek type, and renovations were made throughout the
provinces wherever it was expedient to do so.[60] Renovated theaters may be seen in Athens, Corinth, Epidaurus, Philippi, Pergamum, and Ephesus. When occasion demanded, new theaters on
the Roman model were built from the foundation up.[61] Some of
these were built, like their Greek prototypes, into hillsides, as at
Philadelphia (Amman), Gerasa, and Umm Qeis (Gadara) in Jordan, and at the Asklepieion in Pergamum.

However, most purely Roman theaters were constructed on
level places, usually near the heart of the city, because activities
other than play production occurred here, such as official civic
gatherings and spontaneous assemblies of citizens like the one
prompted by Paul's preaching in Ephesus (Acts 19:29).[62] Through
their mastery of the arch, the Romans were able to build theaters
whose auditoriums or seating areas (*caveae*) rested upon barrel
vaults or groin vaults, and were thus not limited to hillsides as the
Greeks had been. This greater versatility enabled the Romans to
integrate their theaters more fully into the life of the city. Theaters
of this type may be seen, among other places, at Caesarea Maritima and Beth Shean in Israel, as well as Salamis on Cyprus.[63]

The Romans made two major innovations in Greek theaters:
(1) The orchestra was reduced to a semicircle, and the stage

extended from one side of the seating to the other. Correspondingly, the cavea was modified from the shape of a horseshoe to a semicircle. Actors now performed entirely on the elevated stage, and the orchestra, which contained no altar to Dionysus, was used for extra seating. Further, Roman theaters exhibited an elaborate system of seating by sex, age, profession, and rank. Women, soldiers, and married male plebeians, for example, were assigned special areas in the theater by Augustus. The first few rows and the entire orchestra in many theaters were reserved for senators and guests of honor. (2) The extension of the stage (*pulpitum*) to the cavea closed off the passageways (parodoi) which had existed in Greek theaters. The result was the unification of the stage and auditorium into an integrated structure. The vaults supporting the auditorium were then used to provide entrances to the semicircular orchestra, and a vaulted passageway circling the rear of the auditorium gave access to the seating areas through narrow hallways. Entrance thus shifted largely from the parodoi in Greek theaters to the rear entrances in Roman theaters.

The fronts of the elevated stages in Roman theaters were elaborately decorated, usually with alternating rectangular and semicircular niches separated by small columns. One of the best examples is in Philadelphia (Amman). And even more elaborately done was the *scaenae frons* ("back wall of the stage"), which sometimes reached as high as three or four stories. Unlike the open Greek theaters, which allowed a full view of the area outside, the top of the scaenae frons in Roman theaters typically rose to the level of the top of the cavea. A considerable portion of this wall still stands in the Odeum of Herodes Atticus in Athens; and at the theater at Aspendos in Pamphylia (second century A.D.) the scaenae frons, which may have been copied directly from the one in Ephesus, is virtually intact. These stage walls had either three or five doors on the first floor and usually three on the second floor, where actors stood while performing. The scaenae frons was elaborately decorated with numerous columns and capitals in one of the Greek styles of architecture.

Awnings were spread over the theaters to protect spectators against both sun and rain.[64] These are described by Pliny as made of linen and introduced into Rome by Quintus Catulus (in 78 B.C.).[65] They were often colored yellow, red, or dark blue.[66] Pliny says that Caesar stretched such awnings over the entire Roman Forum! They were supported by masts attached to the outer walls of the theater. The sockets into which the masts were inserted may still be seen in Pompeii and the well-preserved theater in Orange, France. Crossbeams between the masts allowed the unfurling of the awnings.

It has been argued that both the Gospel of Mark and the Book of Revelation reflect the format of Greek tragedy and could have been performed in an ancient theater.[67] The popularity of the the-

Roman odeum in
Athens.

ater in almost every city in New Testament times lends credibility
to this hypothesis.

Odea

An *odeum* or *odeion* (ᾠδεῖον) was a type of theater devoted to
musical productions, a concert hall built by the Greeks as early as
the fifth century B.C., and probably earlier. The Odeum of Pericles
was built in Athens about 450 B.C. adjacent to the Theater of
Dionysus. It was used as a rehearsal and performance hall, a
meeting place for small civic functions, and a general-purpose
auditorium. Wherever a large theater was located, a smaller
odeum was usually built nearby.

Copying and occasionally modifying the Greek models, the
Romans built odea throughout the empire. The Roman odea were
built of stone and, more often than not, were simply miniature
theaters that were closely linked architecturally with their larger
counterparts. Pompeii and Corinth have such structures in close
proximity to one another. The odeum at Pompeii represents a variation in that it was rectangular and roofed. The odeum in Ephesus, near the civic agora, may originally have been a bouleterion
(a renovation not uncommon in the Roman world), and may have
continued to do double duty as a place of civic assembly as well as
of cultural entertainment. Such was probably true of most Roman
odea, which were used for lectures and readings as well as concerts.[68] The largest known structure of this kind is the three-thou-
sand-seat odeum in Athens built in the second century A.D. by
Herodes Atticus, the man who also built the odeum in Corinth.

Circuses

The Roman appetite for brutal and inhumane games became more and more degenerate as the republic gave way to the empire. To match such competition, the legitimate theater was modified by the third century A.D. to allow the performance of similar spectacles. In fact, theaters had earlier resorted to lewd mime shows involving casts of hundreds.

The obsession of the public with gladiatorial games (*munera*) enabled the rulers and wealthy aristocrats to use them as a form of narcotic to keep the people contented. All the emperors except Tiberius supported and attended them. However, gladiatorial combat was not a part of the original games, which reach back to the seventh century B.C. The oldest games recorded included vicious boxing matches, wrestling, footraces, acrobatics, mock cavalry battles, horse races, trick riding, exhibitions of wild and trained animals, baiting of wild animals (*venationes*), and—the most popular of all—chariot races.[69] Popular as these became, they were not equally fascinating to everyone. Pliny the Younger at the end of the first century A.D. remarked: "When I think about this futile, stupid and monotonous entertainment, I derive a certain joy from the fact that I get no joy at all from the [horse] races!"

These activities took place on long, narrow surfaces which were enclosed by seats on three sides, the fourth being left open

Natural beauty surrounded human brutality at Delphi's circus.

for the entrance of the chariots and the various participants. The oldest of these structures (its rudiments date from the late seventh or early sixth century B.C.) is the Circus Maximus, built between the Palatine and Aventine hills in Rome. It was 2000 feet long and 650 feet wide. A moat originally protected the crowd from the wild animals used in the games, but it was replaced eventually by an iron fence. In the center of the arena, at a slightly oblique angle to give more room for the chariots at the beginning of the race, was a *spina* ("dividing wall"); there were three *metae* ("cones" around which the racers had to turn) at each end. Some of these may still be seen in the huge circus or hippodrome (ἱπποδρομος, "a place where horses run") at Caesarea Maritima on the coast of Israel. Various decorative objects stood on the spina between the metae, such as statues and obelisks, one of which lies fallen on the arena at Caesarea.

The Circus Maximus seated about sixty thousand spectators at the time of Augustus, but was enlarged continually until in the time of Constantine (early fourth century) it held two hundred thousand. Twelve starting gates allowed twelve chariots to race at one time, although four was the usual number, or sometimes eight. James Butler comments, "The circus stirred the rivalries and passions of the Roman mob to an almost unbelievable pitch and ultimately helped to undermine the moral and social fabric of the Empire."[70] It was probably here that most of the Christian martyrdoms occurred in the period prior to Constantine.

Amphitheaters

Amphitheaters, unlike theaters, were freestanding, oval-shaped structures which completely surrounded arenas. They had no known Greek precedent, for they were built specifically for the degenerate Roman games, which were not tolerated in Athens. Amphitheaters were never common in Greece and the eastern Mediterranean, although they were built everywhere in the Latin West. Their origin seems to have been in Etruria, where gladiatorial games developed from the funeral games honoring dead heroes. They were not introduced into Rome until 264 B.C. The oldest surviving amphitheater was built in Pompeii soon after 80 B.C.[71] Rome did not build a stone amphitheater until forty years later.

The Pompeian structure was about 460 feet long by 345 feet wide and seated about twenty thousand spectators. Entrance to the upper tiers of seats was by outside staircases, while access to the lower tiers was provided by vaulted passageways that led under the upper seats into a central corridor which encircled the building between the second and third tiers. The arena is sunk below ground level and was entered by a broad corridor at each end. Mount Vesuvius, which destroyed the city in A.D. 79, provided a scenic background to the events staged here.

The best-known and most impressive building of this type, however, was the Flavian Amphitheater in Rome; it was called the Colosseum because of the colossal statue of Nero which stood nearby.[72] It was begun by the emperor Vespasian (A.D. 69–79) and completed by Titus (79–81) and Domitian (81–96). The Colosseum measured 617 feet by 512 feet and seated about forty-five thousand people. The arena (floor) was 289 feet by 180 feet.

A supreme example of the best in Roman architecture, the exterior of the building is still breathtaking. The outer wall rests on eighty piers connected by barrel vaults made of stone. Three concentric rows of piers on the lowest three levels provided two parallel passageways which encircled the building. The external facing on each pier utilized the three basic patterns of Greek architecture in the form of columns with bases and capitals in the Doric, Ionic, and Corinthian orders on the first, second, and third stories respectively. A fourth level, added in the early third century and bringing the height of the Colosseum from 120 to 157 feet, consisted of a plain wall with alternating square Corinthian pilasters and open windows.

An elaborate network of underground rooms and corridors , which housed animals, gladiators, and scenery, all of which could be brought rapidly to the surface by an ingenious system of elevators using counterweights, was dug 20 feet below the arena. As in most sophisticated amphitheaters with subterranean networks, a wide opening (*media via*) ran right through the middle of the building. Other examples of this feature may be seen at Capua and Pozzuoli, though not at Pompeii. The entire arena could be sealed off and filled with water for the

The Flavian Amphitheater in Rome, better known as the Colosseum, was an elaborate structure designed using all three architectural orders.

production of mock navy battles (*naumachiae*). Many amphitheaters in the Empire were eventually modified in the third century A.D. for this purpose.

A huge awning operated by a detachment of sailors housed nearby provided shade for the spectators. The corbels that held the awnings may still be seen. Pliny the Elder has furnished a fascinating note: "Recently awnings actually of sky blue and spangled with stars have been stretched with ropes even in the emperor Nero's amphitheaters."[73]

Apart from occasional depictions in mosaic, it is not within the power of archaeological remains to portray the bloodthirsty scenes that took place in these ancient slaughterhouses. But the literary sources provide appalling descriptions of human suffering and the moral, spiritual, and intellectual degradation of the myriads who delighted in watching such perversity of human nature.[74] These connoisseurs of horror who day after day, from morning till night, took pleasure in the slaughter that occurred in the amphitheaters, must bear responsibility for the moral decline which eventuated in the fall of the Roman Empire.

A steady stream of gladiators was supplied from the ranks of slaves, prisoners of war, criminals sentenced to death, and even occasionally from Roman citizens perversely seeking excitement. Human life was regarded as cheap, and murder was justified on the assumption that such people deserved to die, indeed had already forfeited their place in human society. But can a society that took pleasure in such degeneracy be called human? More debased than the gladiatorial combat between two men, one armed with a net and trident spear and the other with a sword and rectangular shield, or the combat between men and beasts, were the pairings of the *gladiatores meridiani* described with disgust by Seneca.[75] Jerome Carcopino summarizes:

> The pitiable contingent of the doomed was driven into the arena. The first pair were brought forth, one man armed and one dressed simply in a tunic. The business of the first was to kill the second, which he never failed to do. After this feat he was disarmed and led out to confront a newcomer armed to the teeth, and so the inexorable butchery continued until the last head had rolled in the dust.[76]

The kind of sub-human activity that occurred in these ancient torture chambers called amphitheaters is movingly recreated from ancient sources in J. G. Davies's account of the martyrdom of a Christian woman, Victoria, during the reign of Diocletian.[77] The popularity of amphitheaters led to the virtual abandonment of the theaters, which were seldom repaired after the third century. It was the Christian gospel that finally put an end to the horrid games in the amphitheaters. The butcheries of the arena were stopped by Christian emperors. In 326 Constantine effectively dried up the main source of supply of gladiators when he issued a decree that forbad the condemnation of criminals to the beasts. By the end of the century, gladiatorial games ceased to exist in the East; and in 404 Honorius issued an edict forbidding gladiatorial combat in the West.

Religious and Domestic Structures

Religious Structures

Synagogues

The synagogue was the "religious, cultural and social center of the Jewish community in every settlement of the Roman and Byzantine Period."[1] Although synagogues have been found in the Diaspora,[2] they are best studied in Israel, where more than one hundred have been found since excavations began in 1905. Over half of these sites are in Galilee and the Golan Heights. Although more than fifty of these structures have a discernible plan, no two are identical.

A direct correlation existed between the size of the Jewish population in an area and the number of synagogues; large cities often had many. The Talmud reports that at the time of the Jewish revolt there were "480 synagogues in Jerusalem . . . and Vespasian destroyed them all."[3] This may be an exaggeration since John Wilkinson estimates that in the late second-temple period 365 synagogues existed in Jerusalem.[4] By the third and fourth centuries, Tiberias is reported to have had thirteen synagogues, Sepphoris eighteen, and Rome eleven.[5]

The word "synagogue" (συναγωγή) originally referred to a gathering of people as well as to a building or institution.[6] Which is meant is not always clear in either the New Testament or other literature. Archaeological excavations, however, provide important chronological information about the physical structure, including how early the Jews began to construct buildings exclusively dedicated to synagogue worship. Those at Masada and Herodium, which date to the reign of Herod the Great, were renovated structures, such as dining halls.[7] A Greek inscription uncovered on Jerusalem stonework from before A.D. 70 states that Theodotus had built the synagogue at that site for the reading of the law.[8] Another building, erected before the mid-first century A.D., probably to be a synagogue, was excavated at Gamla.[9] It was among those destroyed during the revolt in A.D. 66–67.[10]

Most synagogues uncovered in Israel are from the third century A.D. and later. Few earlier remains have been found, perhaps because the economy of the Jewish population was obliterated over the period of the first and second revolts (A.D. 66–135), requiring a long time for recovery and rebuilding. It was widely believed that Jewish life steadily declined after the revolts to centuries of cultural poverty.[11] Excavations in Israel, especially

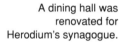

A dining hall was renovated for Herodium's synagogue.

Galilee, however, point instead to a prosperous Jewish culture during the Byzantine period.[12] The Jews in Lower Galilee, where trade routes abounded and Greek was the language of culture,[13] seem to have prospered through commercial enterprise. Lavish synagogues of Greek architectural decoration[14] often boasted floor mosaics, impressive works of art in their own right, that might depict the Torah Ark, a zodiac, animals, or human figures.[15] Synagogues in Upper Galilee, on the other hand, were decorated more conservatively with menorahs, eagles, and other simple elements. Rarely were colored mosaics used.[16]

By 1978 enough evidence had accumulated to force reevaluation of long-held theories. Until then a strong assumption held that chronological periods of synagogue construction could readily be discerned from architectural types. Four periods were thus categorized:

1. Prototypes: Reused Buildings (1st century A.D.). Examples cited were synagogues at Herodium and Masada. Such reused-building synagogues oriented seats to face the center of the room, featured roofs supported by columns, and had no matroneum section for women and children. According to the theory they did not face Jerusalem until after the destruction of the city in 70 A.D.

2. Early Synagogues: Galilean or Basilical (2d–3d centuries). Examples cited were at Capernaum, Bar'am, Chorazin, and Meiron. These buildings were rectangular, constructed from ashlar stones, and paved with flagstones rather than mosaics. Three entrances on the short side faced Jerusalem, and the external facade was elaborately decorated. The interiors had almost no decoration. There were stone benches along the walls, columns along three walls, and often a second story which may have been a matroneum. There was no fixed Torah Ark nor bema pulpit.

3. Transitional Synagogues: Broadhouse (4th–5th centuries). Examples cited were at Eshtemoa and Susiya. The congregation was oriented toward Jerusalem, as were the benches and a fixed niche or bema that faced the holy city. Entrances were moved to the sides not facing Jerusalem. Construction with ashlar walls featured a roof supported by wooden beams, and no columns cluttered the interior. Mosaic floors replaced flagstone.

4. Late Synagogues: Apsidal (5th–7th centuries). Examples cited were at Beth Alfa and Hammath-Tiberias. These buildings were basilica-type designs, often with an apse facing Jerusalem. Transverse columns were removed for the bema, and there were permanent bemas and Torah Arks. Most ornamentation was inside, including floor mosaics of

Figure 4
Types of Synagogues

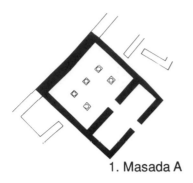

1. Masada A

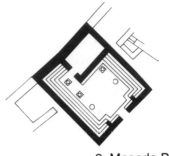

2. Masada B

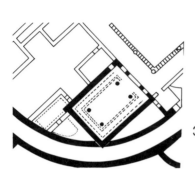

3. Herodium

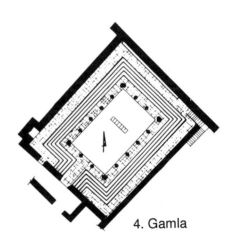

4. Gamla

5. Delos

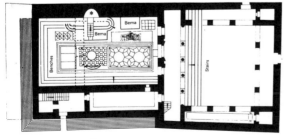

6. Susiya

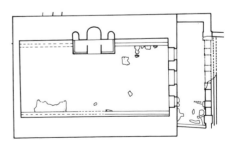

7. Eshtemoa

1–5 Renovated buildings (1st cent. A.D.)
6–8 Broadhouse types
9 Basilica (Galilean) types
10–11 Basilica types with apses

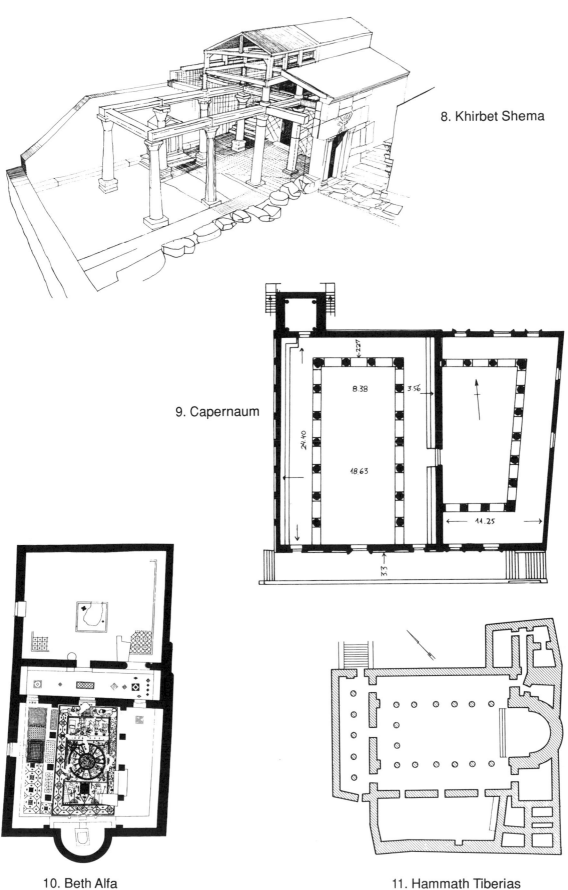

8. Khirbet Shema

9. Capernaum

8.38
3.56
227
24.40
18.63
11.25
33

10. Beth Alfa

11. Hammath Tiberias

zodiacs, animals, and humans. There is no evidence of monumental facades.

The reevaluation of this line of reasoning was devastating to all type theories, and since 1978 opinions have varied widely as to the origin of structures used for synagogue meetings.[17] First, Galilean-type synagogues previously thought to have been second century (for example, Capernaum and Meiron) have been shown to be later.[18] Second, a mixture of types within the same time period has emerged at Khirbet Shema in southern Galilee. There a third- or fourth-century broadhouse synagogue was found only 600 meters from a basilical (Galilean) type at Meiron from the same time period.[19] This mixture of types is seen at Eshtemoa and Susiya where broadhouse synagogues were built in the fourth or fifth centuries while at Engedi a third-century synagogue was rebuilt in the fourth century along basilical lines.[20] In Galilee basilical synagogues were being built with stone floors in the fourth century while at Tiberias a beautiful mosaic floor was constructed in the rebuilt synagogue.[21] Synagogues in the Golan from the fourth and fifth centuries show a mixture of types.[22] At Nabratein in Upper Galilee a broadhouse synagogue was dated to the second century by its excavator, 200 years earlier, though some argue for a fourth-century dating of the building.[23] At Sardis in Turkey, a third-century synagogue shows an apse with a bema on one end, two Torah Arks on the other end, and an

Reused-building synagogue at Hammath-Tiberias is of the basilica type.

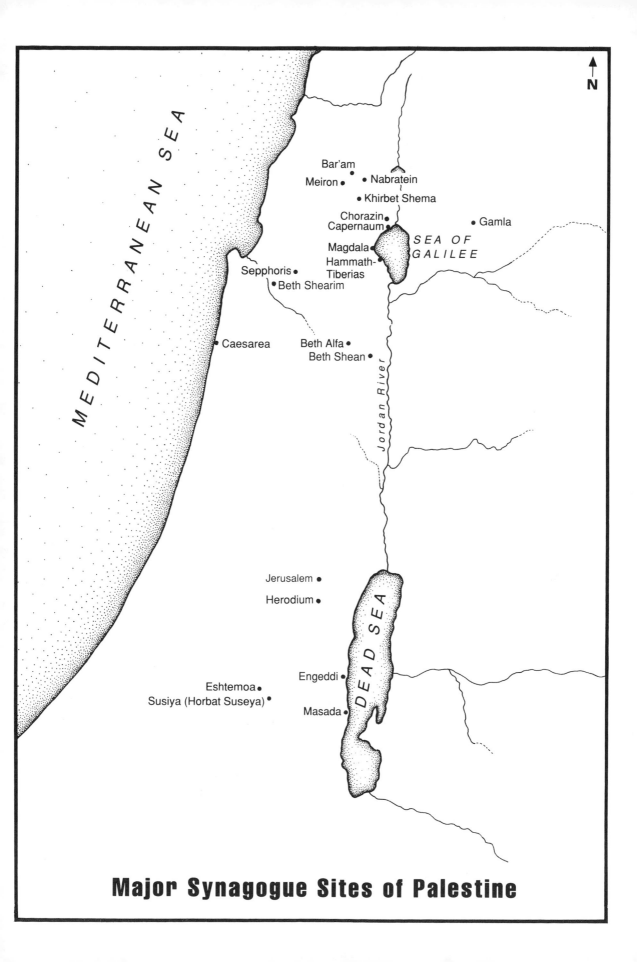

Major Synagogue Sites of Palestine

elaborate atrium.[24] Finally, first-century buildings that were probably built as synagogues have been found at Gamla, Magdala, and Capernaum.[25]

Clearly we cannot now link exact architectural types to a fixed chronology.[26] We know a good deal about synagogues of the fourth century and later, but there is still little archaeological evidence about those of the New Testament era. The best examples are at Herodium, Masada (see p. 139), and Gamla.[27] Opinions differ as to the origin of structures used for synagogue meetings.[28] Lee Levine discusses the similarities and differences among the four synagogues from before A.D. 70: Masada, Herodium, and Gamla in Israel, and the island of Delos in the south Aegean Sea.[29] Two others—the synagogue at Magdala and the earlier Capernaum building, foundations of which have been found beneath the reconstructed fourth century synagogue—should probably be added to the discussion.[30] There is no evident uniformity among any of these synagogues regarding entrances, orientation, benches, main prayer hall, bema, or setting. Most were renovated buildings that had previously served a different function. During the New Testament period, synagogical gatherings in small villages were probably in private homes, as was undoubtedly true of early Christian assemblies. Information is still sparse on the phenomena of Christian synagogues.[31]

Churches

Evidence of Christian meeting places from the New Testament period is as limited as evidence of synagogues. Ecclesiastical architecture did not exist at that time; Christianity was not a legal religion in the time of the early empire so Christians could not corporately own property. Such New Testament references to meeting places of Christians as 1 Corinthians 16:19; Romans 16:5; Philemon 2, and Colossians 4:15 (note also the description of the upper room in Mark 14:15, and the lecture hall in Ephesus of Acts 19:9) indicate that the gatherings took place in homes or rented rooms.[32] Also, there is evidence that early Jewish Christians sometimes met in synagogues.[33] The New Testament letter of James refers to Christians (undoubtedly Jewish) meeting in a synagogue (2:2), but bear in mind that at this time Jews probably met most often in homes and rented halls.

Churches were first built during the reign of Constantine (306–37), the first Roman emperor to adopt Christianity (although it had been the favored religion in Armenia from the conversion of King Tiridates III in 303).[34] With the advent of the Byzantine Empire (324), Christian influence prevailed, and basilica-type church buildings sprouted throughout the Mediterranean

Church of the Nativity, Bethlehem.

world, particularly over sacred sites. In the Holy Land almost two hundred Byzantine churches (from the first half of the fourth century to the beginning of the eighth) have been excavated.[35] Eusebius has described the patronage of Constantine and his mother in some better known projects.[36]

Temples

In New Testament times the vast majority of people in the Roman Empire were pagans, given to polytheism and idolatry. Paul contrasted the pagan deities worshiped in the temples of Athens with the true spiritual reality of the God of Jews and Christians, who "does not live in shrines made by man" (Acts 17:24). Jesus (John 4:21–24) contrasted worship in the Samaritan temple on Mount Gerizim and in the Jewish temple in Jerusalem with worship of God "in spirit and truth" (v. 24), worship that is irrespective of geography and religious architecture.

Temples, commonplace structures in the ancient world, were usually located near the heart of a city or on its acropolis, the most prominent elevation. As Paul spoke to the Athenians (Acts 17:19–34) his view included the temple dedicated to Athena, the Parthenon. It still stands majestically on Athens' acropolis. As Jesus spoke to the woman at Sychar (John 4:1–42) he could see the Samaritan temple perched on the northern spur of Mount Gerizim. Excavations on the spur, now called Tel er-Ras, have revealed foundations of the ancient temple (see p. 182). Towering over the city for a millennium, the Jerusalem temples of Solomon and Zerubbabel stood on Mount Moriah. The temple of Aphrodite on top of the Acrocorinth (the acropolis of Corinth) was visible for miles. Ancient cities probably held no feature more evident or impressive than these magnificently constructed temples.

Unlike synagogues and churches, temples were not primarily places of corporate worship and study. Rather, they were residences of the gods. Worship took the form of offerings of animal and/or monetary sacrifices. Sacred prostitution was often connected with the temple priests and priestesses. The gods had to be placated in order for life to function normally; accordingly, their abodes were usually the best that money could buy.

Temples were usually built of huge cut stones laid on foundations of bedrock. A typical structure consisted of one or more rooms in which stood statues of the gods or emperors. Often a portico was constructed around the perimeter of the building.

Figure 5
Greek Orders

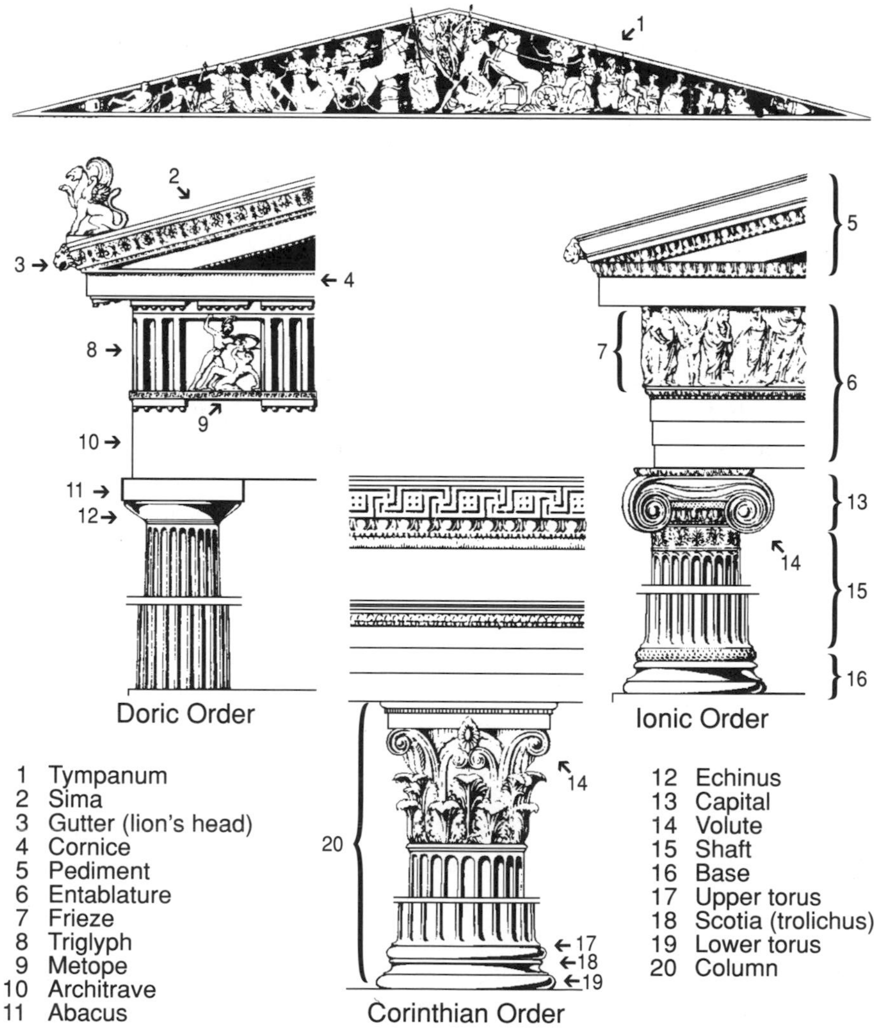

Doric Order

Corinthian Order

Ionic Order

1	Tympanum	12	Echinus
2	Sima	13	Capital
3	Gutter (lion's head)	14	Volute
4	Cornice	15	Shaft
5	Pediment	16	Base
6	Entablature	17	Upper torus
7	Frieze	18	Scotia (trolichus)
8	Triglyph	19	Lower torus
9	Metope	20	Column
10	Architrave		
11	Abacus		

Doric Temple of Hera, Paestum.

Temples were designed according to the various styles of standard Greek architecture: Doric (earliest examples from the eighth century B.C.), Ionic (earliest examples from the sixth century B.C.), and Corinthian (earliest examples from the fifth century B.C.). However, during the period of the Roman Empire Doric architecture was no longer used in the construction of temples. It was reserved almost exclusively for the engaged columns or pilasters of secular buildings.[37]

Many temples standing during the New Testament period had been built hundreds of years before. Some of them still stand. Among the most impressive surviving Doric temples are those in Corinth (Venus or Apollo), Athens (Parthenon of Athena), and Paestum (Hera, sometimes called Poseidon). Examples of the Ionic temple, some of which have been beautifully restored, may be seen in Rome (Temple of Fortuna Virilis); Athens (Erectheum and the Temple of Athena Nike or Athena Apteros, "Wingless Victory"), and Sardis (Temple of Artemis).

Ionic temple, Athens.

Corinthian temple, Athens.

Corinthian temples have survived in Athens (Jupiter, also known as the Olympeion of Hadrian); Baalbek in Lebanon (temples of Bacchus and Jupiter), and Rome (Pantheon). A number of well-preserved Corinthian temples were dedicated to the emperor Augustus. They are located in Nîmes, France (the Maison Carrée); Vienna, Austria; Pula, Yugoslavia; Rome (the Round Temple by the Tiber), and Petra, Jordan (called *Al-Khazneh* and cut into the side of a rock mountain).

Domestic Structures

Villas and Palaces

Homes built for wealthy citizens in New Testament times are the best-preserved examples of domestic architecture from the period we have. This would be expected since the key to preservation is the nature of their original construction. Large stone structures, whether private or civic, endure the ravages of time better than small houses built of field stone, dried brick, or clay. Mansions and palaces have been found all over the empire, and many have been thoroughly excavated.[38] Recently two lovely painted rooms of a late Hellenistic house were excavated at Amphipolis in Greece (see pp. 291–292).

Hadrian's Villa, about 15 miles from Rome, is one of the most impressive and beautiful palaces surviving from antiquity (see p. 347). Built by order of the emperor over a ten-year period (A.D. 125 to 135), this villa was the largest and richest imperial quarters in the Roman Empire. Situated on about 750 acres, a huge imperial palace stood near a Greek theater, a Roman odeum, and two

Statuary and esthetic beauty marked life at this Pompeii villa.

bathhouses (the Great Thermae and the Small Thermae). An expansive rectangular peristyle was patterned after the "Painted Porch" in the agora of Athens. The Canopus, a replica of the Egyptian temple of Serapis near Alexandria, included a statue-garnished pool bordered by recreational booths. A canal resembling some built by Herod the Great in Judea surrounded a luxurious circular pavilion which has been called in recent times the "Maritime Theater." It was in no sense a theater and probably served as a retreat for the emperor. The palace compound also featured several fountains (*nymphea*), libraries, barracks, and a large palestra and a piazza.

Palatial dwellings, of course, dotted Rome and any area throughout the empire where royalty elected to build their residences.[39] Herod built his major palace on the western perimeter of Jerusalem; he supplemented it with desert palace-fortresses in several Judean cities (see pp. 129–139). Roman officials who governed the provinces (praetors and propraetors) did not normally live in dwellings we might label palaces, but they did enjoy elegant quarters, such as the praetorium at Caesarea Maritima (see pp. 139–145).

Wealthy Roman citizens built sumptuous homes in the most coveted sections of a city, as is customary today. Even in a comparatively poor country, such as Judea, homes for wealthy aristocrats have been found in recent excavations.[40] In the Upper City of Jerusalem construction was abundant, with houses built very close together. However, each spacious house and courtyard could properly be called a luxury villa. Opulently ornamented with fresco walls and mosaic floors, the houses contained elaborate bathing facilities and expensive utensils. The excavator concluded that "this was an upper class quarter, where the noble families of Jerusalem lived, with the High Priest at their head. . . .

It can be assumed that this quarter was occupied chiefly by Sadducees."[41] A residence from the days of Herod the Great has been excavated on the Western Hill of Jerusalem's Upper City, overlooking the Temple Mount. The dwelling, covering more than 650 square feet, was made up of rooms arranged around a central courtyard, which contained four sunken ovens. Within the house were a large cistern for storing water, a ritual bath, and a number of living rooms, the largest of which had three cupboards built into one wall. The quality of the household pottery found in the dwelling clearly demonstrates that it was inhabited by a well-to-do family.[42]

Just southeast of this house, near the eastern edge of the Western Hill, Nahman Avigad uncovered a much larger dwelling. Built as a single unit with numerous rooms surrounding a central courtyard, the house covered almost 2000 square feet. Avigad, concluding that the house belonged to a "wealthy patrician family of some stature in Jerusalem society,"[43] explained that, "while modesty has led us to call it 'the Mansion,' its scale would justify referring to it as a palace."[44] West of the central courtyard a vestibule with a mosaic floor gave access from outside to the courtyard and the western wing. This wing contained a large reception room, which had doors on its western side opening to three smaller rooms. The northernmost of these rooms was a small bathroom, tiled with colored mosaics and equipped with a sunken sitting-bath in one corner. The eastern wing was a story lower than the western. Its rooms included two ritual baths (*miqwaot*). The presence of both domestic and ritual baths is evidence that the owners were both wealthy and quite religious. Those involved with the temple, such as the Sadducees, had to be in a constant state of ritual purity. Public ritual baths, such as the poor would use, were as acceptable but not so convenient.

Less than 200 feet north of the palatial mansion, Avigad found a more modest structure. Because it was covered with soot, having been burned in the destruction of the city in A.D. 70, he called it the "Burnt House."[45] It was the first of a number of dwellings eventually uncovered in the area. The plan was similar to many found from the period; three medium-sized rooms, a small room, a small kitchen, and a small, stepped ritual bath enclosed three sides of a small, stone-paved courtyard. The stone walls were thinly coated with white lime plaster, but the floors were beaten earth. An inscription identifies the structure as belonging to the Bar Kathros family, a well-known, but little-admired, priestly family.

The rooms of the Burnt House were on the basement level and contained several ovens, suggesting that this was not a residential

Figure 6
Schematic of Palatial Mansion in Jerusalem

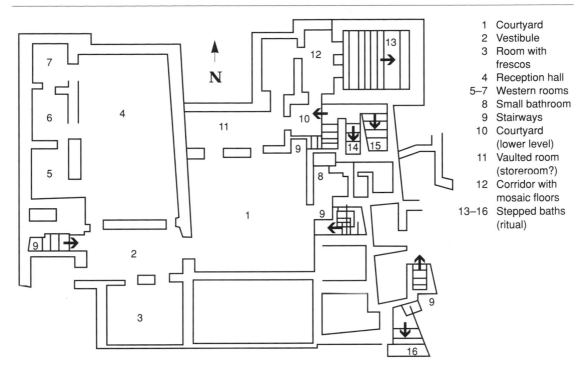

1 Courtyard
2 Vestibule
3 Room with frescos
4 Reception hall
5–7 Western rooms
8 Small bathroom
9 Stairways
10 Courtyard (lower level)
11 Vaulted room (storeroom?)
12 Corridor with mosaic floors
13–16 Stepped baths (ritual)

dwelling but a workshop connected with one of the larger residences nearby. Most likely the kitchen produced spices or incense for the neighboring temple. A number of stone vessels were found in the house. Some had been carved by hand, while others had been turned on a lathe. The bowls, plates, cups, goblets, inkwells, and cylindrical weights testify to the wealth of the owners. Basalt mortars and pestles were discovered, as well as a beautiful rectangular stone table (the first of several to be found in the area), which was subsequently restored.

Dining rooms were characteristic of middle- and upper-class homes of the Roman Empire, though houses of the poor did not have them. These rooms were furnished with couches or benches (usually three but sometimes six in number) placed together in a ⊔ shape that surrounded three sides of the table. Both the couches and the room in which they were housed are known as a *triclinium*. In the triclinium diners would eat as they reclined on one elbow. Such posture is indicated in John's account of the Last Supper, in which a disciple is described as "lying" (ἀναπεσών) close to the breast of Jesus (13:25). The well-known painting by Leonardo da Vinci is based on later European dining customs.

No triclinia have yet been found in Syria-Palestine, even in wealthy residences, but there are beautifully preserved small triclinia in Pompeii. Some of the dining rooms had built-in benches;

Triclinium at Pompeii.

other triclinia were dining areas in which freestanding benches were placed under outdoor arbors. In Judea a Roman-style house of the wealthy or a large rented hall might have several small triclinia or one large one with several ⊔-shaped groups of portable couches. Poor people in Jesus' time who wished to host a number of guests would rent or borrow dining facilities, such as the "large upper room furnished and ready" (Mark 14:15) where Jesus and his disciples ate the Passover.

Portable couches in dining rooms (and elsewhere, no doubt) are depicted on Greek vases from the Classical period as also used for sexual purposes (see pp. 317). Standard beds are rarely, if ever, depicted in sexual scenes by the Greeks. Multiple dining rooms associated with the worship of Demeter have been excavated in both Samothrace and Corinth, and may have been used in fertility rites (see pp. 315–317). We can only surmise that such use of the couches continued among the Romans.

Homes of the Middle and Lower Classes

Individual Houses

As exciting as these discoveries may be, it should be remembered that the average resident of the eastern Mediterranean did not enjoy such a lavish lifestyle. Few homes of the poorer class have been found, due to their flimsy construction and the ease with which they could be destroyed by invaders, earthquakes, or urban renewal.

Work in Capernaum, however, revealed a dwelling the excavator dates to the first century and identifies as conceivably the

Figure 7
Schematic of Peter's House in Capernaum

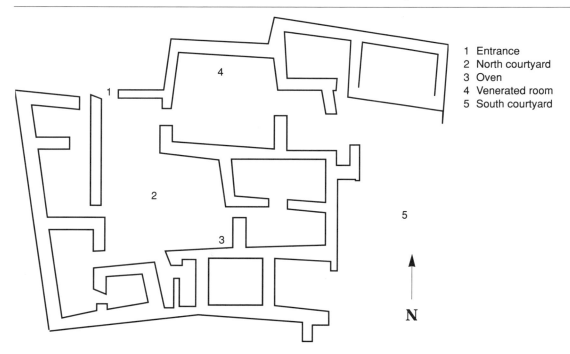

1 Entrance
2 North courtyard
3 Oven
4 Venerated room
5 South courtyard

house of Simon Peter (see pp. 146–166). The house, like several others found nearby, was designed for the pragmatic needs of life in the eastern Mediterranean. A courtyard, which allowed outdoor cooking and even the quartering of small animals, was usually located in the center of surrounding rooms. Rooms opened onto the courtyard, not to the outside, and they had no windows. While these features provided some security, they also meant that the rooms had little light, perhaps explaining why the woman who lost one of her coins lit a lamp to search for it (Luke 15:8). The rooms were used primarily for storage and sleeping. In the summer people used their rooftops for such activities as sleeping, eating, meditating, praying, conversing, and visiting with neighbors. Simon Peter was praying on a rooftop in Jaffa when he had a heavenly vision (Acts 10:9). People who could afford to dug cisterns for storing water beneath the courtyard or rooms of their house. Many examples of these cisterns, plastered with mortar made of lime mixed with ash, have been found in Jerusalem and Sepphoris.

Indoor toilet facilities were nonexistent among the poor, who had to use pots or go outside the house. In large cities, public facilities were available to those who could afford the nominal charge.[46] Public latrines from the New Testament period have been well preserved in Philippi and Ostia, and some have been found in Athens, Corinth, Dion, and Sardis. Bathing among the poor, other than sponge bathing, normally took place in pools, lakes, streams, or public bathhouses. Individual bathtubs have been found in the homes of the upper-class citizens in Hasmonean Jericho and frequently in residences in the western part of the empire (for instance, Pompeii and Herculaneum).

In biblical lands, the poor slept on straw mats or animal-skin rugs, usually lying on floors of beaten earth. Roman-style homes of those with greater means had small bedrooms; in them were bedsteads of wood or bronze, laced with ropes on which mats were laid. Though most beds (*lecti*) were singles, married couples used double beds (*lecti geniales*). In Pompeii and Herculaneum the beds usually were positioned to cover one end of the bedroom, reaching from wall to wall.

Apartment Houses

As Paul traveled from city to city he would have observed a phenomenon quite different from that he was accustomed to seeing in the villages of the Levant (eastern shores of the Mediterranean). While the village poor lived in small houses made of clay or narrow stone walls, the poor in large cities of the empire lived in tenements which strongly resembled the large, plain apartment buildings found in modern Rome today. Unlike a *domus* (a large house or mansion belonging to and occupied by a single family), the *insulae*, in which the poor lived comprised small, crowded flats or apartments called *cenaculi*.[47]

Originally, the term *insula* referred to a square or rectangular parcel of ground surrounded by streets, much like a modern city block. Gradually, however, the meaning was extended to denote what essentially were apartment buildings. Some of these structures had been built as tenements, and others were constructed by renovating large mansions strategically located in the heart of the city. By the fourth century there was only one private house for every twenty-six blocks of apartment houses in Rome.[48] Whereas the domus was designed with an inward orientation toward its atrium, the insula was oriented outward with its openings to the street. By the time of the empire, insulae had reached such heights and had been built in such shoddy fashion that a height limit was set by imperial decree. Augustus forbade the buildings to reach 70 feet;[49] Trajan later lowered the limit to 59 feet.[50]

Two types of insulae were found in Rome. In the more luxurious the entire first floor—sometimes called a *domus*—was rented by a single tenant. The other type was far more characteristic among the masses. Its ground floor was divided into shops, *tabernae*, above which the proprietors lived in one-room lofts which were accessible by a wooden ladder. Such shop-loft construction

has been found east of the theater in Corinth.[51] The upper floors of either type were not connected with the ground floor; outside or inside staircases opened only to the streets. Each floor was divided into several flats, which were subdivided into separate suites as economic necessity demanded. Each suite had one or two main rooms that were larger than the others. The Romans had developed the use of *opus caementicum* (concrete) by the second century B.C., so buildings could support multiple floors of apartments.[52] Vitruvius, the Roman architect and engineer in the time of Augustus, recorded the impetus for and method of construction:

> Yet with the greatness of the city and the unlimited crowding of citizens, it is necessary to provide very numerous dwellings. Therefore since a level site could not receive such a multitude to dwell in the city, circumstances themselves have compelled the resort to raising the height of the buildings. And so by means of stone pillars, walls of burnt brick, party walls of rubble, towers [buildings were five and six stories high] have been raised, and these being joined together by frequent board floors produce upper stories with fine views over the city to the utmost advantage. Therefore walls are raised to a great height through various stories, and the Roman people have excellent dwellings without hindrance.[53]

Strabo, the Greek geographer, wrote that "the houses [in Tyre], it is said, have many stories, even more than the houses at Rome."[54]

These apartment buildings of the New Testament period had few of the comforts to which we in the modern Western world are accustomed. There was no natural light in the dwellings except that which came through large, open windows. In all probability, Eutychus fell from such a window in an insula in Troas (Acts 20:8–12). Although in some locations the windows may have contained glass,[55] the openings most often were covered only by cloths or skins, which were wind-blown or rain-saturated in adverse weather. Windows with solid wooden shutters could keep out the weather and provide security, but only if they were closed and locked, which also kept out the light. Private homes also experienced this inconvenience. Pliny the Younger spoke of the darkness and silence in his Tuscan villa that resulted from the closing of his shutters.[56]

Adding further to the discomfort of the insulae was the absence of furnaces or fireplaces. In excavations of the dwellings no evidence has been discovered of the kind of central heating units (consisting of a *hypocaust* and *suspensura*) such as were found in bathhouses and in the bathrooms of some mansions and palaces. Literature does not mention such units. The privilege of gathering around an open, log fire in the center of a room or in front of a log fireplace, such as peasants in the villages enjoyed, was not allowed tenants of the insulae. In addition to the danger of fire, there was no adequate chimney venting system for the smoke. The best they had was a copper or bronze brazier, which was used for cooking and produced very little heat. Small ovens used for baking emitted virtually no excess heat. Cakes were cooked in a covered oven while other food simmered over the small, open braziers. Thus, during cold and unpleasant winters, the only refuge was the confines of a room darkened by closed shutters, a small, ineffectual brazier, and whatever warm clothing finances would allow. Even the homes of the wealthy provided none of the warmth and comfort available to modern tenement dwellers.

Lack of water facilities made life in these congested apartment buildings even more dreary. Aqueducts brought water only to the ground floors, though an exception to this was found at Ephesus (see p. 88). In the Latin West, insulae residents had to carry water from fountains to their own high-rise apartments, a chore which undoubtedly discouraged personal hygiene. No apparatus for conveying water to upper stories has been found in excavations or mentioned in ancient texts. Juvenal spoke of water-carriers (*aquarii*) as the scum of the slave population,[57] but undoubtedly their task was important for those who wanted or needed someone else to carry water for them. Eventually becoming as much a part of the building as the porters and sweepers, aquarii were inherited with the building by the heirs or legatees.

The inconvenience of the insulae that might be resented most by modern tenants was the lack of sewage drainage for indoor toilets. Evidently the apartments were never connected to Rome's sewer system. The occupant of a first floor domus might have the advantage of an indoor latrine with running water, which would sweep the refuse away to a sewer or, if sewers were too far away, into a nearby cess trench. The trenches were emptied by manure merchants, who had obtained the right, probably under Vespasian to recycle it as fertilizer. Regarding this arrangement Suetonius wrote that "Titus complained of the tax which Vespasian had imposed on the contents of the public toilets."[58]

Public toilets were used by the poor in the insulae who could spare the small admission fee. People using these facilities conversed about daily matters without embarrassment while seated next to each other on stone commodes without partitions. Water flowed continuously in little channels along the front of the seats. These seats and channels are well preserved in Philippi and Ostia, among other places. It was customary for fullers to place large earthen jars outside the front of their shops, on the main sidewalk, for use as open-air urinals. The alkalai produced

Urinals along a street in Pompeii.

A latrine in Philippi.

helped separate dirt from the cloth in washing. Such jars still stand in front of shops in ancient Pompeii. Similar urinals, built on public sidewalks, are used in modern Florence, Italy, but the urine is washed away in a sewer rather than kept. Misers and the very poor used the jars at the fullers' shops and the neighboring dungheaps. It was not uncommon for them to empty their chamber pots from an upper-story window. When the contents landed on an unsuspecting passerby, offenders were often sought out and punished according to the law, which was strictly enforced by sympathetic judges who had to walk the same streets. Financial settlements were awarded if injuries resulted from the incident.[59]

Problems of comfort and hygiene were especially difficult to deal with at night because the streets of Rome and other ancient cities were totally dark. There were no functioning street lights of any sort. When night fell everyone stayed home behind locked doors and shuttered windows. If the rich went out, they were accompanied by slaves bearing torches. In the parable of the wise and foolish virgins (Matt. 25:1–13), the five wise virgins took extra containers of oil with them to the wedding feast. Perhaps this was as much for the return trip home as for participation in the wedding itself.

Most vehicular traffic, except for construction contractors, was not allowed in Rome or in the market areas of some other cities during the daylight hours. In Pompeii huge stone road barriers may still be seen at intersections. This meant merchants had to move goods by night, creating serious obstacles for pedestrians venturing into the darkness. It also meant that the streets were extremely noisy at night, particularly in the summer when shutters on the upper floors might be left open for coolness. Juvenal wrote that Romans were condemned to incessant insomnia: "The crossing of wagons in the narrow, winding streets, the swearing of drovers brought to a standstill would snatch sleep from a sea-calf or the emperor Claudius himself."[60] No doubt, sleep was difficult and quiet meditation virtually impossible under these circumstances. How much more desirable would be a villa in the countryside where the silence described by Pliny could be enjoyed behind closed shutters.[61]

Without evidence of bathrooms, latrines, fireplaces, and kitchens in excavated apartment dwellings we must assume that life in most large ancient cities was rather spartan by modern standards. A somewhat better situation seems to have existed in Asia Minor. Until recently it was thought that Roman insulae originated in Italy, rather than in the East, where shops were

Warm drinks were served at this Herculaneum *thermopolium*.

located in the fora or clustered along main streets. Multistory buildings had been found in Syria, Carthage, and Alexandria but were not regarded as prototypes for the insulae.[62] On the northern slopes of Mount Koressos (Bulbudag) in Ephesus, however, excavations uncovered extensive remains of two huge insulae from the first century A.D. Built on a three-terraced hillside, the dwellings had water piped to apartments on every level, unlike those of Rome and Ostia. The clay pipes ran under the pavement of a stepped passageway, more than 9 feet wide, that separated the eastern block from the western block. Under the pavement also was a vaulted drainage channel, almost 6 feet high, which served both sections of insulae.

The ground floor of the eastern insula housed twelve rectangular vaulted shops, which opened onto the Street of the Kuretes (*Via Curetes*). One was a *thermopolium*, a shop that sold warm beverages; examples of such shops are well preserved in Pompeii and Herculaneum. On the lower terrace, above and behind the shops, a series of interior apartments were situated for shopkeepers and the poor. A huge two-storied mansion was built around a peristyle on the second terrace. Adjacent to the peristyle was a large living room (Lat. *oecus*; Gk. οἶκος), and a "baronial dining hall" (*cenatorium equestre*). The rest of the second and third levels of the eastern block was composed of smaller middle-class apartments, which opened off an alley to the east.

The western half of the Ephesian insulae consisted of five huge luxury apartments which were renovated after the fourth-century earthquake. They had multiple rooms with mosaic floors and frescoed walls. In the northeastern section of the insula some frescos from the first century are extant. Thus, we have an example in Ephesus of the rich, the poor, and the middle class, living in close proximity.[63]

PART 2

The Building Program
of Herod the Great

Herodian Jerusalem

The Beneficence of Herod

Archaeological excavations have uncovered a surprisingly large amount of evidence pertaining to Herod the Great. Since "Jesus was born in Bethlehem of Judea in the days of Herod the king" (Matt. 2:1), more than a passing interest is due the rich written and physical record of this man and his time.

Herod the Great was an Idumean who, in 41 B.C., was granted provisional rule of Galilee by Mark Antony. To make his rule permanent he had to subjugate his enemies and consolidate his power; he easily satisfied this requirement in 37 B.C. when he conquered Jerusalem. In 30 B.C. Octavian (Caesar Augustus) affirmed Herod's rule over Judaea, Samaria, and Galilee despite Octavian's victory over Antony at Actium. Herod remained in power until his death in 4 B.C.; thus Christ was born in Bethlehem prior to that date. A stone weight purchased in 1967 from an antiquities dealer by Israel's Department of Antiquities and Museums provides information on the dating of Herod's reign. Inscribed with an abbreviation for "Herod," in full it reads: "Year 32 of King Herod, the Benefactor, Loyal to Caesar. Inspector of Markets. Three Minas." The year 32 probably corresponds to 9 B.C.[1]

The beneficence of Herod is extolled by Josephus, who enumerates the many cities where Herod endowed building projects. Josephus also records that Athens and other cities were "filled with Herod's offerings."[2] Two little-known inscriptions found between the Propylaea and the Erechtheum on the Athenian Acropolis bolster the historian's claim:

Inscription 1	*Inscription 2*
ο δημος	ο δαμος
ρομαιον ευεργεσιας	[βασι]λεα Ηρωδην Ευσεβη
ενεκεν και ευνοιας	και φιλοκαισαρα [α]ρετης
εις εαυτον	ενεκα και ευεργεσιας
The people	The people
[erect this monument to]	[erect this monument to]
King Herod, Lover	King Herod, Devout
of Romans, because of the benefaction	and a Lover of Caesar, because
and good will	of his virtue and benefaction.[4]
[shown] by him.[3]	

Another fragmentary inscription was found in 1935 on a base of Hymettian marble that had been reused for a modern wall in Athens. Once restored its inscription matched inscription 2 above.[5]

Herod was involved in building projects at twenty or more sites in Israel and at least thirteen outside its borders.[6] In Israel he built at Jerusalem, Caesarea Maritima, Sebaste (Samaria), Herodium, Masada, Jericho, Cypros (near Jericho), Macherus, Hyrcania, Alexandrium, Esbus (Heshbon), Antipatris, Anthedon, Phasaelis, Bathyra, Gaba, Paneas, Sepphoris, Livias, and Hebron. Beyond his kingdom he built at Ascalon, Ptolemais, Tyre, Sidon, Damascus, Berytus, Byblos, Tripolis, Laodicea (Syria), Antioch (Syria), Rhodes, Chios, and Nicopolis.[7] The building program included renovation of the temple in Jerusalem. It raised villages, cities, palaces, fortresses, ports, squares, colonnaded streets, theaters, stadia, hippodromes, gymnasia, public baths, monuments, agricultural and urban water systems, formal gardens, vaulted warehouses, reservoirs, and pagan sanctuaries.[8] Whether Herod actively involved himself in architectural planning and project management details is debated, but his influence upon them is unmistakable. Undoubtedly the locations for his desert palace-fortresses were chosen by Herod himself for political and military reasons. And although Herod was partly Jewish in ancestry, his love for things Roman dominated his building activities. He was truly a Romanophile.[9]

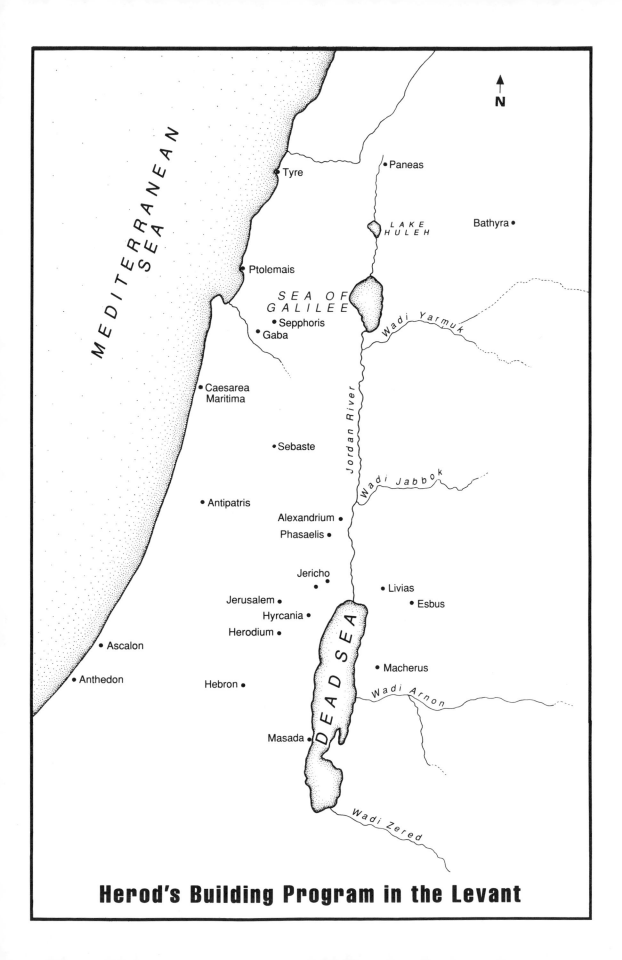

Herod's Building Program in the Levant

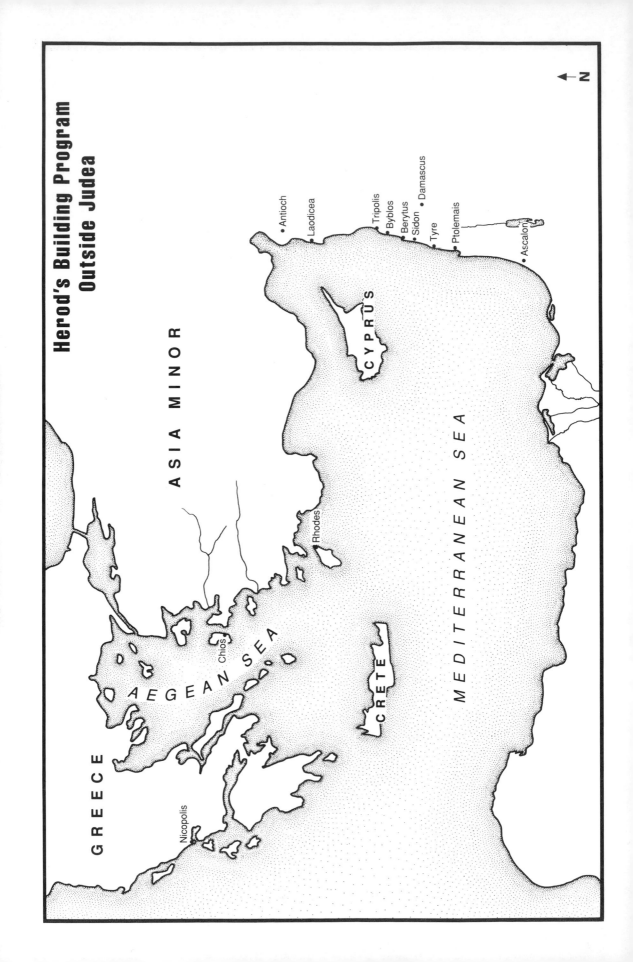

Herod's Building Program Outside Judea

GREECE

ASIA MINOR

AEGEAN SEA

Nicopolis

Chios

Rhodes

CRETE

CYPRUS

MEDITERRANEAN SEA

Antioch

Laodicea

Tripolis

Byblos

Berytus

Sidon • Damascus

Tyre

Ptolemais

Ascalon

N

The Nature of Herod's Construction

Two primary sources tell us most of what we know about Herod's building program: the writings of Flavius Josephus, the first-century Jewish historian, and the dramatic results of archaeological excavations.[10] Ehud Netzer, director of excavations at Herodium and Herodian Jericho and codirector of the Duke University excavations at Sepphoris, is without question the leading authority on Herodian architecture. It is Netzer's opinion that Herod built primarily for utilitarian and practical purposes, imposing his own ideas on the work of his Roman architects. Josephus mentions workers on only one project, the temple renovation in Jerusalem, and says nothing of the architect or architects in charge.[11] Clearly the plan to extend the podium of the Temple Mount southward by constructing a platform (the Pinnacle of the Temple) over huge Roman arches required imperial approval. Herod at least granted permission and may have originated the idea. The large number of projects and the unusual combination of functions many of the structures served lead Netzer to conclude that Herod must have personally been involved with their design and construction. Indeed, Josephus remarked that "with the construction of the porticos and the outer courts [Herod] did busy himself."[12]

His desert palaces are so extravagant and the stones used in some of his larger public projects (e.g., in Jerusalem and Hebron) so monumental that Herod has been regarded as a megalomaniac who built primarily for personal glory and immortality. However, it is erroneous to assume that the ashlar stone is characteristic of all Herod's building.[13] These beautiful stones, bossed with a smooth border and most visible in Jerusalem's Eastern Wall, are typical only of Herod's larger public works. One ashlar stone found in the "Rabbinical Tunnel" along the western side of the Temple Mount is 46 feet by 10 feet by 10 feet; it weighs about 415 tons![14] The largest megalith at Stonehenge, England, weights only 40 tons, and the stones used in the Great Pyramid of Cheops in Giza weigh only 15 tons.[15] How such mammoth stones could have been moved is a mystery. They may have been quarried as circular columns and rolled to the spot where they were put in place and then squared.[16]

Most of Herod's private projects were not composed of such large and costly stones. Masada, Herodium, and the winter palaces in Jericho, for example, were constructed mostly with conventional-sized stone blocks, sun-dried brick, cement, and plaster. Some Herodian architecture used *opus reticulatum* (a network of small bricks laid into cement in a diagonal pattern) and *opus quadratum* (rectangular bricks laid horizontally around doorways and windows as support for the opus reticulatum). The

Herod's ashlar stonework is displayed prominently in Jerusalem's Eastern Wall.

use of opus reticulatum and opus quadratum is noteworthy. Although this type of construction is found in Roman buildings at Herculaneum, Pompeii, and Ostia, there are no known examples in Israel except in Herodian projects (the palace at Jericho, a building in Paneas [Banias] and a round structure northwest of the Damascus Gate). Clear evidence of the use of Roman engineering and architecture, opus reticulatum and opus quadratum were especially good surfaces to plaster. That Herod was particularly fond of decorating walls with beautiful frescos and floors with ornate mosaics is shown in examples of this decor at Jericho, Masada, and Herodium.

It is in private building projects, primarily palaces and fortresses, that Herod's flair for innovation and creative genius are most evident. His choice of building sites and architecture suitable to the various geographical settings is truly remarkable. For example, the three-tiered Northern Palace at Masada clings to the side of the cliff, a unique architecture for ancient Israel. Today the remains are not particularly impressive, but the view over the cliff stirs the imagination as to what once stood there. The Masada palace may have influenced the Roman emperor Tiberius to build a similar "cliffhanger" palace on the island of Capri near Naples, Italy.

Opus quadratum construction in the Jericho palace.

Another feature uniquely Herod's in the Israel of his day was circular construction. One round structure found north of the Damascus Gate in Jerusalem may prove to be the Herod family tomb, which tradition has heretofore identified with a Roman tomb beside the King David Hotel.[17] All other examples of concentric design in Israel are definitely his. This layout is found in a room of Herod's bathhouse at what is called the "Third Palace" in Jericho; in a *tholos*-type pavilion surrounded by his large pool at Herodium, and in the second level of his Northern Palace at

Concentric structure in the bathhouse at Jericho.

Masada. These round structures may have inspired the Maritime Theater in Hadrian's palace in Tivoli (see pp. 76–77). On the other hand, both structures are similar to the Ionic monopteral Temple of Rome and Augustus located near the east end of the Parthenon in Athens.[18] That circular, open-air temple was built about 27 B.C., shortly before Herod's building programs, and he may have been influenced by this type of Roman architecture, which is common in the Mediterranean world. Circular peripteral temples were introduced into Roman architecture in the first century B.C. as an innovation modeled on Greek peripteral temples (e.g., the temples of Vesta in Rome and Tivoli).[19]

The great innovations in Roman engineering came after the death of Herod, reaching a climax in the time of Nero and later. Josephus remarks that some problems in the foundations Herod laid for the renovation and expansion of the temple in Jerusalem were corrected during the reign of Nero.[20] The palace Herod built at Herodium was the largest in the Mediterranean world until Nero built his mammoth complex in Rome. Herod's palace was also surpassed later by Hadrian's Villa in Tivoli but remains the third largest in the ancient world. To some extent, Herod anticipated later advances in his occasional use of vaulted roofs and arches, in floors of *opus sectile* (finely cut and polished marble laid as mosaics), and in the use of hypocausts to heat his bathhouses. Otherwise, he built theaters, bathhouses, hippodromes, amphitheaters, aqueducts, basilicas, and temples in accordance with prevailing styles. The beautifully bordered ashlar limestones provided massive support where required, but otherwise the construction methods were conventional.

Herod's greatness as a builder probably lay more in his attitude that architecture should be motivated by pragmatic concerns. Each of his large constructions had utilitarian value. Northwest of the temple, the huge tower of the Antonia Fortress guarded the Temple Mount. The three towers at the Jaffa Gate, on the northern end of Herod's palace in Jerusalem, also served as fortifications. Titus, the Roman conqueror, left them standing in 70 A.D. "as a monument of his good fortune" to show that "we certainly had God for our assistant in this war."[21] Part of one of these, the Tower of Phasael (or Hippicus?), still stands.[22] The huge eastern tower of Herod's mountain palace at upper Herodium was also a reservoir. Even the Royal Colonnade or Portico, which Josephus said "deserves to be mentioned better than any other under the sun,"[23] served as an esplanade on the southern extremity of the Temple Mount.

Whether Herod built for practicality or self-aggrandizement, he built beautifully. Pliny the Elder spoke of Jerusalem as "the most famous city of the East, and not of Judaea only."[24] The Babylonian Talmud exclaimed, "Whoever has not seen Jerusalem in its splendor has never seen a fine city."[25] Josephus asserted that the

Figure 8
Herodian Architecture

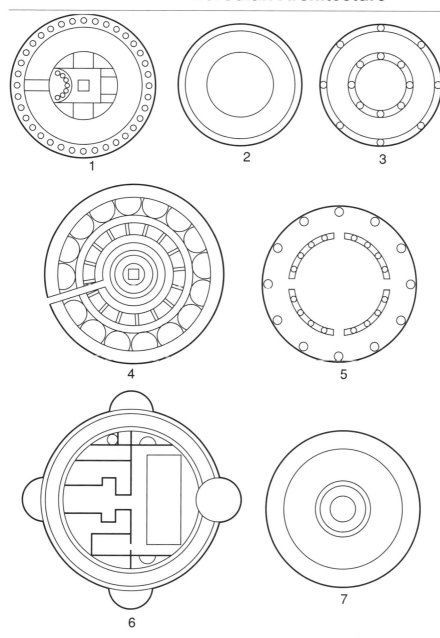

1 Library, Hadrian's villa, Rome
2 West room, Jericho
3 Middle terrace pavillion, Masada
4 Tomb of Augustus, Rome
5 Pool pavillion, Herodium
6 Fortress-palace, Herodium
7 Herod family tomb, Jerusalem

construction of the Royal Porch of the Temple Mount "caused an amazement [to visitors] by reason of the grandeur of the whole."[26] By the time Mark Twain visited Jerusalem, however, the glory had long since departed. "Renowned Jerusalem itself, the stateliest name in history, has lost its ancient grandeur, and is become a pauper village. . . . The wonderful temple which was the pride and glory of Israel is gone."[27]

Today, among the silent ruins in a modern bustling city, the

Herod's circular styling may have inspired Hadrian's Maritime Theater at Tivoli.

Ionic monopteral temple, Athens.

archaeologist seeks the clues that will allow reconstruction, on paper at least, of the splendors with which Herod ornamented the ancient land of Israel. Other, less-active cities of the land are also yielding their long-kept secrets of Herodian grandeur under the incessant attack of the excavator's spade.

Circular pavilion,
Masada.

The Temple Mount

Undoubtedly Herod's best-known building projects are associated with the Temple Mount in Jerusalem.[28] Solomon first built the magnificent temple to the God of Israel on Mount Moriah, just north of the Ophel Hill where the city was located (2 Chron. 3:1). Zerubbabel erected a new temple on the spot after the Solomonic one was destroyed (Ezra 3:8–13). Herod renovated and expanded this second temple, following a plan far more ambitious than either Solomon's or Zerubbabel's.[29] Construction

Figure 9
Temple Enclosure in the Herodian Period

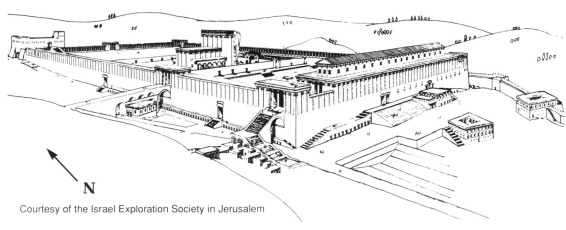

N

Courtesy of the Israel Exploration Society in Jerusalem

Sections of wall remain from Herod's magnificent Temple Mount in Jerusalem.

had already been in progress for 46 years when Jesus was there (John 2:20). Roughly rectangular in shape, the platform of New Testament times was twice the size of the original temple grounds.[30] The wall enclosing the temple platform measured 1591 feet on the west, 1033 feet on the north, 1542 feet on the east, and 918 feet on the south. This constitutes an area covering 1,527,920 square feet or roughly 35 acres. The circumference of the entire city, according to Josephus, was about 3.8 miles.[31]

Josephus also records a date of 23–22 B.C. for the earliest work on the project.[32] An inscription of a donor to the construction of a pavement has been found which probably establishes the accuracy of Josephus's date. Benjamin Mazar, who uncovered the inscription in excavation south of the plaza and below the Double Gate, supports the historian's claim.[33]

The Pinnacle of the Temple

Herod was able to expand the temple grounds by extending the platform out onto the slopes surrounding the temple to the east, south, and west. Huge retaining walls were built to support the fill upon which the platform stood. Only to the northwest did Herod need to shave off some rock that stood higher than the platform level. To the south he had to construct huge arches upon which to rest the stone platform; today these are popularly, but erroneously, called "Solomon's Stables." In the southeastern sector of the Temple Mount, covering 1800 square feet, massive vaults were supported by eighty-eight pillars. The pillars rested on huge Herodian blocks and formed twelve rows of galleries.[34] Although these foundation blocks may still be seen below the pavement level in the southeastern corner, the upper portions were destroyed in the fall of Jerusalem in A.D. 70 and lay in ruins throughout the Roman and Byzantine periods (see discussion of the Triple Gate on pp. 105–106). Only in the seventh and eighth centuries, under the Muslim Omayyads, was the area renovated when two mosques, which are still standing, were constructed. The Crusaders made further renovations at the beginning of the twelfth century, using the area as stables for their horses.[35]

The southeastern corner of the Temple Mount with its massive stone platform was probably the area of the pinnacle of the temple where Jesus was tempted by Satan (Luke 4:9). The pinnacle was probably either the corner of the building that stood on the platform or the corner of the wall itself. Josephus reports that the "height of the portico standing over it [the corner of the wall] was so very great that if anyone looked down from its rooftop, combining the two elevations, he would become dizzy and his vision would be unable to reach the end of so measureless a depth."[36] However, similar statements by Josephus about the views from both Masada and Macherus have prompted one scholar to suggest that Josephus may have been nearsighted.[37] After the destruction of A.D. 70, most of the area stretching 244 feet west from the southeastern corner and 183 feet north (with the possible exception of the very corner itself), was dismantled. What

Arches under the pinnacle of the temple.

The pinnacle of the temple, viewed from the south, shows its height.

Double Gate in the Southern Wall of the Temple Mount.

Walkway in front of the
Double Gate.

remained were the Herodian foundation blocks supporting the eighty-eight pillars still visible today.

The Triple Gate in the Southern Wall marked the western extremity of Solomon's Stables. Though the gate was destroyed, it was rebuilt in Omayyad times and may be seen today, filled in with masonry, on the face of the Southern Wall.[38] The eastern extremity was the southeast-corner walls, which extended 79 feet below the present surface of the ground, according to Kathleen Kenyon's estimation.[39] At least twenty-eight courses of Herodian stones rose to 128 feet from a bedrock foundation. This corner was the highest portion of wall left standing by the Romans, and what remains reaches to within 20 feet of the top of the later Ottoman wall. The top course is unusually large and constitutes the master course, which lay at the level of the entrance into the Triple and Double gates. Portions of seven additional courses containing Herodian stone rise from this master course, making a total of thirty-five.[40] The upper seven courses have suffered damage and deterioration, but they appear to be *in situ*. It is difficult to imagine that these upper seven courses of huge ashlars were replaced in the Omayyad period.

The Double Gate was the other entrance Herod built through the Southern Wall; in the Mishnah the Double and Triple gates are jointly referred to as the Huldah Gates.[41] The Double Gate is

Steps leading to the Double Gate.

43 feet wide, slightly narrower than the 50-foot-wide Triple Gate. Its large, square vestibule of Herodian stone and 78-foot tunnel leading north to the temple platform, 39 feet higher, are still well preserved.[42] The Double Gate was not destroyed in the Roman conquest; in fact it was used until the Crusaders closed it and constructed a building against it, which still covers the western half of the gate. The Crusaders also opened the Single Gate, located at the eastern end of the Southern Wall at a slightly lower level, to provide access to Solomon's Stables.

The Area South of the Temple

Along the Southern Wall in front of these gates, Herod built a stone-paved road 21 feet wide, which was uncovered in Mazar's excavations.[43] From this road immense stairways led down to a plaza 22 feet below. The largest of the stairways descends from in front of the Double Gates and is 215 feet wide. Its thirty steps are made of trimmed and smoothed stone paving blocks.[44] Restored to much of its original beauty, the stairway is used today.

What may have been a ritual bath complex has been found in the area between the Huldah Gates, south of the road. The complex, consisting of a number of miqwaot (Jewish ritual baths), pools, and plastered cisterns, was large enough to accommodate the individual purification needs of large crowds of pilgrims who gathered on the plaza before going to worship in the temple.[45] Mazar, who excavated the area, comments that "during the entire Herodian period this area played a very important role as a centre of public life in Jerusalem and as a focal point for the masses of Jerusalemites and pilgrims before the gates of the Temple Enclosure."[46] In the Mishnah it is said that temple worshippers entered on the right and exited on the left.[47] This statement may relate to the purification process involved. At Qumran, for example, small partitions in the stairways of the ritual baths kept those purified from being defiled by those who were yet unclean. A Talmudic passage refers to Gamaliel (the teacher of the apostle Paul, Acts 22:3) and the elders standing on top of the stairs at the Temple Mount.[48] Thus, entrance to the Temple Mount may have been through the Double Gates and exit through the Triple Gates.[49]

Stairways and baths are not the only features found south of the temple. One subterranean tunnel has been located south of the Double Gate. The tunnel runs north towards the gate and has niches in its walls for oil lamps carved into its walls. According to

A partition protected purity of the ceremonially clean in steps to miqwaot south of Southern Wall of the Temple Mount.

the Mishnah, the tunnel may have extended all the way to the Tadi Gate, in the north of the city.[50] Another tunnel, 3 feet wide and 11.5 feet high, was found east of the Triple Gate, 112 feet west of the southeastern corner. The passageway was built of beautifully cut Herodian ashlars. From the entrance at a vaulted chamber under the Single Gate, the tunnel extended northward for 69 feet to a doorway leading to a hall beneath Solomon's Stables.[51] Mazar suggests that the passageway "may well have led to the subterranean system of treasure chambers within the Temple Mount."[52] Another tunnel, this one rock-hewn, was discovered beneath the Triple Gate. It extended northward to a reservoir which has been abandoned.[53]

The Area West of the Temple

The main street constructed by Herod for the temple area was forty-one feet wide and ran along the Western Wall of the Temple Mount. Sections of the street have been found intact. Excavations have shown that it ran along the eighteenth course of Herodian stone (counting up from bedrock).[54] Five courses of stones were visible before 1967, when two lower layers were exposed. Nineteen Herodian courses still lie underground in this area.[55]

Robinson's Arch stood about 40 feet north of the southwestern corner of the temple wall. A road coming from the south forked to the northwest at a point just north of Robinson's Arch, eventually making its way past a major marketplace in the upper city to the Damascus Gate in the Northern Wall. This is about the same path as the modern el Wad Street. The eastern extension of the fork, Herod's main street, proceeded northward along the side of the Western Wall to the Antonia Fortress.[56] About 25 feet below this street has been found a massive Herodian aqueduct; it slopes downward toward the pools to the south and runs the full length of the street. The aqueduct carried rainwater collected by various channels in the Temple Mount and in the street system.[57] Dan Bahat, Jerusalem's chief archaeologist, reports another find. A quarter-mile-long passageway running along the 350-yard extension of the Western Wall toward the north has been discovered deep below the surface. Efforts being made to open the passageway to the public are being met with resistance from the Arab populace living above the two-millennia-old tunnel.[58]

Four gates described by Josephus in the Western Wall have been identified.[59] Two gates entered the mount from the walkways of Robinson's Arch and Wilson's Arch, both of which were considerably higher than the main street (*cardo*) running beneath

Interior of Wilson's Arch, which spanned Jerusalem's Tyropoeon Valley.

them. The third gate, the so-called Warren's Gate, stands about 150 feet north of the Wilson's Arch. The fourth gate, called Barclay's Gate is partially visible at the southern end of the women's portion of the Western Wall, now called the Wailing Wall.[60] It should be noted that gates and other features are often named for their discoverers.

Wilson's Arch supported a 44-foot-wide street that connected the Upper City (the Western Hill) with the Temple Mount at a point about 600 feet north of the Southern Wall. The street was built of huge Herodian stones, most of which still lie in their places, below the modern pavement. The upper arch, destroyed in A.D. 70, was rebuilt, probably in the Omayyad period. The restoration is almost indistinguishable from the original Herodian construction. Today visitors may enter the area through the men's section of the Wailing Wall. The area is a marvelous place to experience the thrill of Herodian engineering as it would have appeared before its destruction. The present pavement under the arch is Omayyad and stands 13 feet above the Herodian pavement, on which numerous ashlars fell when the original arch was destroyed in A.D. 70.[61]

Excavations have shown that Robinson's Arch did not span the Tyropoeon Valley as had been believed. Wilson's Arch spanned the Tyropoeon Valley, but Robinson's Arch spanned the main street and rested on a huge pier adjacent to the street. Its path wound up to the Royal Porch high above. The arch, 51 feet wide, was built on large supporting arches which housed ancient shops. The shops apparently supplied the needs of those who came to the temple.[62]

The Royal Porch

Often called the Royal Porch, the Royal Colonnade, or the Royal Portico, this structure was indeed "royal." Situated along the Southern Wall of the Temple Mount with an east-west orientation, the Royal Porch was one of Herod's most stunning achievements. Josephus considered it "more noteworthy than any under the sun."[63] Each of 162 monolithic columns, 27 feet high and 4.6 feet in diameter, stretched in four rows. These columns were crowned with Corinthian capitals, the most ornate variety of all Greek capitals.[64] Several column and capital fragments have been found, along with pieces of upper sections of decoration, some painted gold.

The Sanhedrin may have moved to the Royal Porch about the time of the death of Christ; according to the Babylonian Talmud it was "forty years before the destruction of the Temple"[65] that the Sanhedrin moved from its former meeting place at the Chamber of Hewn Stone, which the Mishnah states was "in the Temple Court."[66] It is possible that the trial of Jesus before the Sanhedrin was held at the Xystus, an open space adjacent to the western end of Wilson's Arch, to which some argue the Sanhedrin had already relocated.[67] The southeastern corner of this Royal Porch also may have been the pinnacle of the temple where Jesus was tempted by Satan (see p. 103).

At the southwestern corner of the Royal Porch, a trimmed

Model of the temple shows Robinson's Arch and the Royal Porch.

stone block was discovered, lying where it had fallen from a tower high above. On the block were carved in Hebrew the words "To the Place of Trumpeting to herald."[68] From Josephus we learn that at the beginning of the Sabbath a priest ascended to just such a high place and announced the start of the holy day by blowing a trumpet.[69] The tower was three stories high, and its lower level may have housed animals kept for temple sacrifices at the time of Jesus.[70]

The Eastern Wall of the Temple Mount

Expansion of the Eastern Wall of the Temple Mount was limited by the deep Kidron Valley, which lay between it and the Mount of Olives. A mystery attaches to what has been found. Herodian stone stands in the lower courses of the wall, both in the south and the north. The central portion has not been excavated because Muslim cemeteries lie against it. The questions surround James Fleming's discovery of a gate below the Golden Gate.[71] Josephus writes of Herod's work only on the north, south, and west of the mount.[72] The Golden Gate in the Eastern Wall, as it now stands, was built in Byzantine or early Muslim times. When Süleyman I built the modern walls in the 16th century, he found the Golden Gate intact and rebuilt the walls north and south of it.

The Golden Gate in the Eastern Wall.

111

Straight joint or seam in the Eastern Wall.

But what of this lower gate? Fleming found that its architecture differs from that of such late Roman arches as the Ecce Homo Arch and the lower Damascus Gate Arch, both from the second century. The stone in this lower gate matches stone on the north side of the "straight joint" or "seam" about 105 feet north of the southeastern corner. The seam indicates that a section of wall was added to the Southern Wall since the stones do not interlock with the rest of the wall. There is simply a straight, vertical seam. The stones in this wall extension are clearly Herodian. Some archaeologists think the stones on both sides of the seam are Herodian and represent two phases of construction.[73] Mazar maintains, though, that the older stonework is an earlier Hasmonean addition to the Temple Mount. He believes the Hasmonean section extends for about 130 feet north of the seam to an original bend in the Eastern Wall.[74] Y. Tsafrir regards the stone extension as possibly part of the Akra built in Seleucid times (169 B.C.).[75]

The definitive story of the gate and its kindred section of wall are yet to be told. Since Josephus gives no clear indication that Herod built any of the Eastern Wall,[76] we may assume that only the extension south of the seam—the Royal Porch and the arches beneath the porch, now called Solomon's Stables—can be Herodian. The wall north of the seam, as well as the gate below the Golden Gate must be more ancient. Ernest-Marie Laperrousaz argues that this section was built by Solomon.[77]

The Location of the Temple

Fleming's discovery of the gate below the Golden Gate affects another highly debated aspect of Herod's building program: the location of the temple. Herod did not relocate the temple built by Zerubbabel. But where was it located? The Golden Gate and the one just discovered immediately below it do not line up with the mosque, the Dome of the Rock, which is commonly thought to have been built where the temple once stood.[78] Entering these gates from the east and proceeding due west takes one to a point about 100 yards north of the mosque.

At this point in the northwestern sector of the Haram es-Sharif, foundation cuttings in bedrock have been found that, according to Asher Kaufman, indicate the use of cubits measuring 42.8 centimeters and 43.7 centimeters long.[79] These are the "yardsticks" used in the construction of the first and second temples, respectively. Portions of a wall 6.5 feet deep and 16 feet long, made of well-dressed ashlars were identified by Zeev Yeivin in 1970, and may belong to the eastern wall of the Herodian temple.[80] Furthermore, the modern "Dome of the Spirits," or "Dome of the Tablets," is in the precise location where the Holy of Holies would have stood according to lines projected from the foundation cuttings.[81] The little dome rests on bedrock, although the remainder of the platform on the mount is built of large flagstones. The bedrock under the little dome is 2437 feet above sea level, only 3 feet lower than the rock under the Dome of the Rock. Because of a sacred tradition that the Holy of Holies had stood there, the bedrock may have been left exposed by the Muslims who built the little dome. Accordingly, they may have named it the Dome of the Spirits because of the holiness of the area and Dome of the Tablets because copies of the Ten Commandments and the Pentateuch had been kept in the Ark of the Covenant in the Holy of Holies.

It is important to remember that the Temple Mount was totally destroyed by Hadrian in the second century. When he built his new temple, there was nothing left of the previous one. In the second century Dio Cassius wrote, "At Jerusalem he [Hadrian] founded a city in place of the one which had been razed to the ground, naming it Aelia Capitolina, and on the site of the temple of the god [the Jewish Temple] he raised a new temple to Jupiter."[82] It would certainly satisfy the statement of Dio Cassius if the temple of Jupiter stood within a hundred yards of where the Jewish temple had actually stood. The entire Temple Mount could be considered the site of the temple, and that may be how Cassius considered it.

Four converging lines of evidence suggest that in New Testament times the temple stood about 100 yards north of the Dome of the Rock: (1) the newly discovered gate beneath the Golden Gate; (2) the foundation cuttings; (3) the portion of the second temple's eastern wall found by Yeivin, and (4) the location of the Dome of the Spirits. Lawrence Sporty supports this location by

The Temple Mount as seen from Olivet, east of the Golden Gate.

his study of the literary evidence from the first century.[83] Nevertheless, David Jacobson argues on the basis of symmetry that the sanctuary of the temple would have stood over the rock under the modern Dome of the Rock, with the altar of burnt offering immediately to the east. His argument is based on the symmetry of other Herodian sites in Israel and assumptions regarding the Temple Mount. Specifically, he assumes that only the southern and western walls of the mount were associated with the temple and its precincts, that the northern and eastern walls were parallel to these other two, and that diagonal lines drawn from opposite corners of the reconstructed rectangular walls cross each other at the exact point where the altar would have stood.[84] It is not clear, however, why the temple of Herod would correspond to other Herodian sites since the location of the altar and the sanctuary were already determined by their positions in the Zerubbabel temple, which Herod merely remodeled.

The Judgment Pavement of Pilate

In the north wall of the Temple Mount, Herod built the Fortress Antonia in honor of Mark Antony.[85] L. H. Vincent has argued that the floor of Herod's fortress and the pavement on which Jesus stood before Pilate (John 19:13) are beneath the modern Convent of the Sisters of Sion on the supposed Via

Dolorosa. Vincent has further maintained that the fortress was quite large and had been constructed with four towers, as depicted in the model at the Holy Land Hotel.[86] These views are shared by Jack Finegan, who recommends them on rather shaky grounds: "the correlation of the situation described in the Gospels with the known circumstances of the time, and the weight of early pilgrim tradition."[87]

Several developments seriously challenge the views of Finegan and Vincent:

1. Père Benoit has shown that the pavement beneath the convent is of the same period as the huge vaults of the Struthion Pools underneath.[88] The pavement could not have been built before the Roman siege in A.D. 70 if Josephus is correct, because he states that the Romans built a ramp through the middle of ($\kappa\alpha\tau\grave{\alpha}\ \mu\acute{\epsilon}\sigma\text{ov}$) the pools in order to bring siege machines against the Antonia Fortress.[89] Since the pools must have been open and lay outside the fortress for that to have occurred, the pavement could not have covered them in A.D. 70.

2. The Ecce Homo Arch, which spans the modern Via Dolorosa in front of the convent and extends inside to the chapel, rests its northern pier on bedrock rather than on the pavement. Excavation in 1966 revealed this and disproved Vincent's assumption that the arch rested on top of the pave-

Model of Antonia Fortress.

Alleged floor of Antonia Fortress.

ment. Had the stone pavement been in place when the arch was constructed, by necessity the pier would have been built on the pavement. Instead, the pavement was built with the top of its stone surface level with the bottom of the lowest stone in the pier, which rested on bedrock. It is likely, therefore, that the arch and pavement were built by the same architect. They may date to the time of Hadrian (ca. A.D. 135). Benoit insists the pavement is Hadrianic, but has suggested that the arch may have been built by Herod Agrippa I (A.D. 41–44). This idea is based on a study of arches by one of his students.[90]

3. Benoit finds no evidence whatsoever of a large, four-towered Antonia Fortress. He is certain that the fortress consisted only of the southeastern tower shown in models and stood on the site of the modern Omariyya School. Josephus, however, mentions that there were towers on each corner.[91]

4. An alternative location for the judgment pavement has been suggested: the floor of the Herodian palace in what is today called the Citadel. It is south of the Jaffa Gate in the Western Wall, better fitting the situation as recorded in John's Gospel.[92]

To understand the argument for this alternative location, a bit of background information is needed.

Figure 10
Jaffa Gate Area

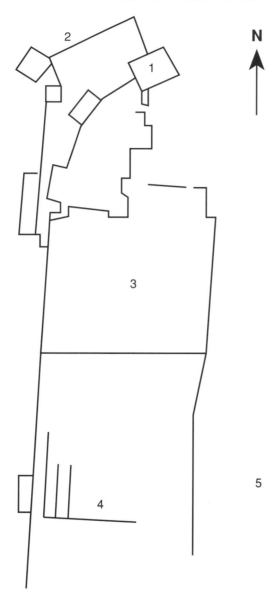

N

1 Herodian tower
  (Phasael's)
2 Jaffa Gate
3 Police barracks
4 Foundation walls
  from Herod's time
5 Armenian convent

Within his western palace Herod buit three large towers, named in honor of friends and relatives: Hippicus, Phasael, and Mariamne.[93] These were the towers that Titus left standing "as a monument to his good fortune" when he destroyed Jerusalem (see p. 98).[94] One of them, which most authorities regard as Phasael, now stands at the modern Jaffa Gate. The lower portion of the tower has been preserved from the time of Herod; the upper part, built of smaller stones, is much later. The tower is a 66-foot square and stands 66 feet high, exactly as Josephus described it: "its breadth and its height equal, each of them forty cubits."[95] Portions of the Herodian city wall with towers have been found inside the northern part of the Citadel. Foundations for a large Herodian podium have been found to the south in the Armenian Quarter, indicating that the original palace of Herod stretched from the Citadel southward along a modern Turkish wall to the point where the Turkish wall turns east. The podium, on which a stone pavement once stood, was built almost 12 feet higher than previous Hasmonean foundations uncovered at that spot. The superstructure for this pavement must have been approximately 1100 feet, north to south, by 200 feet, east to west. Nothing of it was found by Magen Broshi, who excavated the area.[96]

Pilate, it has been argued, may have resided in the Antonia when Christ appeared before him, but this now seems highly unlikely. The Antonia was scarcely comparable in the luxuriousness of its accommodations to the palace of Herod, even though Josephus remarked of the Antonia that "by its magnificence it seemed a palace."[97] However, of the palace of Herod he said: it "exceeds all my ability to describe it."[98] The palace had bedrooms that would house hundreds of guests, gold and silver vessels in the rooms, many porches, groves of trees with long walks through them, and deep canals that kept everything green. There is little doubt where Pilate would choose to live while in Jerusalem. He normally lived in Caesarea Maritima.

Philo, a contemporary of Jesus, writes plainly that Pilate was living in Herod's palace during one of the Jewish feasts, describing it as "the residence of the prefects."[99] Gessius Florus, who became prefect in A.D. 64, lived in the palace just before the

Tower of Phasael at the Jaffa Gate.

Model showing the three towers of Herod's Palace.

revolt, which began in 66. Mark 15:16 states that the soldiers led Jesus into the palace, "which is the praetorium." The praetorium (i.e. residence of the Roman authority) must have been in the Herodian palace. Therefore, the large podium Broshi found must have been that on which Jesus stood before Pilate. In Greek it was called the "stone pavement" (λιθόστρωτον) and in Hebrew an "elevated place" (*Gabbatha*, John 19:13).[100] Like the one still standing in Corinth where Paul stood before Gallio (Acts 18:12), a tribunal platform or bema (βῆμα) must have been built in the open for purposes of addressing the crowds. Matthew noted that Pilate was seated on one (ἐπὶ τοῦ βήματος, 27:19). Apparently a bema was built by the prefect on the stone pavement for the purpose of receiving his subjects. Josephus said that the populace "surrounded the bema" (περιστάντες τὸ βῆμα) where Pilate was seated on one occasion.[101] Pilate also had a bema in the great stadium (στάδιον), or perhaps it was the "marketplace."[102]

The Northern Wall

Very little is known for sure about the Northern Wall Herod built around Jerusalem, and archaeologists' opinions differ widely as to the identity and location of the second (Herodian) and third (Agrippa-Hadrian) walls.[103] Josephus's description contains ref-

The date of construction for the Lower Damascus Gate is uncertain.

erences to places still unknown to us and is rarely in accord with the few archaeological data available.[104] The modern Northern Wall of the city was almost certainly built over Herod Agrippa I's expansion wall of A.D. 44 when Josephus was only seven years old. He would not likely remember much about the walls of his young childhood.

At the Damascus Gate there is a lower excavated gate east of the modern entrance, which is built of Herodian-style stone and contains a rebuilt arch from the time of Hadrian. Menahem Magen has assumed a Hadrianic date for the entire gate, which has been excavated, but he produces little evidence to justify his assumption.[105]

The lower portions of the Northern Wall, containing typical Herodian stones, are now generally conceded to have been constructed by Agrippa rather than Herod. Bruce Schein has argued convincingly that none of Herod's Northern Wall has been found, discrediting the generally accepted Vincent section.[106] From an ancient quarry lying under the modern Muristan Quarter, we learn something about the location of Herod's wall. It must have run east from the palace (Jaffa Gate), along the southern edge of the quarry (modern David Street), then turned north at the eastern edge of the quarry (on the line of modern Suq Khan Es-Zeit Street). From there it would have run northward to the northern edge of the quarry (just north of the modern Lutheran Church of the Redeemer),

Figure 11
Northern Quarry

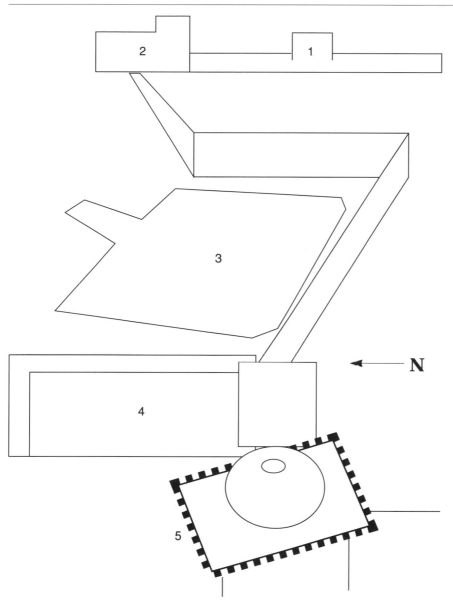

1 Temple
2 Antonia Fortress
3 Quarry
4 Pool of the Towers
5 Jaffa Gate

angling from that point northeast to the Antonia Fortress. This fits Josephus's statement that it "went up as far as Antonia."[107]

The Water Supply

Herod's building projects in Jerusalem included providing water for the city, which he was greatly expanding. Population estimates for Jerusalem at this time vary. Joachim Jeremias and

John Wilkinson suggest there were between twenty-five thousand and thirty-five thousand people.[108] Broshi estimates about forty thousand[109] and Michael Avi-Yonah ninety thousand.[110] The often-quoted figure of one hundred twenty thousand for the city at the time of its destruction in A.D. 70 is from Josephus.[111] Those endorsing this estimate overlook the fact that Josephus was quoting Hecataeus of Abdera, who lived in the fourth to third century

Figure 12
Water Cisterns on the Temple Mount

1–37 Underground passages and cisterns
38 Double Gates
39 Triple Gates
40 Single Gate
41 Stairway
42 Robinson's Arch and Gate
43 Barclay Gate
44 Wilson Arch and Gate
45 Warren Gate
46 Golden Gate

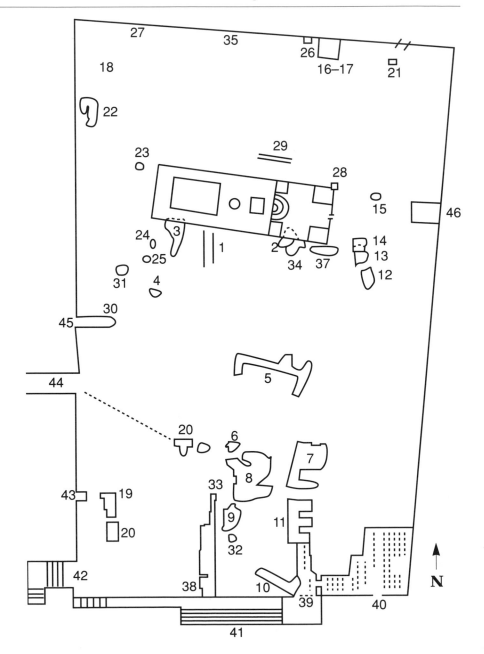

B.C. and whose population figures were for the time of Alexander the Great.[112] Estimates for the population of the entire country at this time range from 1 million to 6 million people, based on a variety of methods of computation.[113] Herod's water installations could have raised the population ceiling of Jerusalem to perhaps twice the number of the smaller estimates.

The Temple Mount is honeycombed with thirty-seven underground chambers cut into solid rock (see diagram on p. 122).[114] Some of them are passageways, but most are reservoirs, which Gaalyah Cornfeld estimates could hold as much as 10 million gallons of water.[115] Rivka Gonen has argued that these chambers were part of a cemetery in the Middle Bronze I Age (2200–2000 B.C.) similar to Hebron's Machpelah Cave and the burial caves at Jebel Qa'aqir near Hebron.[116] Whatever their origin, these cavities were used as cisterns in the Herodian period. Combined with the ever-flowing Gihon Spring and Pool of Siloam, they were still not adequate to meet the needs of the city, so Herod built huge public pools and cisterns.[117]

The double Struthion Pools were built near the Antonia Fortress (and may be seen beneath the Convent of the Sisters of Sion). The Pool of the Towers, or the Pool of Hezekiah, was constructed north of Herod's palace by the Jaffa Gate. It may be seen by ascending the stairs of the Petra Hotel just inside the gate. The Pool of Israel (now a parking lot) was built adjacent to the Northern Wall of the Temple Mount, just south of the Sheep Pool near the Bethesda porches (see John 5:2 NEB for a helpful rendering of the Greek description). Large underground pools cut into rock have been found recently in excavations south of the Double Gate in the Southern Wall of the Temple Mount. And a massive underground

Pilate's aqueduct at Bethlehem.

Figure 13
Pools in Jerusalem

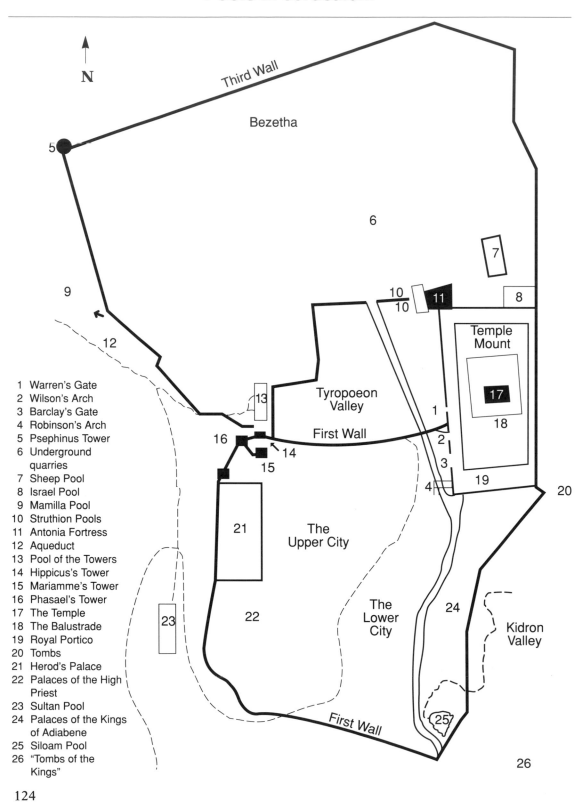

1 Warren's Gate
2 Wilson's Arch
3 Barclay's Gate
4 Robinson's Arch
5 Psephinus Tower
6 Underground quarries
7 Sheep Pool
8 Israel Pool
9 Mamilla Pool
10 Struthion Pools
11 Antonia Fortress
12 Aqueduct
13 Pool of the Towers
14 Hippicus's Tower
15 Mariamme's Tower
16 Phasael's Tower
17 The Temple
18 The Balustrade
19 Royal Portico
20 Tombs
21 Herod's Palace
22 Palaces of the High Priest
23 Sultan Pool
24 Palaces of the Kings of Adiabene
25 Siloam Pool
26 "Tombs of the Kings"

One of Solomon's pools near Bethlehem.

reservoir was discovered in 1974 in the Upper City (on Melchizedek Street near the Dung Gate).[118] Its date has not been determined, but it may turn out to be Herodian. The Mamilla Pool west of the Jaffa Gate in Independence Garden, was probably already in existence and may be the Serpent's Pool mentioned by Josephus.[119]

Josephus makes no mention of any Herodian aqueducts, nor is there any clear evidence that he built any, according to Amihai Mazar, who explored the existing aqueduct system.[120] Outside Jerusalem Herod did build one aqueduct from the spring at Artas east of Solomon's Pools (south of Bethlehem) to his palace fortress at Herodium, which was investigated by Ehud Netzer, Herodium's excavator. Pontius Pilate later built one which may be seen in Bethlehem.[121] Cisterns to collect rain water were located beneath all houses during the New Testament period. Most houses in Jerusalem still have cisterns, even though they hooked up to modern water facilities. Numerous cisterns of various sizes have been found in excavations around the Temple Mount and in the Upper City on the Western Hill (modern Zion Hill).

The Theater

According to Josephus, Herod built a theater in Jerusalem.[122] The well-known model of the city at the Holy Land Hotel places the theater inside the city walls and just west of the Temple Mount. However, no archaeological evidence supports a site located anywhere inside the city's ancient walls; it is highly unlikely that Herod would so blatantly offend his Jewish constituency by building a theater within the city walls—certainly not adjacent to the temple![123] A likely candidate for this theater was discovered by Conrad Schick and published in a preliminary

Figure 14
Herodian Theater

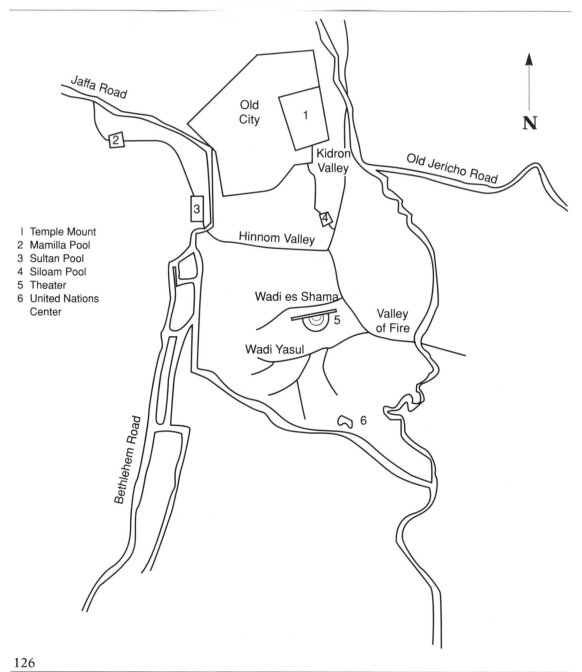

I Temple Mount
2 Mamilla Pool
3 Sultan Pool
4 Siloam Pool
5 Theater
6 United Nations Center

report in 1887.[124] This site is an appropriate distance south of the temple between two valleys, Wadi Yasul on the south and Wadi es Shama on the north, north of the present United Nations facility. Within a semicircular wall, 200 feet in diameter, the cavea (the semicircular seating area) opened to the north, toward Jerusalem. Its orchestra would have been about 132 feet across. The revised edition of Emil Schürer's definitive work on Judaism in the New Testament period asserts that: "the identification of Schick's theatre with that of Herod is therefore quite possible and even probable."[125] A future excavation of the structure will have to await a more favorable political situation.

Josephus's references to a hippodrome in the south of Jerusalem are enigmatic.[126] If a theater near the temple would have offended the Jews, a hippodrome, stadium, amphitheatre (circus), or theater would have been just as offensive. Josephus recorded that Herod built a "very large amphitheatre in the plain."[127] The meaning of "in the plain" ($\dot{\epsilon}\nu\ \tau\tilde{\omega}\ \pi\epsilon\delta\acute{\iota}\omega$) is unclear but hardly fits the Tyropoeon Valley adjacent to the temple on the west side of Mount Ophel. His references to similar kinds of structures at Caesarea Maritima are just as confusing (see p. 141). Archaeological evidence of these structures, except for the theater, has not been forthcoming.

Herod's Tomb

A structure northwest of the Damascus Gate recently investigated by Netzer has been tentatively identified as the family tomb of Herod the Great.[128] Like the circular palace-fortress, the round structure in the center of the pool at Herodium, the round center pavilion in the palace at Masada, and the round structure in Herod's bathhouse at Jericho, this tomb has concentric walls, unique in style within Israel to the architecture of Herod. Also, it was built using the distinctively Herodian opus reticulatum pattern of bricklaying. Though the structure cannot be fully excavated because it lies under modern Arab housing, we know its style is like that of the Tomb of Augustus in Rome, which may have served as its model. There is no evidence supporting the identification of the Roman-type tomb adjacent to the King David Hotel in Jerusalem as that of Herod's family. Herod himself was buried in Herodium.[129]

Herodian Construction Outside Jerusalem

4

Herodium

Jericho

Masada

Caesarea Maritima

Samaria

Hebron

Herodium

Of Herod's twenty-one building activities in Israel (beside those in Jerusalem), six deserve special mention. Herodium, the place where, according to Josephus, Herod was buried with great pomp,[1] was 24 miles southwest of Jericho, where he died. At Herodium, seven miles south of Jerusalem and three miles southeast of Bethlehem, Herod built a desert palace-fortress in about 23 B.C. It was the third largest palace ever to be constructed in the entire Roman world.[2] At this writing excavations are underway, conducted by Ehud Netzer of Hebrew University in Jerusalem. Herod's palace rises up to a point 2460 feet above sea level, looking in profile very much like a volcano.[3] Josephus described the location as "a hill . . . rounded off in the shape of a breast."[4] On top of the natural hill, Herod built a cylindrical structure, which arose about 90 feet above bedrock. There were two concentric circular walls, the outer wall approximately 200 feet in diameter, which was separated from the inner wall by a corridor which was approximately 11.5 feet wide. Dirt and gravel then was piled around the outer walls to bury about two-thirds of their height for defensive purposes. This made the hill and its citadel look even more like a cone-shaped volcano.

An interior view of the Herodium palace indicates its massive scope.

Inside this volcano, Herod built a seven-story quarters with five floors above the ground level and two below. Access from the valley, 180 feet below, was provided by a steep stairway nearly 500 feet long on the north side of the mountain. Within the cylindrical palace, Herod built a rectangular outdoor garden courtyard, surrounded by columns and containing niches for statues. In the western half of the cylinder was a *triclinium* or dining hall, 45 feet by 30 feet, which was converted into a synagogue by Jewish Zealots (see pp. 66–68). A full Roman bath with hot, cold, and warm rooms was built adjacent to the living quarters. The impressive stone cupola of the warm room is still standing. Four large underground cisterns, built to store needed water, have been excavated on the northeast side of the mound.[5] Another cistern was built above ground and may be seen at the top of the huge, otherwise-solid eastern tower, which stood impressively higher than three other semicircular structures. The four towers were placed at the points of the compass in the circular wall.

As impressive as this hill-top citadel was, it was only a part of the 45-acre palace that was worked into the northern slopes and stretched some distance to the north of the hill's base. At the foot of the hill a 400-foot-long building stood; probably it was the central palace for its dimensions are twice as large as the one on top of the hill. In front of this poorly preserved structure is a "course,"

Figure 15
Schematic of Herodium

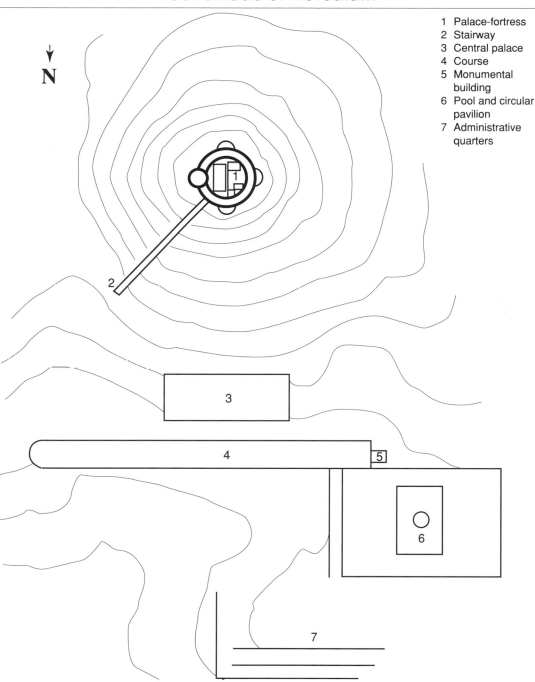

1 Palace-fortress
2 Stairway
3 Central palace
4 Course
5 Monumental building
6 Pool and circular pavilion
7 Administrative quarters

which measures 1100 feet east to west and is 80 feet wide. It may have functioned as an esplanade for the funeral of Herod, for it is too small to have been a hippodrome.

Near the western end of this course Herod built a huge pool, 210 feet long, 135 feet wide, and over 9 feet deep. A circular "party" pavilion, 40 feet in diameter, was built on an island in the center of this pool. It apparently had to be reached by boat, since no evidence of a bridge was found. Water was brought by aqueduct from Artas, about 4 miles to the west.[6] The magnificent colonnade that ran along the elevated southern and western sides of the pool are being restored and the pool is being cleaned. The purpose of the lake must have been to provide the palace with luxury typical of Roman culture. Even in the deserts of Judea, Herod could satisfy his aesthetic needs and entertain his guests. Excavations in the summer of 1985 produced evidence of a bathhouse that served the administrative staff for the large complex. Remains of the administrative quarters lie across the modern road to the north along a large east-west embankment. A Byzantine church has been excavated by the site to the west.

Hopes of locating Herod's tomb in the summer of 1985 were dashed by the highjacking of an airliner and its passengers after departure from Athens. Publicity over the incident caused cancellation of most of our digging teams, and we were forced to limit work to the bathhouse described above. Netzer believes the tomb may lie in the vicinity of a 45-foot-square building at the western end of the course. The northern and southern walls of this building are more than 10 feet thick. Huge, smooth-cut ashlar stones in the typical Herodian style, with wide margins and raised centers (bosses), were found in part of this building. They are unlike any other stone found at Herodium and could well belong to the sort of monumental structure Herod's tomb would require. Then long after Herod's palace had been destroyed the stones were reused in other buildings. Some of the stones show evidence of having been part of a Doric-style frieze, such as in decorated tombs of Herod's time in Jerusalem. Absalom's Tomb and the Tombs of the Kings (i.e., Queen Helen of Adiabene's Tomb) are examples. The use of subsurface interface radar, as at Sepphoris in 1983, and later at Lahav,[7] could facilitate locating underground cavities.

Until we learn where Herod the Great was buried, the words of Josephus will intrigue us:

> There was a solid gold bier, adorned with precious stones and draped with the richest purple. On it lay the body wrapped in crimson, with a diadem resting on the head and above that a golden crown and the scepter by the right hand. The bier was escorted by Herod's sons and the whole body of his kinsmen, followed by his Spearmen and the Thracian company, Germans and Gauls, all in full battle order, headed by their commanders and all the officers, and followed by five hundred of the house slaves and freedmen carrying spices. The body was borne twenty-four miles

to Herodium, where by the late king's command it was buried. So ends the story of Herod.[8]

Jericho

But if the story ends there for Herod, it does not for us; we must look at the city where he died, Jericho. Fourteen miles east of Jerusalem, the city was ideal for a winter palace, since its temperature averages 20 to 30 degrees warmer than that of Jerusalem. Before Herod, the Hasmoneans built their palace four miles south of the city. Today Jericho is known as Tulul Abu el-'Alayiq. Excavations were conducted in 1950 by James Kelso[9] and in 1951 by James Pritchard,[10] but their work was tarnished by inaccurate identification of structures. Netzer's continuing work at the site, which began in 1973, has corrected these problems.[11]

It is now clear that in Jericho Herod was responsible for construction in three areas. The older Hasmonean palace (Josephus mentions a "former palacc"[12]) in the northwest part of the modern town was about 165 feet square. In this general area, the Hasmoneans constructed several residences for themselves and guests. In these have been found pools, stone bathtubs, and six *miqwaot*, the earliest yet found of these ritual baths in Israel.[13] Herod rebuilt the Hasmonean palace at Jericho on a smaller

The floor for the reception hall at Herod's winter palace at Jericho.

scale, probably as a villa. Beside this villa on the east is a large swimming pool from the period—over 100 feet long, 60 feet wide, and 12 feet deep. The pool was divided at its center by an 18-foot-wide partition of earth which was only six feet high, thus only half as high as the pool itself. At this pool Herod's 17-year-old brother-in-law and rival, Aristobulus III, drowned.[14] Partial restoration of the pool was made possible by the archaeological preservation fund of the *Biblical Archaeology Review*.

A second area of Herodian construction around Jericho is located on the south bank of the Wadi Qelt. Adjacent to the wadi was a huge sunken garden, 360 feet long, with twenty-four niches (probably for statues). Some of these niches have been well preserved. Six feet above the garden's east and west sides were double-colonnaded porches, decorated with frescos and molded stucco. In the center of the southern wall of the garden was an exedra or hemicycle with benches, which is visible in photographs of the 1950 excavation report by Kelso.[15] During the 1974 excavation a large swimming pool, 130 feet by 300 feet, was found adjacent to this garden on the east.

South of the southeastern corner of the sunken garden, Herod raised a mound on which was constructed a 66-foot-square structure of Roman concrete. Inside was a large, round hall, 52 feet in diameter. The building may have been another villa, a pavilion, a reception hall, or even an elaborate, elevated Roman bath. About 1000 feet to the east are the remains of a 575-by-475-foot pool that may have been built by Herod. The pool now is called Birket Mousa. Water was brought to the various facilities at Jericho by aqueducts from springs at Ein Duq, Ein Nureimah (ancient Na'aran), and Ein Qelt. Portions of the aqueducts may still be seen.

The third and last building program in Jericho lay on the northern bank of the Wadi Qelt, where Herod built his most impressive palace. The palace's northern wing included a large reception hall or triclinium, 95 feet by 62 feet, with *opus sectile* and mosaic floors. By this hall's east side, Herod built one of two open courtyards. This courtyard was roughly round, about 62 feet in diameter and had a northern semicircular apse almost 30 feet in diameter. This courtyard was Ionic in style while the other was Corinthian.

Adjoining the courtyard on the east was a five-room Roman bath. One of the rooms of the bath is well-preserved and circular, similar in design to the central pavilion of the Masada palace. This circular room may have been the *frigidarium*, although this is not certain since the channels beneath the floor were not plastered (see discussion on frigidariums, p. 45). The room is 26 feet in diameter with four semicircular niches, each 6 feet wide. Perhaps a large basin stood on the central circular founda-

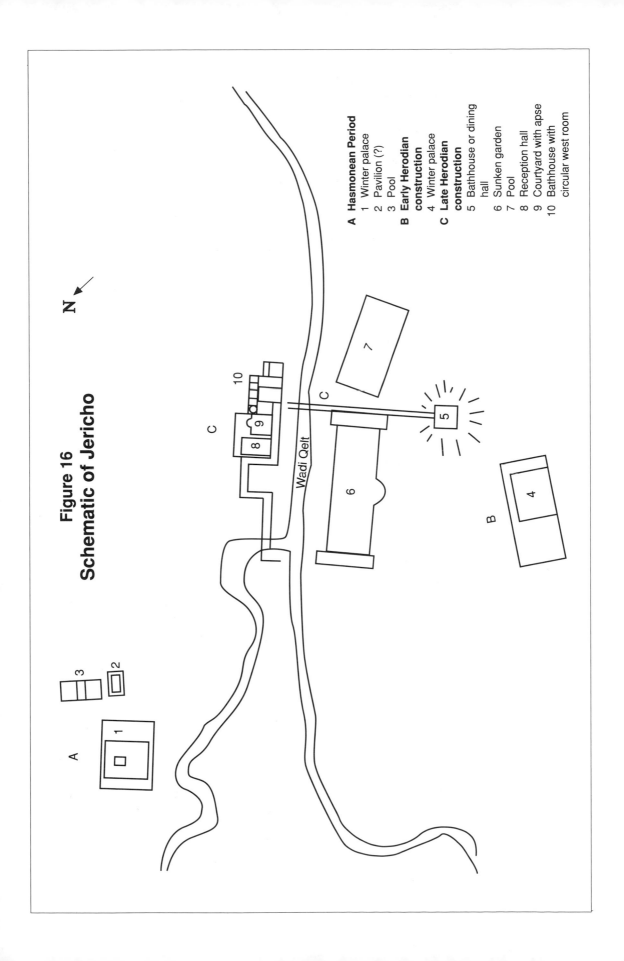

Figure 16
Schematic of Jericho

N

Wadi Qelt

A Hasmonean Period
1 Winter palace
2 Pavilion (?)
3 Pool
B Early Herodian construction
4 Winter palace
C Late Herodian construction
5 Bathhouse or dining hall
6 Sunken garden
7 Pool
8 Reception hall
9 Courtyard with apse
10 Bathhouse with circular west room

tion, which is 6 feet in diameter. The bathhouse was large, about 50 feet by 33 feet. North of the palace Herod built an unusual hippodrome (about 1033 feet by 280 feet) with a theater in its north end.[16]

The use of *opus quadratum* and *opus reticulatum* at this palace is clear indication of imported Roman engineering. This method of building walls from small stones laid in a diamond pattern, over which plaster was spread, is found in Israel only in the buildings of Herod. The frescos this type of construction facilitated are found in all of Herod's building projects, along with elaborate mosaics and cut marble (opus sectile) designs in the floors. In his earliest report on Jericho, Kelso well described the impression one has of Herod's Roman-style building: "Indeed, one might say that here in New Testament Jericho is a section of Augustan Rome that has been miraculously transferred on a magic carpet from the banks of the Tiber to the banks of the Wadi Kelt."

Masada

Perhaps no archaeological site in the past several decades has captivated our attention so dramatically as Masada. There on the west side of the Dead Sea, about 30 miles south of its northern end, Herod built another of his desert palace-fortresses. Masada is an isolated butte rising 1380 feet above the level of the Dead Sea. Its platform is roughly in the shape of a ship, 1900 feet from north to south and 1000 feet from east to west at its widest point. During the years 40 to 30 B.C., Herod built over previous structures from the second century B.C. and added some of his own unique construction. In A.D. 73, under Roman siege, 960 Jewish Zealots—men, women, and children—committed suicide rather than surrender Masada. The site thus was important to modern archaeologists for several reasons and was excavated from 1963 to 1965 by one of Israel's premier archaeologists, the late Yigael Yadin, who supervised an average crew of 300 during a total of eleven months' excavation.[17]

Understandably, Masada has become a symbol of freedom to Jewish people all over the world. In a real sense it is Israel's Alamo. But part of the fascination stems from Masada's architectural magnificence, which was achieved by the greatest builder in Jewish history, Herod the Great. He built a casemate wall (a double wall with partitions) around its perimeter that was 13 feet wide with 110 towers. A three-tiered northern palace was constructed on the sheer slopes. Massive retaining walls, used to support the lower terrace, created a platform 54 feet square. Beautiful colonnades with artificial fluting accompanied multicolored

Figure 17
Schematic of Masada

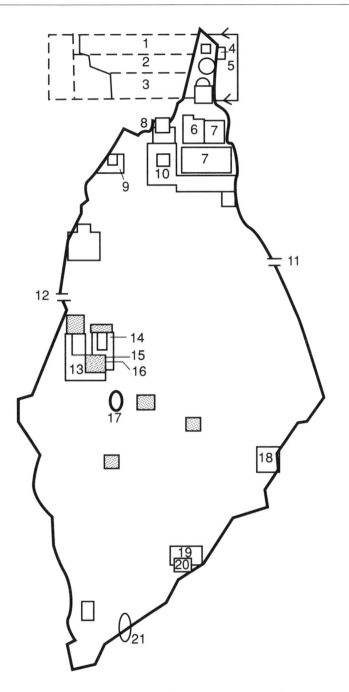

1 Lower terrace
2 Middle terrace
3 Upper terrace; living quarters
4 Small bathhouse
5 Herod's three-tiered palace-fortress
6 Large bathhouse
7 Storerooms
8 Water gate
9 Synagogue
10 Administrative building
11 Snake-path gate
12 West gate
13 Herod's western palace
14 service wing
15 Multicolored mosaic
16 Throne room
17 Swimming pool
18 Zealots' living quarters
19 Mikveh
20 Southern water gate
21 Underground cistern

frescos on the walls to create the impression of a Roman villa. Also supported by retaining walls, a circular pavilion with concentric walls rose 45 feet above the lower terrace (similar to structures at Herodium, Jericho, and Jerusalem). It was plastered and painted using the same marble patterns as in the lower terrace. A staircase led to the upper terrace. On this top level, complete with a semicircular platform 27 feet in diameter from which to view the Dead Sea to the north, Herod built a residence. Private and protected, it was situated on the north side of a huge wall that blocked the severe southern winds. Its four rooms were paved with black and white mosaic floors in simple geometric patterns and are partially preserved *in situ*.

South of this residence on the upper terrace Herod built a public bath 35 feet by 30 feet (remains of a private bath were found in the lower terrace). The complex comprised all the regular components of a Roman bath, including an outer court that may have served as a dressing room (*apodyterium*). The bath and outer court together measured 75 feet by 60 feet. Huge storerooms were built to the south and to the east of the bathhouse, which are mentioned by Josephus in his description of Masada.[18] An administrative center was built to the west of the bath.

In the center of the fortress, along the western edge, Herod built his Western Palace, which included a residence for the king himself, servant quarters, workshops, and storerooms. In the

The Herodian palace fortress at Masada stands near the Dead Sea.

southeastern corner of the palace, Herod built his throne room. Beautiful mosaic floors in geometric patterns have been preserved in related rooms. Outside the palace, near its southeast corner, a large pool for swimming or possibly a bath has been excavated. Niches for clothing may be seen in the eastern wall of the pool's enclosure.

In order to bring water to the site, Herod built a dam across the wadi to the north. Two aqueducts carried water to twelve large reservoirs capable of holding 1.4 million cubic feet. During one of the winters of excavation Yadin witnessed a driving rain storm and wrote that "if the aqueducts had still been in good repair, all the cisterns excavated in the slope of the Masada rock would have filled up in only a few hours."[19]

In the western wall near the northern administrative buildings a synagogue has been found. Though it probably was constructed by Zealots during the occupation of Masada in the years before Jerusalem fell,[20] it may originally have been a Herodian dining hall. The synagogue is one of the oldest ones yet discovered in Israel, along with those at Herodium,[21] and Gamla[22] (see pp. 66–67).

Caesarea Maritima

Jerusalem, Herodium, Jericho, and Masada—Herod's work in these places gives the impression that he was a lavish builder who generally combined practicality with magnificence. On a far different scale, however, is a city that provided revenue for the lavish building and one of his greatest successes.[23] Unlike other cities we have considered, Caesarea Maritima was built completely new, from the ground up, by Herod. On the coast, halfway between Tel Aviv and Haifa, the city in Herod's time covered about 164 acres. Here had stood Strato's Tower, a town Josephus said was "in a state of decay." Josephus said that Herod "rebuilt it entirely with limestone and adorned it with a most splendid palace. Nowhere did he show more clearly the liveliness of his imagination."[24] Netzer believes the palace was located on the promontory between the theater and the sea, where something resembling swimming pools cut into rock may now be seen.[25]

Herod was evidently a man of passionate obsessions. Doubtless he was brutal, but he was also overcome by a beneficence that induced him "to be magnificent, wherever there appeared any hopes of a future memorial, or of reputation at present."[26] Beginning in 23 or 22 B.C., Herod built at Caesarea Maritima for ten[27] or twelve[28] years and upon its completion dedicated his new city, named in honor of Caesar, with characteristically great sumptuousness.[29] I was on the supervisory staff at Caesarea from the beginning of full-scale excavation in 1972 until 1982.[30] An initial probe was done in 1971. Our work has largely confirmed the impression given by Josephus in both his *Wars* and *Antiquities*, of the grand scale on which Herod built to satisfy his own vanity and that of the emperor Augustus.[31]

On a coastline with only one natural harbor (at Haifa) Herod built a magnificent installation that Josephus declares was bigger than the Athenian harbor at Piraeus.[32] Herod engineered the first artificial harbor in the ancient world. It was built with the latest technology—the first extensive use of hydraulic concrete in the eastern Mediterranean. This concrete, made with a volcanic sand known as pozzuolana and available in almost limitless quantity on the island of Santorini, was described by the first-century architect Vitruvius as being capable of hardening under water.[33] One block found that had been formed from this poured concrete underwater measures 39 feet by 49 feet by 5 feet.[34]

Underwater excavations of the Herodian harbor have been conducted by the Caesarea Ancient Harbor Excavation Project (CAHEP) since 1979.[35] This project, sponsored by the Center for Maritime Studies at the University of Haifa in Israel, continues work begun in 1960 by the Link Expedition.[36] CAHEP has shown that Josephus's description of the design and size of Caesarea Maritima's harbor is substantially accurate.[37] Beneath the visible Crusader harbor lie underwater remains of the much larger Herodian harbor, which may be seen in aerial photography. Excavations have shown that the harbor was formed by two breakwaters extending 1500 feet out into the water, the northern one 150 feet wide and the southern one 200 feet wide. The meeting point of the breakwaters, northwest of the harbor proper, was designed to form a 60-foot-wide entrance. Blocks weighing more than 50 tons and larger than those described by Josephus have been found in the breakwaters. Josephus neglected to mention an inner quay which has been found extending 500 feet into the vaulted warehouse section (see below). Portions of two loading docks have been located. The quay was connected to the larger outer harbor by a channel through which stevedores or tugboats moved the vessels.

A small medallion depicting this harbor, or possibly the one in Alexandria, was found by the Link expedition. There can be no doubt that this harbor was the center of extensive trade between the East and the West. Herod was able to finance his building projects through shipping revenues as well as by heavy taxation.

Clear evidence of the vast tonnage that passed through the city came to light in excavations of the Joint Expedition to Caesarea Maritima in 1973. About one hundred huge vaults—five sections of twenty vaults each—were found to stretch along the coast from inside the later Crusader Fort south to the theater. They were

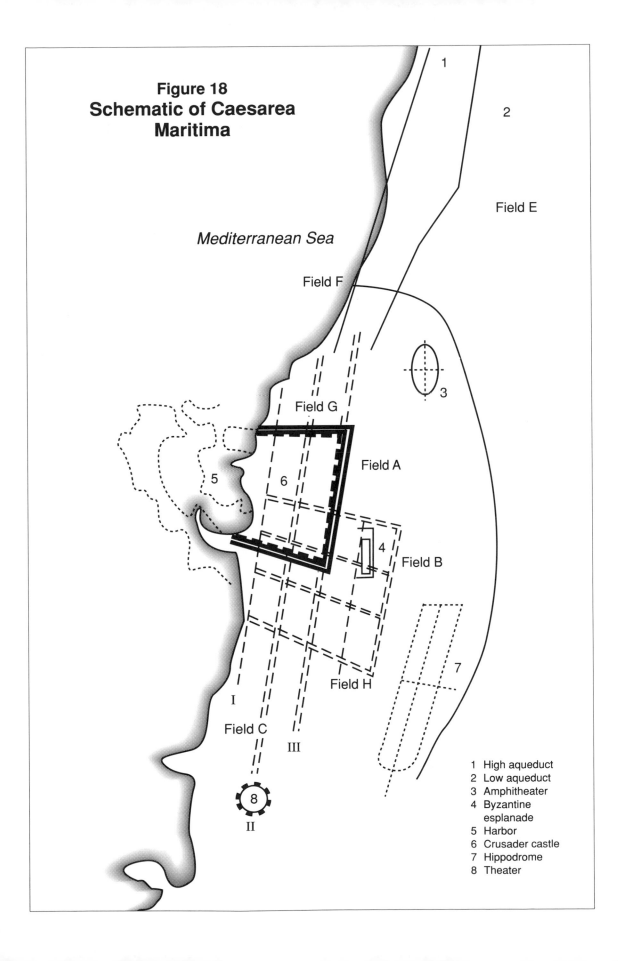

Figure 18
Schematic of Caesarea Maritima

Mediterranean Sea

Field E

Field F

Field G

Field A

Field B

Field H

Field C

I

II

III

1 High aqueduct
2 Low aqueduct
3 Amphitheater
4 Byzantine
   esplanade
5 Harbor
6 Crusader castle
7 Hippodrome
8 Theater

An aerial view of the harbor complex at Caesarea Maritima.

later repaired and rebuilt; one of them, 96 feet long, 16.5 feet wide, and 15 feet high, was clearly used in the third century, as a Mithraeum.[38] Originally, however, they were definitely Herodian warehouses built on bedrock, and coins and pottery from the first century could be harvested from the beaten earth floor. Since there must have been the distance of a city block or *insula* between these vaults and the ancient seashore, many more vaults likely stood here in Herod's time. A major north-south street, 18 feet wide, was found on the western side of these vaults. The street stretches along the modern sea coast and can be clearly seen farther north by the aqueducts, although it has suffered greatly from erosion.

To meet the needs of his new city, Herod built an aqueduct, partially at ground level and partially on arches.[39] In 1972 Robert Bull, the director of the excavation, Jerry Berlin, Neil Christy and I drove to Caesarea from Jerusalem after a farmer reported finding a stone shaft with a stairway leading down to a tunnel on his property. Here, about ten miles due east of Caesarea, was a shaft 8 feet by 5 feet by about 33 feet deep, leading down to a tunnel cut out of solid limestone and measuring about 3.5 feet by 4 feet. It had carried water from a source about 6 miles to the northeast. The water surfaced 6.5 miles east of Caesarea, and a ground-level aqueduct channeled it west to the coast where it gradually was elevated on arches and turned southward to Caesarea, a total distance of about 13 miles. This high-level aqueduct, (a low-level aqueduct was built in Byzantine times) reached an elevation of about 20 feet along the coast. Sections of Roman clay pipe set in concrete remain. No portion of it was open to the elements. The aqueduct is one of the best-known landmarks along the entire coast of Israel—a continuing monument to the work of Herod the Great.

After the time of Herod, Caesarea continued to grow, reaching its zenith in Byzantine times. The need for twice the amount of water provided by Herod's aqueduct was evident as early as the second century when a second aqueduct was built against its western side. An inscription on the western (seaward) side mentions Hadrian and the Tenth Legion so the second aqueduct was probably built about 130 A.D., the time of Hadrian.[40] Other inscriptions refer to the Second and Sixth legions. Legions were noted for their architectural work, including the making of ceramic roof tiles. A cornice on the seaward side of the eastern (Herodian) aqueduct is clearly visible since a large section of the western aqueduct fell down in 1983. The cornice shows that the aqueduct was meant to be freestanding. Evidently Muslim conquerors destroyed a large section of the aqueduct. Since then the unceasing northeastern motion of the savage current has cut the shore farther inland.

Excavation of the streets of Herodian Caesarea provides an idea of the layout of the city. It was thought that the city was designed to match the curved harbor. Ephesus was laid out to match the terrain of mounts Pion and Koressos. Excavation, however, seems to again vindicate the accuracy of Josephus, who wrote that the "streets were laid at equal distances apart."[41] For example, the *cardo maximus* (major north-south street) was 13 feet (4 meters) wide, paved with stone in herringbone pattern.

Aqueduct at Caesarea.

Mosaic sidewalks 18 feet wide (5.5 meters) were paved with mosaics. The *cardo* stretched about 1300 feet north from the theatre to where the Crusader Fort interrupted its original course. It had extended about 1 mile into the northern part of the ancient city. The street was lined with about 700 columns, many of which now lie in the harbor. The cardo maximus parallels the thoroughfare along the western side of the seaside vaults.

A third street ran southward from twin towers in the city's northern Herodian wall. These towers, the foundations of which extend to 23 feet below the modern surface, were considered to be Herodian since period pottery was associated with the foundation of connecting walls.[42] Now, however, the towers and walls are thought to have been reused by Herod from a second-century-B.C. fortified city. Known as Strato's (or Straton's) Tower, the city possessed two safe harbor basins within its walls.[43] The third street, if projected southward, would parallel the other two roads equidistantly south of the Crusader Fort, forming typical Roman insulae. Admittedly, the evidence for the building and repair of the streets is Byzantine or possibly late Roman, but the fact that the streets parallel each other, that one is built alongside Herodian warehouses on the shore, that the cardo maximus extends northward from the entrance to the Herodian theater, and that one passes through the Herodian northern gates of the city, clearly argues that the streets were built upon the previous Herodian system.

A theater Herod built at Caesarea, mentioned by Josephus, was undoubtedly the predecessor of the one now standing on the seashore along the southern coast.[44] In those same passages Josephus refers to an amphitheater, which we have located by aerial infrared photography in the northern sector of Caesarea. Apparently Josephus was confused because he places the amphitheater to the south of the harbor, but the theater stands in that location.[45] He speaks of a stadium in Caesarea,[46] which is possibly the amphitheater, since excavations revealed that the hippodrome was not built until the third century. Gustav Dalman assumes that Josephus confused the structures and that the amphitheater must be thought of as a hippodrome or stadium.[47] He obviously confused the location of the theater in the south and the amphitheater in the north.

The reconstructed *cavea* of the theater at Caesarea was about 300 feet in diameter and seated approximately four thousand. There in A.D. 44 Herod Agrippa I put on a robe made of silver thread and gave an oration to the people as the early morning sun glistened off his garment. Upon accepting their acclamation that he was a god in such stunning circumstances, Herod Agrippa was immediately stricken with a severely painful ailment and had to be taken from the theater. He died within five days.[48] Never again did the theater match that kind of drama!

Much of the visible structure of the theater—the cavea primarily—was rebuilt after the time of Herod. In fact Italian excavators have dated it to the second century.[49] The orchestra (the semicircular floor), however, bears a different tale. Israeli excavators in 1962 found it to have thirteen floors beneath it, all made, one after the other, of colored mortar.[50] These were determined to be Herodian. Rather than being made of the more expensive marble, the floors were made of plaster, which was periodically replaced when they became worn and faded. The geometric design of the last one laid was still visible.

In the steps of the theater the excavators found a Latin inscription carved in stone: "Pontius Pilate, Prefect of Judea, has dedicated to the people of Caesarea a temple in honor of Tiberius."[51] The word *Tiberium* in the inscription refers to a building, probably a temple or shrine, dedicated to the emperor Tiberius (A.D. 14–37) by Pilate, who was procurator from 26 to 36. Foundations of the temple which Herod built to Augustus still stand inside the Crusader Fort.[52] Other writing has been uncovered in Caesarea. Two mosaic floor inscriptions of Romans 13:3 (see p. 373) were found in the floor of a large building (perhaps a praetorium or archives building) near the sea.

Samaria

Farther to the east, in the heart of the district of Samaria, Herod rebuilt the Hellenistic city of Samaria, which he renamed Sebaste (from the Greek translation of the Latin title *Augustus*). The reference is to Octavian, who was Augustus Caesar. Herod had named his harbor in Caesarea after this same Roman emperor. The new city was built as a fortress, and Herod surrounded its two-mile circumference with "strong walls."[53] Two of the round towers in the wall still stand impressively at the western entrance to the city. They are 46 feet in diameter and have been preserved at points to a height of 36 feet.[54] The northern tower which remains stands on four courses of a square Hellenistic tower. If a similar Hellenistic structure once stood beneath the southern tower, it was either destroyed before the Herodian tower was built or was removed by the builders. The walls of the gate between the towers were rebuilt in the second century during the reign of Septimius Severus.

Another tower is located in the wall 174 feet west of the two gate towers. This "corner tower," 36 feet in diameter and almost 27 feet on its inner side, stood at the time of its excavation. It is "the best example of the construction, as it was wholly of the

Hellenistic towers at the western gate at Samaria.

Herodian period, and had . . . no restorations."[55] The lowest course was composed of headers, while the other courses were laid in alternate rows of headers and stretchers. Never were headers and stretchers mixed within a course, as we find in some architecture in the country. The stones were cut with large bosses (protrusions in the centers of the stones) and smooth margins (flat borders around the stone), evidently not for appearance but to accurately fit the stones against one another. In the original excavation reports the three towers were drawn and color-coded to differentiate their times of construction by Clarence Fisher; however, the "corner tower" was not photographed with the other two since it lay some distance away.[56]

The road that ran between the north and south gate towers was bordered by columns and ran eastward along the southern slope of the hill on which Samaria is situated, entering the forum from the east. The columns were monoliths standing on a stylobate with centers placed 10.5 feet apart.[57] Evidence of six hundred of them was found in the excavations[58] but most are no longer present. Measured from the center of the columns on each side, the width of the road was approximately 52 feet. The road was bordered by shops, as was typical of roads leading to fora in Ephesus, Corinth, Philippi, and elsewhere. Slight differences in construction are noticeable between shops on the north side and those on the south.[59]

On the acropolis of Samaria lie foundations of a temple built initially by Herod in honor of Augustus and rebuilt by Severus.

Some of the large ashlars from the walls, dressed in typical Herodian style—bosses and wide margins—are still visible. The temple was 115 by 79 feet with a much larger forecourt to the north. The two were connected by a 90-foot-wide staircase which was rebuilt in the second century and may still be seen.[60] Josephus commented that the temple was one "which in size and beauty was among the most renowned."[61] Its plan is much like a first-century Temple of Jupiter at Baalbek in the Bekaa Valley of Lebanon, which was elevated on a podium 44 feet above the great court, with columns rising another 65 feet to capitals crowned with an entablature 13 feet high.

Samaria stands atop a high hill in a basin between higher ridges. On the eastern side of this hill Herod built a 225-foot-by-105-foot, Corinthian-style basilica as a public center for trade, commerce, banking, and law.[62] This structure was destroyed in the revolts that plagued Sebaste (and Israel as a whole) in the first century A.D. Severus restored the building in the late second century, and remains of it are impressive still. Adjoining the basilica on the east was a rectangular forum, which measured 420 by 240 feet.[63] Only the forum's western edge was excavated, and today the area is a parking lot. At the time of the excavations it was a threshing floor for the village.

A massive stadium, 755 feet by 197 feet, was also built within the Herodian walls of Samaria. Soundings revealed the Doric-style construction for this stadium 242 feet down the slope and to

The Roman forum in Samaria.

the north of the forum.[64] It has been dated to Herod's time. A second phase of building belonged to the Corinthian order and was from the second century. The stadium was a lovely structure with a *peribolos* (an area enclosed by walls or columns) formed by twenty columns on the short sides and sixty-five on the long sides. Although Herod instituted games at Caesarea and Jerusalem, it is odd that no reference exists in the early literature to games being conducted at the stadium in Sebaste.

As a whole Herodian Samaria contained, as André Parrot has written, "all that western civilization expected to find at the heart of a great city: temples, a theatre, a forum, colonnaded streets, a stadium."[65] Josephus's observation regarding Sebaste is an appropriate description of all of Herod's work: "He also made it [Sebaste] splendid in order to leave to posterity a monument of the humanity that arose from his love of beauty."[66]

Hebron

The stone in the Herodian wall at Hebron is like that in the wall of the Temple Mount.

In Hebron a monumental wall around the Cave of Machpelah is the only Herodian structure still intact. Viewing it gives some idea of the beauty of Herodian architecture. Herod built the wall to honor the burial place of Abraham, Isaac, Jacob, and their wives (Sarah, Rebekah, and Leah, but not Rachel). The beauti-

fully dressed Herodian stone, with a slight boss protruding from a smooth margin, is laid with a smooth surface halfway up the wall. Above that point slight alternating indentations produce the effect of pilasters reaching to the top. This design is identical to the one Herod used on the enclosure wall of the Temple Mount in Jerusalem.[67]

The discoveries surveyed in chapters 3 and 4 have convinced most archaeologists and historians that Herod is the greatest builder in Jewish history, surpassing even King Solomon. Herod's legacy is written in the ruins of his building projects, and although he may have earned his appellation as "Great" because he was a splendid builder or because he was the most politically important among the Herods, that greatness was tarnished by his cruelty, greed, ambition, inhumanity, and sheer madness. He will be remembered more for the slaughter of the babies in Bethlehem than for his building program.

PART 3

Archaeology and the Life of Christ

Jesus' Youth and Ministry in Galilee

Birth and Youth of Jesus

Ancient Literary References to Jesus

Archaeology directly contributes to a complete understanding of few events of Jesus' life and ministry. This is, of course, to be expected regarding a carpenter's son and itinerant teacher with a reputation for doing miracles. We would hardly expect that Jesus captivated the attention of ancient historians. Nevertheless, Josephus refers to him in a Greek text of *The Antiquities of the Jews*.[1] The authenticity of this Greek text has been widely rejected because of its apparent Christian witness to Jesus' divinity. It is likely that a zealous believer did add to Josephus's so-called *Testimonium Flavianum* in an effort to "Christianize" the document, but it is also likely that the rest of the facts presented are authentic, since other texts of *Antiquities of the Jews* include the *Testimonium Flavianum* without the reference to divinity. Schlomo Pines argues that the same information, without the questionable testimony, is found in a tenth-century historical work in Arabic, entitled *Kitab al-Unwan*.[2] The Arabic history thus provides independent witness to that of the Greek, and supports the credibility of the historical portions of Josephus's references to Jesus. In another place, the historian also names Jesus as the brother of James.[3]

Brief mention of Jesus may also be found in Suetonius's *Lives of the Caesars*,[4] Tacitus's *Annals*,[5] a history of Greece written about A.D. 52 by Thallus and referred to by Julius Africanus, an epistle of Pliny the Younger (no. 96) to the emperor Trajan, the Jewish Talmud,[6] and the *Death of Peregrine* by Lucian, a second-century Greek satirist.[7]

The Census

Although archaeology has unearthed little that relates directly to Jesus, it contributes to our understanding of the Gospels through references to people, events, and places associated with him. Some recent archaeological evidence has shed new light on an old and vexing problem relating to the birth of Jesus. According to Luke 2:2, Jesus was born during the time when a census was being conducted by Quirinius, governor of Syria. Since Jesus was born during the lifetime of Herod the Great, who died in 4 B.C., this Quirinius cannot be the one whose census was dated by Josephus to A.D. 6, "the thirty-seventh year of Caesar's defeat of Antony at Actium [on Sept. 2, 31 B.C.]."[8] Jerry Vardaman has discovered the name of Quirinius on a coin in micrographic letters, placing him as proconsul of Syria and Cilicia from 11 B.C. until after the death of Herod. The evidence contributed by Vardaman supports the view that there were two Quiriniuses, furthermore, he believes Jesus was born in 12 B.C.[9] Interestingly, the name *Quirinius*, in the form of κυρηνιος (*kyrēnios*), has been found in an epitaph that is probably from the second century A.D.[10] It is also in a first- or second-century inscription in the form κυιρινος (*kuirinos*).[11] Neither inscription refers to the New Testament personage, however, and the name may as likely stand for Cyrenius as for Quirinius.

The censuses to which Luke refers, both in his Gospel and in Acts 5:37, have been illuminated by discoveries of ancient papyrus census forms. The sequence of known dates for the censuses clearly demonstrates that one was taken in the empire every fourteen years. There is a form in the British Museum dated by George Milligan and Adolf Deissmann to A.D. 104.[12] Although we have nothing as yet from the years 90 and 76, there is one from 62.[13] Another is dated by Milligan to 48,[14] and yet another dates to 34.[15] A fifth census form, although it contains no date, is considered by its editor to have been produced in 20.[16] Acts 5:37 and Josephus in *Antiquities* refer to another in the year 6, to which year B. P. Grenfell[17] and A. S. Hunt date Oxyrhynchus papyrus 256.[18] Finally, Tertullian records a census when Sentius Saturninus (9–6 B.C.) was governor of Syria, which would have been in the year 9 B.C. according to the fourteen-year cycle established by the dated papyri.[19] This census suggests the possibility of an earlier date for the birth of Jesus than is commonly assumed. Vardaman argues for 11 or 10 B.C. at the latest; however, a census begun in Syria in 9 B.C. may have taken a long time to be completed in Palestine. It is clear that Jesus was born during an official imperial decree of Caesar Augustus (see Luke 2:1), and the fourteen-year cycle for such censuses suggests a date around 9 B.C. What is not clear is whether the census noted by Luke was part of the cycle or was a special one. The archaeological data seems to indicate an ordinary imperial census.

Two census orders that have been found show an interesting correlation with the wording of the birth narrative of Jesus. One, British Museum papyrus 904, is from the year A.D. 104:

> Gaius Vibius Maximus, Prefect of Egypt [says]: Seeing that the time has come for the house to house census, it is necessary to compel all those who for any cause whatsoever are residing out of their provinces to *return to their own homes* [emphasis added], that they may both carry out the regular order of the census and may also attend diligently to the cultivation of their allotments.[20]

The second, Oxyrhynchus papyrus 255, is a census return from the year A.D. 48, the ninth year of Claudius:

> I the above-mentioned Thermoutharion along with my guardian the said Apollonius swear by Tiberius Claudius Caesar Augustus Germanicus Emperor that assuredly the preceding document makes a sound and true return of *those living with me* [emphasis added], and that there is no one else living with me, neither a stranger, nor an Alexandrian citizen, nor a freedman, nor a Roman citizen, nor an Egyptian in addition to the aforesaid. If I am swearing truly, may it be well with me, but if falsely, the reverse. In the ninth year of Tiberius Claudius Caesar Augustus Germanicus Emperor.[21]

Bethlehem

The place where Jesus was born has never been seriously disputed. Both Jerome[22] and Paulinus of Nola[23] provide evidence that the cave in Bethlehem, under the present Church of the Nativity, was identified as the birthplace before the time of Hadrian—thus almost into the first century. Hadrian (117–38) marked the site by planting a grove of trees there in honor of the Roman god Adonis. In the second century Justin Martyr wrote, "When the Child was born in Bethlehem, since Joseph could not find lodging in that village, he took up his quarters in a certain cave near the village; and while they were there Mary brought forth the Christ and placed him in a manger, and here the Magi who came from Arabia found him."[24] The second-century Protevangelium of James preserves the same information.[25] Origen wrote that the cave at Bethlehem and the manger of that cave were "famous in these parts even among the people alien to the faith, since it was in this cave that . . . Jesus . . . was born."[26] Eusebius wrote that the emperor and his mother Helena built a church over the cave, adorning the place with lavish magnificence.[27] A later chapter in Eusebius's work states that Helena erected the church,[28] a point confirmed by Sozomen in about 430,[29] as well as by Sulpicius Severus in about 395.[30]

The Church of the Nativity, Bethlehem.

Excavations were conducted in Bethlehem in 1934 by William

Harvey and in 1948 to 1951 by the Franciscan Custody of the Holy Land. Beneath the present church were found remains of the foundations of the Constantinian church. About two feet below the present floor a beautiful mosaic floor may belong to the original church but also may be a fifth-century addition since it is higher than the level of the original bases that supported the columns of the church of Constantine. Square with sides 87 feet long, Constantine's basilica was divided by four nine-column rows. At the east end of the basilica, directly above the cave, Helena built an octagonal building, 26 feet long on each side. It was connected to the basilica, forming a two-part structure—the octagon containing the holy shrine and the basilica serving as a meeting place for Christians. The Church of the Holy Sepulchre in Jerusalem, also built by Constantine at the probable site of the crucifixion and burial of Jesus, is similar in design. The twofold pattern copied the monumental mausoleum architecture of the Roman emperors (e.g., that of Diocletian at Spalato), and was used by early Christian churches built in honor of martyrs. The impressive building that today greets visitors to Bethlehem was built by the Byzantine emperor Justinian (527–65). Some medieval alterations were made, such as the closed arch above the modern rectangular doorway.

Jerome, the well-known translator of the Latin Vulgate Bible, moved to Bethlehem in 385 and lived in a cave adjacent to the birth grotto until his death thirty-five years later. The tradition that Jesus' birth took place in Bethlehem is long and solid. There appears little reason to doubt its essential trustworthiness.

Nazareth

Nazareth's comparative unimportance is indicated in John's Gospel by the remark of Nathanael, "Can any good thing come out of Nazareth?"(1:46 NASB). Jesus spent his youth in the village, which is located in the southern end of the hills of Lower Galilee at about 1200 feet above sea level. Archaeological excavations in Nazareth at the turn of the century and by Bellarmino Bagatti in 1955 when the new Church of the Annunciation was erected, have provided some information about the village that is not mentioned in the Old Testament, Josephus's writings, or the Talmud.

The excavations conducted by Bagatti, revealed that Nazareth of Jesus' day was an agricultural settlement with numerous winepresses, olive presses, caves for storing grain, and cisterns for water and wine. Situated below the Annunciation Church and the Church of Saint Joseph to the north, some of these structures are connected by ancient tradition with the habita-

The Church of the Annunciation, Nazareth.

tions of Joseph and Mary. Pottery found in the village dates from Iron Age II (900–600 B.C.) to the Byzantine period (330–640), including Roman pieces from the time of Christ. The location of twenty-three tombs several hundred yards to the north, west, and south of the Annunciation Church indicates the limits of the town during the Hellenistic and Roman periods, for tombs were built outside towns.

The first church built in Nazareth seems to have been constructed by Joseph of Tiberias, an eminent Jew who converted to Christianity and was granted the privilege of building churches in Galilee by Constantine.[31] However, Bagatti has published evidence from his excavations beneath the floor of the Annunciation Church that reveals the Byzantine church was preceded by another religious structure. Considerable remains of architectural features still exist. On the basis of style and structure Bagatti dates these to the third century and thinks the structure was a Jewish-Christian synagogue. He calls it a "synagogue church."[32] The synagogue referred to in Luke 4:16 may have stood here, or perhaps on the site now occupied by the "Place of the Forty" in the Muslim cemetery between the Church of Joseph and Mary's Well.

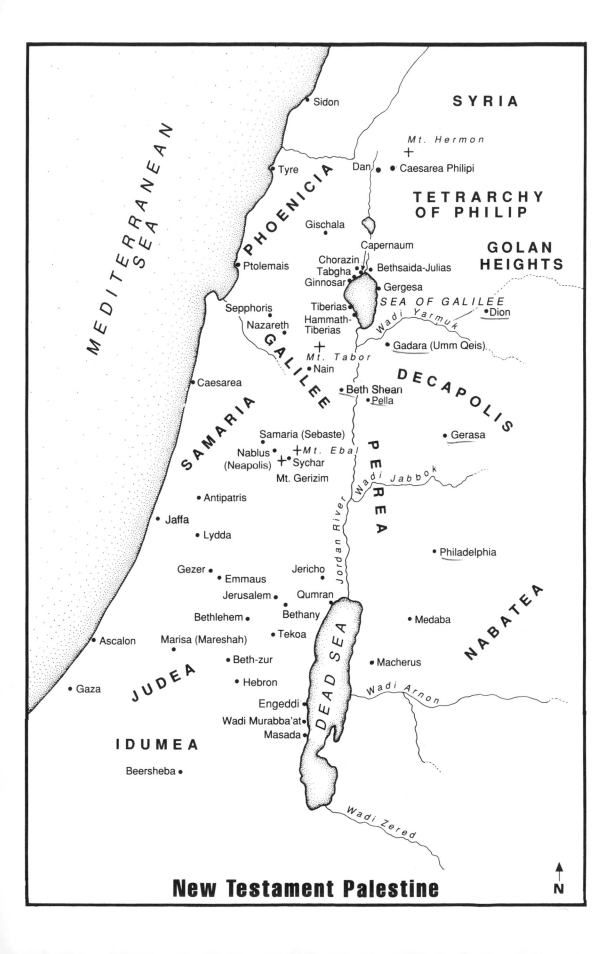

New Testament Palestine

The Public Ministry of Jesus: Galilee

Date

The beginning of Jesus' public ministry is dated by synchronisms in the Gospel of Luke (3:1–2). A date of A.D. 27 seems likely, although Vardaman argues for A.D. 15.[33] The dates mentioned by Luke are rather well established, but the statement that "Lysanias was tetrarch of Abilene" (3:1 NASB) has been controverted because the only Lysanias known for centuries was ruler of Chalcis a half-century earlier (40–36 B.C.). However, an inscription has been found from the time of Tiberius (A.D. 14–37) that names Lysanias as tetrarch in Abila near Damascus.[34]

The Baptism of Jesus

The ministry of Jesus began when he was baptized by John at "Bethany beyond the Jordan" (John 1:28). The exact location of this place has long been disputed. In a personal note I received from William F. Albright he wrote, "The whole problem of 'Bethany' and 'Bethabara' remains very obscure. In my own opinion, this 'Bethany' is a corruption of 'Bethabara,' and 'Bethabara' was in the southern Jordan Valley."[35] Rainer Riesner has recently resurrected a centuries-old argument by John Lightfoot and C. R. Conder that this Bethany was located in the extreme southwestern section of Batanaea in northern Transjordan.[36] John the Baptist was likely associated at one time with members of the Qumran community,[37] who were almost certainly Essenes and who have ties to the Dead Sea Scrolls found in caves linked with the Qumran community. John shared many things in common with the group:

1. He used Isaiah 40:3 ("In the wilderness prepare the way of the Lord" [NRSV]) as his primary justification for preaching in the Wilderness of Judea. The Qumran community used that passage in their literature for the same purpose,[38] but with a different application.
2. Both John and the Qumran group were living and working in the narrow strip of desert along the western side of the southern Jordan Valley known as the Wilderness of Judea.
3. John was popularly known as the *baptist* (literally, the "Dipper"), a term describing his custom of immersing in water those who accepted his teaching—a practice not known in the Old Testament but observed by the Qumran community. Their literature and the many large cisterns excavated since 1956 confirm this practice. William LaSor argues convincingly that "the archaeological and Mishnaic evidence seems to support the argument for immersion. That is clearly what occurred in the contemporaneous Jewish *miqva'ot*."[39]

Steps descend to the baptistries at Qumran.

4. John's parents were so old that a miracle was required to make his birth possible (Luke 1:5–25), justifying the speculation that they probably died while John was young. Since the Qumran community cared for orphaned children, it is not unthinkable that John could have been reared by these nonconformist Jews in the wilderness.
5. John's diet, including locusts (Matt. 3:4; Mark 1:6) is paralleled in the Cairo Damascus Document,[40] fragments of which were found in three of Qumran's caves. This seemingly unusual diet would not be unique to John or the Qumran sect, however, since the locust was considered a clean insect (Lev. 11:22).

The conclusion to be drawn from these observations is that John the Baptist fits beautifully into the *Sitz-im-Leben* of both Qumran and the Gospels. That John's understanding of community and repentance was different from that of the people of Qumran does not argue that he could not have been connected with the community;[41] only that he may have disagreed with them. That very disagreement could have led to his expulsion or his voluntary departure from the sect.

The Temptation of Jesus

After his baptism, Jesus was taken into the wilderness to be tempted by Satan (Matt 4:1; Mark 1:12–13; Luke 4:1–2). The traditional location of the wilderness is due west of Jericho in the

Wilderness of Judea. On top of the most imposing peak of these hills are the walls and foundations of an unfinished church, which was evidently planned to replace the Byzantine church whose ruins stand on the summit. This hill is known by its Arabic name, *Jebel Quarantal* ("Mount of the Forty"), recalling the forty days of temptation Jesus endured here; however, the exact location of the temptation cannot be determined.

One of the three temptations of Jesus took place at the pinnacle of the temple in Jerusalem (Matt. 4:5; Luke 4:9). This is the southeast corner of the Temple Mount, perhaps the Royal Porch's southeast corner, which stood on the temple platform during Jesus' time. Josephus speaks of the area:

> For while the depth of the ravine [the Kidron Valley] was great, and no one who bent over to look into it from above could bear to look down to the bottom, the height of the portico standing over it was so very great that if anyone looked down from its rooftop, combining the two elevations, he would become dizzy and his vision would be unable to reach to the end of so measureless a depth.[42]

The present platform of the Temple Mount cannot be the one involved in the Gospel account because the platform of Herod's Temple was destroyed in the Roman wars (see pp. 102–106 for a discussion of the archaeological and historical aspects of the pinnacle).

Capernaum

After his return to Galilee and rejection in the Nazareth synagogue, Jesus went to live in Capernaum on the north shore of the Sea of Galilee (Luke 4:31; Matt. 4:13), only a short distance west of the Jordan River. Probably living with Simon Peter (Matt. 8:14–16; Mark 2:1), Jesus taught and performed healings in the synagogue in the city (Mark 1:21; 3:1–5; John 6:59). The site now designated as Capernaum, Tell Hum, or Kfar Tanhum of the Talmud, has long been considered authentic. In the foreword to a little volume written about its history and archaeology before 1967, Yigael Yadin wrote: "Capernaum is one of the best known sites in the Holy Land, precious to Jews and Christians alike."[43]

Until quite recently, it was thought that the limestone remains which so far have been identified and studied from the synagogue in Capernaum belonged to the first century, but excavations since 1968 by Virgilio Corbo and Stanislao Loffreda seriously challenge that view.[44] In 1970 they published the first hint of a later date for the synagogue.[45] G. Foerster replied to this in the *Israel Exploration Journal* (*IEJ*) almost immediately,[46] and Loffreda's response to Foerster was published in *Liber Annuus* (*LA*) the next

Beneath a fourth- or fifth-century limestone synagogue in Capernaum, evidence has been found of an earlier building, likely the synagogue where Jesus preached.

year and in the *IEJ* the year after that.[47] The *IEJ* response included an editorial by Michael Avi-Yonah.[48] Finally Loffreda rounded out the controversy with a reply to Avi-Yonah.[49]

Ten thousand coins found beneath the limestone pavements, some of them embedded in the mortar under the pavement, clearly date the structure to the Byzantine period, the synagogue prayer hall to the fourth century, and the attached room on the east to the fifth century.[50] I vividly remember talking one day with Loffreda at Capernaum about the thousands of coins he had found in the excavations, and was shocked when he said the coins were used as gravel in preparing mortar for the synagogue. When he saw the incredulous look on my face he reached over with his trowel and easily dislodged five coins from the mortar between two stones.

Since 1975, when the excavators published their report on the discovery of black basalt walls under all four corners of the later limestone synagogue, we have been given impressive evidence of what is certainly the remains of the synagogue in which Jesus preached.[51] The basalt walls, though lying under the fourth- and fifth-century walls, are slightly out of line with them and are not, therefore, foundations for the later synagogue. These walls are 4 feet thick—much too thick for a private dwelling. In 1981 a basalt cobblestone floor, contemporaneous with the earlier walls, was found under the nave of the synagogue. Beneath the floor, pottery from the first century A.D. was found, which established that date for construction of the floor.[52] The synagogue was 60 feet wide by 79 feet long, essentially the same as the later one above it. Like the later one, it was divided into three areas, a large nave and two narrow aisles on the east and west. The basalt cobblestone floor covered the entire area. No outside doors are evident. These walls and floor do not extend under the east wing of the limestone synagogue, which was added in the fifth century. Here, then, we have evidence of what may have been the synagogue in which Jesus preached, the one built by a Roman centurion for the Jewish nation he loved (Luke 7:1–5).

No less startling, if perhaps less convincing, is the discovery of what may be the house of Simon Peter in Capernaum (see pp. 80–81).[53] The identification of the house as Peter's definitely has champions. James Charlesworth, for example, writes that "Peter's house in which Jesus lived when he moved to Capernaum from Nazareth has probably been discovered."[54] Eighty-four feet south of the synagogue, an octagonal building with mosaic floors stood in partial remains for centuries. Since octagonal buildings were raised in the Byzantine period to venerate particularly holy places, in 1968 excavators of the synagogue investigated this structure and discovered multiple levels of occupation in the strata beneath it. The octagon itself is like several Byzantine churches built over the birthplace of Jesus in Bethlehem and other places of similar significance. Beneath this fifth-century building, which contained a baptistery in a southern apse, was found a fourth-century church, as evidenced by graffiti on the walls.[55] The structure was almost square, its central hall measuring 25 feet by 27 feet. This hall was part of an earlier house built, according to the excavators, in the mid-first century A.D.

The earlier house, whose walls were eventually identified, was made of the same basalt stone as found in the first-century synagogue. Unlike in the synagogue, these walls were narrow and would not support a second story or a masonry roof. The roof would have been made of wooden branches covered with earth, in all probability similar to the one in Capernaum described by Mark (2:4), through which a hole was dug in order to let the paralytic down to Jesus.[56] Simon Peter was praying on such a roof at the house of Simon the Tanner in Jaffa when visitors came from Caesarea (Acts 10:9). The first-century house was built around two courtyards with the outside entrance opening indirectly into

The first-century remains at the site traditionally identified as Peter's house in Capernaum.

one of the courtyards. A *taboun* (round oven) was found in this courtyard, which indicates it was used as the main family room. The southern courtyard may have been used for animals or as a working area. In either size or building material, the house is not unlike all the other houses found in Capernaum (See figure 7, p. 81).

Sometime in the mid-first century the large room (20 feet by 21 feet) at the center of the house was plastered, along with its ceiling and floors. It is the only house discovered there so far that had plastered walls, and these were replastered, along with the floors, at least twice. During the mid-first century the pottery used in the room ceased to be of the typical domestic variety. Only storage jars and oil lamps were found from after this point. Thus the use of the room must have changed from normal residential living. More than one hundred fifty inscriptions were scratched on its walls in Greek, Syriac, Hebrew, Aramaic, and Latin from this time until the fourth century.[57] Whether the name of Peter is among the graffiti, as suggested by the official publication,[58] is impossible to say with certainty.[59] But even if the name was used, there is no certainty it would have referred to Simon Peter.

Sometime after the first century two pillars were erected to raise the roof of the large central room, creating an impressively high ceiling. The fifth-century octagonal chapel was built with the center of its concentric walls directly over this room. Evidence now available suggests that this chapel was built over a first-century house which was set apart in the middle of that century as a public area. It was made into a church and at some point came to be venerated as the house of Peter. It would not be prudent to apply the data beyond that.[60]

In the eastern sector of Capernaum, that part controlled by the Greek Orthodox Church, excavations conducted since 1978 by Vasillios Tzaferis resulted in the discovery of what appears to be the main part of the Roman city.[61] Remains from the seventh to the tenth centuries of the city's occupation were uncovered over 1984 and 1985 in this eastern area. The earliest level revealed foundation walls that "rested directly over an occupation level containing pottery of the Early Roman Period (first century A.D.); the occupation level was lying directly on virgin soil."[62] Remains of a Roman bathhouse, constructed in the first century B.C., were found to the east. A number of buildings oriented in the same direction as the bathhouse, and dating to the first century A.D., were discovered farther to the north.

This information should help put the synagogue and "House of Peter" in a broader context and clarifies the nature of the city itself. There are still those who regard Capernaum's identification with Tell Hum (Kfar Tanhum of the Talmud) to be uncertain.[63] This is due partially to the fact that Josephus seems to equate Capernaum with the Tabgha Springs, a few hundred yards west of Tell Hum.[64]

Gergesa

About 9 miles farther southeast of Tell Hum, around the Sea of Galilee, Tzaferis excavated the remains of a Byzantine church found in 1970 during construction of a new road.[65] The church stands about 300 yards from the unexcavated tell of an ancient urban city known now as Tell el-Kursi. In the small bay nearby lie remains of a well-constructed harbor. In 1971 Tzaferis began work on the basilica-type church, which had three aisles, a narthex, a large inner court, a small outer court, chapels, domestic rooms, and a beautiful mosaic pavement depicting birds, fruits, and flowers.[66] A dedicatory inscription in the pavement at the entry to the baptistery dates construction of the pavement to 585.[67] The work done to reconstruct the Byzantine church and its surroundings is impressive.

I am convinced that this site, known in modern times variously as El Kursi, Khersa, Chersa, Koursi, or Kersi, is Gergesa, the village visited by Jesus on the other side of the Jordan River (Mark 5:1; Matt. 8:28; Luke 8:26). There are at least six reasons for the identification:

1. Eusebius, in the fourth century, identifies the location in these words: "Gergesa where the Lord healed the demons. A village is even now situated on the mountain beside the sea of Tiberias into which also the swine were cast headlong."[68]

2. The lavish expenditure on the Byzantine church manifests the builders' view that it marked an important Christian place or event. The church and monastery were built in the fifth century. In 491, Saint Saba visited the holy places across the Sea of Galilee and prayed in the church at Chorsia (Koursi), according to Cyril of Scythopolis.[69] Efforts were made to identify this site as Gergesa, even before there was archaeological evidence to support it.[70]

3. Halfway up the steep hill behind the monastic compound containing the church there is a two-part building which consists of a small mosaic-paved chapel with an apse in one part and the base of a towerlike structure in the other. The latter structure encloses a huge boulder, 22 feet high, which the building may have been erected to preserve. Tzaferis thinks this memorial tower and chapel, as well as the monastery compound below, were constructed in the late fifth or early sixth century to mark the spot as the place of the miracle.[71]

4. The exorcism of the demoniac and subsequent entrance of the demons into the herd of swine occurred on what the text calls "the other side of the sea" (Matt. 8:28; Mark 5:1; Luke 8:26). Such a description fits this site. An alternative site suggested on the southwest shore of the sea is not on "the other side of the lake" (Luke 8:22) from Capernaum, but is also in Galilee. Since the site of the exorcism was "in the country of the Gergesenes, which is *opposite* (ἀντιπέρα) Galilee" (Luke 8:26 NEB) the event could not have taken place in Galilee.

5. The pigs ran off a "steep bank" (κρημνός) (Mark 5:13; Matt. 8:32; Luke 8:33) into the sea and drowned. El Koursi is the only spot on the entire eastern side of the Sea of Galilee where there is a steep bank coming out to the sea. Almost a century ago William Sanday argued that this was the probable location on the basis of two points: "Not only are there tombs near at hand, but here alone is there a cliff that falls sheer almost into the lake."[72]

6. The names given as the site of the miracle in the Gospels (Gergesa, Gadara and Gerasa) are irreconcilable.[73] The event could not have occurred in three different places at the same time. Let's consider the latter two. Gerasa, modern Jerash in Jordan, is 37 miles southeast of the sea—quite a run for the pigs! Gadara, modern Umm Qeis in Jordan, is 5 miles southeast of the sea, presenting the same distance problem.

Modern El-Kursi is probably the Gergesa near which demons entered a herd of swine.

Though some contend that the "territory" of these cities extended all the way to the sea, the argument is forced and does not give proper consideration to the mention of the "steep bank."

Bethsaida-Julias and Tabgha

The place where Jesus fed the five thousand with the loaves and fish (Matt. 14:13–21; Mark 6:30–44; Luke 9:10–17; John 6:1–13) is still in doubt, and differing identifications of the site have been made through the centuries. In the tenth century, Eutychius of Alexandria recorded that the church at Koursi, on the east side of the sea, was considered a witness to the feeding in that area.[74] (A section in his work that describes Christian holy places in Israel and surrounding areas is probably based on earlier documents.) Recently, Bargil Pixner has defended modern Tabgha, on the northern shore of the Sea of Galilee, as the site.[75]

The feeding of the five thousand and four thousand must have occurred on the eastern side of the sea since Jesus returned "to the other side" (Matt. 14:22; Mark 6:45) after the feeding. Furthermore, Jesus and the disciples landed at Gennesaret (Matt. 14:34; Mark 6:53), which is on the west side. Following the account of the feeding of the multitude is the story of the storm at sea (Mark 6:45–52; Matt. 14:22–33; John 6:14–21). A feeding at Tabgha would be impossible to reconcile with this chain of events. The prevailing winds blow from west to east in Galilee. If the boat left Tabgha, there is no way it would have landed to the *west* at Gennesaret after having been blown *eastward* by the wind.

In 1932, excavations were conducted by Andreas Mader and Alfons Schneider at Tabgha, the traditional site of the feeding west of Capernaum.[76] Their work revealed portions of a fifth-century church. In 1936, Bernhard Gauer discovered a fourth-century church beneath the later one.[77] Loffreda began work at Tabgha in 1968 and examined the remains of the early church in 1970.[78] More work was done in 1976, 1979, and 1980 by Renate Rosenthal and Malka Hershkovitz for the Israel Department of Antiquities prior to construction of the new Center of Christian Life and the new German Church of the Multiplication.[79] Pottery sealed under the atrium floor confirmed a construction date in the second half of the fifth century for the second building. There is no convincing evidence prior to the mid-fourth century placing the miracle here.[80]

It is more likely that the multitude was fed somewhere near Bethsaida-Julias, which was on "the other side of the Sea of Galilee" (John 6:1; cf. Luke 9:10). The village of Bethsaida had been raised to the status of city by Herod Philip and named Julias in honor of the emperor Augustus's daughter.[81] Josephus's account of a battle during the first revolt against Rome describes Julias as close to the River Jordan[82] and possibly having a harbor to which reinforcements were shipped.[83] It lay on the northern shore of the sea.[84] The most probable location for the site is et-Tell, which is about 700 feet north of the sea on the east bank of the Jordan River. The modern es-Saki lagoon may have once extended north to et-Tell, thus placing the tell virtually on the shore of the Sea of Galilee. The lagoon appears to be part of a delta, and there is evidence that in antiquity the Jordan River probably entered the sea east of where it empties today.

It has been suggested that el-Araj, which in antiquity would have been on the western (Galilean) side of the Jordan, may have been Bethsaida of Galilee (John 12:21). It would have been politically separated from et-Tell (Bethsaida-Julias) when the Jordan River became the border between Herod Antipas's Galilee and Herod Philip's territories.[85] This explanation would fit the geographical demands of the Gospel narrative connected with the feeding and the subsequent storm at sea. Jesus was in or at Bethsaida when he fed the multitude (Luke 9:10), after which he put his disciples into a boat and sent them "to the other side, to Bethsaida" (Mark 6:45). A storm from the west, which is normal, would have prevented their landing in Bethsaida of Galilee. After Jesus stilled the sea, they crossed over and came to land at Gennesaret (Mark 6:53; Matt. 14:34), which is the plain west of Capernaum.

An example of the sort of boat Jesus and the disciples used was found buried in mud on the northern shore of the Sea of Galilee in January 1986. It is the first work boat found on an inland lake in the entire Mediterranean area.[86] The boat, dating between the first century B.C. and the end of the first century A.D., was excavated that February and found to measure 26.5 feet long, 7.5 feet wide and 4.5 feet high. It would have accommodated about fifteen average-sized men of Jesus' Galilee (about 5 feet, five inches tall, weighing 140 pounds). Originally it had a mast for sailing and two oars on each side. Jesus and his disciples could easily fit into such a boat and their use is mentioned or inferred often in the Gospels.[87] The excavators reinforced the fragile vessel with fiberglass and polyester resin frames, wrapped it in thin plastic sheeting, and sprayed polyurethane liquid to encase the wood in a protective shell. It was then transported 550 yards by sea from its point of discovery just west of the Kibbutz Ginnosar to the Yigal Allon Museum at Ginnosar for proper treatment to ensure preservation. The depiction of a similar boat was found in a first-century mosaic from the city of Migdal (Magdala),[88] only a mile west.[89]

Archaeology has been able to provide little information on the location of Bethsaida because et-Tell has not been excavated. Pixner has found evidence of a wall built of dressed stones at the site, and a large lintel with a design of a linear configuration enclosing rosettes has been found. Hellenistic, Roman, Byzantine, and Arabic potteries have been found in surveys done by the Israelis in 1967 and 1968 and by Pixner from 1981 to 1984.[90] The site evidently was occupied in the time of Christ. El-Araj, similarly, has produced evidence of ancient stone buildings, as well as capitals, pieces of basalt architraves, and fragments of mosaics. We can only hope that eventually both sites will be excavated to confirm what may be deduced from the writings of Josephus.

Chorazin

The Gospels of Matthew and Luke record that Jesus cursed three cities: Capernaum, Bethsaida, and Chorazin (Matt. 11:20–24; Luke 10:12–16). The latter is identified as Khirbet Kerazeh, a site in the hills 2.5 miles northwest of Capernaum. At the beginning of the fourth century Eusebius of Caesarea located it 2 Roman miles from Capernaum and described it as desolate (ἔρημος).[91] Excavations have shown that during its prime the city covered about 12 acres. Initial work was done at Khirbet Kerazeh in 1905–7 by the Germans, who were followed by the Israelis in 1926. Zeev Yeiven resumed work in 1962-63.[92] In 1980–84, for the Israel Department of Antiquities, he prepared the site for reconstruction, which has been impressively done.[93] None of the excavations has produced evidence of the town in the time of Jesus. Beneath the paved stone floor of the synagogue, which is similar in plan to the one in nearby Capernaum, Yeiven found two coins, which establish the earliest date for the foundation of the synagogue in the late third or early fourth century. However, the latter date is not likely. Assuming the synagogue wasn't destroyed immediately after its construction, some time must have elapsed before Eusebius, in the early fourth-century, characterized the city as desolate. Nothing has been found to date any structure in the town earlier than the third century.

Caesarea Philippi

The northernmost town in Galilee visited by Jesus was Caesarea Philippi. It is distinguished from Caesarea on the Sea by Josephus.[94] In Caesarea Philippi, Simon Peter made the confession of Jesus as the Christ, the Son of the living God (Matt: 16:13–20; cf. Mark 8:27–30 and Luke 9:18–21). The city was built by Philip, one of the sons of Herod the Great, who obviously named it after himself and Caesar. Josephus says, "Philip built Caesarea near the sources of the Jordan, in the district of Paneas."[95] In another place, he says that Philip "made improvements at Paneas."[96] This reference is to a cave, located in the mountains due east of Dan, with a deep pool below it. Josephus calls the area Panion or Paneion.[97] The cave was sacred to the Roman god Pan, the god of the forest, whose name is preserved in an inscription beneath one of three niches cut into the stone mountain. A statue of the god stood in the niches; the words "to

Little has been done until the mid-1980s to investigate remains at Caesarea Philippi.

Pan and the Nymphs" are still discernible in the *tabula ansata* beneath the niche nearest the huge cave.[98]

The beauty of Caesarea Philippi has been extolled through the ages. In 1877 H. H. Kitchener described the site: "Little streams seem to be running in every direction, cooling the air, and making this one of the most lovely spots in Palestine."[99] It is one of three sources of the Jordan River. Josephus spoke of the "natural beauties of Panion," which had been enhanced by Agrippa's "royal munificence."[100] What a beautiful setting for the revelation given to Simon Peter.

Caesarea Philippi was enlarged by Agrippa, who renamed it "Neronias" in honor of Nero.[101] This was to be expected since "there was no one after Agrippa whom Caesar held in greater esteem than Herod, while Agrippa gave Herod the first place in his friendship after Caesar."[102] On the *Tabula Peutingeriana*, a map which may represent the land in the fourth century, the name of the town appears as "Caesareapaneas," a name which combines the Herodian name, Caesarea Philippi, with its original name, Paneas.[103] However, Eusebius and Jerome called it Paneas.[104] Banias, the modern Arabic name of the place, is derived from Paneas through a corruption in the pronunciation of the first letter, which is difficult for indigenous Arabs to pronounce. This peculiarity is also responsible for the modern pronunciation and spelling of the city of Nablus, which is derived from the ancient Neapolis.

Standing virtually on the Lebanese border, Banias has been largely ignored until recently, though neighboring Dan has been under excavation by Abraham Biran for many years. Interest is now being shown in Banias, however, by the Israel Department of Antiquities, which has declared Banias a nature preserve. A detailed survey of the site has been produced since 1983.[105] Conducted by the survey team of the northern Golan, the survey was designed to establish the city boundaries, which had been mapped previously only on the north, the east, and the south. Several sectors of the city were identified. These exhibited evidence of residential quarters with plastered walls, patterned mosaic floors in black and white, and covered conduits and clay pipes for carrying water or sewage. Public buildings were found in the vicinity of the spring. The Department of Antiquities has set up a team responsible for the archaeological development of the site, consisting of Tzaferis, Z. Ma'oz (Department of Antiquities), Ehud Netzer (Hebrew University) and Ya'akov Meshorer (Israel Museum).[106] A consortium of schools is currently digging the site under the direction of Tzaferis. Preliminary results indicate that Banias was not occupied before the early Roman period. A 2-kilometer portion of an aqueduct was discovered on the cliff north of the city and was surveyed, but its date could not be established. A salvage excavation was conducted south of Nahal Hermon in 1984, opposite the "Officer's Pool." A large structure, probably a house, and another structure, which may be part of a semicircular bathhouse, were revealed. Pottery, glass, and coins suggest a date in the late Roman and the early Byzantine periods.

Two short seasons of salvage excavations were conducted in 1985 by Tzaferis. West of the main entrance to the site, these produced evidence of continuous occupation from the early Roman period to modern times.[107] What appear to be ruined public buildings of the early Roman period lie on the surface. In the first full season of work in 1988, a massive subterranean system of vaulted Roman buildings was found. Each vault has a 25-foot-high ceiling and a window, which once contained iron bars, on the back wall.

At Caesarea Philippi, Herod Philip erected "a very beautiful temple of white stone" or "white marble" in honor of Caesar soon after the emperor had given him a large amount of additional territory to govern.[108] This temple is undoubtedly the one portrayed on a coin first publicized in 1951 by the late A. R. Reifenberg.[109] The coin may also be seen in Meshorer's book on Jewish coins.[110] The view is of the facade of a tetrastyle temple with an ornamental pediment. The name *Philip Tetrarch* is largely preserved on the coin. More recently, A. Kindler of the Kadman Numismatic Museum has published two similar specimens, one of them furnished by Meshorer subsequent to the publication of his book.[111] Nothing of this temple has yet been identified in the ruins.

Other coins associated with Caesarea Philippi have been found. Some depict the mouth of the sacred cave with a railing in front of it; some depict Pan leaning on a tree and playing the flute. One coin has preserved the town's title "Caesarea—August, Sacred and with Rights of Sanctuary—under Paneion." This title probably indicates that Pan was worshiped in the sacred cave at the same time that divine worship or recognition was given to Caesar in the white marble temple, which may have stood on the cliff high above the cave. These coins were published by F. de Saulcy.[112]

Cana of Galilee

Despite tourist appeal, there is no compelling evidence to accept Kefr Kenna, Arabic for "City of Cana," as the Cana where Jesus performed the first miracle of his ministry (John 2:1–11). The little picturesque village situated about 5 miles northeast of Nazareth on the road to Tiberias has two churches, one Greek and one Roman Catholic, that claim to preserve some traditions relative to the miracle in that place. A first-century date for the construction beneath the Roman church has never been established, and the Aramaic inscription in the mosaic floor beneath the nave of the modern church is probably not earlier than the third or fourth century. It reads, "Honored be the memory of Yoseh, son of Tanhum, son of Buta, and his sons, who made this mosaic, may it be a blessing for them, Amen."[113] There is nothing indicative of Jewish Christianity in this inscription.

A more likely choice for ancient Cana is Khirbet Kana ("Ruins of Cana") about 9 miles north of Nazareth on the north side of the Beit Netofa Valley. On a main route from Sepphoris to Damascus via Tiberias and the Sea of Galilee, it is where Josephus resided just before the outbreak of the first revolt: "My quarters at the time were at a village of Galilee called Cana."[114] Leaving Sepphoris in the early morning, I have leisurely walked the ancient route to Tiberias in two days, arriving at the Sea of Galilee after dark on the second day. The ruins called Khirbet Kana are impressive, though as yet untouched by the archaeologist's spade. I have observed lengthy portions of walls still standing just above ground level, as well as what appear to be tombs and perhaps a columbarium or dovecote on the hillside. On the surface at the site I have even found potsherds of Roman *terra sigallata* typical of the time of Christ. A full description of the location of Cana may be found in Gustaf Dalman's work, which also cites his evidence for showing that the tradition at Kefr Kenna cannot be documented earlier than the seventeenth century.[115] Although Khirbet Kana is limited in area, it fits the current trend of digging and publishing smaller sites. We hope that the importance of the place to Christian history and tradition will

Khirbet Kana is the less attractive but more likely Cana of Galilee that Jesus knew.

soon offset the comparative isolation and obscurity of Khirbet Kana and cry out for its excavation.

Sepphoris

Five miles west of Khirbet Kana and three miles northwest of Nazareth, the mound of ancient Sepphoris guards the western end of the Beit Netofa Valley. This ancient city, which Josephus called "the ornament of all Galilee,"[116] became an important district capital after Pompey conquered the country in 63 B.C. and divided it into five districts.[117] Herod the Great took Sepphoris at the beginning of his reign during a snowstorm.[118] After his death a rebellion in the city caused the Roman general Varus to burn it and sell its inhabitants into slavery.[119] When Herod's kingdom was partitioned, all of Galilee, including Sepphoris, was given to his son Herod Antipas, who immediately rebuilt it. Antipas intended the city to be subordinate to Tiberias,[120] which he eventually built on the Sea of Galilee and named for the emperor Tiberius.[121] According to Josephus, Sepphoris was virtually entirely Jewish at this time.[122] Under Agrippa I Sepphoris became the "capital of Galilee and the seat of the royal bank and the archives."[123]

The building program of Antipas at Sepphoris is a potential point of contact with Jesus of Nazareth. It is difficult to imagine that Joseph and Jesus, living in nearby Nazareth, would not have found work in Sepphoris during its building boom. What might they have done? We cannot say for certain that Jesus was a carpenter. The Greek term translated "carpenter" (τέκτων) occurs only twice in the New Testament, and in one of these, Matthew 13:55, Jesus is called the "son of the carpenter" (ὁ τοῦ τέκτονος υἱός). The text of Mark 6:3, the other reference, has variant readings. The major fourth- and fifth-century manuscripts call him "the carpenter," but enough letters survive in the mutilated Chester Beatty papyrus to show that it contained the reading "son of the carpenter."[124] Richard Batey has rightly argued that Jesus

Jesus could have worked as a carpenter on building projects at Sepphoris.

would certainly have learned the trade as a child and, in all probability, would have assisted his father in his work until he left home.[125] Shirley Jackson Case suggested, in 1926, the intriguing possibility that Jesus worked on the construction of a theater at Sepphoris.[126]

Sepphoris is identified with modern Saffuriyeh or Tzippori, which stands on a very prominent mound exhibiting considerable evidence of the town's earlier expansion into the surrounding valleys.[127] In 1948 the Arab village was completely destroyed in the Arab-Israeli war, and on the site today there stands only the small Jewish kibbutz Zippori, which preserves the root name. The first excavations of Sepphoris, conducted in 1931 by Leroy Waterman of the University of Michigan, lasted only two months.[128] He unearthed what he called a Christian basilica, built in the fourth century and destroyed in the sixth by one of the twenty earthquakes that struck the land during that century. Waterman thought the walls beneath the present Crusader fort belonged to the work of Herod Antipas, but in 1983 we were able to show that the walls were built in the Byzantine period, near the end of the fourth or beginning of the fifth century. In the northwest corner stands a possible remnant of a Roman building; it consists of four large ashlars laid on bedrock, and its orientation does not quite match that of the citadel.

Waterman dug part of a theater uncovered in the eastern portion of the tell, adjacent to the Crusader building. The discovery of Hasmonean coins around the stage led Yeivin, who worked with Waterman, to date the theater's construction to the time of Antipas. Waterman, on the other hand, felt that it might have been built by Herod the Great and then later enlarged and embellished by his son Antipas during his extensive building program in the city, which covered two decades. Albright, upon a brief investigation of the structure, suggested a date in the second century.

Our own stratigraphic excavations in the four- to five-thousand-seat theater in 1983 produced pottery beneath the robbed-out seats (seats whose stone was removed for reuse elsewhere), dating no later than the second century. This suggests that the theater was either founded or rebuilt in that century. James Strange from the University of South Florida directed the first two seasons of recent excavations; basing his tentative hypothesis on excavations in 1983 and 1985, he suggests the theater was built in the first century, "most likely in the Herodian period." He believes it underwent major reconstructions in the middle Roman and early Byzantine periods.[129] A 1985 expedition, sponsored jointly by Duke University under the direction of Eric Meyers and the Hebrew University of Jerusalem under the direction of Netzer, excavated separate areas of the tell.[130] Their findings indicate that the theater was initially built by Antipas and destroyed in the late Roman or early Byzantine periods.[131]

In work of a different nature, Batey has explored the possibility of literary allusions to the theater in the Gospels.[132] The American-Israeli expedition also found the tell honeycombed with remains of what turned out to be at least thirty-nine underground caves and cisterns. In 1983 the University of South Florida expedition, with which I was working, had discovered some of these. Strange, who explored twenty-five chambers in 1986,[133] dates only four to the first century A.D.[134] The work of the joint expedition yielded only a few that Netzer would date to the first century.[135] The large number of Jewish miqwaot raises the question as to whether these are evidence of an Ebionite (Jewish Christian) community meeting in secret, underground dwellings. There was a strong Jewish population in second-century Sepphoris. Toward the close of that century the Mishnah was codified there by Judah ha-Nasi.[136] As in so many other cases, the answer to the Ebionite question "lies below" and we will have to await further excavation.

An extraordinary discovery was made by the Meyers/Netzer expedition in the summer of 1987 when a "Mona Lisa of Palestine" was unearthed.[137] It is a mosaic panel that was in the floor of a public building in the late third or early fourth century. The panel comprises about 54 square feet (9 feet by 6 feet). That it is 75 percent complete is remarkable, for mosaics are usually badly damaged due to earthquakes or rebuilding activity after military conquests. This stunning portrait depicts a woman of enchanting beauty, not unlike one we found in Caesarea Maritima dating to the same period. The opposite end of the panel contained another such portrait, but it was substantially damaged. Consisting of fif-

A Wheaton College team works at Sepphoris.

teen separate scenes, the panel, in all probability, depicted the life of Dionysus, the Greco-Roman god of wine and debauchery, and adorned the floor of a banquet hall.

Tiberias

Little is known from archaeology about the city of Tiberias, and it is mentioned only once in the New Testament (John 6:23; cf. 6:1; 21:1). We must rely heavily on Josephus for information about the city. Today, Tiberias encompasses both ancient Tiberias and Hammath, two cities originally surrounded by separate walls. Though once a mile apart,[138] the cities apparently were combined into a single city during the first century A.D.[139] Sometime between A.D. 18 and 23,[140] Herod Antipas built Tiberias to serve as his capital, replacing Sepphoris.[141] Harold Hoehner argues from numismatics that the city was begun when Tiberius became emperor in A.D. 14 and was finished nine years later. Tiberias never exceeded Sepphoris in size, however, for Josephus says Sepphoris was the largest city of Galilee and an exceptionally strong fortress at the time of the first revolt in 66.[142]

Earlier excavations at Tiberias revealed several superimposed synagogues dating from the fourth to the eighth centuries.[143] Recent work in the area south of the synagogues has revealed a paved road and city gate from the time of the founding of the city by Antipas. The gate complex consisted of the gate itself and two round towers, each 23 feet in diameter, which stood south of the gate. In the Roman period the complex seems to have been isolated, serving as an outer gate and having no connection with a wall. No archaeological evidence for walls of the period has yet been found, although literary allusions suggest that there may have been one. The extant walls connected with the gate complex are from a later period. Several courses of the stone from the towers are preserved. The road leading northward from this gate is paved with rectangular slabs laid parallel to each other near the gate and in an oblique pattern a short distance from the city.[144] Plans are now complete for a full-scale excavation of the city by Yizhar Hirschfeld.[145]

Beth Shean

Beth Shean, known as Sythopolis in the Greco-Roman period, was about 20 miles south of Tiberias near the Jordan River. The city was inhabited six thousand years ago, and was of considerable importance in Old Testament Israel, especially at the time of King Saul (1 Sam. 31:10–12; 2 Sam. 21:12; 1 Chron. 10:10–12). Although Beth Shean is not mentioned in the New Testament it is the largest and best-preserved late Roman period city in Israel.

Excavations began at Beth Shean in 1986 after two salvage digs in 1980 and 1981.[146] Since then intensive excavation has been underway in the area between the Old Testament mound on the north and the theater on the south. A colonnaded basalt street, probably built in the fourth century A.D., is well preserved with herringbone-pattern stonework.[147] The street runs northeast to the northern mound and southwest to the theater, where it broadened into a theater square or open plaza. A colonnaded walkway with shops bordered the street along its western side. Beneath this street lies evidence of both early and late levels of Roman occupation. Mosaic pavements from the late Roman period were also discovered beneath the floors of all the shops. Baths and a palestra found from the early Byzantine period were built in the style of imperial Roman baths.

South of the theater an amphitheater has been uncovered which seated 5000 to 7000 spectators on eleven to thirteen rows of seats. A large temple, a nympheum, a basilica, and an unidentified monumental civic structure stood at the foot of the mound where the central colonnaded street intersected another colonnaded street running northwest to southeast. A small odeion and a large Roman theater complete the picture of a typical Roman-Byzantine city. Remains of two late Byzantine synagogues were uncovered at the site in 1962, one of which may have been a Samaritan synagogue.[148] At this point in the excavations almost nothing has been found from the New Testament period except a few pieces of pottery, a few coins, the lower portions of the municipal basilica, and two small altars. One of them, the altar of Dionysus, bears a date corresponding to A.D. 12.

What has been found are the remains of a late Roman and early Byzantine city. Like one of its sister Decapolis cities, Jerash in Jordan, it apparently reached its zenith by the second century A.D.[149] and maintained some measure of greatness until it was destroyed by a major earthquake in 749. Rebuilt in the Abbasid period (750 to 969) it never regained its prominence.

Sychar

There is little recorded activity of Jesus in Samaria, which is to be expected due to the feelings of hostility that persisted between Jews and Samaritans at that time. These feelings surfaced in a conversation Jesus had with a woman of Samaria at the Well of Jacob (John 4:1–42), which is located in the eastern part of modern Nablus. At one time the well was covered by a vault of cut stones. Though the vault, whose date is not known, is now gone, it was seen by travelers in the nineteenth century. Below ground level the vault may have been part of the crypt of a Byzantine church, which later stood over the well.

Water still may be drunk from Jacob's well at Sychar.

In the mid-fourth century Eusebius mentions the well but no church.[150] Jerome's translation of the *Onomastikon* in 380 adds the phrase *"ubi nunc ecclesia fabricata est"* ("where now a church has been built").[151] Thus, there was a church building at the well by that date. Conder and Kitchener's *Survey of Western Palestine*, published in 1882, contains a very interesting discussion of the well as they saw it, along with letters from others who saw it at about the same time.[152] The Byzantine church had long since been destroyed, probably in the Persian (614) or Muslim (638) invasions, and had been replaced by a Crusader church. The Greek Orthodox Church bought the well and its surrounding property in 1885 and excavated the area, finding nothing earlier than the Crusader period (twelfth century). In 1903 they began building a new church, which reached the proportions seen today by 1960; it is still unfinished.

Arculf, a Frankish bishop and pilgrim, visited the Well of Jacob in about 670 and saw a cruciform crypt built over it. The crypt was probably all that was left after the upper church was destroyed.[153] (Today the well sits considerably below ground level.) He described the well as being 240 feet deep. According to Conder and Kitchener, Edward Robinson found the well to be 105 feet deep in 1838,[154] although Robinson himself wrote that he was unable to measure it on his first visit.[155] In 1875 Conder found the depth to be 75 feet. It is evident that across the centuries debris accumulated in the bottom of the well and the water level fluctuated. In 1687 Henry Maundrell found 15 feet of water in it; Robinson found 10 to 12 feet in 1839. But in May of 1881 the well was dry. It is apparently fed by underground rainwater.[156] During annual visits over the past twenty years, I have always found cold, refreshing water in the well. Clearly, the well is deep, as the Gospel of John records (14:11). And although, to my knowledge, there is no literary evidence confirming the identity of the well before the time of Eusebius, this is one of the few sites whose identity is agreed upon by Jews, Christians, Muslims, and Samaritans alike.

Over the mouth of the well, there was a massive hard white limestone block with a hole in the center through which a vessel was lowered into the water. In 1881 C. W. Barclay published the following dimensions for the stone and the well:[157]

Length of the stone	3 feet, 9 inches
Breadth of the stone	2 feet, 7 inches
Thickness of the stone	1 foot, 6 inches
Height of the stone above the pavement	1 foot, 1 inch
Width of the opening to the well	1 foot, 5.5 inches
Depth of the well	67 feet
Width of the well shaft	7 feet, 6 inches

Several Roman tombs have been found at Nablus.

Foundations mark the Samaritan temple on Mount Gerizim.

The stone, which is pictured in Conder's and Kitchener's *Survey of Western Palestine*,[158] does not match the one standing over the well today.

After the Samaritan woman's conversation with Jesus, she went into the village of Sychar to proclaim what she had heard from him (John 4:5, 28–29). The village of 'Askar, situated on the southern slopes of Mount Ebal, one-half mile north of the well, is generally, and probably correctly, identified with Sychar. From the Well of Jacob the village is clearly visible, and one can easily imagine the ensuing scenario as Jesus observed the people coming to him out of the village. The sight of so many coming to hear him teach prompted Jesus' remark to his disciples: "Lift up your eyes and look at the fields, for they are already white for harvest" (John 4:35, NKJV).

In the process of digging a channel for a large water pipe in 1972, a mausoleum of the Roman period was found in 'Askar. This mausoleum contained ten stone sarcophagi ornamented with snakes, laurel wreaths, vine shoots, garlands, bucrania (bulls' heads), and rosettes. E. Damati suggests that "this mausoleum belonged to a wealthy Samaritan family residing in Neapolis at the end of the second or the beginning of the third century A.D."[159] The burial chamber measures 16 feet by 16 feet, and has a facade facing south, in the center of which is an ornamented stone door. This door is similar to some in a nearby Roman burial ground, which was accidentally discovered in 1966 at Khirbet Blibous in the heart of modern Nablus.[160] There three Roman tombs were cut into the rock on a hillside, and an ashlar stone facade was built facing the south; for each tomb, a swivel door opens into a paved forecourt. Nine sarcophagi were found in tombs 2 and 3. Tomb 1 was empty.

The remains of what must be the temple of Gerizim, referred to by Josephus[161] and involved in Jesus' discussion with the Samaritan woman (John 4:20), are situated on a northern spur (Tel er-Ras) of Gerizim. These ruins include a large building of uncut stones, 66 feet long, by 66 feet wide by 30 feet high, laid without cement and without internal structuring. The foundation rests on bedrock in the center of a 135-foot rectilinear courtyard, which was built with walls of unhewn stone. On the basis of pottery the excavator dates the temple to no later than the third century B.C. and identifies it as the Samaritan altar of sacrifice.[162]

Jesus' Ministry and Last Days in Judea

The Public Ministry of Jesus: Judea

Most of Jesus' ministry took place in Galilee. The birth narratives and the passion narratives, which comprise a large part of the gospel, took place in southern Judea, but the time covered by Jesus' birth and death was short. The birth stories involve only the time before the flight to Egypt, and the passion narratives deal primarily with the last week before the crucifixion. The comparative importance of the two events, however, commands a large amount of space in the biblical text. In addition to the nativity and passion, the Gospels record only an occasional visit of Jesus to Judea.

The Pool of Bethesda

The Gospel of John (5:1–15) records one of Jesus' visits to Judea. He had gone to Jerusalem for a festival, and while there he healed an invalid at the Pool of Bethesda. John 5:2 poses several problems regarding the place of the miracle, not the least of which is whether the name was Bethesda, Bethzatha, or Bethsaida. Which name belongs in the text and how each should be identified is unclear. Also, the syntax of 5:2 seems to require the addition of a word, either *gate* or *place*. Translators have resolved the problem in different ways. The New American Standard and Revised Standard versions render the first part: "Now there is in Jerusalem by the sheep gate a pool."[1] The New English Bible, considering *pool* (κολυμβήθρα) to be in the dative rather than the nominative case, offers the translation: "Now at the Sheep-Pool in Jerusalem there is a place." The question is whether Jesus performed the miracle at a pool or, as John Wilkinson argues, in a nearby building.[2]

Evidence of the existence of a place with a pool called Bethesda has been found in the Copper Scroll from Qumran,[3] which was written between A.D. 25 and 68.[4] In a list of places in

Jesus' miracle at the Pool of Bethesda likely took place here, although some believe it occurred in a nearby building.

Jerusalem we find the description: "At Beth Eshdathayin, in the pool where you enter its small[er] reservoir . . . near there at the west entry of the porch of the triclinium [i.e., dining room]."[5] The Hebrew name *Beth Eshdathayin* may mean "House of the Twin Pools."[6] This may be the pool referred to in a fourth-century parchment from Oxyrhynchus as the Pool of David in which people bathed for purification "in the poured-out waters."[7]

About 100 yards north of the Temple Mount's Northern Wall and about that same distance west of the Lion Gate (also called Stephen's Gate), excavations were begun near the Church of Saint Anne at the turn of the century by the White Fathers.[8] This exploration identified two large pools that had been cut into rock and plastered. These lie close to the church on its west side. The larger, southern pool is estimated to be 215 feet wide at its southern side and 190 feet across at its northern edge. The east and west sides measure about 160 feet. The smaller northern pool is estimated at 175 feet on its southern side, 165 feet on the north, and 130 feet on the east and west. Together the pools may have provided as much as 5000 square yards of water surface.[9] Many fragments of column bases, capitals, and drums were found, which probably belonged to the five porches (i.e. porticos or colonnaded walkways) of the pool John mentions.

Excavators dug a wide, deep trench along the northern end of the southern pool, revealing a partition about 20 feet wide separating the two pools; it was made of dressed stone from Roman times and built upon bedrock. Perhaps a road of the Herodian city ran east and west across this dike.[10] The north-south *cardo maximus* of Jerusalem, depicted in the Madeba Mosaic Map, has been found and dated to the Roman period by Y. Tsafrir,[11] and to the Byzantine period by Nahman Avigad.[12] The pools were probably fed by rainwater and underground springs. Over the southeastern corner of the northern pool is a cistern with a vaulted chamber about 50 feet long and 20 feet wide. Water continues to stand in the cistern today, but only about a foot deep and stagnant. There is no good reason to doubt that these are the Sheep Pool referred to by Eusebius[13] and the "twin pools" mentioned by the Bordeaux Pilgrim,[14] both in the early fourth century. The pools are located near the ancient Sheep Gate, as we would expect by the name. Benjamin Mazar attributes the construction of the Bethesda Pool to Simon the Just in the third century B.C.[15]

Wilkinson's arguments that the miracle did not occur at the pool but in an adjacent building that stood over some of the several cisterns east of the pool are forced, without solid evidence, and unconvincing. Evidence that the site may have been a pagan center for healing in subsequent centuries has no bearing on the text of the New Testament. The impression conveyed by the

Gospel of John is clear: The invalid was near a pool with steps, around which people congregated, and they prevented him from getting to the water when it bubbled. No remains of the building conjectured by Wilkinson have been found, nor is one needed to fit the text.

The Pool of Siloam

Another pool in Jerusalem was immortalized when Jesus put clay on the eyes of a blind man and told him to wash his eyes in its water (John 9:1–41). It is called the Pool of Siloam in the Gospel of John (v. 7), a Greek equivalent of the Hebrew *Shiloah* (see Isa. 8:6), and was built by King Hezekiah in the eighth century B.C. at the southern end of a long tunnel he cut through solid rock to bring water from Gihon Spring to the pool inside the city walls (2 Kings 20:20). A walk through the 1749-foot tunnel is a popular tourist attraction.

The appearance of the pool has changed through the centuries; it has become considerably smaller (50 feet long by 15 feet wide) than originally. In 1897 F. J. Bliss and A. C. Dickie uncovered a court about 75 feet square, in the center of which was the pool. It was probably surrounded by a colonnaded portico, which must have been the one described by the Pilgrim of Bordeaux in 333 as a *quadriporticus* (a courtyard enclosed on all four sides with porticos).[16] Presumably the portico and an adjacent church were destroyed during the Persian invasion in the seventh century. After the 1897 excavations, the people of the village of Silwan (an Arabic rendering of *Siloam*) built a mosque with a minaret over the northwest corner of the pool, and it still stands above the pool. The identity of a pool lying at the mouth of such a large tunnel would seem to be indisputable. However, confusion regarding the Pool of Siloam has resulted because a second pool, the modern Birket el-Hamra, was located just to the south of this one, and Josephus seems to locate the Pool of Siloam outside the city wall.[17] Since Birket el-Hamra has been assumed to lie outside the wall, it has been suggested that it may have been the pool of which Josephus spoke. Wilkinson remarks, "If . . . we heed Josephus, this lower pool, now called Birket el-Hamra, must have been the 'Pool of Siloam' mentioned in John's Gospel."[18]

The problem with this approach is that it does violence to Josephus's sense of direction. Translations of the passage at issue (*Jewish Wars* 5.4.2) by Gaalyah Cornfeld, G. A. Williamson, H. St.J. Thackeray and (to a lesser extent) by William Whiston contribute to this confusion.[19] While these translations indicate correctly that the Northern Wall of the city terminated at the western portico of the temple and the Eastern Wall joined the eastern portico of the temple, the intervening text, in which Josephus

The Pool of Siloam is smaller today, but this is probably the spot mentioned by John.

discusses the lines of the Western and Southern walls contradict his statements elsewhere, as well as the geography of Jerusalem. For example, the translations illogically suggest in rendering line 145 that the Western Wall began at the Hippicus Tower, moved south to the Essene Gate and then "turned southward." Nor is it possible for the Southern Wall to extend from the Essene Gate eastward toward Solomon's Pool and then, by-passing both the Pool of Siloam and Ophlas, to terminate at the eastern portico of the Temple." There must be a northward turn of the Southern Wall past the Pool of Siloam in order to reach the Temple Mount. This is readily evident in the diagram of the Herodian city.

Yet this passage can be translated in a way that resolves the contradictions while preserving the integrity of the text:

> On the north, beginning from the Tower of Hippicus and extending to the Xystus, [the wall] joined the council chamber and terminated at the western porch of the temple.

Figure 19
Pool of Siloam Area and Josephus's Wall

1 Temple
2 Western Porch
3 Eastern Porch
4 Xystus
5 Hippicus's Tower
6 Ophlas
7 Gihon Spring
8 Pool of Siloam
9 Birket el-Hamra
10 Bethso
11 Essene Gate

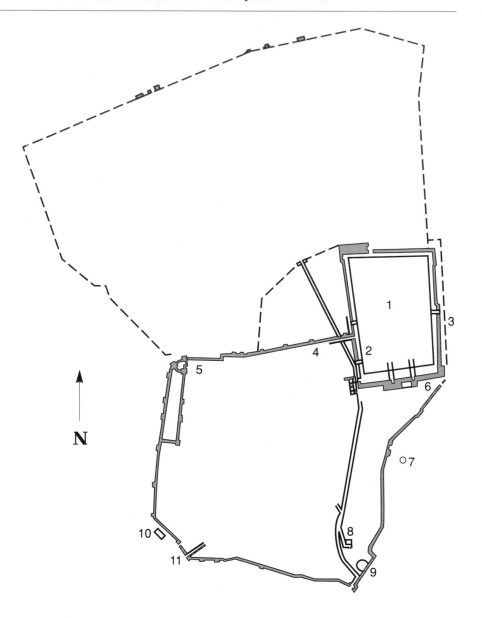

N

In the other direction, on the west, beginning at the same point, [the wall] descended to the Gate of the Essenes. And then, on the south beyond the Siloam Fountain [or Spring], it turned and from there inclined again, on the east, to the Solomon Pool. After passing a place which they call Ophlas, it joined the eastern porch of the temple.

Wilkinson's translation is close to this, except for the phrase "beyond . . . Siloam," which he renders "above Siloam."[20]

Hezekiah's tunnel brought water from the Gihon Spring to the Pool of Siloam.

Josephus's reference to the Solomon Pool adds to the difficulty. It is clear that the pool lay between the Siloam Pool and the Temple Mount. Possibly he was referring to the Gihon Spring, where Solomon was anointed king by the priest Zadok (1 Kings 1:38–40). Too much can be made of Josephus's differentiation between a *spring* and a *pool*. On the one hand, any pool fed by spring water may be regarded as a spring. Siloam is fed by the Gihon Spring through Hezekiah's Tunnel. On the other hand, the Gihon Spring itself issues into a pool, from which Solomon ran an aqueduct. This aqueduct coursed along the eastern side of Mount Ophel and fed a lower pool and gardens. It would be perfectly natural for Josephus to refer to the rock basin of Gihon as Solomon's Pool.

However, a pool excavated in 1977 immediately east of the Siloam Pool may have the greatest claim to being Solomon's Pool.[21] Parts of two sides of the pool were found, along with part of the floor on the northern end, all of which were plastered. It was fed by the overflow from the Siloam Pool through a canal, which has also been found. The pool did, indeed, lie between the Siloam Pool and Ophlas. Furthermore, the constant overflow of water from the Siloam Pool into this pool justifies calling it a fountain.

Strangely, in all of Josephus's descriptions there is no reference to Hezekiah's Tunnel. Perhaps portions of it were blocked by the historian's time, although at least a small water channel remained through it. The tunnel could have been blocked at the point of its entrance (Gihon Spring) or its exit (Siloam Pool), not allowing access to people but still allowing water to flow. His discussion of the conquest of Jerusalem by David is clearly based on 1 Chronicles 11:4–9 and does not mention the water shaft that figured in David's strategy (2 Sam. 5:8). Josephus writes that Joab climbed the citadel and, reaching the top, was rewarded, as David had promised.[22] Josephus seems unaware of 2 Samuel, which says that David took the citadel by sending his men up the water shaft to reach the inside of the city. Such a shaft, now called Warren's Shaft, lay inside what became Hezekiah's Tunnel, 72 feet from the spring. It was blocked with debris at its excavation by Yigal Shiloh, 1978 to 1982.[23] Shiloh, incidentally, does not believe the Hebrew word *ṣinnôr* in 2 Samuel 5:8 refers to a water shaft because he thinks the shaft was not built until the tenth century B.C., after David's conquest.[24] His evidence is not conclusive, however, and the alternatives leave us with even greater problems.

What sense can we make of Josephus's writings and the archaeological evidence? A retranslation of Josephus solves the problem of the direction of the walls around the south end of the city, and if we translate the text to describe the southern wall at its eastern extremity as running "beyond Siloam" rather than "above Siloam" there is no need to place any one of these pools of the lower city outside the walls. Nor is there any reason to doubt that the modern Pool of Siloam is the one referred to in John 9:7. Josephus's silence about Hezekiah's Tunnel and Warren's Shaft are puzzling in view of his residence in Jerusalem. But there is no good reason why his "Solomon Pool" may not be identified with either the pool at the Gihon Spring or, more likely, with the newly found pool east of Siloam. He only mentions the Gihon Spring in *Antiquities* 7.14.5 (355), where he recalls the Old Testament account of the anointing of Solomon.

Josephus's other references to the Siloam Spring are not particularly helpful in determining its relation to the city wall.[25] No portion of the Southern Wall as it stood in the time of Josephus has been found. Eilat Mazar reports the discovery of what may be a gate from the time of Solomon.[26] At the time this book went to press the news of this gate was still preliminary, but it was located a few yards south of the southeast corner of the Temple Mount. It resembles gates found at Megiddo, Hazor, and Gezer. The wall of Josephus's time could have been built in line with or near this gate.

Tyre and Sidon

Matthew 15:21–28 and Mark 7:24–30 record that toward the end of his ministry Jesus visited the Gentile territory of Tyre and Sidon in the territory of Syria and Phoenicia (modern Lebanon). Although he intended to preach to Jews (Matt. 15:24), Jesus responded to a plea by a woman of the district to heal her daughter, for he was impressed by this Gentile woman's faith. The story is a remarkable demonstration of the cultural context in which Jesus lived and worked and provides theological insight into the ministry of Jesus to the Jews. Archaeology can do nothing to enhance the drama of that supercharged moment, but it can identify the locale and provide physical clues to its culture.

Political tensions between Israel and Lebanon made journeys difficult in the 1980s. My visits to Tyre and Sidon in previous years, though, left lasting memories of a massive, systematic excavation. Work began at Tyre in 1947 under the direction of Maurice Chehab, director-general of the Lebanese Department of Antiquities. Roman remains have been found beneath the impressive ruins from the Byzantine period. Although none of these date to the period of the New Testament, there are remains from the second century A.D., including a monumental arch, which has been partially restored. Beyond the arch and beneath the Byzantine pavement, the excavators found a Roman road. Located just outside Tyre, the road was lined with tombs, as was typical along other Roman highways; the road outside Tyre is reminiscent of the Appian Way at Rome. Excavation of the necropolis at Tyre produced scores of beautiful marble sarcophagi with carved inscriptions. One of the largest and best-preserved hippodromes in the Mediterranean world was found in the city, as well as a large bathhouse and forum (or perhaps palestra). Colonnades are being reconstructed on streets which, in Byzantine times, were about 70 feet wide, including the sidewalks. The Roman street beneath must have been about the same width.

Tyre's companion city, Sidon, was 28 miles to the north—31 miles south of Beirut. Around 1900 many tombs dating from the fourth century B.C. to the Byzantine period were excavated, including numerous white marble anthropoid sarcophagi, which are now in the National Museum in Beirut. Underwater investigations of the harbor of Sidon were made in 1946 and 1950 by A. Poidebard and J. Lauffray. Phoenician layers at Sidon were uncovered by P. Bikai in the 1970s. No finds from the New Testament era have been reported. The best known and most evident ancient remain in Sidon is the crusader castle on the sea coast.

Roman and Byzantine remains uncovered at Tyre date to as early as the second century.

The Corban Vow

In the same chapter that describes Jesus' visit to Tyre and Sidon, Mark records a criticism leveled by Jesus against the Pharisees (7:9–13). These Pharisees had forsaken their obligation to support their parents, claiming the money that would have been used for this purpose was *corban*, that is, "an offering" to God (Mark 7:11). Two archaeological discoveries help us understand the corban vow and its use in ancient society.

In the Kidron Valley, southeast of Jerusalem, a sarcophagus from the early Christian period was found in a Jewish tomb.[27] An inscription in Hebrew on the lid of the sarcophagus includes the word "corban." Joseph Fitzmyer's translation of the inscription reads, "All that a man may find to his profit in this ossuary [is] an offering (corban) to God from him who is within it."[28] The inscription seems to be addressed to potential grave robbers, who should understand that the contents in the tomb have been dedicated by vow to God and cannot be used for any other purpose without sacrilege. Knowledge of the vow might dissuade a person of religious conscience from disturbing the tomb. (The obvious question is: Would a man of religious conscience be robbing a tomb?) According to Fitzmyer the inscription provides "a perfect contemporary parallel" to the sense of corban in Matthew and

Mark. In effect, the word "puts a ban on something, reserving it for sacred use and withdrawing it from the profane."[29]

In 1968, during excavations at the Double Gate in the Southern Wall of the Temple Mount in Jerusalem, the leg of a stone vessel (jar?) was found with "corban" inscribed on it in Hebrew.[30] Two upside-down birds, either doves or pigeons, were also incised on the vessel. Birds were traditional offerings at the birth of a child, especially among the poor (Lev. 12:6–8). This was the offering that Mary brought on the occasion of her purification after the birth of Jesus (Luke 2:22–24). The contents of an earthenware vessel with such an inscription were deemed to be an offering consecrated to God.[31]

But one could not "swear on an oath" to transgress religious duties.[32] We learn from Mark 7:9–13 that Jesus certainly considered the honoring of one's father and mother to be a religious duty; the rules of the corban vow did not offset other God-ordained obligations.

The Last Days of Jesus

Bethany

Six days before the final Passover of his life, Jesus went to Bethany, where he had raised Lazarus from the dead (John 12:1; cf. 11:1–44). Bethany is to be identified with the modern village of el-'Azariyeh, which is located about 2 miles from Jerusalem on the eastern slopes of Mount Olivet. Eusebius described Bethany as "a village at the second milestone from Aelia [Jerusalem], in a steep bank of the Mount of Olives, where Christ raised Lazarus. The place of Lazarus is being shown even until now."[33] Almost seventeen hundred years after Eusebius that tomb, which tradition assigns to the raising of Lazarus, is still shown to visitors. The original entrance to the tomb was on the east. The present entrance on the north, facing an alley behind the modern church building, is a modification made in the Muslim period when a renovation of the adjacent crypt into a mosque required the sealing of the eastern entryway. The tomb is not large. A northern opening in the small vestibule leads through a narrow, 5-foot-long passage into the burial chamber, which is about eight feet square (For a discussion of Roman-period tombs see pp. 208–210). There is no way to identify the tomb as that of Lazarus. Tomb typology is still in a state of infancy and hazarding a guess as to its date on the basis of its type is precarious.

Apparently there was no church at the site when Eusebius wrote his *Onomastikon* in 330, for he refers to the "place" (τόπος) where Lazarus was buried.[34] By the time Jerome translated Eusebius into Latin in 390, a church had been recently built, so Jerome added the words *"ecclesia nunc ibidem extructa"* ("a church which has now been constructed there").[35] Prior to the construction of the modern Church of Saint Lazarus, S. Saller and Stanislao Loffreda excavated the site for the Franciscan Custody of the Holy Land.[36] Their work revealed considerable portions of the beautiful mosaic floor of the mid-fourth-century church. In the floor of the nave were small crosses in the tessellation. These crosses attest to a date in the fourth century, for the Byzantine emperor Theodosius prohibited the use of crosses in Christian art in 427. The church of which Jerome spoke was destroyed, probably by an earthquake, and was rebuilt and mod-

Since the time of Eusebius this tomb at Bethany has been identified as that of Lazarus.

ified in the following centuries. The modern church, which was dedicated in 1954, stands over the ruins of these previous constructions.[37]

Dominus Flevit Church

During his last days, Jesus made a triumphal entry into Jerusalem from the Mount of Olives (Matt. 21:1–11; Mark 11:1–11; Luke 19:29–44). Luke writes that "he was now drawing near, at the descent of the Mount of Olives. . . . And when he drew near and saw the city he wept over it" (Luke 19:37, 41 RSV). Coming from Bethany, through the probable location of Bethphage on top of the mount, Jesus would likely have passed the site traditionally identified as the place where he wept. On the descent into the Kidron Valley, the place is about halfway down the western side of the mount, and is marked by Dominus Flevit, a Franciscan chapel whose name means "The Lord wept."

Construction of this chapel began in 1953. During the digging of the foundation, tombs were revealed which prompted excavation of the property.[38] Construction of the chapel was then resumed, and it was finished in 1955 over some of the excavations, including the ruins of a Byzantine church found in 1954. The excavations yielded hundreds of graves, most of them dating to two periods of occupation. From the earlier period, 135 B.C. to A.D. 70 (or possibly A.D. 135), were the greatest number of burials.[39] These were built in the *kôkhîm* or *loculi* type characteristic of Jewish burials of the time (for a discussion of tomb typology, see pp. 207–211). From the later period, the third and fourth centuries, came graves of the *arcosolia* type. Various symbols, such as crosses and Constantinian monograms, were carved or traced in charcoal on the stone ossuaries. The symbolism of decorations is discussed by Bellarmino Bagatti in his book on Jewish Christianity.[40] Also found on the ossuaries were forty-three inscriptions. Written in Hebrew, Aramaic, and Greek,[41] the inscriptions contain names familiar to readers of the New Testament—Yeshua (Aramaic for Jesus), Miriam (Mary), Martha, Eleazar (Lazarus), Judas, Salome, Matthew, Joseph, Jairus, John, Mattia (Matthias), Sapphira, Menahem (Manaean), Simeon, and Zechariah.[42]

Vespasian-Titus Inscription

During the last week of his life from somewhere on the Mount of Olives, Jesus predicted the fall of Jerusalem (Matt. 24:1–3; Mark 13:1–3; Luke 21:5–17). Only forty years later the city was captured and partially destroyed by the Roman generals Vespasian and Titus. In the summer of 1970 a stone column bearing their names was discovered. Also mentioned on the stone is Flavius Silva, who commanded the Tenth Legion in 73, capturing Masada and Herodium. The column was excavated in the area of the southern end of the Temple Mount by Benjamin Mazar. Deeply incised Latin letters appear on the beautiful limestone column. The extant letters are noted in the left column below. Its restored inscription is shown in the right column.[43]

IMPCAESAR	IMP[ERATOR] CAESAR
VESPASIAN	VESPASIAN[US]
AUG IMPT	AUG[USTUS] IMP[ERATOR] T[ITUS CAE]
SAR VESPAUG	SAR VESP[ASIANUS] AUG[USTUS] [FILIUS]
L	L[UCIUS FLAVIUS SILVA]
AUG PR PR	AUG[USTI] PR[O-]PR[AETOR]
LEG FR	LEG[IO] FR[ATENSIS]

Vespasian and Titus were both commanding generals of the Roman legions and subsequently became emperors. Vespasian began the conquest of Palestine but was made emperor in A.D. 69 before completing it. His son Titus took command at that time and destroyed Jerusalem the next year. Titus succeeded his father in 79 and reigned only until 81. His exploits at Jerusalem are commemorated on the triumphal Arch of Titus erected in his honor by the senate at the Forum of Rome, where it still stands. A relief on the inside depicts a menorah being carried by soldiers from the temple.

Gethsemane

Down the Mount of Olives to the west of the Dominus Flevit Church is the Gethsemane Church of All Nations. Built on the foundation of a Byzantine church by the Franciscans in 1924, this church marks the spot venerated since at least the fourth century, as the Garden of Gethsemane. Tradition holds that, before his betrayal by Judas, Jesus prayed on the rock that is now in front of the apse (see Matt. 26:36; Mark 14:32; Luke 22:40–41; John 18:1). The rock is referred to by the Bordeaux Pilgrim in 333.[44] The modern church was designed, as was the Byzantine, so that the rock stands in the center of the eastern end of the nave.

Eusebius identified Gethsemane in 330 as a place "at the foot of the Mount of Olives where the faithful now make their prayers diligently."[45] Once again, in his Latin translation of Eusebius's work, Jerome alters the text to reflect his own time. In 390 he added the words *"nunc ecclesia desuper aedificata"* ("a church has now been built over it").[46] It would seem, then, that the Byzantine

Roman commanders Vespasian, Titus, and Flavius Silva are named on a column found near the Temple Mount.

church was built between 330 and 390. After this church was destroyed, probably by the Persian invasion of 614, it was not rebuilt until the Christian presence was again felt. In the twelfth century the Crusaders built a new one slightly to the south of the Byzantine church and partly overlapping its southern side. The Crusader church also was subsequently destroyed.[47]

The Palace of Caiaphas

After his arrest in Gethsemane, Jesus was taken to Annas (John 18:13), the former high priest and to his son-in-law Caiaphas (John 18:24), who was high priest from A.D. 18 to 36. Stone steps, which may date to the time of Jesus, have been found on the north side of the modern Saint Peter of the Cockcrow Church (Saint Peter in Gallicantu). Jesus may have climbed these stairs going from the Last Supper to Gethsemane and from Gethsemane to the house of the high priest. Josephus located the house of the high priest in his day in the Upper City, stating that the residence was burned by brigands during the first revolt.[48] This could have been anywhere on the hill known today as Mount Zion. The Bordeaux Pilgrim in 333 was shown "the house of Caiaphas the priest" on Mount Zion.[49] Efforts to locate the house of Caiaphas, however, must also take into consideration Theodosius's statement in 530 that it was about fifty paces from the Holy Zion Church.[50]

The possibility of locating the Holy Zion Church was enhanced by the discovery of the Madeba Map of the Holy Land, which was constructed as a mosaic floor in a church in Madeba, Jordan. Michael Avi-Yonah dates the map to about 560 in the reign of Justinian.[51] This map locates the Holy Zion Church southwest of the famous New Church of the Theotokos, which was built by Justinian about twenty years before the map was constructed. The Holy Zion Church is depicted as a red-roofed building with yel-

Steps to the fifth-century St. Peter of the Cockcrow Church.

The Madeba Mosaic map, depicting sixth-century Jerusalem.

low doors just southwest of the red-roofed New Church. The foundations of the New Church have been excavated and found to extend through the Southern Wall of the Old City in the Jewish Quarter.[52] Given the location of the New Church, even though distances are not accurate on the Madeba Map, it is probable that the modern Saint Mary Church (Dormition Church) on Mount Zion and the adjacent building housing the tomb of David and the Cenacle (the traditional site of the Last Supper) stand on the ruins of the Holy Zion Church.[53]

In 1899 excavations at what was probably the Byzantine Holy Zion Church by Heinrich Renard determined the building to have been a basilica about 200 feet long by 130 feet wide. Renard built Saint Mary Church (Dormition) over the northwest corner of the ruins.[54] A niche in the north wall of "David's Tomb" is probably a part of the Byzantine church. A portion of the southeastern corner has also been preserved. Holy Zion Church was twice destroyed and was last rebuilt by the Crusaders.

Equipped with Theodosius's comment about the location of the palace of Caiaphas, though Theodosius did not specify a direction, and the probable location of the Holy Zion Church, Magen Broshi and Ehud Netzer conducted excavations in the court of the Armenian Church of Saint Saviour, which is about 50 yards north of the Saint Mary Church. They found the area to be rich in water reservoirs and "occupied densely by buildings of two, and possibly three stories."[55] Dated with certainty to the Roman period—from the first century B.C. to Jerusalem's destruction in A.D. 70—some of these were public buildings and others private dwellings. Some structures had rooms with intact vaulted roofs, courts, and water installations. Broshi writes: "The location of our site on the summit of the Upper City and the elegant sophisticated murals . . . leave no doubt that this quarter was occupied by the more affluent residents of Jerusalem."[56] It might be expected that the high priest lived in such an area, and indeed Josephus says that he did.[57] However, nothing from the excavation identifies with certainty the house of Caiaphas.

The site now occupied by the Saint Peter of the Cockcrow Church is another that has been suggested as the palace of Caiaphas. This tradition is as old as Theodosius, who wrote that the house of Caiaphas "is now the Church of Saint Peter." The building is located a few hundred yards east of the Saint Mary Church on the lower slope of Mount Zion. Early authors who connect the house with the site of the Church of Saint Peter tend to be ambiguous. As noted, Theodosius wrote of the fifty paces from the Holy Zion Church but gave no direction. The modern Saint Peter building is much too far from the Holy Zion to have been the one referred to by Theodosius, assuming the Holy Zion Church has been correctly identified.

Excavations were begun at the site of the modern Church of Saint Peter in 1888. In 1911, ruins of a fifth-century church were found. The modern church was built in 1931 and named for the older one, with the assumption that it was, in fact, the site of the ancient Cockcrow Church. Below the level of the ancient church a central room surrounded by rock-hewn chambers was discovered. These have rings on the wall and stone handles cut out of the walls and above the doors that could have been used for restraining an individual being whipped. Some have identified the room and chambers as a prison and as the place where Jesus was kept until Caiaphas could see him.[58] There is, however, no clear evidence to connect the modern Church of Saint Peter with the one of the same name mentioned in the early sources. According to the Madeba Map the Church of Saint Peter referred to by Theodosius and others must have been north of the modern site and nearer to today's Church of the Holy Zion.

The Upper Room

Early Christian tradition commemorated the Holy Zion Church as the site where, in the upper room of an earlier building, Jesus instituted the Lord's Supper (Mark 14:15; 22:25; Luke 22:12, 17–20; cf. Matt. 26:26–29) and where he appeared to the disciples after his resurrection (Mark 16:14; Luke 24:33–43; John 20:19–25). The Holy Zion Church was also believed to be the site where the disciples were staying when they received the Holy Spirit at Pentecost (Acts 1:13; 2:1–4). Cyril, a bishop of Jerusalem, reflected these traditions in a series of lectures given in 348.[59] Theodosius in 530 identified the Holy Zion Church as the site of the house of Saint Mark the Evangelist (cf. Acts 12:12), locating it two hundred paces from Golgotha.[60] The Holy Zion Church was rebuilt by the Crusaders around 1099, and in 1335 the Franciscans, who acquired it, altered the cenacle above David's Tomb, giving it the Gothic appearance it now possesses.

Holy Zion Church was damaged by a mortar shell in Israel's 1948 War of Independence. Repairs to the building in 1951 afforded an opportunity for Israeli archaeologist Jacob Pinkerfield to excavate, and he found remains of a Roman-period structure beneath the ruins of the Byzantine church which he identified as a Jewish synagogue. The identification was based on discovery of a niche, about 6 feet above floor level, which resembled niches in other synagogues of the period which were installed at this height as a repository for Torah scrolls.

Jack Finegan suggested that this might rather have been a Jewish-Christian church.[61] Bargil Pixner has expanded on Finegan's idea, demonstrating that the remains are from a Roman-period Judeo-Christian synagogue known as the Church of the Apostles.[62] The synagogue, he argues, was built in the decade after 73 when Jewish Christians returned from Pella. They are believed to have reused Herodian stone from the Temple Mount for the structure, orienting the niche toward the Church of the Holy Sepulchre rather than toward the site of the temple, as was the practice for Jewish synagogues built before 70. Some of the Herodian stones have been found in the portion of the first-century wall that still stands. Pixner is convinced that this building signifies the site where the apostles prayed when they returned from the Mount of Olives after Christ's ascent to heaven (Acts 1:1–13) as well as the site of the Last Supper and the Pentecost visitation by the Holy Spirit; outside would have been where Peter preached the Pentecost sermon (Acts 2).

The Pontius Pilate Inscription

Jesus' appearance before Pontius Pilate is recorded by all four Gospels (Matt. 27:2; Mark 15:1–15; Luke 23:1–5; John 18:28–19:16). Prefect from A.D. 26 to 36, Pilate is known from extrabiblical records. In 1961 at Caesarea Maritima, the city of Pilate's residence in Israel, the Italian expedition discovered a stone bearing the prefect's name in the Roman theater.[63] The stone had been reused in the construction of a landing between flights of steps in a tier of seats reserved for guests of honor. Despite the stone's poor condition, three of the original four lines may be partially reconstructed:

```
[     ]S TIBERIEUM
[  PON]TIUS PILATUS
[  PRAEF]ECTUS IUDA[EΛ]E
[                        ]
```

Jerry Vardaman suggests the following free translation of the reconstructed text:

Tiberium [of the Caesareans?]
Pontius Pilate,
Prefect of Judea
[. . . has given . . .][64]

Undoubtedly, the stone was first used as part of some important building called a *Tiberium*, possibly a temple, which was dedicated in honor of the emperor Tiberius. The inscription provides us with the first archaeological evidence of Pilate, before whom Jesus was tried and condemned to death (see pp. 114–119 for consideration of the stone pavement where Jesus stood before Pilate).

Crucifixion: Archaeological Evidence

Although thousands of prisoners and slaves were crucified in antiquity,[65] only one victim of crucifixion has ever been discovered. The victim, a Jewish male who died sometime around the mid-first century A.D., was excavated by Vassilios Tzaferis in 1968.[66] The man's kôkhîm-type tomb was typical of those used by Jews in the Holy Land between the end of the second century B.C. and the fall of Jerusalem in A.D. 70.[67] Osteologists and other doctors from Jerusalem's Hadassah Medical School who examined the bones confirmed that the victim was a male between twenty-four and twenty-eight years old. He stood about 5 feet, 6 inches in height, about average for the Mediterranean people of the time, and had some slight facial defects, due in part to a cleft right palate. An inscription on the ossuary may contain his name: "Yehohanan, the son of Hagakol,"[68] although this translation of the last word is by no means certain.[69]

Differences of opinion exist about the posture of this man during his crucifixion. Nico Haas, in his original publication of the

Figure 20
Positions of Crucifixion

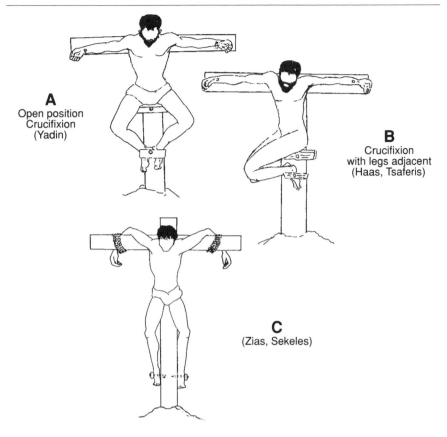

A
Open position
Crucifixion
(Yadin)

B
Crucifixion
with legs adjacent
(Haas, Tsaferis)

C
(Zias, Sekeles)

Courtesy of the Israel Exploration Society in Jerusalem

data, wrote: "The feet were joined almost parallel, both transfixed by the same nail at the heels, with the legs adjacent; the knees were doubled, the right one overlapping the left; the trunk was contorted; the upper limbs were stretched out, each stabbed by a nail in the forearm."[70] Tzaferis has defended this view.[71]

Joseph Zias and Eliezer Sekeles have argued that the victim's arms were tied, rather than nailed, to the crossbeam, and that his legs were apart, each foot nailed to a separate side of the vertical part of the cross.[72] Yigael Yadin also raised questions about some of Haas's conclusions. Believing that the victim was crucified "in an open position, with knees apart," Yadin supports his view by arguing that the inscription should be read as "son of the one hanged with his knees apart," instead of as "son of Hagakol."[73] Yadin further argues that his feet were not nailed to the cross at all and that he might have been crucified head down, with his feet looped over the crossbar beam and nailed together.[74] According to an early tradition, Simon Peter requested that he be crucified in this position,[75] one known in antiquity as exceptionally cruel.[76] Death by crucifixion, it should be remembered, was not the result of nail penetrations. A special communication of the American Medical Association states that "the actual cause of death by crucifixion was multifactorial and varied somewhat with each case, but the two most prominent causes probably were hypovolemic shock and exhaustion asphyxia."[77]

The Burial Place of Jesus

The location of the tomb in which Jesus was buried has been and remains a controversial topic in archaeological studies. Traditionally, two sites have been venerated by Christians. One is the Church of the Holy Sepulchre (also called Holy Resurrection Church) in the Christian Quarter of the Old City of Jerusalem. The other is the Garden Tomb, which is located about 100 yards outside the Damascus Gate, the central and largest gate in the Northern Wall of the Old City. Until recently there was no substantial archaeological evidence to support the claims of either place, but now we are in a better position to evaluate the two sites.

The Garden Tomb, commonly called "Gordon's Tomb" because in 1883 Charles Gordon championed its identification as the tomb of Jesus, has long been held by Protestant and evangelical Christians to be the actual burial place of Christ. However, W. S. McBirnie's defense of the tomb has been rightly criticized by Gabriel Barkay because, among other things, it does not deal with the archaeological evidence.[78] Although the Garden Tomb does have the aesthetic appeal of being located in a lovely garden,

Gordon's Tomb, popularly identified with the Garden Tomb, does not meet the criteria of a careful reading of Scripture and archaeological evidence.

removed from the rush and noise of a bustling and distracting modern city, several lines of evidence argue decisively against its identification as the tomb of Jesus. This evidence can be classified as (1) the location and date of the tomb, (2) the type of tomb, (3) Gordon's method of identification, (4) the use of tomb inscriptions, and (5) the witness of archaeology and early Christian literature.

Location

The Garden Tomb is situated squarely in the midst of a large burial ground north of the present city wall. In 1976 Benjamin Mazar published a report of two tombs found several decades earlier just east of the Damascus Gate outside the wall.[79] The Garden Tomb is only about 100 yards north of these tombs. On the property of the French School (Ecole Biblique et Archéologie Francaise), and adjacent to the Garden Tomb on the north lies the southernmost of two large burial grounds. They lie beneath and beside the Church of Saint Etienne (Stephen). Lying squarely in the center of the massive complex, the Garden Tomb is contemporary to the others. No tombs from the second-temple period have been found anywhere in the vicinity of the Garden Tomb.

Typology

The date assigned to the entire tomb complex can now be determined by a study of tomb typology. The entire network, covering several hundred square feet, belongs to Iron Age II and was constructed sometime from the eighth to the seventh centuries B.C. Excavations in Jerusalem and elsewhere in Israel have produced sufficient evidence to study tombs according to their types. Although still unable to produce an unequivocal pattern of changes in ancient tombs, archaeologists are now able to plot these changes and study them with an increasing degree of confidence in their ability to determine the date of a tomb's construction. Several characteristics of Iron Age tombs, which had two or more chambers, have been identified:[80]

1. They were multichambered tombs featuring a central chamber with peripheral rooms branching from it. The two-chambered tombs were built with an entrance chamber and another room beside it, on the right or left.
2. Low benches usually were cut into three of the rock walls of these peripheral rooms. Bodies were laid on these benches in the primary burial.
3. Walls were smooth, bearing no chisel marks, the result of having been cut with smooth faced instruments.

4. Cut into the benches were repositories for the secondary burial of bones after the flesh had decayed. After this point deceased individuals were considered to be "buried with their fathers" (cf. 2 Kings 8:24; 22:20). The practice continued into the Hellenistic period.
5. Ceilings were flat rather than vaulted.
6. Many benches were equipped with horseshoe-shaped headrests.[81] The four-legged animal figurines (found in tombs in the vicinity of the Garden Tomb) are well-attested only in Iron Age II tombs.[82]

Tombs of the second-temple period (the time of Christ), were built in two-chambered and multichambered styles, yet they had different individual characteristics from earlier types. By the end of this period in A.D. 70 Jerusalem was surrounded by burials, and about 700 second-temple tombs have been surveyed within three miles from the city limits.[83] Some characteristics of these tombs were:

1. Two-chambered tombs were built with one room behind the other, rather than side by side. The burial chamber lay directly behind the entrance chamber.
2. A hewn pit in the center of the burial chamber left a small shelf or ledge around the room in front of the small niches (loculi or kôkhîm), which were cut into the sides of the walls to hold small sarcophagi. Jewish tombs in Jerusalem from the time of Christ have been found in abundance, and most were built with a central chamber surrounded by other rooms which had three or more small niches cut into each of three walls.[84]

Kôkhîm in a Roman tomb at Heshbon, Jordan.

Rolling stone tomb entrance at Heshbon, Jordan.

Rolling stone entrance to Herodian family tomb in Jerusalem.

3. Walls, ceilings, and floors display "combing" (parallel chisel marks), the result of having been cut with iron "comb chisels," which had toothed edges.

4. The practice of primary and secondary burials was continued. Bodies were placed on special benches or in a *kôkh* (*loculus*) until they decomposed; the bones were then placed in small stone sarcophagi or ossuaries.[85] These were usually a little less than 3 feet wide and about 15 inches high. At Marisa, there are repositories cut into the ledge beneath the kôkhîm, presumably for holding bones, but each repository seems to have served two kôkhîm. These are dated by inscriptions in Aramaic, Greek, and Nabatean to the period between the third and first centuries B.C.[86] According to Tzaferis, the practice of putting bones into small stone ossuaries was evidently limited to the period between the rise of the Herodian dynasty and the first half of the second century A.D., as far as present evidence shows.[87] This practice is referred to in the Mishnah: "When the flesh had wasted away, they gathered together the bones and buried them in their own place."[88]

5. Ceilings in this period were often vaulted.

6. As early as Hellenistic times, and continuing into the Byzantine period, tombs employed arcosolia in addition to or in the place of kôkhîm. An *arcosolium* is formed by cutting a ledge or bench into a wall and hewing out an arch-shaped ceiling above it. The use of these arched niches in the Roman period is nowhere more evident than in the Catacombs of Rome. Sarcophagi were placed on the ledge beneath the arch, and frequently several of these arcosolia were cut one above the other on a high wall.

7. Tombs of the period typically had rolling stones in front of them that sealed the entrance to the first chamber. Eugenia Nitowski has studied sixty-one rolling-stone tombs in Israel and Jordan dating from the early Roman through the Byzantine periods (63 B.C.–A.D. 640).[89]

When the Garden Tomb is compared with the various types it clearly corresponds to known Iron Age tombs. It is a two-chambered tomb, the rooms arranged side by side with the burial chamber on the right of the entrance. The walls are smooth and the ceiling flat. Although it was altered in the Byzantine period, when ceilings were normally vaulted, its ceiling was left flat. The Garden Tomb possesses no evidence of arcosolia. The evidence leads to the conclusion that the Garden Tomb is from Iron Age II.

Figure 21
Roman and Iron Age Tombs

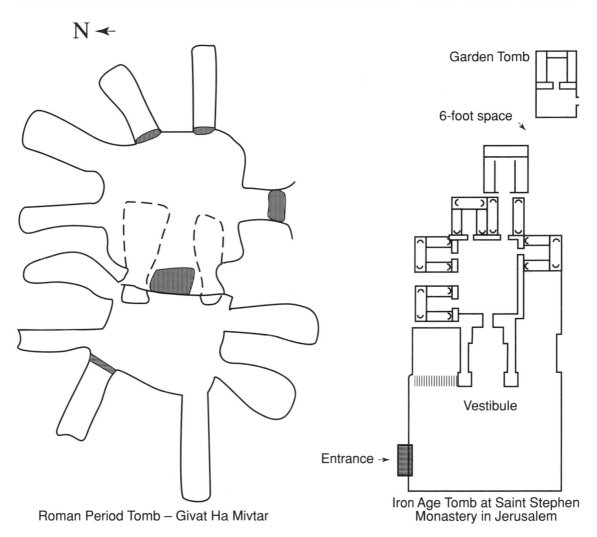

N ←

Garden Tomb

6-foot space

Vestibule

Entrance →

Roman Period Tomb – Givat Ha Mivtar

Iron Age Tomb at Saint Stephen
Monastery in Jerusalem

Initial identification

Insight into the method used by General Gordon to identify the tomb as Jesus' burial place is obtained from a letter Gordon published in 1885 in the *Quarterly Statement* of the Palestine Exploration Fund. He wrote that when he visited the Skull Hill he "felt convinced" that it must be the place of Christ's crucifixion, since it was north of the city. Jesus, he reasoned, would have been slain north of the altar as were the Old Testament sacrificial lambs, of which he was the type (Lev. 1:11). He also determined that the lay of the land supported this analogy. He saw various land formations of Jerusalem as representing a skeleton: Skull Hill (Golgotha or Calvary) and the Garden Tomb represented the head; the land lying between Skull Hill and the Temple Mount was the torso or

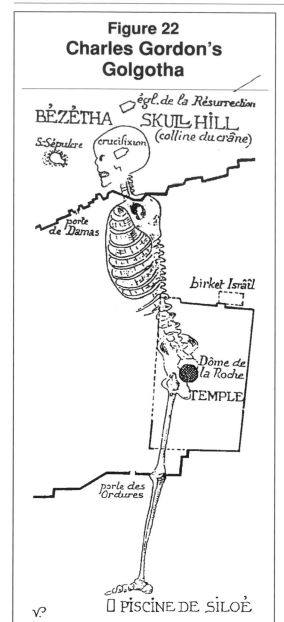

Figure 22
Charles Gordon's
Golgotha

"sides", and the Temple Mount was the pelvis. Had not Psalm 48:2 spoken of "Zion on the *sides* of the north?" (KJV, emphasis added).[90] The legs in Gordon's theory of symbolic geography extended south to the Pool of Siloam.

Obviously, Gordon relied heavily on a personal Biblical typology—a typology manufactured more from emotion than from sound archaeological or biblical interpretation. In his letter Gordon admitted that "unless the types are wrong . . . [the Church of the Holy Sepulchre] should never have been taken as the site." As a matter of fact, the Holy Sepulchre is situated north of where Jerusalem's Northern Wall stood in the days of Jesus—a fact unknown to Gordon. That wall was built no earlier than the time of King Agrippa (see p. 188). He made a similar error when he assumed that the Romans entered Jerusalem through the modern Damascus Gate. Thus, Gordon's vision of a skeleton superimposed on the city of Jerusalem, with its head at the Garden Tomb, is now just one more interesting, if not amusing, piece of the mountain of folk lore which has grown around the Holy City.

Inscriptions

Yet another argument against the Garden Tomb as the burial place of Jesus is the improper, if not fraudulent, use of two tomb inscriptions found nearby in 1885 and 1889 as supporting evidence.[91] One inscription was on a 51-inch-by-31-inch stone slab which covered the entrance to a Byzantine tomb, found in 1889 under the atrium of the Saint Stephen's Monastery. It contained the following inscription:

θηκη διαφερ[ουσα] Νοννου διακ[ονου] Ονισ[ιμου] της αγ[ιας] του Χ[ριστο]υ Α[ναστασεω]ς κ[αι] της μο[νης] αυτης ["The private tomb of the deacon Nonnus Onesimus of the Holy Resurrection of Christ and of this monastery"].

Jerome Murphy-O'Connor believes this inscription was amalgamated, deliberately or unwittingly, with another found in 1885

The tomb enshrined at the Church of the Holy Sepulchre stands near what was a limestone quarry.

in the tomb complex to which the Garden Tomb belongs. This inscription was translated, "Private tomb of the deacon Euthymius Pindiris." News of the inscription reached the United States but whoever reported the find remembered the two inscriptions as one and the deacon's name as Eusebius. By the time the erroneous form was published November 7, 1889, in the *Northern Christian Advocate* of Syracuse, New York, it had become: "I, Eusebius, have desired to be buried in this spot, which I believe to be close to the place where the body of my Lord lay." Murphy-O'Connor observes the actual inscriptions do "not have a single word in common" with the final reproduction. The anonymous correspondent himself called it "a strange rumor" that was afloat and said that the inscription was being translated only "in effect."

Despite the problems with the story, the inscription was used to argue that the tomb of Jesus (called "The Holy Resurrection of Christ") was very close by the place of Euthymius's burial and thus in the Garden Tomb area. This was thought to confirm General Gordon's identification. The actual inscription only affirms that Euthymius was both a monk in the Saint Stephen's Monastery and a deacon of the Holy Resurrection Church (Church of the Holy Sepulchre) and was buried near the former. Others are known to have held the same dual position at the church and monastery.[92]

Archaeological and literary evidence

Archaeological and early Christian literary evidence tend to further substantiate the Church of the Holy Sepulchre as standing on the burial site.[93] Although within the modern city walls, excavation shows that this location was outside the walls in the days of Jesus;[94] therefore it cannot be excluded from consideration as the tomb's site because of its present location. Moreover, excavations by Vergilio Corbo established that the area surrounding the church was a huge limestone quarry in the seventh century B.C.,[95] a fact confirmed by the discovery of Iron Age II pottery. This quarry was in use until the first century B.C.,[96] according to Corbo, at which time it was filled and became a garden. He believes that at least four early-Roman-period tombs were constructed there.[97]

Eusebius wrote in the mid-fourth century that the Roman emperor Hadrian, after suppressing the second Jewish revolt in 135, built a huge rectangular platform of earth over this quarry for a temple dedicated to Venus.[98] During the lifetime of Eusebius, Queen Helena, the mother of the emperor Constantine, went to Jerusalem and was shown "the very spot which witnessed the Savior's sufferings." Eusebius writes that "the emperor now began to rear a monument to the Savior's victory over death, with rich and lavish magnificence [the Church of the Holy Sepulchre]."[99] In a letter to Macarius, the bishop of Jerusalem, Constantine referred to the discovery of the "monument of His most holy passion," which had "remained unknown for so long a series of years."[100] Apparently Constantine meant that the tomb itself, not the general location, had been found.

Jerome supplies more information: "From the time of Hadrian to the reign of Constantine—a period of about one-hundred and eighty years—the spot which had witnessed the resurrection was occupied by a figure of Jupiter."[101] Whether Hadrian's temple had already been destroyed by the time of Constantine is not entirely clear, but in a letter to Macarius Constantine indicates that he may have dismantled a building used in idolatrous worship when he built the church: "The dwelling-places of error, with the statues . . . were overthrown and utterly destroyed. . . both stone and timber . . . that sacred spot, which under Divine direction I have disencumbered as it were of the heavy weight of foul idol worship . . . a spot . . . which now appears holier still, since it has brought to light a clear assurance of our Savior's passion."[102]

The literary witness argues strongly that the memory of the tomb location had persevered through the centuries, even though within fifteen years of Jesus' death Herod Agrippa I had built a new wall on the north side of the city, placing the tomb within the city walls. Unless there had been a compelling reason to do so, no one in the time of Helena would have looked for the burial site inside the crowded walled city. It should be noted that the succession of Christian bishops in Jerusalem was never interrupted during these early centuries. Though the first fifteen Jewish Christian bishops were necessarily succeeded by Gentile Christians after the publication of Hadrian's edict expelling all Jews from Jerusalem,[103] the memory of so sacred a place would never have been forgotten. It was convincing enough to Helena and Constantine that they erected a church on the site.

Whether the emperor or his mother financed construction of the church is not entirely clear. Eusebius attributed it to Constantine, who "judged it incumbent upon him [to build it], being moved in spirit by the Savior himself . . . acting as he did under the guidance of the divine Spirit."[104] Eusebius credited Helena with building the Nativity Church in Bethlehem and the Ascension Church on Mount Olivet.[105] Sozomen (ca. 430) affirmed that Constantine built the Resurrection Church and Helena built the other two.[106] On the other hand, Sulpicius Severus, writing in about 395, recorded that Helena built all three basilicas, a view also presented in the history by Socrates Scholasticus (ca. 430).[107] It is likely that Constantine sent his mother to search out the place of the burial of Jesus in order to construct a church over it, and while there she also decided to build the other two. Scholasticus also provides details about the tomb prior to the construction of the church. He claims that when the ground above the tomb was cleared, three crosses—the cross of Christ and the crosses of the two thieves—were found in the sepulchre. According to the history, the very sign, that was affixed above Christ's head proclaiming him to be "King of the Jews" in three languages was found as well.

Disagreement exists regarding the architecture of Constantine's church.[108] In general, excavation has confirmed the accuracy of Eusebius's description. A round monumental structure stood over the tomb itself. This monument probably resembled the mausoleum for Constantine's daughter in Rome (the rotunda of the Church of Santa Costanza).[109] An atrium or garden adjoined the tomb's east side.[110] East of the garden stood a basilica-style church building,[111] measuring about 165 feet long, east to west, and 115 feet wide, north to south. Overlooking the garden and tomb, the apse faced the west. This is highly unusual, for apses I have seen in other Byzantine churches throughout the Mediterranean world almost always faced the east.

A gold ring found during excavation south of the Temple Mount in 1974 adds to the intriguing mystery, for it is formed in the shape of a structure that, depending on its age, may represent either Constantine's church or the twelfth-century Crusader church that stood on the site. The two may have been similar in outward appearance. The ring may be Byzantine,[112] in which case its representation of a square structure with a dome resembles the depiction of the Constantinian structure on the Madeba Mosaic Map.[113] It also may date to the twelfth to sixteenth centuries,[114] and its form is not unlike the Crusader structure.

Although absolute proof of the location of Jesus' tomb remains beyond our reach, the archaeological and early literary evidence argues strongly for those who associate it with the Church of the Holy Sepulchre. That ground certainly represents the emotional impact the tomb has stirred in the hearts of pilgrims through the centuries. Mark Twain eloquently described that sacred meaning when he called it "the most sacred locality on earth to millions

The Church of the Holy Sepulchre offers long tradition and location as evidence that it encloses the tomb of Christ.

and millions of men, and women, and children, the noble and the humble, bond and free." Christians and even many non-Christians can share in the awe Twain relates:

> In its history from the first, and in its tremendous associations, it is the most illustrious edifice in Christendom. With all its claptrap side-shows and unseemly impostures of every kind, it is still grand, reverend, venerable—for a god died there; for fifteen hundred years its shrines have been wet with the tears of pilgrims from the earth's remotest confines. . . . History is full of this old Church of the Holy Sepulcher—full of blood that was shed because of the respect and the veneration in which men held the last resting place of the meek and lowly, the mild and gentle Prince of Peace![115]

The Shroud of Turin

All three Synoptic Gospels record that when Jesus was taken down from the cross he was wrapped in a "linen shroud" (σινδών; Matt. 27:59; Mark 15:46; Luke 23:53). John 20:6–7 uses more precise terminology, stating that when Peter entered the tomb he saw "the garments" (τὰ ὀθόνια) lying there and "the napkin" (τὸ σου–δάριον) "which had been on his head" lying folded in a separate place from the other garments. John 11:44 also attests to the Jewish custom of using a separate cloth for the face in describing the burial of Lazarus.[116] John's description does not invalidate the Synoptic account, which may be regarded simply as a generic reference to the shroud with no specific notation of the additional face cloth.[117] John 19:40 speaks only of the garments (ὀθονίοις), without referring to the face napkin.

A linen shroud, 14.25 feet long and 3.58 feet wide, was publicly displayed sometime after 1357 in Lirey, France, by a famed knight named Geoffrey de Charny. On the shroud was an image of an unclothed, bearded, long-haired man who bore the marks of one who had been crucified. Since that time the cloth has been considered by many to be the actual burial shroud of Jesus. In 1453 de Charny's granddaughter gave the shroud to the Duke of Savoy, who in 1578 brought it to Turin (Torino), Italy, as he moved the capital of Savoy to that city. Called by Pope Paul VI "the most important relic in the history of Christianity," it was willed to the Vatican in 1983 at the death of Umberto II, the last king of Savoy.[118] The history of the shroud prior to 1357 is not known, although Ian Wilson, a British freelance journalist, has tried to trace it to Jerusalem via Constantinople and Edessa.[119] It may have been brought to France during the Crusades.

In 1898 the shroud was photographed by Secondo Pia, who first observed that the shroud contained a negative rather than a positive image. This has often been regarded as a proof of its authenticity, since it dates back to at least medieval times, hundreds of years before the invention of photography. Pia's amazing discovery sparked scholarly interest in the shroud, which has continued until the present. In 1973 a group of experts, largely Italian, was allowed to examine the shroud and verified that the image was not superficial; no pigment of paint could be seen, even under magnification. A group of American, Italian, and Swiss scientists met in March 1977 in Albuquerque, New Mexico, to form the Shroud of Turin Research Project. They planned a program of detailed, non-destructive experiments on the shroud after its public exhibition on October 8, 1978, the four-hundredth anniversary of its arrival in Turin.

Permission was secured, and a host of scientists converged on the Savoy Royal Palace at Turin.[120] Over five days they used 6 tons of the latest scientific equipment worth more than 2.5 million dollars, to test and experiment on the cloth. Experts of all religious backgrounds and from such institutions as Los Alamos National Scientific Laboratory, the University of Colorado, U.S. Air Force Weapons Lab, Nuclear Technology Corporation, U.S. Air Force Academy, Jet Propulsion Laboratory, and Saint Agnes Medical Center conducted scores of experiments on the shroud. Among other techniques and equipment, they measured ultraviolet fluorescence and used X-rays, spectroscopes, macrophotography, fiber optic photography, photomicrography, and a VP-8 Image Analyzer, a mechanism that transforms the intensity of an image into vertical three-dimensional relief. The *National Geographic* reported that "perhaps never before had an object of art or archaeology been subjected to such exhaustive examination."[121]

This unprecedented scientific investigation was unable to demonstrate the shroud to be a fabrication. Nor was it able to prove its authenticity. Subsequent experiments in the various laboratories have now proven that the shroud contains blood as well as "aragonite, the particular crystalline form of calcium carbonate present both on the shroud fibers and in Jerusalem's first-century tombs."[122] Max Frei, a Swiss criminologist, found forty-eight samples of pollen, seven of which are from halophytic (salt-loving) plants found in saline areas such as the Dead Sea. Others originated in Palestine and Anatolia. It seems more likely that the pollen would have been carried on the cloth than that they would have blown from Palestine to Europe and landed on the shroud, although that is possible. The weave of the cloth was shown to be a herringbone twill, a pattern known to have existed in ancient times, and the thread was hand spun. After about A.D. 1200, European thread was spun by the wheel.[123]

Carbon 14 or radiocarbon testing, the one test that could date the shroud to within 150 years of its production, was not approved by John Paul II and Anastacio Cardinal Ballestrero, archbishop of Turin, until October 1986 because until the 1980s the test required the burning of too large a piece of the cloth. A new technique, however, using an accelerator as a mass spectrometer, required a sample about the size of an adult's fingernail. Laboratories at Oxford, England; Zurich, Switzerland, and the University of Arizona, were approved to perform the tests. A strip .4 inch by 2.8 inches was cut from the cloth on April 21, 1987. Each of the three laboratories received one-third of the strip. The official results of the tests were submitted to the British Museum, which supervised the process, and that October 21 the results were forwarded to the archbishop of Turin.

The verdict: the shroud was dated to the fourteenth century! While those results are generally accepted and the shroud regarded as an amazing forgery, Adam J. Otterbein, the president of the Holy Shroud Guild, remained unsatisfied and told the author before this book went to press that he planned to call for new testing, because of questions about the procedure.[124] A book challenging the procedure used in the testing has already appeared.[125] Many scientists had feared this uncertainty would result from the decision to spare cloth by using three laboratories rather than seven. Also, while the carbon 14 tests may show the shroud to be a medieval forgery they have done nothing to explain how the enigmatic negative image was created. A study of the calcium found on the shroud may have provided a partial explanation. Joseph Kohlbeck and Eugenia Nitowski have shown that such an image could have been created by a change within the cellulose of the flax, not by the particles attached to the fibers.[126] A process known as mercerization occurs when linen reacts to a slightly alkaline solution, leaving a yellowish stain. This solution forms when moisture from the body, consisting of blood and perspiration, mixes with limestone dust. Limestone dust from a first-century tomb in Jerusalem near the traditional tomb of Christ contains aragonite, the particular crystalline form of calcium carbonate present on fibers of the shroud. The shroud might have encountered the limestone dust when the body it covered was laid on a limestone ledge characteristic of Jewish tombs of the Roman period (see the discussion of tomb typology on pp. 207–211).

Ricardo Levi-Setti of the Fermi Institute of the University of Chicago performed a test that also suggests, but does not prove, a Jerusalem milieu for the shroud. He put samples from the shroud and from the tomb in Jerusalem through a high-resolution scanning ion microprobe. The resultant graphs show that the samples are an unusually close match. Kohlbeck and Nitowski have concluded that the body heat produced by crucifixion, combined with the mildly alkaline limestone, "might well have

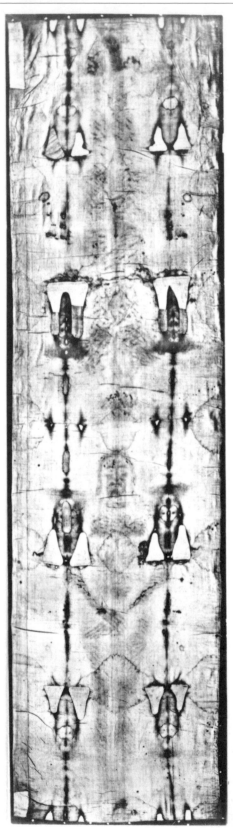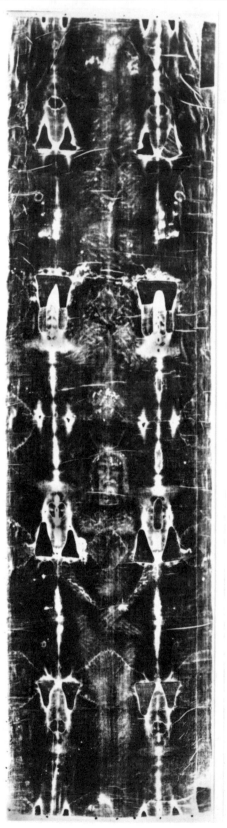

Controversy continues over tests conducted on the Shroud of Turin.

resulted in a mercerization process that attacked the outer skin of the fibers of the shroud, leaving the yellowish-tone color of the image—the same color found when the Jerusalem limestone paste was applied to new linen fibers. . . . In short, the extreme body heat produced by crucifixion may have resulted in a mercerization process with the mildly alkaline aragonite containing traces of iron."[127]

With a fourteenth-century date seemingly confirmed for the shroud, this mysterious image becomes more perplexing. In 1987 a carefully controlled experiment combining calcium, blood, perspiration, and heat as suggested by Kohlbeck and Nitowski, was conducted before television cameras, producing an image similar to that on the shroud.[128] How this could have been done in 1300 remains a mystery. It must be remembered, however, that even if the shroud had been shown to have originated in the first century, it would not have proven, nor could it, that the shroud belonged to Jesus Christ. In addition to its other strange characteristics, at least two problems can be mentioned regarding the claim that coins minted by Pontius Pilate were placed over the eyes of the figure. First, this custom has not been clearly demonstrated for Jewish burials in the first century. Second, no friend of Jesus, such as Joseph of Arimathea or Nicodemus, would likely have put on his eyes the coins of the governor, who condemned him to death.[129]

Emmaus

In addition to locations in and around Jerusalem and on the Sea of Galilee, only Emmaus is specifically mentioned in the Gospels as the site of a resurrection appearance by Jesus (Luke 24:13). Four locations have been suggested for the actual village of Jesus' day, Amwas, el-Qubeibeh, Abu Ghosh, and Motza-Colonia.

Amwas or Imwas is about 20 miles west of Jerusalem on the road to Tel Aviv.[130] It lies immediately north of Latrun, at the point where the central mountain range drops off into the Aijalon Valley. The location almost fits the distance of 160 stadia (about 18 miles) from Jerusalem that is given in Codex Sinaiticus and a few later Greek and Latin manuscripts. Amwas seems to be the town referred to in 1 Maccabees 3:40 and by Josephus,[131] Sozomen,[132] and Eusebius, who calls it "Nicopolis, a famous city of Palestine."[133] The Bordeaux Pilgrim also mentions a place called Nicopolis, locating it 22 Roman miles from Jerusalem.[134] Excavations at Amwas from 1875 to 1930 revealed five buildings at the site: a house, a baptistery, a large and a small basilica dating variously between the third and sixth centuries, and a Crusader church from the twelfth century.

The village of el-Qubeibeh, due west of Nebi Samwil is 7 miles northwest of Jerusalem. Although not supported by as much ancient tradition as Amwas, this distance agrees with the distance of 60 stadia or about 7 miles, given in the third century papyrus Bodmer XIV (**p**[75]), the fourth-century Codex Sinaiticus, the fifth-century Codex Alexandrinus, and others—including a correction in Codex Vaticanus, although the uncorrected text of the Codex Vaticanus read 160 stadia. The committee for the third edition of the United Bible Societies text of the Greek New Testament felt that the reading of 160 stadia arose "in connection with patristic identification of Emmaus with Amwas (modern Nicopolis)," so they accept the shorter distance in their Greek text. They conclude that the longer distance of nearly 20 miles is "too far for the travellers to have re-traversed that same evening (verse 33)."[135]

Wilkinson agrees but rejects both Qubeibeh and Abu Ghosh as New Testament Emmaus, arguing that "there is no evidence that anyone had regarded either of these sites as Emmaus before the arrival of the Crusaders." El Qubeibeh, according to Wilkinson, is first mentioned as the New Testament site only in 1280.[136] Wilkinson, however, suggests Motza-Colonia, even though it is only 4 miles from Jerusalem. He identifies this site with the Amassa in the Latin version of Josephus.[137] However, this conclusion forces Wilkinson to assume an extreme position on the accuracy of the New Testament text. He states that "Motza-Colonia is therefore not certainly the Emmaus of the New Testament, but if it were, then both distances in our biblical texts were wrong. To the present writer this seems the most probable solution to the problem."[138] Charles Schürer identifies Josephus's Emmaus with the New Testament city and regards the distances in both Josephus and the New Testament as "only approximately correct." H. St.J. Thackeray accepts the identification as well.[139]

PART 4

Archaeology
and the Church

Cities in Eastern and Central Asia Minor

Archaeology and Pauline Chronology

The task of establishing dates and time sequence for events within the ministry of Paul is complicated by the fact that Acts makes no reference to any of the apostle's letters. We do know that many of them were written during the years on which Acts reports. John Knox wrote that he finds Acts of no help in efforts to construct a chronology of Paul, so he relies only on primary sources—Paul's letters.[1] Gerd Luedemann dealt with the subject from an even more radical perspective.[2] A more balanced treatment from the pen of Robert Jewett allows a cautious use of Acts.[3] The best recent treatment is that of Jack Finegan, who includes a section on chronology in his second volume on New Testament archaeology.[4] Such works help us at least to understand the many problems inherent in establishing a working chronology of the New Testament, and especially of the events of the Book of Acts and Paul's life.

One example of how archaeology has contributed to establishing a Pauline chronology is that now we can set the approximate beginning of Paul's work in Corinth on his second journey. The key is found in Acts 18:2 where we learn that when Paul arrived in Corinth he found Priscilla and Aquila, who had lately come from Italy, having been banished from Rome in a general expulsion of Jews under Claudius, who reigned from 41 to 54. This event is referred to by Suetonius and others and can be dated to A.D. 49.[5] It may have been a product of the normal conflicts Claudius was having with oriental religions in Rome at the time or it may have been precipitated by some particular event such as the one described in the *Teaching of Addai*. A wife of Claudius, named Protonice in the document,[6] converted to Christianity, made a pilgrimage to Jerusalem, and returned to Rome with a report that the Jews had wrongfully withheld from Christians the possession of Golgotha, Jesus' cross, and his tomb. The reaction of the emperor to this news was: "he commanded all the Jews to leave the country of Italy."[7] Perhaps this was part of the tumult in Rome that was instigated over the person of Christ (Chrestus)[8] to which Suetonius refers. Dio Cassius's comment that Claudius did not drive the Jews out of Rome,[9] may refer to some local incident in the early part of his reign, prior to the event described in Acts and by Suetonius.

This latter expulsion by Claudius, mentioned in Acts and by Suetonius, may have included only those Jews (and Christians) who were involved in the disturbances and not the whole Jewish population of Rome. An action involving some Jews need not be interpreted as necessarily including all Jews. A recent archaeological discovery illustrates the point. A large cemetery, 7 miles long and containing more than 120 tombs, includes a tomb with an inscribed sarcophagus which belonged to "Theodotus,[10] freedman of Queen Agrippina[11]." Agrippina was a wife of Claudius and queen between A.D. 50 to 54. The manumission of this slave by the queen cannot necessarily be taken as an indication of imperial policy. She may have chosen to free Theodotus for personal reasons, prompted possibly by the close relation she is known to have had with the Jewish King Agrippa II (A.D. 53–100).

Paul stayed in Corinth for eighteen months (Acts 18:11); then he was brought before Gallio, probably on the occasion of the proconsul's appointment to office. Again archaeology helps date this event. At Delphi archaeologists found a stone which probably was once attached to the outer wall of the Temple of Apollo. Inscribed in it is a copy of a letter from Claudius to the city of Delphi, naming Gallio as the friend of Claudius and proconsul of Achaia.[12] The Greek inscription reads in part:

Τιβερ[ιος Κλαυδιος Κ]αισ[αρ Σεβαστ]ος Γ[ερμανικος,

αρχιερευς μεγιστος, δημαρχικης εξου]σιας [το ιβ, αυτοκρατωρ τ]ο κ[a digamma follows the kappa]. . . .

Λουκιος Ἰουνιος Γαλλιων ο φ[ιλος] μου κα[ι ανθυ]πατος [της Ἀχαιας]. . . .

"Tiberius Claudius Caesar Augustus Germanicus,

Pontifex Maximus, of tribunician authority for the twelfth time, imperator the twenty-sixth time. . . .

Lucius Junius Gallio, my friend, and the proconsul of Achaia. . . ."[13]

Finegan dates the inscription to A.D. 52, with Gallio having assumed office in the early summer of 51. Since Paul had been in the city for eighteen months he would have arrived in the winter, perhaps January, of 50.[14] Thus the arrival of Priscilla and Aquila in Corinth after the 49 expulsion and just before Paul arrived, coincides well with Paul's arrival at the end of 49 or the beginning of 50.[15]

Yet another find may have bearing on the time frame of Paul's ministry. Until recently, most chronologies have dated the accession of Festus as procurator of Judea to A.D. 59 or later.[16] However, Jerry Vardaman has evidence (at this writing still unpublished) for an accession date in the late spring or early summer of 56. The information comes from graffiti-like micrographics on a coin.[17] This date for Festus coincides with the date given in Jerome's Latin version of the *Chronicle of Eusebius.* If it proves tenable, Paul's Caesarean imprisonment would be earlier and the time between his appearances before Gallio and Festus would be greatly reduced.[18] The two years Paul spent in prison in Rome, would probably extend from his arrival in that city about February of 57 until February of 59.[19]

Cities in Syria and Eastern Asia Minor

Antioch of Syria

As Christianity spread beyond the borders of Palestine to the Diaspora, its focal point was Antioch of Syria. This city on the Orontes River probably had a first-century population of about three hundred thousand.[20] Antioch's Jewish population was unusually large at this time, according to Josephus.[21] Endowing splendidly decorated synagogues, the Jews of Antioch were also wealthy and constantly attracted "to their religious ceremonies multitudes of Greeks."[22] Refugees from the persecution that arose in Jerusalem after the stoning of Stephen were the first Christians to contact the city's Jews (Acts 11:19).[23] Others who initially fled to Cyprus and Cyrene, soon followed and preached to "Greeks" with considerable success (Acts 11:20–21). These Greeks were probably "God-fearers"—Gentiles attracted to Jewish monothe-

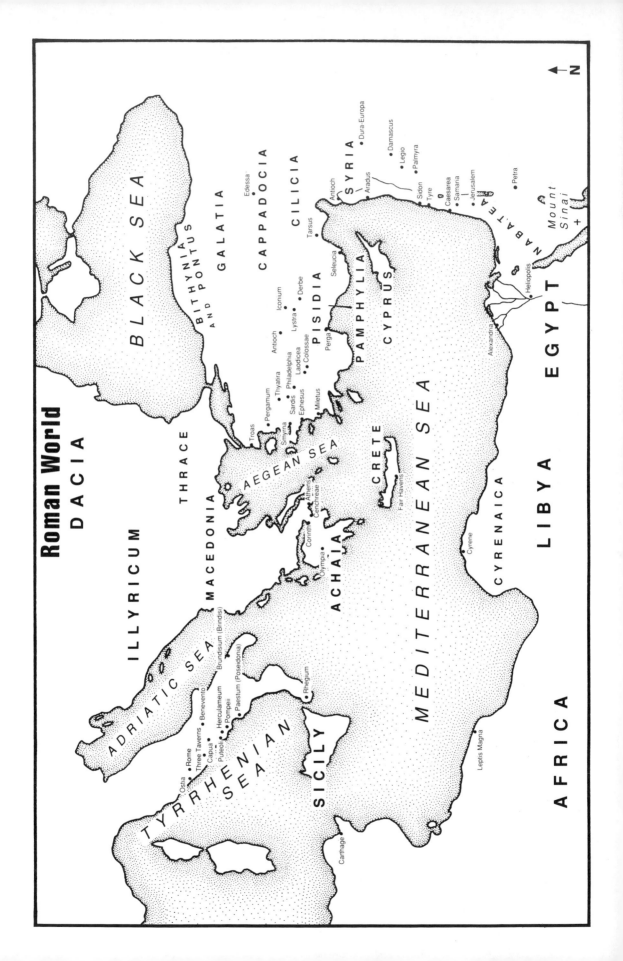

Roman World

N

BLACK SEA

DACIA

ILLYRICUM

THRACE

MACEDONIA

BITHYNIA AND PONTUS

GALATIA

CAPPADOCIA

Edessa

CILICIA

SYRIA

Dura-Europa

Damascus

Legio

Palmyra

Antioch

Tarsus

Aradus

Sidon

Tyre

Caesarea

Samaria

Jerusalem

Petra

NABATEA

Mount Sinai

Heliopolis

Seleucia

PISIDIA

PAMPHYLIA

CYPRUS

Perga

Antioch

Iconum

Derbe

Lystra

Pergamum

Thyatira

Philadelphia

Laodicea

Colossae

Sardis

Ephesus

Miletus

Smyrna

Troas

AEGEAN SEA

Athens

Cenchreae

Corinth

Olympia

ACHAIA

CRETE

Fair Havens

MEDITERRANEAN SEA

EGYPT

Alexandria

LIBYA

CYRENAICA

Cyrene

Leptis Magna

AFRICA

ADRIATIC SEA

Brundisium (Brindisi)

Paestum (Poseidonia)

Benevento

Herculaneum

Pompeii

Three Taverns

Rome

Ostia

Capua

Puteoli

Rhegium

SICILY

TYRRHENIAN SEA

Carthage

ism (Acts 10:22; 13:16, 26, 43; 16:14; 17:4, 17; 18:7). Barnabas, sent by the Jerusalem church to check on the status of these non-Jewish converts, saw their need for leadership and journeyed to Tarsus to persuade Paul to work among them (Acts 11:22–26). Paul and Barnabas spent a full year at Antioch, after which the church there became the base for Paul's missionary journeys (Acts 13:1–3; 15:35–36; 18:22–23) Peter, according to Eusebius, was the first bishop of Antioch.[24] He was succeeded by Evodius and then by Ignatius of Antioch, who was martyred in the reign of Trajan.[25]

Excavations have revealed little of Antioch relating to the New Testament period; however, there is a considerable body of ancient literature dealing with the city with which to compare the archaeological data.[26] We know that the city lay between the Orontes River and Mount Silpius, an area of approximately 1 mile by 2 miles.[27] It was laid out on a Hippodamian grid plan, typical of Hellenistic cities, with *insulae* of 367 by 190 feet.[28] The wall surrounding Antioch was built by Seleucus I, enlarged (probably) by Antiochus Epiphanes, and rebuilt by Tiberius.[29]

The Romans constructed many important public buildings in Antioch.[30] In 67 B.C. Marcius Rex, representing the Roman government, initiated construction of a palace and a circus on an island (which no longer exists) in the Orontes River.[31] Under Julius Caesar in 47 B.C., work began on an aqueduct to provide water for residences built on the side of Mount Silpius. Remains of some of these private residences have been found, as have remains of small

Seen from a nearby mountain, Antioch of Syria was the base for Paul and Barnabas's missionary operations.

bathhouses made possible by the aqueduct. Julius Caesar also constructed a theater in the town's monumental center (the area in which a large number of monuments were constructed) and an amphitheater near the southern gate. Somewhere, undoubtedly near Antioch's center, he built the Kaisareion—perhaps the oldest basilica in the east. The Kaisareion was dedicated to use by the cult of Rome.[32] It bore Caesar's name and housed his statue.[33] The Pantheon in Antioch, which was in a state of deterioration, was rebuilt by Julius Caesar, and on a slope of Mount Silpius he either built or reconstructed a second theater.

A north-south colonnaded street running the length of the city divided Antioch in halves.[34] Arguments continue as to whether this was the first such street ever constructed.[35] It is clear from the texts of Josephus that Herod did more than merely pave a street and build a stoa along part of *one* side, as J. B. Ward-Perkins maintains.[36] Though Josephus's text of the *Jewish War* is somewhat ambiguous, all major translations render it virtually the same: "And the wide street in Syrian Antioch, once avoided because of the mud, did he not pave—two and a quarter miles of it—with polished marble, and to keep the rain off furnish it with a colonnade from end to end?"[37] *Antiquities* describes the street more clearly: "And for the Antiochenes, who inhabit the greatest city in Syria, which has a street running through it lengthwise, he adorned this street with colonnades on either side (ταύτην αὐτὴν στοαῖς κόσμησας παρ' ἑκάτερα), and paved the open part of the road with polished stone."[38]

The Byzantine author Malalas, however, gives credit elsewhere, indicating that Tiberius built the roofed colonnades that lined the street, after Herod had paved it.[39] Glanville Downey affirms that Malalas's information originated in local records. Obviously, both Josephus and Malalas cannot be correct. Furthermore, traces of pavement from the earlier Seleucid period have been found beneath this street, which leads Downey to question whether the street was as muddy before it was paved as Josephus reports.[40] Tiberius built bathhouses in the eastern part of the city,[41] and he may have constructed a huge bathhouse on the island in the Orontes which was destroyed by an earthquake in the time of Trajan and rebuilt in the fourth century.[42] Tiberius is also credited with the construction of *tetrapyla* at each main intersection of streets, expanding the theater, and with completing and improving Epiphania, the section of southern Antioch built by and named for Antiochus Epiphanes.

It is difficult, if not impossible, to clearly differentiate the building program of Augustus from that of Tiberius Augustus in Antioch. Augustus visited twice, and commissioned his architect, Marcus Agrippa, to conduct an extensive building program, funded by the considerable treasure he found in Egypt after the

Figure 23
Schematic of Antioch of Syria

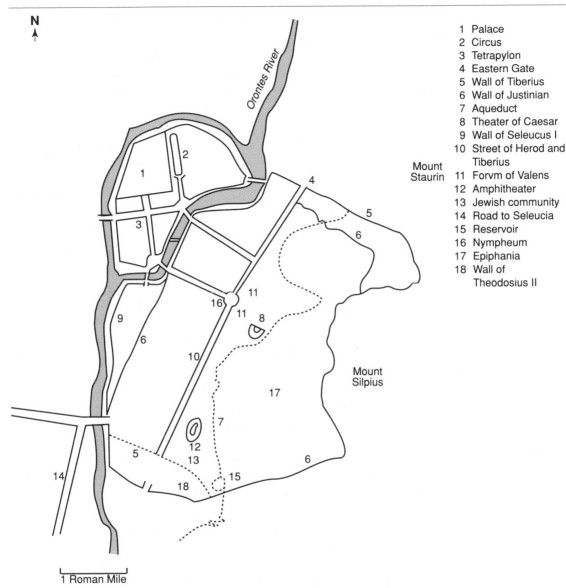

1 Palace
2 Circus
3 Tetrapylon
4 Eastern Gate
5 Wall of Tiberius
6 Wall of Justinian
7 Aqueduct
8 Theater of Caesar
9 Wall of Seleucus I
10 Street of Herod and Tiberius
11 Forvm of Valens
12 Amphitheater
13 Jewish community
14 Road to Seleucia
15 Reservoir
16 Nympheum
17 Epiphania
18 Wall of Theodosius II

defeat of Cleopatra and Antony at Actium in 31 B.C. Several temples built and projects begun by Augustus were attributed to Tiberius. Tiberius may have finished several projects which Augustus started, and he probably needed to undertake other building activities after a fire in A.D. 23 or 24.[43]

Earthquakes often shook Antioch. Two occurred in the New Testament period. The first of these struck on April 9, 37, during the reign of Caligula. He responded quickly and generously, using the considerable surplus left in the treasury at Rome by Tiberius to rebuild the devastated city.[44] The second earthquake occurred during the reign of Claudius, damaged Antioch, Ephesus, Smyrna, and other cities of Asia Minor.[45] Buildings restored in Antioch after this quake included the Temple of Artemis and the Temple of Herakles. The roofed colonnades of the street, reportedly built by Tiberius, may have also been restored, or work may have continued from repairs to the street after the 37 earthquake.[46]

Thus, Antioch was bustling with activity and excitement during a time of rebuilding when Paul first arrived there about A.D. 43, the year the city replaced a no-longer-celebrated festival founded under Augustus with Olympic games.[47] Antioch on the Orontes was a huge, cosmopolitan city where barriers of religion, race, and nationality were easily crossed: the perfect base of operations for a new religion that was rooted in the religion of ancient Israel and internationalized by Jesus of Nazareth. One of the early converts to Christianity was from Antioch, a Jewish proselyte named Nicolaus who was selected as one of the seven leaders of the Hellenist Christians in Jerusalem (Acts 6:5). Paul, the Jew chosen by God to preach the message of Christ to Gentiles (Acts 9:15 and 26:16–18; Gal. 1:15–16; Col. 1:24–27), made this city of heterogeneous cultures his headquarters and the focal point of missionary activity for many years. And in Antioch disciples of Jesus were called Christians for the first time (Acts 11:26).[48] It would be difficult to overstate Antioch's importance, for "with the exception of Jerusalem, Antioch in Syria played a larger part in the life and fortunes of the early Church than any other single city of the Greco-Roman Empire."[49]

An intriguing ancient Christian relic from the city, the "Silver Chalice of Antioch," was purportedly discovered in 1910 while Arab workmen were digging a well in the city.[50] Measuring 7.5 inches high and 6 inches in diameter, it consists of a plain silver inner cup and an outer silver holder, which is heavily gilded. The worked exterior of the outer holder portrays Christ in two scenes, centered in each with five apostles around him. Through spaces in this framework the inner cup is visible. Some have speculated that the reason such a beautiful container holds a rather ordinary silver cup is because this was, indeed, the cup of the last supper. World-class authorities have dated the outer vessel anywhere between the second and sixth centuries. Recent studies prove the cup is not a modern forgery,[51] but neither has it so far been shown to date to the first century.[52]

Damascus

Damascus, Syria, located about 130 miles north of Jerusalem, is one of the oldest, continuously inhabited cities in the world. Paul was converted on the outskirts of the city around A.D. 34 (Acts 9:3–9; 22:6–11; 26:12–18) and spent some time there after his conversion (Acts 9:19b–22; Gal. 1:15–17). About 37, during the time of Aretas IV, he left the city clandestinely (Acts 9:23–25; 2 Cor. 11:32–33).[53] Damascus first came under Roman control in the time of Pompey (64 B.C.).[54] At the time of Paul's visit several synagogues in Damascus (Acts 9:2) served a large Jewish community. Part of this community was in some way affiliated with the Essenes at Qumran.[55] According to Josephus, in A.D. 66 citizens of Damascus reacted to the first Jewish revolt by slaughtering 10,500 Jews.[56]

The importance of Damascus as a cultural and commercial center lie in its location at the meeting of three trade routes, one going south to Mecca, one east to Baghdad, and one west to the Mediterranean Sea, Palestine, and Egypt. The Abana River (modern Nahr el-Barada) flowed east along the north side of the city, and the Pharpar (modern Nahr el-'Awaj) passed within about 10 miles south as it coursed eastward.[57] Damascus, thus, had the water resources to be a verdant oasis; some early writers called it a paradise.[58] The city of New Testament times was located in what is now the southeastern section of the city. It was laid out on a typical Hellenistic grid of *insulae*, measuring 300 feet (east to west) by 150 feet (north to south). The insulae are still discernible in the street plan.

A 50-foot-wide street, the colonnaded *cardo maximus* was probably the "street called Straight" (Acts 9:11)[59] and ran east and

A Roman period gate beneath this later wall is associated with Paul's escape from the city.

west. Some columns of this street have been excavated, and others stand amid the modern shops. Other ancient remains along this street include a theater, a monumental Roman arch, and perhaps a palace. Part of the Roman wall has been found about 1000 feet south of the East Gate (Bab Sharqi) beneath Saint Paul's Chapel and Window. Under the present Ottoman gateway, this small chapel was built by Greek Catholics over a gate from the Roman period. Tradition associates the spot with Paul's escape by a basket that was lowered from a window in the wall (2 Cor. 11:33).

Tarsus

As many ancient cities Tarsus enjoyed the military and commercial benefits of being on an important route (between Rome and Syria) and of its proximity to the sea. Cilicia was notorious in the first century B.C. for pirates who operated for decades along its coast. About 68 B.C., Pompey cleared the province of its notorious plunderers in seventy days: Terence B. Mitford writes that Cilicia was then "the paramount military province of Anatolia and guardian of the great strategic route from Ephesus by way of Iconium and the Cilician Gates to Tarsus and so to Syria."[60] Both Strabo[61] and Dio Chrysostom[62] say the Cydnus River cut through the center of the ancient city. About 5 miles south of Tarsus the river flowed into an ancient lake named Rhegma, very near the sea.[63] Lake Rhegma was merely a wide place in the river in 41 B.C. when Cleopatra sailed through in her gilded barge on her way to meet Mark Antony at Tarsus. It grew in size and importance until Strabo called this lake "the naval station of Tarsus."[64] The Cydnus, incidentally, has since changed its course and now bypasses to the east of both Tarsus and the lake.

The city's importance to this survey, of course, is that Paul was also "Saul of Tarsus." Born there (Acts 9:11; 22:3), his family apparently moved at some point to Gischala, a village in Galilee about 7 miles west of Hazor and remained there until the Romans took it.[65] They then returned to Tarsus.

Tarsus was a significant city at the time of Paul, as Luke affirms (Acts 21:39), and Strabo wrote enthusiastically of the people's high interest in education and philosophy, surpassing, he said, "Athens, Alexandria, or any other place that can be named where there have been schools and lectures of philosophers. . . . Tarsus has all kinds of schools of rhetoric; and in general it not only has a flourishing population but also is most powerful, thus keeping up the reputation of the mother-city."[66] Tarsus was a world-famous center of Stoic philosophy and boasted a number of notable philosophers as native sons, among whom were Athenodorus Canaanites and Nestor, both of whom died in the early first century A.D. Athenodorus Canaanites had among his pupils

the emperor Augustus, under whose reign the city reached the zenith of its fame as an educational and intellectual center. The well-known Neo-Pythagorean philosopher Apollonius of Tyana, studied there in the first century.[67]

Remains of the Hellenistic and Roman city still lie buried, perhaps 20 feet beneath the surface of the modern city. Excavations were conducted on the southeastern fringe of the modern city by Hetty Goldman of Bryn Mawr College at Gözlü Kule just before and after World War II. This work produced nothing significant for the Roman period.[68] Material from the excavation is housed at Adana, about 25 miles east of Tarsus. Occasionally local workmen find artifacts, which are displayed in a small museum in Tarsus, but the general paucity of excavated remains from these periods is disappointing. One of the best studies of the geography and history of the city continues to be the work of Sir William Ramsay;[69] Cilicia's history receives an excellent treatment by Mitford in *Aufstieg und Niedergang der römischen Welt*.[70]

Cities in Central Asia Minor

When Paul journeyed westward to the center of Asia Minor, he encountered a very large area which geographically may be called Anatolia or the Anatolian Plateau and politically was defined by Rome as Galatia ("land of the Gauls or Celts").[71] After Pompey conquered Mithradates VI Eupator in 66 B.C., he built a system of three Roman provinces around the shores of Asia Minor beginning in the north with Bithynia and the coastal area of western Pontus, extending southward through Asia, and including an enlarged Cilicia to the east. The interior regions and the eastern sectors were left under the control of subjugated local rulers.[72] One by one these client kingdoms and petty dynasties were absorbed into the growing district of Galatia.[73] Amyntas ruled most of central Asia Minor after Mark Antony placed it under his control in 36 B.C. Amyntas, however, supported Octavian against Antony at the Battle of Actium, and the victorious Octavian increased Amyntas's holdings to include much of Pisidia, Isauria and the western mountainous part of Cilicia called Tracheia.[74] At the death of Amyntas the entire area was made into the Roman province of Galatia by Octavian (Augustus) in 25 B.C. and placed under a Roman governor.[75] Archelaus, king of Cappadocia, came to govern Cilicia Tracheia.

The Galatia that Paul toured, therefore, was diverse, comprising territories originally held by three gallic tribes,[76] Pisidia, Isauria, and Lycaonia. Part of Pamphylia was also included,[77] as was Inner Paphlagonia, to the north.[78] Paul preached in several cities in this area: Antioch, Iconium, Lystra, Derbe, and Perga (Acts 13, 14). Ramsay's explorations through Central Asia Minor a century ago has been supplemented by later histories and archaeological reports, but there is still not much available on some sites beyond the fact that architectural remains and inscriptions show a patronage to Hellenistic culture.[79]

The Hellenistic way of life prevailed in the cities of Asia Minor but did not penetrate very deeply into the countryside. Paul concentrated his efforts in the Greek-speaking urban culture. Local tongues were also spoken in the various regions of the province. For example, Paul heard the Lycaonian language used in Lystra, a city of Lycaonia, one of the least civilized parts of Anatolia and strongly resistant to outside influences. Celtic tribes had settled in Phrygia and the Celtic language became the common speech in Galatia to the east, especially in the country districts.[80] We surmise that most of the rural population did not use Greek because funerary inscriptions in that language are comparatively rare. The Celtic language is not epigraphically attested in Galatia, but it was probably not a written language.[81] The Pisidian language evidently survived under the Roman Empire, but the only epigraphic evidence of it has been found near Lake Egridir, an area described by Strabo as having a mixed Phrygian and Pisidian population.[82]

Antioch and Lystra, both in Pisidia, were Roman colonies established by Augustus. These privileged communities were independent of direct authority of the imperial legate or proconsul. The colonies were also immune from the imperial tax, and their prosperity was a boon to the older Hellenistic cities in which they were planted. At the time Paul visited Antioch, a distinction was still drawn between "colonists" and "natives."[83] That the worshipers of Paul and Barnabas in Acts 14:11 spoke Lycaonian indicates they were not Roman colonists but the less-educated natives.[84] With the Hellenistic natives and the colonists living in one place their cultures were bound to interact. In Pisidian Antioch, for example, inscriptions attest that Latin had given way to Greek. Greek words gradually replaced Latin ones for Roman institutions; *boulē* (βουλή) replaced *senatus* for "senate" or "council." Coin legends indicate the same kind of change.[85]

Evidence of idolatry has been found in the areas of Iconium (Poseidon and Pluto), Lystra (Pluto), and Antioch (Sanctuary of Men Askaenos, an Anatolian deity), and evidence for the worship of Ares is rather widespread.[86] At Lystra, after Paul healed the man who had been a cripple from birth, he and Barnabas were called Zeus and Hermes, gods who had come down "in the likeness of men" (Acts 14:8–12).

Antioch of Pisidia

Antioch, described by Luke as "of Pisidia" (Acts 13:14) and by Strabo as "near Pisidia" (Ἀντιόχειαν τὴν πρὸς τῇ Πισιδίᾳ),[87] is placed on seven hills about a mile northeast of the modern city of Yalvaç (or Yalovatch) in Turkey.[88] Ramsay worked at the site from the 1880s to the 1920s, primarily on inscriptions.[89] Though his partial excavations in the 1920s revealed remains of the Roman period, these were never adequately published.[90] However, extensive surveys and probes conducted in 1983 and 1984 under the direction of Stephen Mitchell have clarified the existing structures and produced maps and diagrams of the entire area.[91] The full circuit of the city walls has been traced, although only short sections are visible above ground. The walls, between 15 and 18 feet thick, were made of rectangular blocks of limestone ashlar masonry enclosing a core of mortar and rubble. Most of Antioch was built in the Julio-Claudian period, primarily under Tiberius and Claudius, though construction began under Augustus.

Antioch's layout shows typical Roman planning, although the contours of the city prevented strict use of a grid. An east-west cardo maximus ran to the Temple of Augustus. In the Severan period (A.D. 193–217) or before, a theater was built over the cardo in such a way that the street ran through a tunnel beneath the seating. As far as is known this was a unique arrangement in Roman architecture.

A north-south *decumanus maximus* broadened at its northern end into an esplanade which led to a nympheum (public-fountain building), built perhaps in the Flavian period under Vespasian,

Titus, and Domitian (A.D. 69–96). A large bathhouse and *palestra* were found west of the nympheum. In the center of the city a colonnaded street could be identified through an inscription as the Tiberia Platea. A triple-arched gateway or propylon connected the Tiberia Platea with stairs that ascended to a large square. An inscription, of which the *Res Gestae* of Augustus was part[92] was probably attached to the propylon. Originally the gate was assigned to the late second century, but advances in the understanding of architectural styling led to a redating of the gate to the first century A.D. A new reading of the inscription from the architrave suggests that it may have been erected in A.D. 50 or 62.[93]

On the east side of the square in the center of Antioch stood the Temple of Augustus.[94] Principally erected in the reign of Tiberius, the temple was a broad hemicycle. The straight side of the structure formed the rear wall of a large terraced platform. The curved side was a two-story portico, styled in the Ionic order above and the Doric order below. The temple, standing on a lofty podium with a tetrastyle porch across the front, was typically Roman. Remains show that elaborate decorations, stylish at the time of Augustus, were carved on its stones—friezes of acanthus scrollwork and of bulls' heads and garlands are especially impressive.[95] Such embellishments testify to the entrenched wealth and power in this imposing city,[96] which confronted the efforts of the Apostle Paul.

Near the Temple of Augustus in the Sanctuary of Men were two Hellenistic temples. Inscribed on the walls of these structures

Frieze of garlanded bull graces the Temple of Augustus at Antioch of Pisidia.

were several hundred short dedications to Men Askaenos. Both temples stood during the time of Paul. The larger was an Ionic peripteral temple with six columns along the short sides and eleven along the long sides. Built on a high, stepped podium, the temple is described by Mitchell as "among the great hill-top sacred sites of south-western Anatolia."[97]

Thus, in the days of the New Testament emperor worship was well established in Antioch of Pisidia, and much of the building seems to have been concerned with establishing the Imperial cult.[98] Paul's monotheistic preaching must have seemed rather strange and Christian worship in private homes rather transient within such a milieu.[99] Throughout the region, Paul would have confronted such pagan superstition in addition to more traditional polytheistic idolatry.

Iconium, Lystra, and Derbe

Iconium, Lystra, and Derbe, cities in the region of Pisidia and Lycaonia, have not been excavated, although the museum at Konya (Iconium) in Turkey houses artifacts of indigenous Anatolian civilizations. Lystra was located about 18 miles southwest of Iconium. The site was identified by J. R. S. Sterrett in 1885 at Zoldera, near Khatyn Serai.

Most of what has been done concerns Derbe, and so we must confine our remarks to that site. The location of Derbe was identified with the mound of Gudelisin by Ramsay, who affirmed that it was an important city on an "Imperial Road" and was, therefore, a station for collecting customs taxes.[100] Because of its importance to the empire financially, the city was honored with the imperial title Claudio-Derbe. In the 1950s Michael Ballance discovered an inscribed white limestone block, probably a statue base, that mentions the people of Derbe.[101] The relevant part of the inscription reads:

. . . ν, Κλαυδιο[δερβητων η βουλη και ο δ]ημος επι Κορνηλιο . . .
[". . . the council and the people of Claudio-Derbe for Cornelius. . . ."]

A dedication by the council and people of Derbe, the inscription dates to A.D. 157. The limestone block, measuring 41 by 27 by 26.5 inches, was found on the slopes of the mound Kerti Hüyük, about 30 miles east of Ramsay's site. Ballance judged that the stone was too heavy to have been moved very far, so he identified this site as ancient Derbe. In June 1962, however, another inscription mentioning Derbe was found in the nearby village of Suduraya.[102] It probably dates to the late fourth or fifth century and reads:

ο θεοφιλεστατος Μιχαιλ επισκοπος Δερβις ["The most God-loving Michael, bishop of Derbe"][103]

Local people said the inscription was found at Devri Sehri, about 2.5 miles southeast of Kerti Hüyük and Ballance later accepted this as the site for Derbe,[104] as did F. F. Bruce initially.[105] Bastiaan Van Elderen considers the provenance of the inscription to be uncertain and defends Kerti Hüyük as Derbe.[106] Bruce came to reverse his view, accepting Van Elderen's identification.[107]

Perga, Attaleia, and Side of Pamphylia

Along the southern coast of Asia Minor, Paul preached in a city of Pamphylia named Perga at the end of his first journey (Acts 14:25). He had not attempted to evangelize the city on an earlier visit (Acts 13:13). Archaeological remains at the 151-acre site of Perga are impressive,[108] although most of them date to late Roman and Byzantine periods. A Greco-Roman theater, which would seat about fourteen thousand, has been partially excavated and a palestra, measuring about 250 feet square, can be dated by a dedicatory inscription to the emperor Claudius, who was reigning when Paul visited the city. It was dedicated by a C. Julius Cornutus and his wife and children.[109]

Recent work at Perga has been productive. A Roman marketplace, which measures 300 feet by 175 feet, has been found south of the Hellenistic Gate. A nympheum of the imperial period stood west of the marketplace. The city walls and towers, built in the third century B.C., are well preserved and were standing at the time of Paul. A gate shaped like a horseshoe in the south wall is the most striking ruin in Perga. The gate is dated to some time in the Roman period, perhaps to Augustus.[110] Foundations of a temple, probably Hellenistic in date, have been discovered about half a mile south of the city near the end of the street. The deity it was built to honor has not yet been discerned at this writing.[111]

Perga lay 10 miles inland from the Mediterranean and was served by the nearby harbor of Attalia (Antalya), a city of 205 acres.[112] Paul left Asia Minor from this harbor after preaching at Perga (Acts 14:25–26), and it is probable that he had entered the region through the same harbor (Acts 13:13), rather than through Side to the east. Except for the large cylindrical mausoleum, which stands on a square base and overlooks the harbor, little of the first century is left at Attalia.[113] Yet, in the city is one of Turkey's best local museums, for it houses much of the statuary excavated by A. M. Mansell at Perga.

The excavations at Side have been similar to those at Perga, and the two cities share similar histories. The majority of the impressive remains at Side, a site of 112 acres,[114] are from the second to fifth centuries and thus do not relate directly to the New Testament.[115] However, remains of some structures in use in Roman times have been preserved; these include portions of the city wall from the second century B.C., two peristyle houses from the same period, and three shops situated between them. Also found is a small fountain-building constructed in A.D. 71. This structure may show what sort of building stood in Ephesus before the city built its monumental nympheum.[116] A small first-century tetrastyle temple stands on a podium in the city.[117] According to Strabo, Side had a flourishing slave market that "the dockyards stood open to the Cilicians, who would sell their captives at auction there."[118] Pompey eliminated this human trafficking before the time of Paul.

Cities in Western Asia Minor

The Book of Revelation is addressed to seven churches—all located in the province of Asia, in western Asia Minor.[1] Since earliest times the main routes of communication in this area were dictated by natural topography, and today, "when the camel has been displaced by the locomotive and the motor-car, the routes have undergone no essential change."[2] Our study of transportation routes in the province has been facilitated greatly by a major work on Roman roads in Asia Minor by David French.[3] Roads ran up the coast from Ephesus to Smyrna and Pergamum, and from there a road ran through the valleys to Thyatira, Sardis, Philadelphia, and Laodicea.

It is no accident that the letters in Revelation 1–3 are arranged in this same sequence. Beginning with Ephesus, the roads follow a geographical semicircle, extending northward, turning to the east, and continuing southward to Laodicea—thus connecting the cities on what must have functioned as an ancient postal route. Ephesus was the largest and most important city of the province. Situated on a commercial harbor, it undoubtedly was a distribution hub for a wide area, circulating goods and correspondence to the other cities.

For Christians, Ephesus was also a "mother church," the base from which Paul evangelized the entire province of Asia over a two-year period (Acts 19:10). The various cities he visited or addressed by letter must have been secondary postal centers for disseminating information to areas farther inland. Paul, for example, asked the church in Colossae to be certain that the Laodicean church read its letter, and vice versa (Col. 4:16). Clearly, the Book of Revelation was meant to be circulated to at least the seven churches to which it was addressed. And if, as is often suggested, the number "seven" has apocalyptic significance as a symbol, the book may have been intended for the entire province. Paul's letter to the church at Ephesus is probably an encyclical, intended for distribution to a wide group of churches. Our oldest and best manuscripts do not include the address "in Ephesus" (ἐν ᾿Εφέσῳ) in verse 1.[4] However, the letter may have been addressed to the mother church in Ephesus, which copied and distributed it to the others, leaving out the destination. Our current texts, then, may represent manuscripts preserved in both forms.

In 1971 I traveled to the cities of the churches of Revelation, to western Asia Minor. My purpose was to investigate the status of archaeological investigation in the area. As might be expected, some cities have received more attention than others. In fact, Philadelphia and Laodicea have never been excavated. Furthermore, some of the cities have extensive remains from the late Roman and Byzantine periods, but remains from the New Testament period are sparse.

Thyatira, Philadelphia, and Laodicea

Thyatira remained untouched until Rustem Duyuran worked there from 1968 to 1971. Soundings on the acropolis revealed a colonnaded stoa, and part of another public building from the Roman city was found.[5] Inscriptions discovered at Thyatira have been published by G. Petzl,[6] and twenty-one of these were gathered into the collection of the Manisa (Turkey) Museum.[7]

Trade guilds, many of them associated with a strong textile industry,[8] endowed Thyatira with much of its importance. Evidently the guild of dyers was especially prosperous.[9] Lydia, whom Paul converted in Philippi, is identified as a woman from Thyatira who sold purple goods (Acts 16:14). The best purple dye was obtained from the murex shellfish, which were available along much of the eastern Mediterranean seaboard. Murex shells are found frequently in excavations close to the the coastline at Cae-

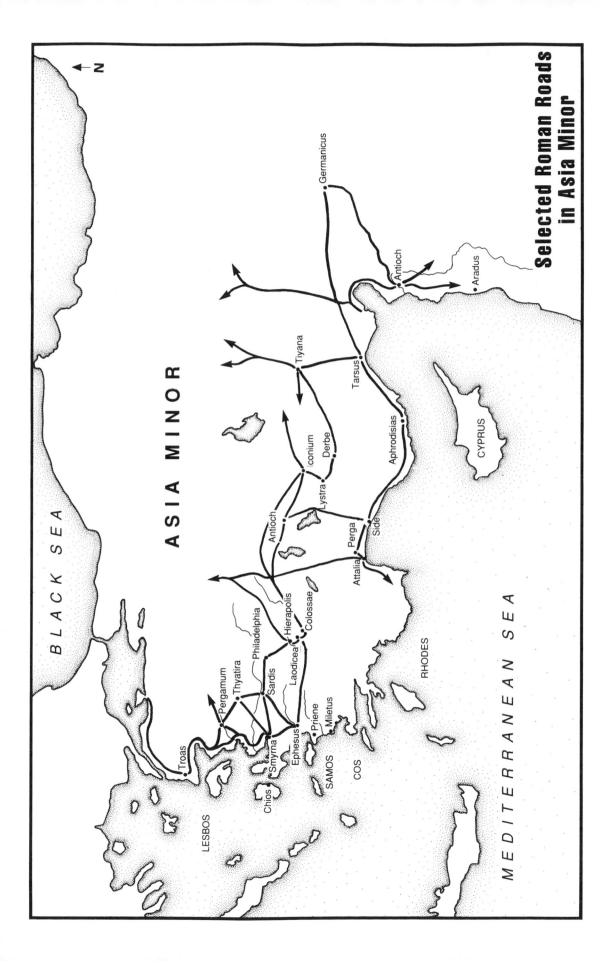

Selected Roman Roads in Asia Minor

N

BLACK SEA

ASIA MINOR

MEDITERRANEAN SEA

Germanicus

Antioch
Aradus

Tiyana

Tarsus

Iconium
Derbe

Aphrodisias

Lystra

Antioch

Perga
Side

Attalia

CYPRUS

Colossae
Hierapolis
Laodicea
Philadelphia
Thyatira
Pergamum
Sardis

Ephesus
Priene
Miletus
Smyrna
Chios

Troas

SAMOS
COS

RHODES

LESBOS

sarea. Phoenicians developed the industry of harvesting shells for dye, and the profitable idea spread through the textile crafts of Asia Minor. The purple dye was expensive, and Lydia was likely a wealthy woman whose business took her as far as Philippi.

Philadelphia remains unexcavated, lying as it does beneath the modern city of Alaşehir, Turkey. Strabo wrote that the city was "ever subject to earthquakes," and that "incessantly the walls of the houses are cracked, different parts of the city being thus affected at different times. For this reason but few people live in the city, and most of them spend their lives as farmers in the country, since they have a fertile soil."[10] As recently as 1969, Alaşehir was near the epicenter of an earthquake.[11] Consequently, any excavations at the site would reveal a chaotic history.

The entire Meander Valley was subject to seismic activity, according to Strabo.[12] Laodicea, situated near where the Lycus River empties into the Meander, was destroyed during the reign of Augustus, who assisted in its reconstruction.[13] In A.D. 17, it was damaged again. and Tiberius helped with the rebuilding.[14] Laodicea was not at first a wealthy city,[15] but by the time of the next serious earthquake in A.D. 60 the Laodiceans rebuilt without any outside aid from Nero.[16] Such a proud, self-sufficient attitude is indicated in the Book of Revelation, where the Laodicean church is depicted as saying, "I am rich, I have prospered, and I need nothing" (3:17 RSV).

Laodicea lies largely unexcavated, a frequent victim of earthquakes in New Testament times.

Laodicea has never been extensively excavated, so we must infer much of our information from coins and inscriptions.[17]

Known originally as Diospolis ("the City of Zeus"), it claimed Zeus as its chief deity.[18] Nothing of the temple has been discovered; only a few traces of the city wall and portions of the city's three gates are visible. The Syrian Gate on the east side of the city is the best preserved of the gates. Two theaters lie on the northeast slope of the low, flat-topped hill on which the city rests. Seats of the larger Greek theater are visible, and the smaller Roman theater which opens to the northwest still contains some of its upper seats. A stadium, about 1250 feet long, is poorly preserved. Cicero in June of 50 B.C. spoke of gladiatorial combat at Laodicea.[19] Inscriptions show that the stadium itself was dedicated to Vespasian in A.D. 79 by a wealthy citizen, and the ceremony of consecration was performed by the proconsul of Asia, the father of the future emperor Trajan.[20] Part of a bathhouse, which was dedicated to the emperor Hadrian and his wife Sabina, still stands. In antiquity it was fed by an aqueduct that connected it to a water tower nearby. Today the water tower stands to a height of about 15 feet, and several miles of the aqueduct may still be traced. A third-century nympheum, also uses water running by pipes from the tower and is the only structure in Laodicea thus far excavated. It was dug by a team of French archaeologists from 1961 to 1963 and dated to the third century A.D.[21]

An inscription erected by a freed slave from Laodicea was dedicated to Marcus Sestius Philemon.[22] It will be recalled that a Philemon who owned the slave Onesimus (Philem. 10)[23] was a leader in the church of Colossae. We cannot identify this Philemon with the slaveholder to whom Paul wrote, but the coincidence of the inscription from the same area is intriguing, especially since it refers to the manumission of a slave.

Hierapolis and Colossae

A similarly interesting inscription reminds us that Laodicea is intertwined with Colossae, and Hierapolis in the New Testament. Christianity was probably brought to all three cities by Epaphras, a companion of Paul and native of Colossae (Col. 1:5–8; 4:12; Philem. 23). The inscription, found in Colossae, mentions the name T. Asinius Epaphroditus.[24] Incidentally, Epaphras is probably a shortened form of Epaphroditus.[25] Since Epaphroditus was another companion of Paul (Phil. 2:25; 4:18), were it not unlikely on other grounds, the two names could refer to the same person.[26] Unfortunately, as in the case with the Philemon inscription, there is no way to connect the name on the inscription found at Colossae either to the region's evangelist or to Epaphroditus.

As one scans the lovely view north across the Lycus Valley from Laodicea, the name for modern Pamukkale seems very appropriate; even 6 miles away the limestone hill of ancient Hierapolis appears very much like a "cotton castle."[27] White mineral deposits collected over millennia around putrid warm springs at this resort town. Perhaps the sensuality of bathing in the spring waters infected residents of neighboring Laodicea and prompted the graphic warning of Revelation 3:16: to declare of the city's conduct, "because you are lukewarm, and neither cold nor hot, I will vomit (ἐμέω) you out of my mouth" (author's translation). Such a reaction is natural when tasting the water of Laodicea and Hierapolis. Water piped into Laodicea by aqueduct from the south was so concentrated with minerals that the Roman engineers designed vents, capped by removable stones, so the aqueduct pipes could periodically be cleared of deposits.

Hierapolis contains a number of impressive ruins, although few can be dated to New Testament times. With Laodicea, Hierapolis was destroyed by the earthquakes of A.D. 17 and 60. As part of the reconstruction that lasted through the Flavian period, Domitian considerably enlarged the city. The central northwest-southeast street was colonnaded; triple-arched gates flanked by round towers marked either end. The northwestern complex of gates and towers, still well-preserved, may be dated to 84 or 85 by a dedicatory inscription to Domitian from the proconsul of Asia, Sextus Julius Frontinus. Along the main street a series of buildings, probably shops, were built in the Flavian period. Part of the city's agora, with a monumental portico on the west and a mon-

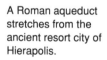

A Roman aqueduct stretches from the ancient resort city of Hierapolis.

umental building (Caesareum) on the east were built at about the same time.

Archaeological work continues at Hierapolis[28] including an impressive reconstruction of the second-century-A.D. theater—one of the better-preserved theaters in Asia Minor. Its *cavea* is about 330 feet wide and contains about fifty rows of seats. The *pulpitum* and *scaenae frons* are also well preserved. Northeast of the theater is an octagonal shrine of the fifth or sixth century, identified either with the Apostle Philip[29] or with Philip the Evangelist (Acts 6:5). Polycrates, a bishop in Ephesus in the late second century, recorded Hierapolis as the burial place for Philip the Evangelist.[30] In either case the Philip could have been part of the large Jewish community known to have lived there by inscriptional evidence.[31]

Excavations have also uncovered the temple of Apollo, the principal deity of Hierapolis. In its present state, the temple dates no earlier than the third century A.D., but it replaced an older one. On the southeast a pagan sanctuary called the Plutoneion adjoined the temple. It may be partially visible in a shelf of the hillside, just below the side wall of the temple. This shelf shows evidence of a roofed chamber about 10 feet square beside a swift stream. Poisonous gases emitted by the spring at the Plutoneion were mentioned by early authors,[32] but they are no longer present.

The site of ancient Colossae has never been excavated, though the Near East Archaeological Society has frequently applied for an excavation permit from the government of Turkey.[33] Inscriptions from the time of Trajan and later have been found on the mound which stands about 75 feet above the valley.[34] Remains of a theater, a necropolis, and various other buildings are barely evident.[35] At one time on the western end of the mound, a square shaft, faced with masonry, was open. When George Bean explored the site his guide claimed to have descended the shaft on a long rope "till he could no longer breathe, without reaching the bottom."[36]

The size of New Testament-era Colossae is not clear. Strabo seems to contrast Colossae, Aphrodisias, and other *polismata* (πολίσματα—"towns") with *poleis* (πόλεις—"cities") such as Laodicea, but a lacuna in the text poses unanswerable questions about the certainty of the reference.[37] For centuries the very location of Colossae was unknown. In fact, a medieval tradition identified Rhodes, an island near the southwestern coast of Turkey, as Colossae, based on a supposed connection between the name of the city (Κολοσσαί) and the name of the huge statue which stood in the harbor of Rhodes, the Colossus (κολοσσός).[38]

Ephesus, Sardis, Pergamum, and Smyrna

Archaeological remains at Ephesus, Sardis, Pergamum, and Smyrna are significantly greater than those at Thyatira, Philadelphia, and Laodicea, but evidence from the New Testament period is typically meager. Recently an article in a leading archaeological journal characterized the remains at Ephesus this way: "Current excavations at Ephesus have revealed an elaborate Roman city of the second to sixth centuries C.E., but evidence of the first-century city remains sparse."[39] One reason why there is so little with which to work is that the Roman cities along the western coast of Asia Minor were renovated Hellenistic cities. George Hanfmann has observed:

> Roman foundations of new cities were rare in western coastlands of Asia Minor and there was little opportunity to use the overall standard Roman colonial plan. A small city like Priene retained a basically Hellenistic appearance until the Byzantine age. It is rather the enlargement and transformation of *existing* towns and cities, their expansion for a growing population, the raising of the standard of living through better supply systems, utilities, and baths, the development of large facilities for social, intellectual, and leisure functions, and the expression of this revitalized, Romanized Greek polis in luxurious, nearly Baroque architectural forms—that made the cities of Asia the envy of the empire.[40]

Indeed, Ephesus, Sardis, Pergamum, and Smyrna were, in many respects, the envy of the empire. They were the four largest cities in the province of Asia.[41] Ephesus was the center of the worship of Diana, boasting one of the Seven Wonders of the Ancient World as her sanctuary. Pergamum contained the world-renowned Asklepieion, a major medical center of the Roman Empire. Sardis possessed an elaborate temple of Artemis, a magnificent gymnasium, and one of the oldest colonnaded streets in the East. Smyrna, along with Ephesus and Pergamum, maintained sanctuaries to the imperial cult.[42]

Ephesus

The city of Ephesus was encompassed by a wall from the time of Lysimachus in the third century B.C.[43] Part of the wall may be seen on both Mount Koressos and Mount Pion, between which the main thoroughfare of the city ran. The only portion of a gate to survive is the Magnesian Gate, which was erected by Vespasian.[44] Ephesus held about two hundred thousand people and was described in one inscription found there as "a most illustrious city" (λαμπροτατος Εφεσιων πολεως).[45] Strabo called it "the greatest emporium in Asia, I mean Asia in the special sense of

Figure 24
Schematic of Ephesus

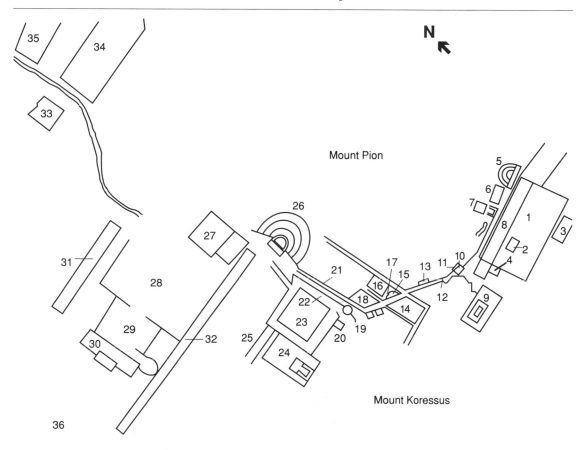

1 State (civic) agora	7 Town hall	14 Private houses	20 Celsus Library
2 Temple of Augustus	8 Basilica	15 Temple of Hadrian	21 Marble Road
3 Fountain	9 Temple of Domitian	16 Scholastica baths	22 Stoa of Nero
4 Pollio fountain	10 Memmius Monument	17 Latrine	23 Commercial agora
5 Odeion (bouleuterion)	11 Fountain	18 Brothel	24 Temple of Serapis
6 Temples of Divus Iulius	12 Curetes Street	19 Auditorium (Lecture hall	(?)
and Dea Roma	13 Nympheum of Trajan	of Tyrannus?)	25 West Gate of Agora
			26 Theater
			27 Gymnasium
			28 Verulan Hall
			29 Palestra of harbor
			gymnasium
			30 Harbor baths
			31 Church of Mary
			32 Arcadius Street
			33 Meat market
			34 Stadium
			35 Vedius gymnasium
			36 Harbor

that term [Asia Minor]."[46] When Paul entered Ephesus, he was confronted with an array of Greco-Roman structures and commercial, religio-political, and civic institutions.[47]

Commercial Facilities of Ephesus

Commerce, trade guilds, and banking made Ephesus preeminent. Money was kept on state property and in the Temple of Artemis, deposited by out-of-town people—private citizens as well as kings—from all over the Mediterranean world.[48] The average Ephesian, however, was "less prosperous than many" citizens of other Asian cities. Much wealth and trade came into Ephesus through its fine harbor, which eventually silted up because inept engineers tried to counter the problem of silting by narrowing the entrance channel.[49] The result of such a counterproductive measure still plagues the harbor, and it remains silt-laden, but at this writing underwater investigations will soon be made to establish the original shape of the 23-foot-deep lagoon.[50]

Excavations in the lower (commercial) agora have determined that the pre-Lysimachan city was laid out on a grid,[51] even though the major processional road ran between Mount Koressos and Mount Pion.[52] The layout of the housing complex (called by excavators "Hanghäus I") southeast of the lower agora and Celsus Library corresponds to the Hippodamian scheme.[53] The main thoroughfare of Ephesus was composed of several streets. The Curetes Street proceeded westward and then northwestward from the Magnesian Gate at the east wall to the lower agora. There it turns northward and becomes the "Marble Road," although marble pavement was added by Eutropius, probably in the fifth century. This portion ran along the full length of the eastern side of the agora. In front of the theater Stadion Street takes over and continued northward. At the theater another major colonnaded thoroughfare, 36 feet wide and almost 2000

Curetes Street, Ephesus.

The Ephesian
commercial agora.

feet long, extended west to the harbor. It was also a later addition, built by the emperor Arcadius (395–408) and named the Arcadian Way. However, the Arcadian Way may have upgraded an existing street. A Hellenistic gate has been found on the axis of this street at the harbor end,[54] and it is reasonable to assume that a street from the harbor to the theater must have been one of the first building projects of the city.

The commercial agora, situated in the heart of Ephesus, was renovated by both Augustus and Nero. It was 360 feet square, surrounded by shops and double-aisled stoas. Some of the shops on the south side remain intact. An elevated doubled-aisled stoa with Doric colonnades, from the time of Nero, lies on the east side. This esplanade was 5.5 feet high, with steps on its north and south ends; affording a lovely view of both the road on the east and the agora on the west.[55] The Mazaeus and Mithridates Gate is being restored as far east as the Neronic stoa.[56] This southeastern gate to the agora was built by the men for whom it was named in 4 or 3 B.C., according to an inscription.[57]

Religious and Political Institutions

Ephesus also had a 525-foot-long state agora in the upper eastern part of the city and enclosed on its north by a 65-foot-wide basilica. The colonnades of the agora feature unique Ionic bull's-head capitals. Written in both Greek and Latin, the bronze dedicatory inscription mentions Augustus and Tiberius (as well as

A statue of Artemis (Diana) was one of three found at the prytaneion.

Artemis), so the state agora may be dated to the early imperial period. Corinthian columns were added in the late empire. Law courts were probably convened on this agora, while state affairs were conducted across the street at a *prytaneion* ("town hall"). A temple, probably Augustan, stood in the center of the agora.

Along with the sanctuary of Hestia Boulaia and the state apartments, the prytaneion was the center for religious and political life. Three statues of Ephesian Artemis found in the prytaneion now reside in the museums of Selÿuk and Izmir in Turkey. These statues, depicting either multiple breasts or eggs, emphasize the goddess's fertility. One of the statues, twice life size, was sculpted in the reign of Domitian. Various banquets, ceremonies, and receptions also were held in the complex. It also housed the city's state clerk, the *grammateus* (γραμματεύς).[58] Several inscriptions found in the city refer to this office, one identifying Laberius Amoenus as "the clerk or secretary of the people" (ο γραμμ[ατευς του δ]ημου).[59] The state clerk of Ephesus came from his headquarters in the prytaneion to the theater on its north side to placate the mob that was protesting the work of Paul (Acts 19:35–41).

It is noteworthy that among Paul's "friends" (φίλοι) in Ephesus, Luke counts political figures of wealth and power called *Asiarchs* (Ἀσιάρχαι; Acts 19:31). At least two men are said to have simultaneously held both the office of clerk of the people and Asiarch.[60] Asiarchs, the "foremost men of the province of Asia, chosen from the wealthiest and the most aristocratic inhabitants of the province,"[61] were elected by the citizens with the expectation that they would personally finance public games and festivals.[62] Ephesus, Strabo said, "is as well peopled as any other city in Asia by people of means (εὐπόρων ἀνθρώπων, *euporōn anthrōpōn*); and always some of its men hold the chief places in the province, being called *Asiarchs*."[63] Asiarch inscriptions have been found in more than forty cities throughout Asia.

Dio Chrysostom, writing at the end of the first century A.D., seemed to suggest that Asiarchs may have been high priests, or at least that a high priest of the imperial cult was chosen from among them.[64] Ephesus, Pergamum, and Smyrna were the most important cities of Asia in which emperor worship was practiced. Considerable disagreement has existed among scholars about the supposed dual function of these officials but recent developments in archaeology have greatly enhanced our ability to evaluate the role of Asiarchs in Asia Minor in the first and second centuries. In 1974, M. Rossner used inscriptions to identify 74 Asiarchs or high priests of Asia in Ephesus. That figure had to be changed, though, with the monumental publication of the repertory of inscriptions from Ephesus, containing 3500 inscriptions,[65] many of them previously unknown and some dating to within fifty years of the events described in Acts 19.[66] The number of Asiarchs in Ephesus now stands at 106, including both men and women.[67] R. A. Kearsley has now shown that the office of asiarch and that of high priest were separate offices in the late first and early second centuries, and that there is no evidence that the asiarch was a priest, although he had some religious functions.[68]

That such men were friends of Paul may suggest that the wealthy and educated people of Ephesus were not as opposed to Paul as the superstitious crowd in the theater, and that Paul's ministry was not exclusively oriented to the poor and uneducated. The relationship probably also suggests that the policy of the

Roman Empire toward Christianity at this time was not one of hostility.[69] But there was opposition in Ephesus to Paul's monotheism, opposition rooted in the long polytheistic history of the city.

It is not difficult to imagine Paul's impressions of Ephesus as he walked through the city and observed its religious institutions, such as the overwhelming beauty of the Temple of the Ephesian Artemis. Firsthand the apostle witnessed the citizens' intense devotion to the pagan idol in the two-hour-long demonstration in the theater in her behalf. The Temple of Artemis in Ephesus had been destroyed and rebuilt more than once, but the most impressive reconstruction is credited to Croesus, the Lydian king of Sardis which began in 560 B.C. The rebuilt temple's architecture was Ionic. Measuring 377 feet by 197 feet, the temple was the first monumental structure ever constructed of marble and the largest building in the Greek world.[70]

The wooden ceiling and inner architrave of the Croesus temple building were burned in 356 B.C. by an arsonist who sought by his act to achieve eternal fame. It was rebuilt by the citizens, who refused the help of Alexander the Great. The new structure essentially retained the dimensions of the older one, although recent studies have shown it to be wider (235 feet).[71] This was the temple standing in New Testament times. It was burned by the Goths in 263 and completely destroyed by Justinian in the sixth century to provide building material for his Saint Sophia Church. Virtually nothing is left of the famed structure except for portions of the foundations constructed by Croesus, recently discovered sections of the north and south faces of Croesus's building,[72] and part of the great altar on the west side of the temple.[73] From what was found the excavator described the altar as a large sacrificial stone table and ramp with walls around three sides and with an opening to the west that formed a courtyard about 100 feet by 50 feet.

A number of other temples dominated the skyline of ancient pagan Ephesus. The temple in the center of the state agora was an Ionic or Corinthian peristyle structure, 36 feet by 20 feet. It may have been built under Augustus as a Sebasteion (Augusteum) rather than as a temple to Isis or Dionysus, as previously thought.[74] North of this agora, between the prytaneion and the odeion, two small temples were built in 29 B.C. to Divus Iulius and Dea Roma. These were constructed by the emperor or, as it now seems, by Mark Antony. A colossal head of Antony was recently found nearby.[75] The extent to which the imperial cult was established in Ephesus is strikingly revealed in life-size marble busts of Augustus (father of the emperor Tiberius) and his wife Livia found *in situ* in excavations of private houses in Ephesus (Insula VII of the *Hanghäuser* excavations). The imperial family seems to have been worshiped even "in a private context as guarantors of peace and prosperity."[76]

A portion of the long-sought Olympeion (Hadrian's Temple of Jupiter) has been found in Ephesus in the area around and under the Church of Saint Mary.[77] A Corinthian-style Temple of Hadrian stands, partially preserved, on Curetes Street, with the figure of a girl depicted on the arch-shaped tympanum over the entrance to the cella. A Temple of Domitian stood adjacent to the state agora on its west side; this temple, surmounting a massive substructure measuring 165 feet by 330 feet, housed a colossal cult statue of Domitian. Sitting, the statue would have been 16 feet high, and standing the figure would have been 23 feet tall. The head and 6-foot-long forearm are preserved in the Izmir Museum.[78]

According to patristic sources, the apostle John was exiled to Patmos from Ephesus during the reign of Domitian, who died in 96.[79] According to these same sources, John returned to Ephesus under Nerva and died there under Trajan, who reigned from 98 to 117.[80] Thus, some of the buildings at Ephesus that date to this time would possibly coincide with the presence of John, whether he be the apostle John or the presbyter John.[81] The Book of Revelation is set against the background of provincial Asia at this time. The Church of Saint John, on a hill northeast of the city, is not earlier than the fourth century, though there are second-century legends that place the burial of John under the apse of this building.[82]

Worship of the Roman emperor through an imperial cult was authorized for the provinces of Asia and Bithynia in 29 B.C. under Augustus, whose temple in Pergamum was the first in Asia built to an emperor.[83] Tiberius, unlike Augustus, resisted emperor worship, but in his desire to maintain the general policies of his predecessor acquiesced to a request by Asia in A.D. 23 and authorized a temple to be built for him, his wife, and the Roman senate.[84] This temple was raised in Smyrna in 26, after three years of squabbling by the Roman senate.[85] The third temple for the imperial cult was constructed in Ephesus, probably in the reign of Claudius.[86]

Sometime in the late first century, probably during the reign of Domitian, Pergamum, Smyrna and Ephesus were honored for their role as seats of emperor worship and were officially designated *neōkoroi* (νεωκόροι—"temple-wardens"),[87] a term used by the Clerk of the City of Ephesus in Acts 19:35. Whereas in Acts the term may only have "referred to the Ephesians as worshippers of Artemis,"[88] in the second century *neōkoros* became a title conferred by Rome on cities in which there was "a temple founded for the worship of the emperors."[89] It appears in its full form νεωκορος των Σεβαστων (*neōkoros tōn Sebastōn* "temple-warden of the Augusti") in numerous inscriptions from the second century and later. For example, an inscription found in Ephesus, dating to between 162 and 164, reads in part:

[εδ]οξεν της πρωτης και με[γιστης μητρ]οπολεως της Ασιας και δις νεωκ[ορου των Σεβα]στων και φιλοσεβαστου Εφε[σιων πολεως τη βο]υλη και τω δημω ["It was decreed by the council and people of the patriotic city of the Ephesians, first and greatest metropolis of Asia, *temple-warden* of the Augusti two times"].[90]

Some cities (e.g. Pergamum, Smyrna, and Ephesus) built two temples and were designated as "twice temple-wardens";[91] a few of the more important cities even became "thrice temple-wardens."[92]

The care of the temples, the handling of the sacred funds, and the recording of public documents (often on the temple walls) were entrusted to a board of men known as *neopoiai* (νεοποιαι—temple-wardens) a term which seems to have been used synonymously with *neōkoioi* in the inscriptions.[93] The term *neopoiai* appears frequently in inscriptions from Ephesus, both in the form *neopoios* (νεοποιος) and *neōpoios* (νεωποιος).[94] Demetrius the silversmith (Acts 19:24) could have been one of these officials. Though one inscription does indeed mention a Demetrius who was a *neopoios*, William Ramsay has rejected the identification of this man with the Demetrius mentioned in Acts.[95] In an inscription from the time of Claudius or later, a man named M. Antonius Hermeias is called a "silversmith" and "Temple-Warden" (αργυροκοπου νεοποιου, *argyrokopou neopoiou*).[96] This same inscription refers to an Ephesian "guild of silversmiths" (συνεδριον των αργυροκοπων, *sunedrion tōn argyrokopōn*) that was commissioned to care for a grave site. Franz Miltner, it has been reported, found the shops of the silversmiths in his excavations in the agora.[97] A number of inscriptions in the *IEph* series contain references to silversmiths, and these references are dated much closer to the time of Acts than the papyrus citations recorded in standard Greek lexicons.[98]

Civic Architecture in Ephesus

The most impressive structure still standing at Ephesus is the theater, whose cavea seated twenty-four thousand on three levels of twenty-two rows each, reaching a height of almost 100 feet. The scaenae frons was three stories high; a large pulpitum and *proskenion* have been partially restored. Originally built in Hellenistic times, the theater was enlarged under Claudius about the time Paul was in the city, and also by Nero.

It has been suggested that the Book of Revelation may have been written to be produced on this very stage.[99] In this theater the crowd, incited by the silversmiths who feared the economic impact of Christianity on their livelihood, gathered to protest the missionary work of Paul.[100] The silversmiths crafted images of Artemis, the Roman Diana (Acts 19:23–41). A Greek and Latin inscription found in the theater, tells that a Roman official provided a silver image of Artemis and other statues to be displayed in the theater when civic meetings were held there.[101] An inscription at Ephesus touches on another trade which was mentioned by Paul, who wrote to Timothy regarding "Alexander the coppersmith," who opposed him while he taught in Ephesus (2 Tim. 4:14–15). Timothy was probably in Ephesus when he received the letter (1 Tim. 1:3). The inscription refers to the workplace of "Diogenes the *charkōmatas*" (χαρκωματας—coppersmith).[102]

Lovely fountains were built by Caius Sextilius Pollio between A.D. 4 and 14. A section of the 3.5-mile, two-tiered aqueduct that brought water to the many fountains from the Marnas River is well preserved.[103] A monumental fountain stood on the south side of the state agora, and southwest of the fountain was a nympheum built in A.D. 80 by the proconsul C. Laecanius Bassus. Running along the west side of the agora, there is a little street leading to the Temple of Domitian, which is appropriately called Domitian Street. Near its junction with Curetes Street, a monument erected in the Augustan period honored Gaius Asinius Pollio, an orator, playwrite, soldier, and statesman who lived from 75 B.C. to 5 A.D. A nympheum was added to this monument in A.D. 93. On the north side of Curetes Street, in the same general area, a late Hellenistic monument honored C. Memmius, grandson of

The Roman theater at Ephesus seated 24,000.

the Roman general and dictator Lucius Cornelius Sulla (138–78 B.C.). A structure identified by inscription as a fountain was placed on its northwest side in the first century A.D. Further west, on the north side of Curetes Street, a fountain was built and dedicated sometime before A.D. 114. A colossal statue of Trajan, more than two stories high, stood in the center of the fountain on a base with a globe. The base, globe, and feet have been restored.

An inscription also has identified a house of prostitution, located on the north side of the intersection of Curetes Street and the Marble Road. The brothel was large enough to be connected to the aqueduct, and was constructed in the latter part of the first century A.D. Recent excavations have determined that it was built over domestic housing from earlier in the century.[104] Around 400 a Christian woman named Scholastica renovated the structure as a bathhouse.

A number of civic structures using the water supply of Ephesus were built just after the New Testament period but are, nevertheless, worth a brief note. The huge Harbor Gymnasium and Bath was constructed on the west side of the harbor, primarily during the reign of Domitian. It was completed under Hadrian with the addition of marble facing for the *palestra*. The much smaller Theater Gymnasium, situated between the Harbor Gymnasium and the theater, was probably constructed in the second century. A private bath on the east side of the odeion, and a gymnasium at the Magnesian Gate were probably built by Flavius Damianus in the third quarter of the second century. The huge Vedius Gymnasium, near the northern wall of the city, is one of the best-preserved buildings in Ephesus. It was erected by Publius Vedius Antoninus, a wealthy Ephesian, in 150.

Ephesus was not without its symbol of pagan lust for human suffering. An inscription found on a part of the north wall of the stadium indicates that it was rebuilt during the reign of Nero. Adjacent to the Vedius Gymnasium in the northern part of the city, the stadium was used for festivals, athletic contests, and the racing of horses and chariots. A circular area at the eastern end was designated for gladiatorial fights and animal baiting. Paul wrote that "humanly speaking" (*kata anthrōpon*, κατὰ ἄνθρωπον), he "fought with wild beasts at Ephesus" (1 Cor. 15:32, author's translation). It is not likely that Paul literally fought beasts in the arena because he was a Roman citizen and could not be forced to engage in this activity reserved for slaves and captives, and had he inadvertently been forced into the arena as he was mistakenly jailed and whipped in Philippi, his deliverance would surely have been a miracle warranting mention in an epistle or in Acts. If arrested he would undoubtedly have appealed to his citizenship, as he did at Philippi and Caesarea, to prevent such combat. Opinions of translators vary slightly, but Paul perhaps compared arena combat with opposition from "beasts" of a human sort (*kata anthrōpon*).[105]

One of the most prominent civic structures in Ephesus was the Library of Celsus, the subject of a recent and impressive reconstruction at its site south of the lower agora. Built to honor Gaius Julius Celsus Polemaeanus by his son, according to Greek and Latin inscriptions on the wings of the front steps[106] the library was begun in A.D. 110 and finished in 135. Celsus was consul in 92 and later proconsul of Asia.[107]

Ekrem Akurgal locates an auditorium or lecture hall (αὐδειτώριον—*audeitōrion*; from Lat. *auditorium*) just east of the front of the library. The hall is mentioned in a first-century inscription[108] and is noteworthy because Luke states that Paul reasoned daily in Ephesus in the hall or school (σχολή) of Tyrannus (Acts 19:9). Colin J. Hemer has argued that the Greek words αὐδειτώριον and σχολή were virtually synonymous.[109] The "Auditorium" is a subject of discussion,[110] but little, if any, of the actual structure has been uncovered, although portions of a circular Hellenistic platform destroyed when the auditorium was constructed have been revealed.[111]

Sardis

Sardis, whose first-century population has been estimated at one hundred twenty thousand, dominated the Hermus Valley.[112] Tributaries to the Hermus River made the Hermus Valley "the broadest and most fertile of all the river-basins of Asia Minor."[113] The city lay to the west of the acropolis which stood on a projecting spur of Mount Tmolus. The Pactolus River, famed for its gold,

Near the lower agora the Ephesian Celsus Library has been reconstructed.

flowed beside the Temple of Artemis.[114] Pliny the Elder wrote that the region of Lydia was famous for the city of Sardis, "situated on the vine-clad side of Mount Tmolus . . . from which the Pactolus flows."[115] In addition to gold, the area was famous for fishnets and textiles.[116]

Ancient literary sources record that an earthquake devastated Sardis in A.D. 17 during the reign of Tiberius.[117] Pliny the Elder called it "the greatest earthquake in human memory,"[118] and Strabo wrote that it "severely harmed Sardis."[119] Both Pliny and Tacitus recorded that twelve cities were destroyed in one night, but Tacitus judged that "the disaster was harshest to the citizens of Sardis and brought them the largest share of pity."[120] It is to be expected that a quake of that dimension would disrupt the continuity of the city's architecture and necessitate reconstruction; such is definitely the case at Sardis, where remains from before the quake are sparse. Effects of the disaster on Sardis were comparable to those of the great fire which destroyed a large segment of Rome in A.D. 64. Both allowed rebuilding on a new pattern. Even landscape forms were altered.

The emperor Tiberius responded with generous aid, and remitted taxes for five years.[121] His grateful people honored Tiberius with erection of a colossus in Rome and undoubtedly with statues at Sardis. In 1979 a statue base inscription feting the emperor as the "Founder of the City" was uncovered.[122] From the time of the earthquake until at least the reign of Claudius, the city called itself Caesareia Sardianeon. Claudius also helped with the rebuilding of Sardis. He completed, among other things, the aqueduct begun by Tiberius.[123] Only traces of the aqueduct have been found.[124]

The new city was not laid out on a grid, but it did follow a plan. The Marble Road divided the city into northern and southern sections and the East Road provided the axis for an east-west division. The reconstruction plan particularly used the Marble Road as a demarcation line. Most public buildings were placed north of this road, while the residential section, comprising an area about twice as large, was set to the south. For the sake of convenience the residential area did include temples, a theater, a stadium, and some other nonresidential buildings. A colonnaded main avenue, the Marble Road, stretched from the river eastward for 4600 feet, running by the south side of the gymnasium area. The 50-foot-wide avenue, paved with marble blocks, was probably begun under Tiberius and finished under Claudius. At the south edge of the road the statue honoring Tiberius[125] stood along a raised pedestrian sidewalk;[126] the colonnade bordering the early Roman street was probably 16 feet wide. Though the Marble Road street ran very near the ancient Persian imperial road from Susa to Sardis,[127] excavations thus far have not revealed remains of the Persian roadway. The East Road intersected the Marble Road at the southeast corner of the gymnasium-bath.

Imperial Sardis is largely unexcavated. The gymnasium-bath complex is the most impressive visible archaeological feature but it touches only slightly on the New Testament era. The building as it was rebuilt in Byzantine times has been carefully reconstructed. It stood in the northern part of the city and rests upon remains of an earlier structure. It is this earlier gymnasium which might be of more importance to this study. The western section of the earlier building probably was built during the last half of the first century or the first half of the second century.[128] Something similar can be said of an adjacent synagogue. There are impressive visible remains that date from after the fourth century;[129] Hellenistic and Roman levels lie beneath them. Earlier levels of the synagogue were part of the pagan gymnasium. The gymnasium was reused as a civic basilica and sometime later, perhaps as early as the third century, was turned over to the Jewish community for use as a synagogue. Between the synagogue and the street a monumental building was contained within the southern portion of the gymnasium complex. The monument was begun in the renewal of the city after the quake, but little of it remains, except the large foundation walls below the stylobate and the

Modern restoration work proceeds on the gymnasium complex at Sardis.

front wall of the Byzantine shops that replaced it. A fragment of a column from the monumental building has been discovered, and this shows that the original columns were larger than those that replaced them in Byzantine times.

The agora was surely set somewhere in this northern, public area of Sardis, but that location is unknown. It must have been in an elevated area because there was a "Downroad from the Agora" (κάθοδος ἀγορᾶς, *kathodos agoras*).[130] Also unidentified is the Temple of Augustus, which was built before 5 B.C. With many other buildings this temple vanishes from history after the earthquake.[131]

South of the Marble road stood the residential district, called the HOB (House of Bronzes) area by excavators. The terrace houses, of modest construction and small courtyards, resemble the Hanghäuser (slope house) style in Ephesus.[132] A first-century stadium was strategically situated between the homes and the public area, just south of the Marble Road and about 3500 feet from the gymnasium-bath. About 600 feet of the fragmented northern wall of a first century A.D. stadium are preserved.[133] On the stadium's south side are the sparse remains of a Hellenistic theater which was rebuilt after A.D. 17.[134] R. L. Vann calculates that it would seat between twelve and fifteen thousand spectators.[135] Neither the theater nor the stadium has been excavated.

A bathhouse found outside the eastern walls may have been added after the earthquake. It was located at an especially good supply of water.

One of the most impressive structures at Sardis is the Temple of Artemis. It was probably begun in the third century B.C. and underwent three constructions, the last over the century and a half following the 17 earthquake.[136] Excavation began in 1910 under the direction of Princeton's Howard Butler, and the results were published in nine of a projected seventeen-volume series.[137] The 328-foot-long temple was pseudodipteral. There were eight Ionic columns along the front and eight along the back. Rows of twenty columns stood along either side. Depictions of lizards, scorpions, snails and slugs are carved into the beautiful Hellenistic bases. Some bases and some Hellenistic capitals were used in the Roman reconstruction following the earthquake and a later flood.[138] The temple's double cella was turned into two imperial cult halls, perhaps to house statues of Augustus and his wife Livia.[139]

During the 1981 and 1982 seasons excavation of the acropolis, on one of the natural terraces at the southern end of the Roman city, another temple was discovered.[140] This prostyle, pseudodipteral building with Ionic columns and Attic bases, was located on the northern slopes of the acropolis[141] and is tenta-

Ionic columns mark the front of the Temple of Artemis in Sardis.

tively dated to the second or third quarter of the first century. Set in a stream bed in the shadow of the north face of the acropolis, the temple was possibly a provincial temple of the cult of a Roman emperor, perhaps Vespasian.[142] The worship of Roman emperors, both locally and provincially, was well established in the first century A.D.[143] Augustus officially sanctioned the worship of himself and Rome (never just himself) on a *provincial* level by the building of a temple in Pergamum, the first such temple in Asia.[144] (The temple built in Sardis in 5 B.C. and dedicated to Augustus was a *local* temple.) Tiberius reluctantly allowed a provincial temple to be built to him in Smyrna,[145] and Caligula authorized one for himself in Miletus.[146]

Sardis, therefore, did not have a provincial temple for the imperial cult during the reigns of the first three emperors. But this raises something of a mystery, for inscriptions and municipal coinage from the time of Septimius Severus name Sardis as a neōkoros ("temple-warden") for the *second* time. The question must be asked, "When did the city become a temple-warden for the *first* time?" A large issue of coins struck in the name of Vespasian, but without the imperial image, depicts a tetrastyle temple which may have been dedicated to the emperor. If so, the coins could be commemorating the first occasion when Sardis became a neōkoros, and the newly discovered temple on the acropolis may be Vespasian's.[147]

Pergamum

Pergamum, another of the seven cities mentioned in Revelation (2:12), was beautifully situated 16 miles from the Aegean Sea, where it was served by the port city of Elaea.[148] The city sat on terraces of a precipitous mountain of rock, 1165 feet above sea level, looking southward over the broad fertile valley of the Caicus River. It was enclosed on the east by the Cetius River and on the west by the Selinus, both cutting deep ravines as they fed the Caicus from the mountains to the north. The acropolis stronghold was thus impregnable, except from the south, and the city was built on two plateaus of this slope.

Tacitus does not list Pergamum among the twelve cities devastated by the A.D. 17 earthquake which destroyed Sardis, although Sardis lay only 60 miles southeast of Pergamum;[149] this beautiful Hellenistic city, therefore, must have come through the disaster relatively unscathed. The city's still-visible structures are mostly from either the tremendous original building program of the second century B.C. (primarily under Eumenes II [197–159 B.C.]) or the renovations of the second century A.D. (under Trajan and Hadrian).

The upper terrace of this well-planned city consisted of city government, military, educational, and religious facilities. Here, on the east side of the central north-side street that ran along the top of the mountain, were located two palaces (one of Eumenes II and one of Attalos I), the barracks and arsenals of the military, and residences of officers. Also at this level Eumenes II built the Doric Temple of Athena, with its large precinct, and Hadrian raised the Corinthian-style Trajaneum Temple to honor Trajan.[150] The discovery of colossal heads of both Trajan and Hadrian in the Trajaneum Temple indicates that both emperors were worshiped here. Pergamum was noted for its statuary, much of which Nero carried off to Rome, as he did most statues on the Acropolis of Athens.[151] The Trajaneum may have been built by the province of Asia, rather than the city of Pergamum, as a provincial temple for the imperial cult. If so, Pergamum would have been twice temple-warden, since it was first declared a neōkoros under Augustus.[152] Coins have been found in Pergamum with temples depicted on both sides, one side bearing an inscription to Augustus and Rome (θεα Ρωμη και θεω Σεβαστω), and the other an inscription to Trajan (Φιλιος Ζευς Αυτ[οκρατωρ] Τραιανο[ς] Σεβ[αστος] Περγ[αμηνων]).[153] Excavations in the Trajaneum are ongoing.[154] A Temple of Dionysus was built on the western slope of the upper city at the northern end of a temple terrace. This terrace also served as an esplanade in front of the theater. The temple, of mixed Doric and Ionic design, dates to the second century B.C. and was renovated in the early third century A.D.

An Altar to Zeus built by Eumenes II stood at the southern end of the upper city. Almost square (112 feet by 118 feet), the marble altar has been partially reconstructed in the Pergamum Museum in East Berlin—a most impressive museum exhibit.[155] Dominating the altar was a huge frieze, 365 feet long and 7.5 feet high, constructed of 118 panels, most of which are preserved. The frieze depicts a battle between gods and giants. Opinions vary, but it may symbolize the second-century-B.C. victory of Pergamum over the Gauls. The assumption is that it was dedicated to Zeus and Athena Nike (goddess of Victory). This temple may have been in the mind of John when he referred to Pergamum as the place "where the throne of Satan is" and "where Satan dwells" (Rev. 2:13, author's translation). However, Revelation was evidently written in the context of emperor worship (the imperial cult), so it is more likely that Pergamum's Temple of Augustus—the first provincial temple built to a Roman Emperor in Asia Minor[156]— was the object of the reference in Revelation 2:13.[157] The Temple of Augustus has not yet been identified in the excavations, but on some coins minted in Pergamum the head of Augustus is cast on one side and the temple on the other. In some issues the temple is pictured on the coinage as hexastyle and in others as tetrastyle.[158]

Eumenes II built one of the ancient world's great libraries in Pergamum's upper city. It opened onto the eastern side of the north stoa of the Athena temple precinct. Portions of it are standing, although the southern wall has disappeared. Vitruvius wrote that "the Attalid kings, impelled by their delight in literature established for a general perusal a fine library at Pergamus."[159] Strabo wrote about the diligence of the Attalids in building the library.[160] Dio Cassius stated that the volumes of the library were "of the greatest number and excellence,"[161] and Plutarch referred to 200,000 volumes in its collection.[162] Only the library in Alexandria, Egypt, founded in the third century B.C.,[163] was in the class with Pergamum's at that time. In fact, Ptolemy Philadelphus enlarged Alexandria's library out of jealousy over the one at Pergamum.[164] According to Dio Cassius, when Caesar besieged Alexandria in 47 B.C. a fire burned the library there, making Pergamum's the world's largest repository.[165] Plutarch repeated a story, which the *Encyclopaedia Britannica* considers a "doubtful tale," that Mark Antony subsequently gave the entire two hundred thousand volumes of the Pergamene library to Cleopatra.[166]

Another indication of the bookish inclinations of the people of Pergamum is that Marcus Varro attributed the invention of parchment to the city.[167] Parchment is animal skin used as "paper" in ancient scrolls, and the Greek word translated into English as *parchment* (περγαμηνά; Lat., *pergamena*) derives from the name *Pergamos* (Πέργαμος).

Altar of Zeus, Pergamum.

Recreated Altar of Zeus in the Berlin Museum.

In the upper city, below the temples of Trajan and Athena, the people of Pergamum built a theater. Built into the side of the mountain overlooking the huge Caicus Valley, the imposing third-century-B.C. theater was renovated in Roman times and would seat about ten thousand. The lower third of the cavea was typical,[168] but the upper portion was modified to fit the shape of

the slope into which it is built, resulting in a somewhat unique appearance among Mediterranean theaters. An 800-foot-long terrace resembling a street ran south to north in front of the theater, leading to the Temple of Dionysus. A wooden stage could be erected as needed on the terrace and then removed to allow unimpeded travel along the terrace. A permanent stone stage was built in Roman times. Along the west side of the terrace a stoa was built so that three stories looked out over the valley and one Doric level faced east toward the mountain. A shorter Doric stoa (245 feet) was built along the east side of the terrace. Thus it was possible to walk to the temple or simply stroll on the open terrace road or under the protection of the stoas.

In the second century B.C. an agora was built, probably by Eumenes II, south of the Altar of Zeus to serve the upper section of Pergamum. It had Doric colonnades on the southwest and southeast sides and a small temple of mixed Doric and Ionic styles in its western part. The agora was bisected by the road that ran from the middle city to the upper city.

Just south of the upper city was Pergamum's middle city, containing large commercial structures and temples. The common people probably frequented this section more often than they did the upper city. Excavations at this writing are uncovering residential dwellings here, north of the Temple of Hera.[169] At the southern extremity of this terrace a lower agora measured 112 feet by 210 feet, which was approached by a road from the north that was lined with shops on either side. North of the agora a huge gymnasium complex was built in Hellenistic times on three levels. A stoa divided the uppermost level of the gymnasium from the lower two. Although the original gymnasium was built of

Pergamum's imposing theater was built into the side of a mountain in the upper city.

269

andesite, as was much of Pergamum, most of what now remains is marble from the Roman renovation; the west baths date to the mid-first century A.D. and the east baths to Hadrian.[170] The upper level of the gymnasium had an earthen courtyard 243 feet by 118 feet, used for athletic training. In Hellenistic times this level was surrounded by Doric stoas which were reconstructed on the Corinthian order in Roman times. A large Roman bathhouse adjoined the courtyard on the east, and on the north there stood a one-thousand-seat auditorium for public meetings. This was not a theater, since there was no orchestra. Adjoining the auditorium on the east was the *ephebeion*, where major ceremonies took place. A large eastern room of this building was reserved for the emperor. The upper part of the gymnasium was reserved for young men, the middle level for adolescent boys, and the lowest for children. These designations are attested by inscriptions in Pergamum, just as they are in Beroea, Greece.[171]

To the northwest of the gymnasium complex lay the Sanctuary of Demeter, which was founded by Philetairos and Eumenes I in the early third century B.C. and altered in Roman times. An altar with an inscription "to the unknown Gods" (see p. 304) in the temple precinct[172] and the many temples that intermingled with civic and commercial structures in the upper and middle sections of Pergamum reminds us that religion was a pervasive influence on the thinking and conduct of the ancients. One is reminded of Paul's comment on Mars Hill that the Athenians were "in every way" (κατὰ πάντα) very religious (Acts 17:22). Paul's remark was prompted by his "passing along and observing" their "objects of worship" in the agoras (Acts 17:23).

The lower city of Pergamum was Roman and stretched between the Selinus River west of the mountain city and the Asklepieion, which was still farther west. This section contained an amphitheater which would seat fifty thousand and a theater slightly south of the amphitheater which would hold thirty thousand.[173] A stadium was built just east of the amphitheater on the banks of the Selinus River, and a huge Serapion (temple to the Egyptian goddess Serapis) was erected in the second century A.D. due east of the theater. The temple, the largest building in Pergamum, was unusual in that it was constructed of brick instead of stone and stood in the east end of a huge rectangular enclosure, almost 600 feet long, beneath which the Selinus flowed through two vaulted tunnels. The entire complex was almost a thousand feet long.

At the western bounds of the lower city and the terminus of a 2700-foot-long Corinthian colonnaded street, lay the Asklepieion. After renovation in the second century A.D., the street was known as the Sacred Way. Beginning as a narrow road in the Roman city, this street broadened into a beautiful road at the theater, and continued on to the Asklepieion. At its widest the street measures 27 feet—60 feet if the colonnaded areas on each side are included. A 450-foot segment of the widest section was excavated and reconstructed so visitors to the site can experience a beautiful approach to the Asklepieion. Dedicated to Asklepios Soter, the god of healing, the Asklepieion was a kind of Mayo Clinic of the ancient world and ranked with similar centers of Asklepios at Epidaurus, Greece, and on Cos, an island off the southwestern coast of Asia Minor. It represented the cutting-edge of medical technology in the New Testament period, although founded much earlier.[174] The development of the Asklepieion under Hadrian was so magnificent that it was listed as one of the Seven Wonders of the Ancient World.[175]

The Asklepieion covers 360 feet by 425 feet, with stoas on its north, west, and south and with several buildings, including the Temple of Asklepios, on the east. Most of the buildings still visible were erected in the second century A.D. The architrave of the north colonnade contains an inscription that dates much of the rebuilding to the latter part of Hadrian's reign[176] or shortly thereafter.[177] The circular temple was almost certainly modeled on the Pantheon of Rome, which was constructed about a decade earlier.[178] Numerous treatment rooms, sleeping rooms (for incubation and autosuggestion in psychiatric treatment), meeting rooms, and temples (Apollo, Asklepios Soter, and Hygeia) were located here. A 260-foot-long tunnel connected the center of the building area with a large, two-story cylindrical structure on the southeast corner, which probably functioned as a treatment center. At the southwest corner of the complex was a large and luxurious latrine, with separate facilities for men and

Odeion in lower Pergamum stands near the Asklepieion.

women. The latrine was built partly of marble. At the northwest corner stood a Roman theater that would seat about thirty-five hundred spectators.

Patients coming to the shrine believed that Asklepios would heal them. There was no perceived dissonance between science and religion in the ancient world or, for that matter, between religion and any activity of everyday life.

Smyrna

Alexander the Great relocated the city of Smyrna from a peninsula to the slopes of Mount Pagos overlooking the beautiful Gulf of Izmir. Strabo wrote that in his time it lay 2.5 miles from the old city.[179] Though some of the city was on the city mound, most of it was on flat land around the harbor[180] on the main road between Ephesus and Pergamum, about 35 miles north of Ephesus.

Little remains of Smyrna from the New-Testament period; thus we are dependent upon literary descriptions for our knowledge of its structures. Strabo described it as "the most beautiful of all" the cities along the coast, having stone-paved streets which were laid out in lines as straight as possible. He noted that the engineers made one major mistake when they paved the streets without providing underground drainage. Therefore, he wrote, "filth covers the surface, and particularly during rains, when the cast-off filth is discharged upon the streets."[181] Orator Aelius Aristides, a second-century-A.D. native of Smyrna, wrote that the two main streets, the Sacred Way and the Golden Road, ran east and west, oriented to the sun and the sea breeze.[182] Excavations revealed a well-paved street, 33 feet wide, which ran east and west. It had a roofed walkway for pedestrians along the side and may have been part of the Sacred Way.[183]

David Magie said he disbelieves estimates which set the population of Roman Smyrna at one hundred thousand.[184] He puts it rather at two hundred thousand, based on the twenty-thousand-seat capacity of the theater.[185] Magie makes the same population estimates for Ephesus and Pergamum.[186] Smyrna's harbor could be closed, and a commercial agora stood near the docks. A gymnasium was also near the harbor. A stadium was located on the west of the city, a theater on the northwest slope of Mount Pagos, and a state agora on the hill above the city. Strabo identified a library and a Homereium, "a quadrangular portico containing a shrine and wooden statue of Homer."[187] That a shrine to the Greek poet might be located in Smyrna is not surprising, for the city was probably Homer's birthplace in the second half of the eighth century B.C.[188]

Smyrna could also boast its share of temples. The Temple of the Mother Goddess was near the harbor.[189] Smyrna was selected out of eleven competing cities for the honor of housing the imperial cult in a provincial Temple of Tiberius. It was first given the title temple-warden under Tiberius.[190] According to an inscription, the people erected a statue to Tiberius[191] and issued a coin bearing the emperor's name and his figure in front of a temple. On the reverse side of the coin were the heads of Livia and the senate and the legend "Augustus, Senate" (Σεβαστη, Συνκλητος— *Sebaste, Sunkletos*).[192] In the second century, Smyrna was referred to as "the second neocorate of the Augusti" (δις νεωκορος των Σεβαστων),[193] establishing that Smyrna had received the honor of temple-warden again under Hadrian.[194]

Nothing remains of the theater or the stadium, and the commercial agora has not been identified. However, the state agora, the only part of the city that has been excavated, is well preserved. It contained a rectangular piazza, 425 feet by at least 250 feet, and was bordered on two or three sides by two-story triple porticos. The north side was enclosed by a two-story basilica, 525 feet by 90 feet,[195] similar to one at Cyrene in North Africa.[196] At the western end of this second-century structure[197] stood a rostrum and beneath the basilica was a magnificent vaulted basement, which is still in excellent condition. The northern aisle of the basement contained shops which probably opened onto a street to the north.

A severe earthquake hit Smyrna in 178. With the help of the emperor Marcus Aurelius, the city was reconstructed, and a portrait of the emperor's wife, Faustina II, was carved into an arch

Smyrna's Roman Forum dates to after the New Testament period.

over the west colonnade around the forum by the thankful people.[198] Unfortunately, almost nothing of the New Testament city of Smyrna is still standing.

Patmos

Archaeology contributes little to our knowledge of Patmos, the island to which John was sent toward the close of the first century (Rev. 1:9). The Roman government had made Patmos a place of banishment for political prisoners, and, according to Eusebius, John was exiled there during the reign of Domitian.[199] Any mention of the island is absent in most works dealing with archaeology and the New Testament, and not without some justification.

Patmos is a small island, only 24 square miles, with a coastline in the shape of a horseshoe. It is actually composed of three pieces of land, joined by two narrow isthmuses. During the New Testament period, the city was located in the center of the island around the large eastern harbor, now known as Skala. An ancient mule path, now a paved road, ascended 2 miles to the town of Patmos (or Khora), which was situated 427 feet above the level of the sea. The Monastery of Saint John stands on a rocky crag above the whitewashed houses, monasteries, churches, and chapels of the town. The panoramic view from the 885-foot summit is breathtaking and conducive to contemplation. The monastery was founded in 1088, and additions were made in succeeding centuries. It houses a library of thirteen thousand docu-

The Island of Patmos is small but offers breathtaking views.

ments, two thousand early printed books, eight hundred ninety manuscript codices, and thirty-five parchment rolls. Also preserved in the library are thirty-three leaves of the early-sixth-century Codex Porphyrius; these constitute most of the Gospel of Mark.

Halfway up the mountain is the Convent of the Apocalypse. According to tradition, John wrote the Book of Revelation in a cave that is now within the convent.

Macedonian Cities and Athens

Macedonia

Paul's Macedonian Call

When Paul received the "Macedonian call" (Acts 16:9) to leave Troas and enter Europe, he must have had some reason to think that Philippi was his destination because he journeyed directly there without stopping to preach along the way (Acts 16:11–12). How he recognized the man in the vision as a Macedonian is not revealed, except that the request to "come over to Macedonia and help us" indicated the man's nationality.[1] There was no clear distinction in dress between the Greek settlers of Aeolia-Ionia on the

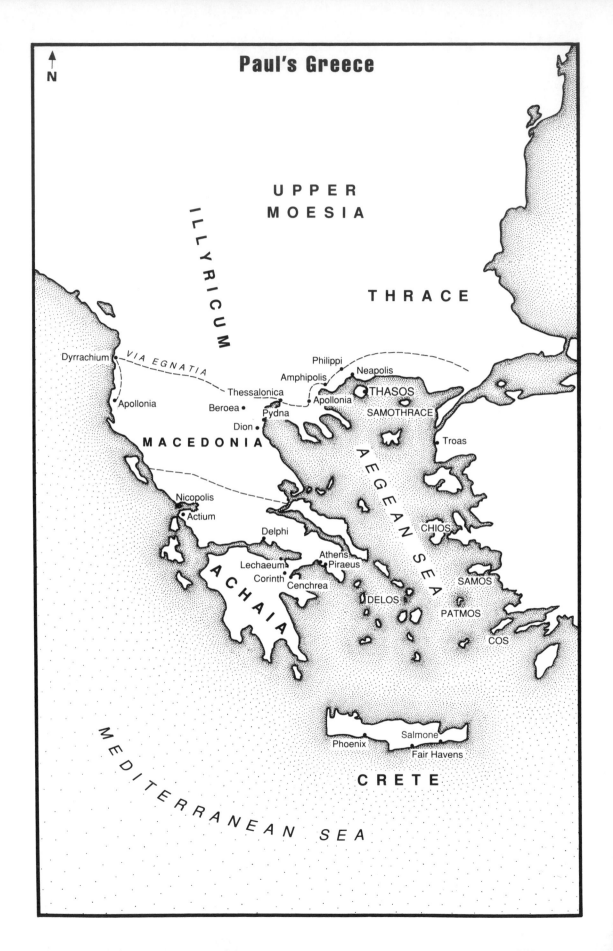

Paul's Greece

western coast of Asia Minor and the inhabitants of Macedonia.[2] There is no good reason to think the man was "Luke the beloved physician" (Col. 4:14), as William M. Ramsay and others have suggested. Luke, who undoubtedly wrote Acts, includes himself among Paul's companions (Acts 16:10).[3]

Samothrace

Luke records that the decision to sail to Macedonia was immediate, based on the conclusion "that God had called us to proclaim the good news to them" (Acts 16:10 NRSV). Paul and his companions took the shortest possible route, stopping at Samothrace and continuing on the following day to Neapolis, the harbor city of Philippi. Whether Paul went ashore that one night in Samothrace is not clear, but he did not remain here even one day to preach to the island's inhabitants. Had he done so he would have been in the midst of a major pagan "Sanctuary of the Great Gods"—whose mysterious rites were held at night and unlike the Eleusinian Mysteries, could be attended by those who were not participants. The rites were open to all, slave or free, without regard to sex, nationality, age, or social status. Since the cult functioned at night, Paul could have observed. He might have known that Alexander the Great's father and mother, Philip and Olympias, met at Samothrace while attending, and perhaps while actually celebrating, one of the festivals.[4]

The Samothracian mysteries revolved around a central female

Round architecture was distinctive to the building of the Samothracian mystery cult.

deity of pre-Greek origin called Demeter (Ceres). Other divinities included her spouse Hermes (Mercury), twin attendant demons known as the Cabiri (who were later fused with the Dioscuri— Castor and Pollux), Hades (Pluto), and Persephone (Proserpina). Pliny the Elder states that Venus (Aphrodite) and Pothos were worshiped at Samothrace "with the most sacred ceremonies."[5] In Paul's time the mystery religion of the Cabiri drew many people to the island and strongly opposed Christianity. All the mystery cults had tremendous appeal; Orphic hymns at Samothrace dedicated to deities claimed that by the gods' power alone "the greatest mystic rites to men at first were shown."[6]

Samothrace is a pleasant island of 69 square miles with lots of farm land and scrubby hills but few trees. The site of the ancient city is today called Palaeopolis ("Old City") and lies on the north side of the island, twenty miles south of the mainland city of Alexandroupolis. French, Austrian, and Swedish teams sporadically dug at ancient Samothrace from 1863 until 1925, but systematic work began in 1938, sponsored by the Institute of Fine Arts at New York University under the directors Karl and Phyllis Lehmann. It continues under James R. McCredie for the American School of Classical Studies in Athens.[7] Its lovely coastline features no natural harbors. The modern harbor on the western tip of the island at Kamariotissa probably would not have been used by first-century ships. However, on the north coast near the ruins of the ancient sanctuary, remains of an old harbor mole may still be seen; Paul's boat surely dropped anchor in this vicinity.

Lying west of the ancient city, the Sanctuary of the Great Gods was entered through a propylon of Thracian marble. This gateway opened onto a beautiful terrace which overlooked the sea and the Rotunda of Queen Arsinoë. At 65 feet across, the Rotunda is the largest circular building known from Greek architecture, an imposing structure dedicated to the Great Gods of the Samothracian mysteries. Its extant foundation remains impressive. A 295-foot-long Doric and Ionic stoa stood on the west side of a hill, across a valley from the Rotunda. This colonnaded porch, which was excavated by an Austrian team, sheltered pilgrims who came to observe or participate in the festivities. The stoa looked down on the Temenos area, comprising several buildings used in cultic initiation ceremonies. These structures included the Hieron (a two-level sanctuary used for the higher initiation ceremonies), the Hall of Votive Gifts, and the Altar Court. A number of dining halls used in the ritual banquets associated with Demeter worship stood on the northeast side of the stoa; similar halls served the same purpose in Corinth. Adjacent on the north side of the Rotunda was the Anaktoron, a large rectangular building used for initiation rites. All of these structures operated in Paul's time and are partially preserved today.

I believe the apostle Paul passed through Samothrace in the fall of A.D. 49, before the hard rains and heavy snowfalls that characterize the island's winter and while the religious rites were in full swing (see the discussion of Pauline chronology, pp. 225–227). This was during the reign of Claudius (41–54). An inscription on a well-preserved stele found on the island by McCredie's expedition in 1986 mentions Claudius as it records a treaty between Maroneia and Rome.[8]

Neapolis

After their one-night stop at Samothrace Paul and his companions sailed on, probably in the same boat, most likely a commercial vessel. They disembarked at Neapolis, a city on the coast of Thrace just inside the border of the Roman province of Macedonia.[9] The port of Neapolis is known today as Kavalla, a corruption of its Ottoman name, *Cavallo*, which originally derived from the Latin word meaning "horse." Cavallo was an important station in the postal service of the Ottoman Empire.[10]

Neapolis was founded by a colony from nearby Thasos, one of the most beautiful and heavily forested of the Aegean Islands. The settlers built their new city in a natural amphitheater and harbor which eventually became a crossroads for both the international east-west highway, the Via Egnatia, connecting Europe with Asia, and the road leading north to the gold mines of Mount Pangaeus. About 350 B.C. the city was taken by Philip II of Macedon to serve as a port for Krenides (the city he conquered, rebuilt, and renamed Philippi six years earlier). In 42 B.C. Brutus and Cassius used the harbor of Neapolis in their unsuccessful battle with Octavian and Mark Antony at Philippi, only 10 miles to the northwest.

The Harbor at Neapolis was a base from which Brutus and Cassius sailed to the Battle of Philippi.

Almost nothing Kavalla of today bears on Pauline archaeology.[11] The magnificent aqueduct reaching across the heart of town is not Roman,[12] although it was built on a Roman model by Süleyman the Magnificent in the sixteenth century[13]. The masonry clearly is not Roman. In 1986 the Greek press reported the discovery of a part of the ancient harbor wall,[14] but an archaeologist at the Kavalla Museum who took part in the excavations, related to the author that what was found was rather a part of the city wall and/or a Roman building. The new Greek Orthodox Church of Saint Paul, which stands a considerable distance from the seashore, makes no claim to ancient tradition.[15] The Church of Saint Nicholas, rebuilt in 1930, predates the Ottoman period, when it was converted into a mosque. Beside the church a column drum marks the traditional spot where Paul first touched European soil—200 yards from the water's edge!

The Via Egnatia

The museum in Kavalla is as devoid of remains from the New Testament period as is the modern-day town. In the yard of the museum are a number of well-preserved Roman milestones, however, reminders that the important Via Egnatia ran through the city. Paul undoubtedly traveled to Philippi on this road, which ran from Apollonia on the west coast of Macedonia to Kypsela (modern Maritza) on the east coast, north of Samothrace.[16] Milestones announced the total distance of this road as 535 Roman miles

The Via Egnatia was a highway for commerce and the gospel across Macedonia.

(493 English miles). Near the Gallikos River, in the vicinity of Thessalonica (modern Salonika), one recently-discovered milestone[17] now housed in the museum of Salonika, is most interesting in that it gives (in Latin and Greek) a distance of 260 Roman miles to both ends of the Via Egnatia.[18] Thessalonica is midway between the terminal points reported by Strabo.

The Via Egnatia was built about 130 B.C.[19] At least the western part was opened between 146 B.C., when Macedonia was made a Roman province, and 120 B.C. when Polybius, who mentioned it in his histories, died.[20] Included on the milestone found near Thessalonica is the name of the builder, the Roman proconsul of Macedonia, Gnaios Egnatios (Lat. Cnaeus Egnatius). The road was an extension of the Via Appia and the maritime route, which began at Brundisium (modern Brindisi) on the southeastern coast of Italy and extended to Dyrrhachium and Apollonia on the eastern coast of Macedonia. Built as a military road the Via Egnatia soon became the international commercial and migratory route between Asia and Europe, since it was the most direct road available. In the Macedonian cities of Amphipolis, Apollonia, and Pella, the presence of Roman and Italian merchants in the first century B.C. is attested by inscriptions.[21] One such inscription mentions Roman residents in Beroea,[22] while another mentions Roman communities in Thessalonica and other Macedonian cities[23]. Good roads such as the Via Egnatia, helped ignite an economic boom in Macedonia during the New Testament era.[24]

Philippi

Paul undoubtedly followed the Via Egnatia from Neapolis to Philippi, his immediate destination upon reaching Macedonia. It was the fastest and most efficient road. Within Philippi Via Egnatia was the *decumanus maximus*, the southeast-northwest route dividing Philippi in half, from the theater built into the southern slopes of Mount Lekani to the forum on the south side. The city itself stretched into the Plain of Philippi, where the historic battle of 42 B.C. occurred. Paul and his friends would have entered Philippi through the eastern Neapolis Gate, and when he departed for Thessalonica (Acts 16:40–17:1), he would have exited at the other end, the Krenides Gate.

Philippi was of little importance until the Via Egnatia was built. Because it had proven so decisively important in the battle of 42 B.C., Octavian refounded the city with veterans from the battle. In 27 B.C., Octavian named it the Roman colony (Acts 16:12) of *Colonia Julia Augusta Philippensis*, a name found on inscriptions from Philippi's East Temple[25] and the Library.[26] Philippi joined Macedonia's three other "Augustan" colonies— Kassandreia, Dion, and Pella. Kassandreia, Dion and Philippi enjoyed the status of *ius italicum*. This entitled the colonies to equal status with communities in Italy and freed their citizens and lands from direct taxation.[27]

Acts 16:12 is usually translated as referring to Philippi as "the leading city of the district of Macedonia," but textual variants and questions relating to the original Greek put that translation in question: First, there is no article before either *city* or *first* in any manuscript. Second, the word *district* (μερὶς) is a technical term for the four sections into which Macedonia was administratively divided in 168 B.C. These sections should not be confused with Macedonia as a whole, which was made a province of Rome in 146 B.C.[28] Third, Philippi was located in the *first* (πρώτη) of these districts, but it was not the capital city. According to Pliny the Elder, that honor belonged to Amphipolis[29] (Thessalonica was the capital of the second district, Pella of the third, and Pelagonia [Herakleia Lynkestis] of the fourth).[30] Coins minted in Amphipolis from between 168 and 146 B.C. carried the inscription *Makedonōn Prōtēs* (ΜΑΚΕΔΟΝΩΝ ΠΡΩΤΗΣ).[31] Fourth, the texts of **p**[74] and codices ℵ, A, and C are problematic, as are those of B and the majority text of the Textus Receptus family (KJV). The conjectural text of Nestle-Aland's twenty-sixth edition, which makes *first* (πρώτης) a genitive, is probably to be preferred. This would allow the reading, "a city of (the) first district of Macedonia."

Excavations by French and Greek archaeologists have been ongoing in Philippi since the early twentieth century.[32] In spite of the impressive remains found, little bears directly on the New Testament. The rectangular forum primarily investigated, measures 325 feet by 164 feet, and was built by Marcus Aurelius about 160 A.D., according to inscriptions. An earlier forum on the

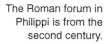

The Roman forum in Philippi is from the second century.

Excavated area on the east side of the Roman forum in Philippi.

same ground was a square of even larger dimension.[33] On the north side of the forum as it stood in Paul's time, a large basilica stood above a row of shops. Excavations by Michel Sève show that the modern road which passes through the site partially covers monumental stairways which connected shops under the basilica with an equal-sized strip of shops on the south side of the forum.[34] Monumental fountains decorated both ends of the north side of the forum, with a tribunal (*bema*) or speaker's platform, centered between them. When Paul was arrested (Acts 16:19–21), he probably stood before the magistrates on this platform as he stood only weeks later before Gallio at the bema in Corinth (Acts 18:12).

The various excavations at Philippi have uncovered some intriguing inscriptions. Paul's visit to Philippi and Corinth took place during the reign of the emperor Claudius (Acts 18:2). Excavations in 1984 adjacent to the east side of the forum produced a dedication to Nero Claudius Drusus, father of Claudius.[35] In other digs outside the east and west city walls, cemeteries were found, containing tile and pit graves from the Roman period and later and some inscriptions.[36] A group of disturbed Roman sarcophagi produced an inscription bearing the name Rufus,[37] a name which also appears in the New Testament (Mark 15:21; Rom. 16:13), though there is no connection between the grave inscription and the New Testament Rufus.[38] Interesting also is a discovery made by the late S. Pelekanides east of the forum. On the mosaic floor of a fourth-century (Constantinian) church—which lay under an

Figure 25
Schematic of Philippi

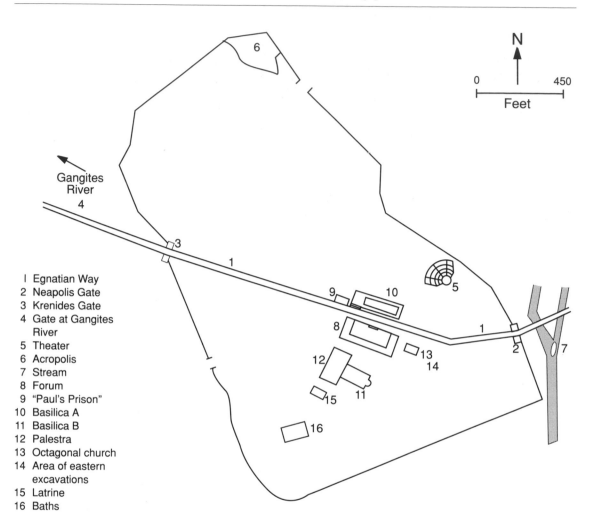

Gangites
River
4

N

0   450

Feet

I Egnatian Way
2 Neapolis Gate
3 Krenides Gate
4 Gate at Gangites
   River
5 Theater
6 Acropolis
7 Stream
8 Forum
9 "Paul's Prison"
10 Basilica A
11 Basilica B
12 Palestra
13 Octagonal church
14 Area of eastern
    excavations
15 Latrine
16 Baths

octagonal sixth-century (Justinian) church—Palekanides found an inscription which can be translated: "Christ, help your servant Priscus with all his house" (ΧΡΙΣΤΕ ΒΟΗΘΙ ΤΟ ΔΟΥΛΟΥ ΣΟΥ ΠΡΙΣΚΟΥ ΣΥΝ ΠΑΝΤΙ ΤΟΥ ΟΙΚΟΥ ΑΥΤΟΥ).[39] Priscus is the masculine form of the feminine name Prisca (Πρίσκα) and its diminutive Priscilla (Πρίσκιλλα) which appear in the New Testament (Acts 18:2, 18, 26; Rom. 16:3; 1 Cor. 16:19; 2 Tim. 4:19).

The setting for the conversion of Lydia, "outside the gate beside the river" (Acts 16:13–15)[40] might be any of three locations. Paul Collart thought the description best fits the Gangites (or Ganga) River bank, just west of a colonial arch. According to a plan of this arch drawn fifty years ago for Collart's publication, it measures 10.77 meters high and 5.79 deep, with a passageway 4.95 meters wide. Appian wrote that the Via Egnatia ran through this arch near where the road forded the Gangites.[41] All evidence of the foundation has disappeared.[42] A major problem with this view is that the river is 3 kilometers (1.9 miles) west of the forum at this point, and it is difficult to imagine a place of regular prayer being so far from the city.

An alternate location, presented by Paul Lemerle, is that the Krenides Gate in the city's west wall was that mentioned in Acts. Nearby flows the abundant, cold water of the Krenides stream,[43] 1 kilometer (about .5 mile) from the forum. The Krenides is referred to locally as "the River of Lydia." Predictably a Hotel Lydia has been built beside the river in the little village which is also called Lydia.[44] Limited excavation in the area has revealed the foundation of a building, pavement for a road that ran westward toward the stream, and some inscribed Roman burial monuments.

The final possibility is that Luke is referring to the eastern Neapolis Gate. On the south side of the modern road, next to the theater, part of the Neapolis Gate has been excavated. Immediately outside the gate a stream bed may still be seen. Pelekanides excavated a fourth-century church beside this stream in 1956 and 1957. Just inside the Neapolis Gate, also on the south side of the road, an octagonal church with mosaic floors was recently discovered. Four church structures stood on this spot, but the earliest was shown stratigraphically to be a basilica of the fourth century.[45] This church, reached through a gate off the nearby Via Egnatia, was dedicated to Paul.[46] The placement of two churches near the eastern gate suggests that as early as the time of Constantine there may have been an ancient recollection that Paul met Lydia in the area.[47]

Ancient Krenides, west of Philippi, a possible site for Lydia's conversion.

Ruins of Philippi's Neapolis Gate, near the modern town of Krenides.

Some time after Lydia's conversion, Paul and Silas were taken before the magistrates and thrown into prison (Acts 16:16–24). On the north side of the modern road, above the northwest corner of the forum and to the west of the forum basilica—what has been called by archaeologists Basilica A—stands a small crypt, which may have been the prison of Paul and Silas. The early Roman architect, Vitruvius, wrote that prisons were normally built near the fora of ancient cities.[48] This structure has been considered Paul's prison since the fifth century.[49] Inside the crypt remains of benches around the walls and later frescos are partially preserved.

The theater in Philippi was standing during Paul's visit. In recent work on the theater, archaeologists have used ceramic typology to date its final use to about the beginning of the fifth century.[50] Originally, it was a Hellenistic theater, built about the time the city was founded. It was remodeled into a Roman theater in the second century A.D., approximately at the time the forum was renovated.[51] Seats in the cavea were restored between 1957 and 1959 for modern use.

Amphipolis

After the release of Paul and Silas from prison, they headed for Thessalonica, apparently passing through Amphipolis and Apollonia without stopping (Acts 17:1). That Paul decided not to preach in these two cities is as interesting as his overnight stay in Samothrace. Paul evidently had a very specific strategy of

Stone crypt by the forum has long been identified as Paul's Philippian jail.

targeted evangelism. Macedonia was essentially a rural region, although urban life reached its peak there during the Roman period.[52] Had he simply sought metropolitan Macedonia, obvious preaching points would have included Samothrace and its Sanctuary of the Great Gods; Amphipolis, the large and prosperous capital of the first district of Macedonia, and Apollonia. One reason Paul might bypass these cities is that each lacked a significant Jewish population, and his practice was to preach to Jews first (Acts 16:13; 17:1, 10, 17; 18:4; 19:8; Rom. 1:16).[53] In Acts 17:1 Luke may refer to such a strategy when he says that "they came to Thessalonica, *where there was a synagogue of the Jews*" (RSV). The inference is that Amphipolis and Apollonia had none. Although extensive work has been done at Samothrace and Amphipolis, I know of no archaeological evidence for a Jewish population in any of these three cities.

Amphipolis, one of the most beautiful sites along the eastern seaboard of Greece, is 505 feet above the east bank of the Strymon River overlooking the sea, which is 3 miles to the south. In the valley below the city and clearly visible from it, the Lion of Amphipolis guards the bridge at the bend in the Strymon. Built near the end of the fourth century B.C., the lion was probably a funerary monument to Laomedon, admiral of Alexander the

The Lion of Amphipolis was restored in 1936 and again guards the ancient city.

Great and governor of Syria. It was destroyed in the medieval period and not reassembled until 1936.[54] As Paul and Silas traveled toward Thessalonica on the Via Egnatia they would certainly have seen this magnificent statue.

Amphipolis was a huge city; soundings at sixty-four points have revealed sections of a wall with a circuit of almost 4.5 miles. With impressive results, excavations have been carried out at Amphipolis by Dimitrios Lazarides for the Greek Archaeological Service (from the 1970s until his death in 1984),[55] by E. Stikas,[56] and by Chaido Koukouli-Chrysanthaki.[57] Lazarides's work has been carried forward since 1985 by his daughter, K. Lazarides.[58] The Ephoria of Kavalla (Neapolis) has been working on the city walls as well.[59]

Excavators have uncovered five impressive fifth- and sixth-century churches (four basilical and one hexagonal), some of them preserving lovely mosaic floors,[60] as well as a gymnasium (identified through seven inscriptions). The gymnasium, located in the eastern part of the city, was built in the third century B.C. and destroyed violently by fire in the first century A.D. It was

standing when Paul passed through. Just south of one of the churches (tagged Basilica A), excavators found the courtyard and handsome mosaic floors of a Roman house.[61] East of this residence is a well-preserved late Hellenistic house. The two-room structure

The gymnasium of Amphipolis burned in a first-century fire.

Amphipolis city walls denote a populous, prosperous community.

has white plaster walls, which were beautifully painted red and black in the First Pompeian style to resemble pseudo-isodomic masonry (in isodomic masonry the stones are cut to standard size and laid in uniform courses). The north wall is preserved to a height of 12 feet.[62]

Several inscriptions have helped us understand life in Amphipolis during the Roman period. An honorific inscription found in a small room south of the west entrance to the gymnasium names Apellas, son of Diogenes, as *gymnasiarch* (superintendent of athletic training).[63] The writing can be dated to the early first century A.D.[64] A lengthy inscription (139 lines) from 21 B.C. contains an *ephebic law* (i.e. a law for youth), which provides detailed information about athletic activities and equipment in the gymnasium.[65] Also on the inscription are references to the city's road system,[66] factories, a theater and an agora which confirm that Amphipolis was a major city. Neither the agora nor the theater has been excavated. A reused marble plaque found in Amphipolis in 1975 contains the title *politarchs*, which suggests how some of the cities of Macedonia were administered.[67] Paul was taken before such officials in Thessalonica.

Apollonia

From Amphipolis Paul journeyed 35 miles southwest on the Via Egnatia to Apollonia, a city on the eastern seaboard with the same name as the one on the western coast of Greece. The highway actually ran about three miles north of the city, but Paul is said to have passed through the city (Acts 17:1), which may mean that he either went into Apollonia or that he merely traveled through its outskirts.

An inscription that may have come from Apollonia refers to the "Boule, the Ekklesia, to Politarchai, Agonothetai, to the Agora and to tribal divisions." These references indicate a town of size and importance in the late Hellenistic and early Roman periods.[68] However, the site of Apollonia has not yet been studied.[69]

Thessalonica

Paul's arrival in Thessalonica (Acts 17:1) put him in the capital city of the second district of Macedonia and from the time of Pompey, the seat of the governor of the entire province.[70] Placed under senatorial jurisdiction in A.D. 44, the metropolis enjoyed the status of *civitas libera* ("free city"),[71] as well. Under Claudius (A.D. 41–54) coins were first minted in Macedonia,[72] so prosperity was everywhere evident about the time Paul arrived in the late fall of 49. Among the first Thessalonican converts were "Greek women of high standing," who took their place in a society that boasted great families possessing enormous wealth. Indications of such prosperous families has been found at Thessalonica, Beroea, and Philippi.[73]

Thessalonica lies in a natural amphitheater at the head of the Thermaic Gulf, on the slopes of Mount Khortiatis. Founded on the site of ancient Therme in 316 B.C. by Cassander, one of Alexander the Great's generals, the city was named Thessalonica after Cassander's wife, the half-sister of Alexander.[74] When Macedonia became a province, Thessalonica was made its capital. Due to its strategic location on both the Via Egnatia and the commercial sea routes, it became a world cultural center where "poets, philosophers and rhetors came to teach or to address a cultivated audience."[75]

Here there was a significant Jewish population so Paul began his preaching in the synagogue (Acts 17:1) and then to the Greeks. Paul's message that all people are equal before God, through Christ, whether Jew or Greek, slave or free, male or female, barbarian or Scythian (Gal. 3:28; Col. 3:11; 1 Cor. 12:13), was especially apt here, because "of all other periods in the history of ancient Macedonia the early imperial age was the one in which the process of social levelling was most intense."[76] This does not mean, however, that all were equal in Macedonian society. At least a part of the wealth of Macedonia, as in most ancient societies, was based on trade in human beings. A yet-unpublished inscription from Beroea contains rules for the sale of slaves in the markets of the province.[77]

Little is to be seen at Thessalonica from the time of Paul, for modern Salonika, the second largest city in Greece, functions busily over the buried remains of Roman Thessalonica.[78] A fire in

Modern Thessalonica surrounds the imperial Roman Forum of the second largest city in ancient Greece.

1917 destroyed a large area that was subsequently used as a bus station. When the station was moved in 1962 excavation revealed part of the imperial Roman forum, which may not be earlier than the second century A.D.[79] Systematic excavations were done for the Greek Archaeological Service by Photius Petsas, who uncovered a typical rectangular forum with a paved, open court and small odeum.[80] Beneath the stoa which surrounded the open court was an underground stoa (*cryptoporticus*), reminiscent of a subterranean structure found at Smyrna. We know very little of other public buildings in the city—the gymnasium, Serapion, baths, nympheum, hippodrome, and secondary structures.[81] All over the city modern construction has stumbled across discoveries relating to these buildings, as well as ancient walls and streets, but the evidence is fragmentary and not fully published.[82] Also lacking is evidence of the religious institutions in Thessalonica. Since the time of Augustus a Temple of Divine Caesar was in the city,[83] and an inscription discovered in 1980 documents that the temple to the August Gods (θεοι Σεβαστοι) shared a temple with or was a fellow sanctuary with (συνναοι) the temple of Serapis and Isis.[84]

Inscription provides proof of the rule of politarchs at Thessalonica.

Although archaeological evidence has been limited, one find has helped answer a question regarding Paul's contact with Thessalonica. Critics of the New Testament asserted for many years that Luke was mistaken in his use of the term "politarchs" (πολιτάρχης) for the officials of Thessalonica before whom Paul was taken (Acts 17:6). An inscription using this term, however, was found on the Vardar Arch at the west end of the modern Odos Egnatia Street (once known as Vardar Street). The first-century A.D. arch was torn down in 1867 to be used in the repair of the city's walls. The inscription from the arch, which was subsequently found and is now in the British Museum, begins "In the time of the Politarchs."

The popular perception of the inscription's importance, as expressed by Jack Finegan, is that the term *politarch* "is otherwise unknown in extant Greek literature."[85] However, in 1960, Carl Schuler published a list of thirty-two inscriptions which contain this term.[86] Nineteen of Schuler's inscriptions come from Thessalonica, and Numbers 8, 9, and 10 date to the first century A.D., as well as one from Beroea. The Beroean inscription on an impressive stele in the Beroea Museum has been the subject of recent study by J. M. R. Cormack.[87] Three more inscriptions may be added to the Schuler list: One in the Thessalonica Museum was apparently discovered in Mygdonian Apollonia and was published by K. Sismanides.[88] James H. Oliver discusses another inscription that appeared on the base of a statue erected in Beroea for the emperor Claudius. This refers to a board of five politarchs in Beroea, naming each.[89] It was first published in modern Greek by J. Touratsoglou.[90] Finally, in January 1975, a reused marble plaque was discovered at Amphipolis in Basilica A which contains the word "politarchs" in line 7. Koukouli-Chrysanthaki of the Kavalla Museum states that the inscription from Amphipolis can definitely be dated to the reign of Perseus, who ascended the throne in 179 B.C. It "demonstrates that the institution of the politarchs existed in Macedonia at least as early as the reign of King Perseus."[91] How interesting that scholarly discussion has shifted from whether politarchs existed at all to when the institution originated![92] It is incontrovertible that politarchs existed in Macedonia long before the time of the apostle Paul.

Beroea

From Thessalonica Paul journeyed a short distance westward on the Via Egnatia and then turned southward to Beroea, where there was a synagogue (Acts 17:10). The appearance of the modern city of Beroea (Verroia) has been aptly described as "changing rapidly from ramshackle vernacular to undistinguished modernity."[93] As at Thessalonica, the building development has produced most of the archaeological discoveries.[94] Primarily these finds have been the remains of houses from Hellenistic and Roman times, public buildings, graves and statuary.[95] Portions of Roman roads were uncovered, which tend to follow the same routes as modern streets and lead to the same exits from the city.[96] Due to the nature of the discoveries in the city, the excavations have been carried out by numerous archaeologists including A. Rhomiopoulou, J. Touratsoglou, P. Lazarides, and K. Tzanavani, among others. Results have been piecemeal and are not yet integrated into a cohesive pattern.[97]

The museum in Verroia is literally full of high-quality Roman statues, inscriptions, and funerary altars. Artifacts overflow into a cluttered courtyard. Were these pieces properly displayed, the museum could be one of the best in Greece. Works of a family of Beroean sculptors are scattered over Macedonia from Larissa to Yugoslavia. Perhaps the most important inscription yet found in the city is the "gymnasiarchal law of Beroea," which was published in 1951, and recently was restudied.[98] According to the rules of the gymnasium, the participating youths were grouped by age:

1. *paides*, up to age 15
2. *ephēboi*, ages 15–17
3. *neoi* or *neaniskoi*, ages 18–22.

This grouping may indicate the age of Timothy as a young evangelist being counseled by Paul, who in 1 Timothy 4:12 refers to his protégé as a *neotēs* (νεότης, "youth").

Impressive statuary litters the museum yard in Verroia.

Like many other cities in biblical lands, Verroia is not without "recent traditions." One shrine in the heart of town purports to contain some steps from a podium or bema on which Paul preached. The steps would appear to date no earlier than 1961.[99]

Dion and Paul's Sea Voyage

Paul's route out of Beroea is not clear. Acts 17:14 simply states that he went "to the sea" (RSV; Gk., ἕως ἐπὶ τὴν θάλασσαν), which may imply that he continued his journey to Athens by boat.[100] Codex Bezae, a fifth-century Greek manuscript of the Gospels and Acts, does add a phrase to verse 15 that "he passed through Thessaly, because he was forbidden to preach the word to them."[101] This is an inferior text, about 30 percent longer than the better Alexandrian text, so we can assume that it is a late addition and go on to ask where Paul would likely have put to sea. A map in N. G. L. Hammond's *Atlas of the Greek and Roman World in Antiquity* shows a road from Beroea 30 miles southeast to Dion, near the coast, and another from Beroea northeast, which circles the northern end of Mount Pieria and then turns south, passing through Dion after a total of 50 miles.[102] The existence of the more direct road has been questioned by M. B. Hatzopoulos, who omits it on his map of the central Macedonian plain.[103] If such a road existed Paul undoubtedly would have traveled it. Dion was four miles from the sea up the Baphyras River, a stream made navigable in the Hellenistic period to serve Dion. If the road did not exist, Paul would likely have journeyed the northeasterly route to any of three harbors north of Dion: (1) Methone, which the ancient Athenians used as a base against the Macedonians; (2) Makrigialos, 3 miles south of Methone. At Makrigialos Hammond's *Atlas* locates ancient Pydna, or (3) Aliki, almost four miles south of Makrigialos. Aliki was probably the harbor of Pydna in Paul's time, though the city itself was moved 5 miles northwest to Alonia, according to Hammond's *Atlas*.

Although Paul perhaps did not go 20 miles out of his way to use the port of Dion, it was an important city. It was reestablished as a Roman colony, *Colonia Julia Diensis,* after the decisive battle of Pydna in 168 B.C. Excavations were conducted from 1928 to 1931 by G. Soteriades and renewed in 1962 by G. Bakalakis. Since 1973, Dimitrios Pantermalis of the Aristotelian University of Thessaloniki has directed work there, which has revealed a large, beautiful Roman city measuring about 1500 feet by 1600 feet.[104] Both the site and the museum are models for how such facilities should be arranged for public viewing.

Dion's *cardo maximus* has been cleared to its full length; at least twenty other streets have been identified and several of them are cleared.[105] Two theaters have been found[106] as well as a com-

Streets, public buildings, and temples have been cleared at the port of Dion.

plex of public bathhouses covering over 13,000 square feet.[107] Many statues of pagan idols and some sanctuaries have come to light, showing a pervasive influence of polytheism. Especially impressive is the Sanctuary of Isis, which was uncovered outside the southeast corner of the city walls, under more than six feet of water after earth tremors. Two cult statues and an honorary-portrait statue were found still standing on their bases.[108]

Athens

The Harbors of Athens

Whether from Dion or some point to the north, Paul evidently departed by sea, for Athens. Several harbors existed near Athens, though the city itself is not on the sea; therefore where Paul arrived is also somewhat uncertain. The original port of Athens and closest natural harbor is at *Phaleron*, about 5 miles south of the heart of town. There the Greeks beached their triremes until the fifth century B.C., in full view of the Athenians on Philappapos

Paul may have embarked at the harbor at Makrigialos.

Hill. Local tradition says Paul landed farther south at the resort city of *Glifada*, a picturesque bay on whose shores lie the unimpressive remains of an early church building, probably Byzantine. But there seems little reason to doubt that Paul would have landed rather at *Piraeus*, which since classical times, has remained the harbor of Athens. In addition to the large main harbor, there are two small adjacent havens—Zea and Mounikhias. Themistocles, beginning in 493 B.C., built a navy of 200 ships and fortified Piraeus, which he chose as his harbor. It was destroyed by Sulla in 86 B.C., but was revived in early imperial times and was functioning when Paul was in Athens. Apollonius and Pausanias both seem to have entered Athens from Piraeus.[109]

The City of Athens

Extensive archaeological excavation and numerous ancient literary sources have made it possible to reconstruct the Athens of the New Testament period. Some seventy-five hundred inscriptions have been found in the Agora, and much information has been gained through stratigraphical excavation of structures.[110]

What this wealth of information shows is a city quite unlike such great urban centers of the time as Antioch of Syria, Ephesus, Alexandria, Rome, and even Corinth. Athens was a city from which the glory had departed. After five hundred years of political and military misfortunes, which induced haphazard growth, Athens was a "provincial backwater,"[111] a small university town

Figure 26
Schematic of Athens

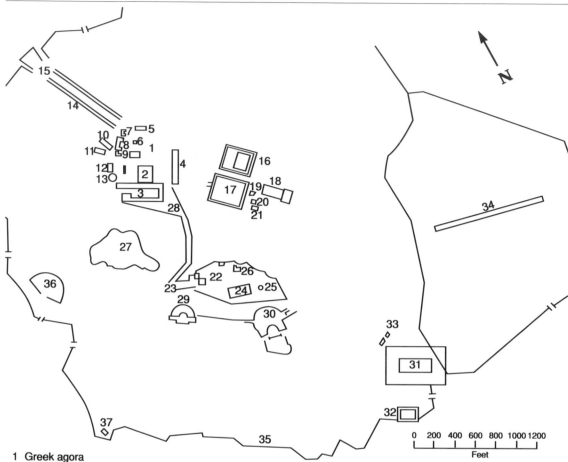

1 Greek agora
2 Odeion of Agrippa
3 Middle stoa and civic offices
4 Stoa of Attalos
5 Painted porch (Stoa Poikile)
6 Altar of the Twelve Gods
7 Royal stoa
8 Stoa of Zeus
9 Apollo Patroos
10 Arsenal
11 Hephaestion (Theseion)
12 Bouleuterion (council chamber)
13 Tholos
14 Road west
15 Double Gates
16 Library of Hadrian
17 Roman forum
18 Pantheion
19 Latrine

20 Tower of the Winds
21 Agoranomeion (?)
22 Acropolis
23 Propylaea
24 Parthenon
25 Circular monopteral temple of Rome and Augustus

26 Erechtheion
27 Areopagus (Mars Hill)
28 Panathenaic Way
29 Odeion of Herodes Atticus
30 Theater of Dionysus
31 Olympeium (Temple of Zeus/Jupiter)

32 Panhellenium
33 Gate of Hadrian
34 Lyceum
35 Wall of Themistocles
36 Pnyx
37 Philoppapus Monument

more concerned with ideas than commerce, whose people basked only in the memories of a glorious history. The gloomy state of Athenian culture in the first century is revealed by the evidence of archaeological investigation.[112] However, Paul's visit came during a brief resurgence of building activity, the likes of which the city had not seen since the reign of Augustus and would not see again until the extensive program of Hadrian the Hellenophile in the second century.[113] No fewer than ninety-four altars are known to have been dedicated to Hadrian in Athens,[114] which became a significant city again under Hadrian and his successors. Hadrian's enormous spending spree on the city produced an economic renaissance.[115]

The Acropolis of Athens

When a Jewish-Christian traveler such as Paul arrived in Athens he must have felt admiration mixed with revulsion at the sight of the Acropolis—admiration for the splendor of the architectural achievements of the Parthenon but revulsion for the polytheism and pagan idolatry it had represented for a half millennium. During a visit to the summit he would have ascended the marble staircase built by Claudius, only about seven years (A.D. 42) before he arrived,[116] past a monument of Marcus Agrippa on the left,[117] and through the Propylaea, to the monuments and temples on top. The Propylaea or "Porch" and most of the other well-known structures on the summit were built in the early classical period; these include the Temple of Athena Nike, the Parthenon (Temple of Athena), and the Erechtheion.[118] Forty steps from the Propylaea was a colossal bronze statue of Athena Promachos by Phidias, finished in about 458 B.C.

More significant for the New Testament period was the Ionic monopteral Temple of Rome and Augustus a few yards east of the Parthenon. Built soon after 27 B.C.,[119] the temple is identified through a dedicatory inscription which may still be seen lying at the site.[120] This temple dedicated to the goddess Roma and the emperor Augustus emphasizes the importance of emperor worship in the New Testament period. Even off the Acropolis, thirteen small altars bearing the name of Augustus in the genitive or dative case have been found in the lower city.[121] Linguistic case is significant, for deity is clearly implied when dedicatory base

The splendor of pagan temples Paul saw on the Athenian Acropolis still inspires awe.

inscriptions appear in the dative case; an altar on which is inscribed the honored name in the genitive case clearly implies divinity.[122] Most statue bases inscribed with the name of Augustus thus infer his divinity.[123] A dedication from the agora assimilates Claudius, a generous and important benefactor of Athens, into the personage of Apollo Patroos, an important divinity in Athens. A series of statues designate Claudius "preserver and benefactor" (σωτηρα και ευεργετην). He earned the honor of Athens when he restored many of Athens's Attic sanctuaries. He moved to the city what Leslie Shear calls "migratory monuments," statuary which had stood elsewhere since the fifth-century B.C. Evidence of these donations has been found in agora excavations, and both Pausanias and Dio Cassius record the gifts.[124]

The Greek Agora

That Paul visited the Acropolis is a legitimate assumption, but his daily discussions in the agora are a matter of record (Acts 17:17). A Greek agora and a Roman forum stood in Athens when Paul visited the city; more precisely, these were two sections of one large agora. Agora and forum had been "a single indivisible unit" until the Stoa of Attalos was built, dividing them in the second century B.C.[125] The older, larger section to the west is the more familiar, lying due north of the Areopagus and including the prominent Hephaestion and the reconstructed Stoa of Attalos.[126] The other section lay 250 feet to the east, as confirmed by two inscriptions, one on the architrave of the Gate of Athena, a Doric tetrastyle propylon that allowed entrance to the Greek agora;[127] the other on the base of a statue of Lucius Caesar, Augustus's grandson.[128] Augustus, in fact, completed the Roman section in the last decade of the first century B.C. after work was begun by Julius Caesar.[129] It is now customarily referred to as the "Market of Caesar and Augustus."

During the imperial period dramatic changes in Athens reflected themselves in the altered function of the agora. The ancient city-state had reserved the agora for political purposes. John M. Camp states that "in its simplest form the agora was a large open square reserved for public functions."[130] For five centuries in democratic Athens, the square had been kept free of public and private buildings. Civic structures, such as the Bouleuterion, the Tholos, the Royal Stoa, and the law courts were allowed only around its perimeter. However, "a conquered city had little need for democratic assemblies,"[131] and, from the reign of Augustus buildings and monuments began to fill the public square. One structure remaining from earlier years was the bema, which stood in front of the Stoa of Attalos. From this speaker's platform "orators harangued the crowds."[132] Built between 150

Figure 27
Athenian Agora (A.D. 50)

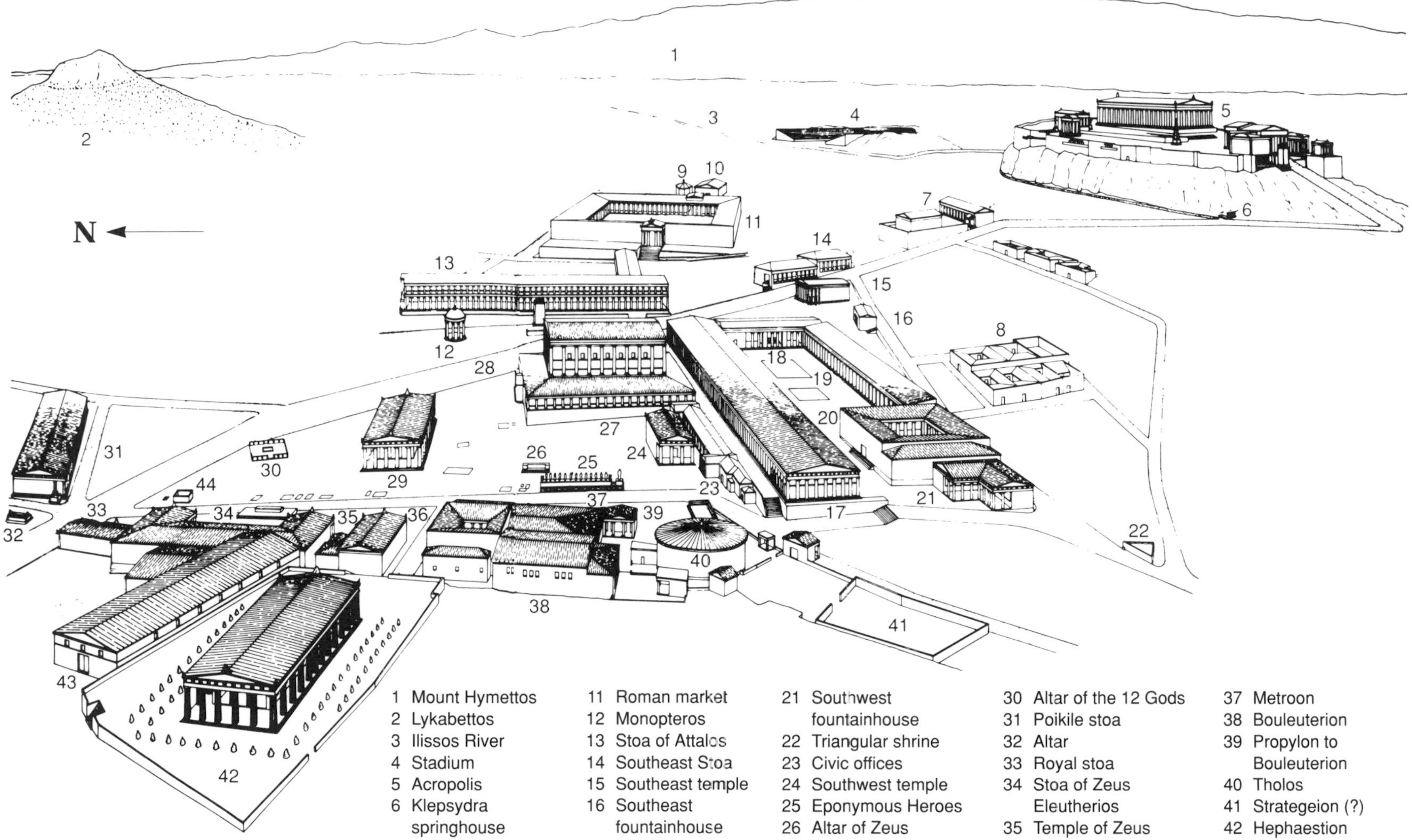

N →

1	Mount Hymettos
2	Lykabettos
3	Ilissos River
4	Stadium
5	Acropolis
6	Klepsydra springhouse
7	Eleusinion
8	Houses
9	Tower of the winds
10	Agoranomion

11	Roman market
12	Monopteros
13	Stoa of Attalos
14	Southeast Stoa
15	Southeast temple
16	Southeast fountainhouse
17	Middle stoa
18	East building
19	South stoa II
20	Heliaia (?)

21	Southwest fountainhouse
22	Triangular shrine
23	Civic offices
24	Southwest temple
25	Eponymous Heroes
26	Altar of Zeus Agoraios (?)
27	Odeion
28	Panathenic Way
29	Temple of Ares

30	Altar of the 12 Gods
31	Poikile stoa
32	Altar
33	Royal stoa
34	Stoa of Zeus Eleutherios
35	Temple of Zeus Phratrios and Athena Phratria
36	Temple of Apollo Patroos

37	Metroon
38	Bouleuterion
39	Propylon to Bouleuterion
40	Tholos
41	Strategeion (?)
42	Hephaestion
43	Arsenal (?)
44	Cross-road sanctuary

Courtesy of the American School of Classical Studies at Athens. Adapted from a reconstruction by W. B. Dinsmoor.

and 88 B.C.,[133] it could have been used by Paul, but there was almost no political activity in the Greek agora after the death of Augustus,[134] so Paul probably spent most of his time in the commercial agora to the east.

Since this eastern market, the Agora of Caesar and Augustus, was used primarily for commercial purposes and since the Greek Agora was no longer needed for democratic functions, the latter had "assumed something of the aspect of a museum."[135] By the mid-first century A.D. the agora had become a repository for altars, statues, and temples. With the imperial emperor worship and Greek mythological idolatry on display, Petronius, the satirist, remarked that it was easier to find a god than a man in Athens!

Paul was impressed that among so many objects of pagan superstition, there should actually be an altar dedicated to an "unknown god" (Acts 17:23). He was one of many who noticed this particular altar of the pantheon. Pausanias, who visited Athens between 143 and 159 A.D., saw such altars. In describing his trip from the harbor to Athens he wrote: "The Temple of Athene Skiras is also here, and one of Zeus further off, and altars of the 'Unknown gods.'"[136] Similarly, at Olympia, he described the Altar of Olympian Zeus as near "an altar of the Unknown gods."[137] Apollonius of Tyana, who died in A.D. 98, spoke of Athens as the place "where altars are set up in honor even of unknown gods" (ἀγνώστων δαιμόνων βωμοί).[138] Diogenes Laertius wrote of altars being erected "to the god whom it may concern" (τῷ προσήκοντι θεῷ).[139] Oecumenius records an altar dedicated to "the gods of Asia, Europe and Libya, to the Unknown and Strange God."[140] An altar to an "unknown god," was purportedly located in Athens by Pope Innocent III in 1208.[141]

When William Dorpfeld cleared the sacred precinct of Demeter at Pergamum in 1909, he found an altar with a partially defective inscription, which was restored by Hugo Hepding and Adolf Deissmann to read: θεοις αγν[ωστοις] Καπιτω[ν] δαδουχο[ς] ("To unknown gods, Capito, torchbearer").[142] Undoubtedly, some of these references are to multiple altars, which may have singular as well as plural references to god. There is no reason to assume, as Edward Norden, that every altar was to a plurality of "gods."[143] One clear reference to a Greek referring to "god" in the singular is found in the very words of the poet Aratus quoted by Paul in his sermon in Athens: "For we are indeed his offspring" (Acts 17:28, RSV; Gk., Τοῦ γὰρ καὶ γένος ἐσμέν).[144] The adherents of ancient polytheistic religion, characterized as they were by superstitious ignorance, may have simply erected altars to unknown gods "so that no deity might be offended by human neglect."[145]

The first two large structures to inhabit the Greek agora under the Roman empire occupied most of the area west of the Panathenaic Way: the Agrippeion and the Temple of Ares. The largest

In the Greek agora, here shown surrounded by modern Athens, Paul noticed many altars, including one to "an unknown god."

of all the Roman additions was the Agrippeion, an odeum built about 15 B.C. by Marcus V. Agrippa, son-in-law of Augustus.[146] It seated about one thousand people and was built primarily as a concert hall (for a discussion of the characteristics of odea, see p. 58).[147] By the mid-second century A.D. the ceiling of the Agrippeion collapsed for it had no central supports, and was rebuilt to about half its original size. The larger size was no longer needed because at about this time (160 A.D.) an Athenian millionaire named Herodes Atticus built a large new Roman theater on the south slopes of the Acropolis. Moreover, according to Philostratus, the smaller seating capacity reflected a change in the use for the building;[148] it had become largely a lecture hall for "sophists and philosophers who had replaced generals and orators as the most notable citizens."[149]

The Temple of Ares also altered the interior of the Greek agora. Located just northwest of the Agrippeion, it was built elsewhere in the fifth century B.C., then moved, stone by stone, to the agora during the rebuilding program under Augustus. It seems to have been finished and dedicated in A.D. 2.[150] Besides the Agrippeion and Temple of Ares, other structures added to the Greek agora included a small temple built during the reign of Claudius. Now called the Southwest Temple,[151] it apparently was dedicated to Livia, the consort of Augustus and mother of Tiberius. The dedication identifies Livia with Artemis Boulaia.[152] Another small temple also stood in the southeastern section of the agora from Claudius's reign. Either Augustus or Claudius transferred the fourth-century B.C. marble Altar of Zeus Agoraios from the Pnyx to just south of the Temple of Ares and added to the Stoa of Zeus. Thus, what Paul saw in the agora had become somewhat of a religious and civic showplace.

The Roman Forum

A walkway connecting the Greek and Roman sections was not colonnaded until the time of Hadrian; Athens had no colonnaded streets at all until Hadrian's building program.[153] In contrast with the Greek agora, the Roman Forum (the eastern section of the old agora) was alive with commercial activity. Here Paul would more likely have found the ear of the ordinary citizen of Athens. Called the Eretria by Strabo,[154] the Forum was 364 feet long by 321 feet wide, about the same size as the Forum of Julius Caesar (*Forum Iulium*) in Rome, which measured 430 by 295 feet.[155] The Forum in Rome was designated for public business, according to Appian,[156] whereas the Forum in Athens was used for commercial purposes.

This Forum, excavated by the Greek Archaeological Society and the Archaeological Service of Greece,[157] is seen much less frequently by the modern visitor to Athens than the Greek section to the west. This is unfortunate for those who are interested in New Testament period archaeology, because one of the best preserved ancient monuments in Greece is located there. Popularly called the "Tower of the Winds," it is a tall octagonal marble tower with sculpted images of the eight winds near the top of its eight sides. Its official name is probably the one cited by Varro, Horologion, indicating that it contained some kind of clock.[158] It was, in fact, a huge water-clock, sundial, and weather vane,[159] built by Andronicus of Cyrrhus in the last half of the first century B.C., and served as a public time piece for the city.[160] The Horologion stood

Athens' commercial center, the Roman Forum.

Tower of the Winds, a marble clock tower and weather vane.

at the east end of the Forum of Caesar and Augustus, its location selected, undoubtedly, to make the clock accessible at any hour to the largest number of people possible. That it stood in this spot may testify to the central position of the eastern part of the agora, even before the construction of Caesar and Augustus.

A sixty-six-seat public latrine was built beside the Horologion in the first century A.D. Another building, whose function is not known, was built adjacent to the Horologion's south side, in the mid-first century. It was thought to be a caretaker's residence (*agoranomion*),[161] but that probably was just outside the western Gate of Athena Archegetis, along the road connecting the two agoras.[162]

Under Trajan, about the time the apostle John died at Ephesus, the Greek agora and the Roman Forum both began to receive extensive additions.[163] Between 98 and 102 the Library of Pantainos was erected at the south end of the Stoa of Attalos, between the two agoras. The library was dedicated, by inscription, to Trajan, Athena Polias, and the city of the Athenians.[164]

Colonnaded stoas were built along its west and north sides. Colonnades also were added along the street connecting the agoras, and the street was paved with marble about A.D. 100. Later Hadrian added colonnaded stoas on both sides of the northern entrance to the Greek agora. Between 114 and 116, on the hill southwest of the Acropolis, the Athenians built an impressive tomb monument to C. Julius Antiochos Philopappos. Philopappos had been king of Commagene in northern Syria and later became a great benefactor of Athens, serving as consul in 109. Hadrian built a huge library, styled somewhat after the design of the Market of Caesar and Augustus by the north side of the Forum. Nearby, to the east, he built the gigantic Pantheon, which was larger than the Parthenon. A section of the Pantheon was recently discovered and may be seen on Hadrianou Street.

The Olympeion of Hadrian

About 1200 feet due east of the Pantheon, Hadrian built his "New Athens" (Hadrianopolis), a district that included gymnasiums, parks, baths, and villas for the wealthy. Today Hadrianopolis takes in the area of Syntagma Square, the National Gardens, and the Zappeion. On the south edge of his development, Hadrian constructed the huge Temple of Olympian Zeus; its fluted columns crowned by Corinthian capitals may still be seen. The Gate of Hadrian, which provided entrance to the temple area, still stands beside Amalias Boulevard. This gate marked the eastern limit of the old city of Athens where it joined New Athens. On the northwest side of the gate, an inscription reads; "This is Athens, the ancient city of Theseus;" while the opposite side reads: "This is the city of Hadrian and not of Theseus."

Between the Temple of Olympian Zeus and the Ilissos River, remains of Hadrian's Panhellenium (Temple of Hera and Zeus Panhellenios) have been discovered. Close by to the south stood a large gymnasium (one of many in the city) from the building program. Remains of the channel of an aqueduct that brought water to a reservoir on the lower slopes of Mount Lykabettos can be seen behind the Gennadion Library of the American School. The reservoir itself has disappeared. Hadrian also added colonnaded stoas on either side of the northern entrance to the Greek Agora.

The Areopagus

While preaching in the agora, Paul was seized and taken before the Areopagus (Acts 17:19), which in the decades preceding Paul's arrival had been reinstated by Sulla as the governing body of the city.[165] We know that the council of the Areopagus had judicial authority, and the Areopagites seem to have begun to act as municipal senators by the time of their confrontation with Paul.[166] During the Roman period, the official address of this body was "the council (βουλή) of the Areopagus, the council of the five (or six) hundred and the municipality (δῆμος) of the Athenians," a formula that appears on many monuments of the period. The council of the Areopagus had come to dominate Athenian government.[167] Questions regarding the teaching of Paul, who had been speaking of "foreign divinities" (Acts 17:18), fell under the jurisdiction of the Areopagus, which had "surveillance over the introduction of foreign divinities," according to Daniel J. Geagan.[168]

The meeting place of the Areopagus at this time is not certain. In the classical period it met in various locations—the Royal Stoa in the fourth century B.C., for example.[169] It sat in Eleusis during the Eleusinian mysteries.[170] But "Areopagus" means literally "the hill of Ares" (Lat., "Mars") so the traditional location on the Areopagus or Mars Hill,[171] seems to fit the evidence from Lucian that jury panels were assigned to hear trials at this site.[172] However, while there is no good reason to deny that Paul stood before the Areopagus council on the Areopagus, it is by no means certain that he did.

One of the men who heard Paul speak and believed his message was a member of the Areopagus named Dionysius (Acts 17:34). He became the first bishop of Athens, was martyred under Domitian, was canonized by the Orthodox Church and today is regarded as the patron saint of Athens. Paul's success in Athens was so modest that it is ironically appropriate that one of his few

Mar's Hill is probably, but not definitely, the place where Paul confronted the Areopagus.

converts, rather than Paul himself, became the patron saint of the city. Tradition has attributed the founding and perhaps the building of the original Church of Saint Dionysius the Areopagite, on the northern slopes of Mars Hill, to his influence. Only the foundations of the sixteenth-century church building are still visible. Excavations since 1963 by the American School have been unable to find anything but private houses beneath the foundation level. However, adjoining the building, a seventh-century palace of the archbishop was uncovered and identified by inscription.[173] Complicating matters is that tradition seems to confuse the original Dionysius the Areopagite with three other leaders of the same name: Dionysius, bishop of Corinth; a later "Pseudo-Dionysius" who penned spurious writings in the name of Paul's disciple, and still later, Dionysius or Denys, bishop of Paris.[174]

Among the groups of philosophers who heard Paul was the Stoics. Their name derived from the Stoa Poikile (Painted Porch) on which they met. The foundations of the building were found in 1981 in the northwest corner of the agora.[175] Excavations in 1982 confirmed the date of construction to be the decade between 470 and 460 B.C., and Pausanias was shown, once more, to be remarkably accurate in his topographical descriptions.[176]

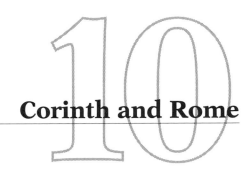

Corinth and Rome

Corinth

The Geography of Corinth

Paul's limited success at Athens, in contrast to the substantial success and consequent persecution he experienced in other cities, presumably caused him to leave Athens and go to Corinth, where he began his preaching, as usual, in the synagogue (Acts

18:1, 4–5). Rejection of his message by the Jews caused him to turn once again, though not permanently, to the Gentiles of the city (Acts 18:6; cf. 19:8–9). Archaeological and literary evidence together give a detailed picture of the Corinth Paul knew.

Corinth is about 50 miles west of Athens, a pleasant drive of 1.5 hours along the coast.[1] Remains of the ancient city lie in the midst of the village of Old Corinth, but this quaint town was destroyed by earthquake in 1858; then New Corinth was built 3.5 miles northeast of the old city. New Corinth was placed on the coast, 1.5 miles west of the Corinthian Canal. Ancient Corinth, the city which Paul visited stood between the northern slopes of the 1886-foot-high Acrocorinth and the Gulf of Corinth, 4 miles to the north. Corinth's population exceeded that of Athens, numbering perhaps 300,000 or more citizens and 460,000 slaves, according to Athenaeus, who lived during the second century A.D.[2] The walls are known to have extended for 6 miles around the city. Excavations have been conducted in ancient Corinth since 1886.[3]

Corinth was already a prosperous city in the second century B.C. when it headed the Achaean League and attempted to break away from Rome. The rebellion was mercilessly put down by the Roman general Lucius Mummius in 146 B.C., and Corinth lay in ruins until rebuilt by Julius Caesar in about 44 B.C., although James Wiseman argues that Corinth's destruction was less extensive than scholars have thought.[4] Strabo, who visited Corinth in 44 and again in 29 B.C., described it as "wealthy because of its

The Acrocorinth provides a view of the intermingling of ancient and modern Corinth.

commerce."[5] This is significant because the city had been rebuilt for only thirty-seven years when he finished his *Geography* in 7 B.C. How the city could have achieved this remarkable comeback, which is supported by archaeological remains as well as literary sources, is probably due to the same reason Julius Caesar began to rebuild it. It became wealthy, Strabo explains, because "it is situated on the Isthmus and is master of two harbors, of which the one [Cenchreae] leads straight to Asia, and the other [Lechaion] to Italy; and it makes easy the exchange of merchandise."[6] As recorded by Strabo, other important sources of revenue included the city's famed immorality, and the quality of its statesmen and craftsmen.[7] The Isthmian Games, according to Strabo, as well as Plutarch and Pausanias, must have provided enormous income also, just as do the modern Olympic Games.[8]

The Diolkos

Archaeological evidence now supplements literary allusions[9] to the commercial and military traffic that crossed this 3.5-mile neck of land. From 1956 to 1959, N. M. Verdelis of the Greek Archaeological Service excavated a stone-paved roadway, called the *diolkos,* that was built across the Isthmus in the sixth century B.C.[10] Although the initial purpose for its construction could have been military,[11] its primary users quickly became commercial traffic.[12] Brian MacDonald has argued that only cargo—not the ships themselves—was moved over the roadway. He believes that the diolkos was intended mainly for commerce from the start.[13]

Excavations seem to agree that the road was used as a portage for cargo only, which was loaded onto a different vessel across the isthmus. Channels in the stone pavement, along which the load-bearing platform (*holkos*) moved, are only five feet apart, so only small boats could fit.[14] Both Thucydides and Polybius mention light-weight boats using the diolkos.[15] MacDonald writes that "cargo was probably transported on a wooden platform fitted with wheels or rollers that were guided along the parallel tracks: oxen may have provided the drawing power."[16] Marble, timber, building stone, roof tiles, metals, pottery, and foodstuffs were probably all transported along the road. A wide stone dock where these were loaded and unloaded at the western end of the diolkos has been uncovered by the Verdelis excavation.[17] About 750 feet of the roadway have been uncovered on the Peloponnesian side of the entrance to the modern canal from the Corinthian Gulf. The width varies at this point from 11 feet to 18 feet. Another section, more than 670 feet long and measuring 18 to 19 feet wide, has been found on the northern side of the canal on the grounds of the Military Survey School.

Cargo and even small ships made the portage across the diolkos near Corinth.

It was probably during the reign of Periander, tyrant of Corinth in the early sixth century B.C. (ca. 625–585 B.C.) that the diolkos was built, and he is the first person in recorded history to have conceived the idea of cutting a canal across the isthmus.[18] Philostratus thought such an accomplishment would be both "undying and incredible in its very nature . . . a job more for Poseidon than a mortal man."[19] Some of the Roman emperors, who considered themselves to be somewhat more than mortal, attempted the feat, including Julius Caesar, Caligula, and Nero.[20] The apostle Paul could not have imagined as he first crossed the isthmus in 49 that in September of 67, only eighteen years later, 6000 Jewish slaves would be brought by Vespasian from Tiberias in Israel to work on this canal.[21] According to Philostratus, Nero was finally dissuaded from the project after digging only a short distance.[22] A French company finally completed the canal project after working from 1881 until 1883. The finished canal is 3.9 miles long, which includes a channel totalling 1772 feet that extends into the gulfs at both ends. At sea level the canal is 80.7 feet wide; at the highest point of the isthmus, walls of sheer rock rise to 259 feet above the canal's surface.[23]

Immorality at Corinth

Another factor in Corinth's wealth mentioned by Strabo was the great immorality of the city. The Temple of Aphrodite on the Acrocorinth, he said, "owned a thousand temple-slaves, prostitutes, whom both men and women had dedicated to the goddess;" because of these, he maintained, "the city was crowded with people and grew rich."[24] Thus, there was a popular proverb: "Not for every man is the voyage to Corinth!"[25] Though Strabo's words are indeed puzzling on first reading, they are not necessarily a complete fabrication based on his acquaintance with temple prostitution elsewhere, as Jerome Murphy-O'Connor has argued, but with unconvincing evidence.[26]

Archaeological evidence relating to immorality at Corinth is scanty. However, a careful rereading of Strabo and exploration of the top of the Acrocorinth have led me to believe that the prostitution was carried on in the city. Consider the evidence:

1. Strabo says the "city," not the "temple," was crowded with people because of the prostitutes.
2. He says the temple "owned" the prostitutes; he does not say that the prostitutes either lived or functioned in the temple. It would seem reasonable that the temple-owned prostitutes functioned in the city where the crowds were.
3. Anyone who has ascended the Acrocorinth knows that a mass migration of people to and from this peak for any purpose is unlikely. The notion of hundreds of people frequently making a two-hour climb to the top, even if hundreds of donkeys were used, is simply not credible. Such a sight would have evoked a greater response from Strabo than the one he actually made! Helen Miller describes, regrettably without documentation, what must indeed have been the real situation in Corinth: "Of an evening, these hetairai gathered at the great fountain house [Fountain of Peirene] in the lower city."[27]
4. The excavations of the Acrocorinth by Carl Blegen for the American School found sufficient evidence of foundations, scanty as they were, to estimate the size of the Temple of Aphrodite at no larger than 33 feet by 52 feet.[28] Although a temple of these dimensions would not be large enough to "house" a thousand functioning prostitutes, housing them would not have been necessary since living quarters in a

sanctuary for priestesses and prostitutes would have been separate from the temple. At nearby Cenchreae, for example, excavators found what may have been the living quarters of the priestesses but no trace of a temple.[29] No trace of such quarters has been found on the Acrocorinth.

The Sanctuary of Demeter and Kore, on the northern base of the Acrocorinth, was an important center for ritual dining in connection with fertility worship in the sixth to fourth centuries B.C. The temple itself was ruined in the destruction of 146,[30] and it is difficult to say to what extent the worship functioned. Even before the temple was destroyed, excavator Ronald Stroud maintains, no more than thirty-two of the fifty excavated dining halls were in use at any one time. With one possible exception, none was in use in the time of Paul.[31] But that does not mean that sexual immorality was not practiced at this point, which was not so inaccessible as the top of the Acrocorinth. Nor did dining associated with this worship cease. Indications are that visitors to the sanctuary at the mid-first century did dine in tents or even the open air and the association of sexual practices with eating is strong in such agriculture-related worship.

There is some evidence that sexual immorality was associated with the Sanctuary of Demeter and Kore, as well as in the city and perhaps to a limited extent up the hill: First, the rite of the great cult of Demeter and Persephone—the Eleusinian mysteries—was so secret "that the efforts of scholars have scarcely been able to unravel its exact nature."[32] We know almost nothing from

The Temple of Aphrodite on the Acrocorinth.

The Sanctuary of Demeter and Kore on the base of the Acrocorinth.

literary references about the ritual.[33] Second, as I noted above, fifty small dining rooms were excavated in the sanctuary at Corinth. In discussing the triclinium in chapter 2 (pp. 79–80) it was observed that the sexual use of dining couches (κλῖναι) is widely portrayed on stone, pottery, and gems in museums throughout Greece.[34] In many of these depictions food is shown on nearby dining tables, perhaps indicating that the sensual pleasures of eating and sexual intercourse may commonly have been combined. Third, the dining areas were connected with worship of Demeter who was closely associated with Dionysus; that in itself strongly implies that sexual immorality was involved. Dionysus was the deity under whose powers came the fertility of vineyards, wine and "every type of life-giving moisture."[35] His was a fertility cult, and worshipers carried representations of a phallus in processions.[36] One sign of their religious superstition was that ancient Greek couples sometimes had sexual relations lying on barren sections of their land in the hope that doing so would increase the soil's fertility.[37]

Most of this evidence is drawn from before Paul's time, but it is doubtful that the worship of Demeter, much less human nature, changed over the Roman period. Worshipers can function without buildings; these devotees probably used tents.[38]

The Isthmian Games

Isthmia was one of four permanent sites for the Panhellenic games of Greece; games were also held at Olympia, Delphi, and

Nemea. All four local economies benefitted greatly from the athletic events. Isthmia was less than 10 miles east of Old Corinth and immediately west of the Corinthian Canal, .5 mile south of today's Athens-Corinth road. The Isthmian Games were administered from their beginning by Corinth, but after Corinth was destroyed in 146 the games were moved to Sikyon, west of Corinth.[39] They were returned to Isthmia and Corinthian administration again, however, in the last decade of the first century B.C.[40]

Oscar Broneer, who began excavating Isthmia for the University of Chicago in 1952,[41] thinks these games were the motivating reason Paul chose to "settle down" in Corinth and to make it the "pilot plant for his work on Greek soil."[42] Paul was in Corinth in A.D. 51, and there is evidence that the festival of games was held that year.[43]

However, there are problems with Broneer's view. First, Paul's primary concern was to reach Jews first with the Gospel and from them to branch out to Gentiles. The number of Jews in Isthmia is not known, but Paul *immediately* worked among Jews in Corinth (Acts 18:4–5). Wiseman agrees that "Paul must have been attracted to Corinth for a number of reasons: the large size of its Jewish community, swollen by the edict of Claudius. . . ."[44] Second, the games did not occur until more than a year after Paul arrived in Corinth. Third, there was little in Isthmia itself that would attract Paul, outside the games. Excavations have shown that, apart from the stadium in which the games were held and the sanctuaries of Poseidon and Palaimon, there were few buildings still standing at the site at the midpoint of the first century. The theater was not renovated for use until the seating was needed for a visit by Nero in 66.[45] The facilities that were in use related to the temple cults and the games.[46]

A fourth suggestion is that the games may, in fact, have been partly involved in the crisis that caused Paul to leave Corinth. He appeared before Gallio in the spring or summer of 51. The Jews may have taken advantage of the high feeling of loyalty to Poseidon that was part of the spirit of the Isthmian Games to accuse Paul of improperly worshiping God. Those games, would recently have been completed or were about to begin. Murphy-O'Connor notes that "Greek national consciousness was one of the by-products of the panhellenic games."[47]

It must be recognized that the worship of the Roman emperor, which Paul found so prominent in Athens, was prevalent in the area around Corinth as well, for Isthmia was also a center of emperor worship.[48] The fact that Isthmia contained many temples and altars to pagan idols, including the Temple of Poseidon in whose honor as chief deity of the Isthmian Sanctuary the games were held, would provide Paul with a challenge similar to that faced in Athens. No doubt Paul would have seized the opportunity to work with the huge crowds at the games while he was in Corinth,[49] but his choice of Corinth as a base must have been based on something more substantial than a few days of sports competition.

The Jewish Presence in Corinth

Surely Paul went on to Corinth because it was the largest and most important city in Greece, with ports to both the east and the west, and contained a sizable Jewish population.[50] There were Jews in Corinth as early as the reign of Caligula (37–41),[51] and others came in 49 during the expulsion of Jews from Rome under Claudius (Acts 18:2).[52] Jewish inscriptions have been found occasionally in the area of Corinth from 1951 to 1976 and were gathered only recently for publication. Most of these are funerary inscriptions from the Christian period, and one of them (no. 29) is bilingual, in Hebrew and Greek.[53]

A partially preserved inscription mentioning a "synagogue of the Hebrews" was found in Corinth in 1898 and published in 1903 by Benjamin Powell, who thought it came from the synagogue in which Paul preached.[54] After further study by the excavation team of Corinth, however, it was dated "considerably later than the time of Saint Paul" on the basis of its style of lettering.[55] Since it was found on the Lechaion Road at the foot of the marble steps leading to the Propylaea, the synagogue from which it came likely stood north of the Propylaea and the Fountain of

Corinth's synagogue stood along the Lechaion Road. In the background lies the Acrocorinth.

Peirene. The synagogue in which Paul preached probably lies under the later one, since Jews in ancient Israel tended to rebuild synagogues over previously destroyed ones.

Interestingly, a Samaritan amulet inscription was noticed by Jacob Kaplan among those published in the Corinth excavations. It dates to the fourth century A.D. Corinth may now join Athens, Thessalonica and Rome on the the list of Samaritan migrant communities.[56]

Paul's Arrival in Corinth

When Paul arrived, Corinth like Athens, was in the midst of a building boom. Had he come a few decades earlier, he would have beheld the ruins of Mummius's conquest and felt perhaps as did William Haygarth, who wrote in 1814, after viewing Corinth's later ruins:

> "Hard is his heart, O Corinth! who beholds
> Thee bow'd to dust, nor sheds one pitying
>   tear."[57]

But the Corinth of Paul's time was not "bow'd to dust" but a proud, international center of commerce and entertainment; Horace could write in the time of Augustus, *"Non cuivis homini contigit adire Corinthum"*: "It is not the privilege of every man to go to Corinth."[58]

The official name for the Roman colony founded by Julius Caesar was *Colonia Laus Julia Corinthiensis*.[59] Continuing excavation of the site since 1896 by the American School of Classical Studies at Athens has drawn a rather good picture of its appearance in the mid-first century, particularly the Forum and the Sanctuary of Demeter and Kore. Reports of the excavators have appeared in *Hesperia* and the *American Journal of Archaeology*; the major publication of the excavations is the multi-volume *Corinth: Results of Excavations Conducted by the American School of Classical Studies at Athens*.[60] Work on the site has also been conducted by the University of Texas at Austin and Case Western Reserve University.[61]

Paul probably first entered Corinth from the north on the graveled Lechaion Road.[62] As he walked along the street the surrounding architecture reflected the transition from a culture that had been Greek for half of a millennium to that of a Roman colony. The institutions of Roman society were all there—religious, commercial, civic, and athletic—just as they had been at Philippi, another Roman colony in which he had found an openness to God's message. After his disappointing experience in Athens, Paul's sensitivities must have been heightened, his reli-

Figure 28
Schematic of Corinth

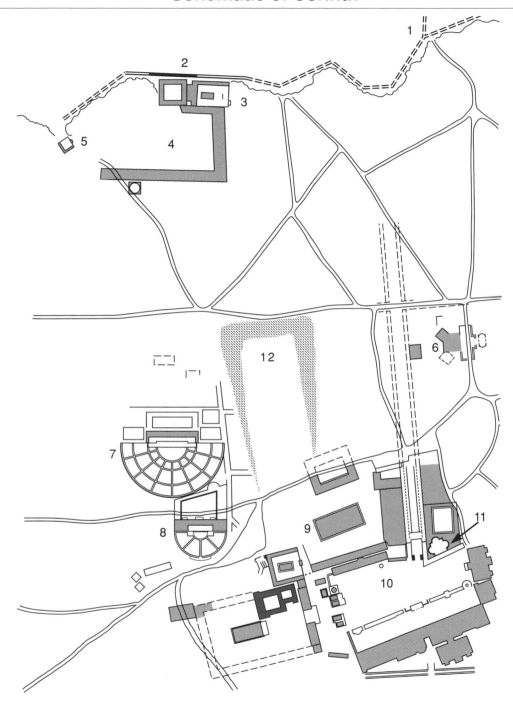

1 West long wall	7 Theater
2 City wall	8 Odeion
3 Asklepieion	9 Archaic temple
4 Gymnasium	10 Forum
5 Bath and fountain	11 Peirene
6 Roman bath	12 Excavation Dump

gious insights outraged, and his sense of imminent cultural conflict sharpened.

Religious Architecture of Corinth

The stark contrast between Roman polytheism and monotheistic Jewish Christianity must have been Paul's most immediate impression. Just inside the northern city wall on the west side of the road he passed the Sanctuary of Asklepios, one of the premier medical centers of the day, where medicine was practiced in the context of pagan idolatry. As at Pergamum (see p. 271), Asklepios received credit for the healing that occurred in this large temple. The medical clinic was on the west side of the lower level.[63] Three dining rooms were built into the east side of the lower level, probably for sacred banqueting.[64] A special room in the Corinth Museum houses scores of ceramic representations of body parts called *ex votos* from the temple.

Also west of the Lechaion Road, although nearer the Forum, the Temple of either Apollo or Athena[65] stood on a high promontory. One of the oldest temples in Greece, it was built in the sixth century B.C. on the Doric order and was peripteral with 38 columns. The design had fifteen columns across and six columns deep; seven of these monolithic columns still stand. By the time Paul arrived in Corinth, the temple had been restored. Also, the

The museum at Corinth has a large collection of ex votos from the Sanctuary of Asklepios.

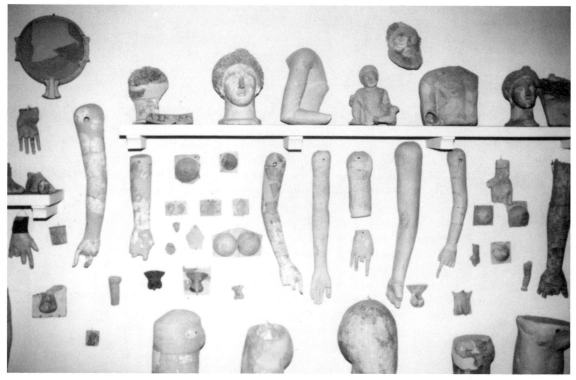

322

A Doric temple to Apollo or Athena near the Forum at Corinth is one of Greece's oldest.

interior columns had been removed for use on a stylobate that stood west of the south stoa.[66]

A focal point of religious observance, of course, was the Acrocorinth. Most noticeable on its summit today are the remains of 1.5 miles of walls built by Byzantines, Franks, Venetians, and Turks. On the south side of the summit, there are considerable remains of the Roman period, including the Upper Peirene Fountain, which was described by Strabo as "beneath the summit," and by Pausanias as "behind the temple."[67] It is "behind" (i.e., south of) the Temple of Aphrodite when one stands on the Acrocorinth and faces north toward Corinth. Pausanias was writing with reference to the city.[68] When Paul was in the city the Sanctuary of Demeter and Kore had been remodeled. One of its buildings served as the temple, while ritual dining was served outside (see pp. 316–317).

Several smaller temples also stood at the western end of the Forum (see diagram of the Forum).[69] The Temple of Tyche and the Temple of Apollo had been standing from the time of Augustus. A circular base for a statue stood adjacent to the Temple of Tyche on its south side. By the mid-first century the Temple of Aphrodite was built adjacent to the south side of the Temple to Apollo.[70] Another structure among the temples may also be a temple, but its date is undetermined.[71]

Charles Williams, II, the current director of the American School excavations in the Forum, has argued that the huge structure at the western end of the Forum, known as the "Corinthian Temple," was built during the reign of Tiberius or earlier. Probably built to house the imperial cult, the temple testifies to the shift in emphasis during the first century A.D. from worship of the Olympian gods to that of the emperor.[72] Adjacent to the northeast corner of the *temenos* of the Corinthian temple stood yet another religious structure. Though Robert Scranton has identified it as the Sanctuary of Hera Acraea,[73] this is "highly conjectural, and there is little archaeological evidence for support."[74]

Commercial Facilities of Corinth

In addition to the imposing religious architecture of Corinth, Paul would no doubt have been greatly impressed with its commercial facilities. The forum arrangement in Corinth was somewhat similar to that in Athens. The old Greek agora is thought by Williams, the excavator, to lie under the modern shopping district, which is north of the Fountain of Peirene and the Peribolos of Apollo. In the first century A.D. the Forum was relocated to just south of Temple Hill.[75] The lay of the land divided this area naturally into two forum sections. The entire forum area lay roughly between a South Stoa and a Northwest Stoa. The Upper Forum, used primarily for the administrative needs of the city, was built on the terrace north of the South Stoa. Until the destruction by Mummius in 146 B.C., this section had been occupied by monuments. Corinthians could descend from this terrace to a Lower Forum. Its large area was bounded on the east by the shopping area in and around the Julian Basilica to the temples on the west. On its north end rose the Temple Hill and on its south the Central Shops. The area of the Lower Forum was a racetrack before 146 B.C., so it did not have to be cleared by the builders of the new Roman colony. Starting blocks can still be seen carved into the rock on its east end.

Considerable space was provided for shops and markets around the Lower Forum and in other areas throughout central Corinth. Food was probably most available at the North Market, which has been so-named because it lay well down the north slope of the Temple Hill. It was built in the first half of the first century A.D. so it was relatively new when Paul likely purchased food from its vendors. Even more recent in Paul's time were two identical basilicas, the South Basilica and the Julian Basilica, built in about 40. These buildings were designed so that goods could be displayed on elevated platforms, with storage space for excess merchandise under these floors in the ground-level *cryptoporticus*. The floors to these markets were supported by arches. The Peribolos of Apollo, a large courtyard with colonnades and shops on three sides and a terrace wall on the east, was built during the reign of Augustus immediately northeast of the Lower Fountain of Peirene. Shops extended from this district along both sides of the nearby Lechaion Road. Under the eastern side of a

Figure 29
Roman Forum in Corinth

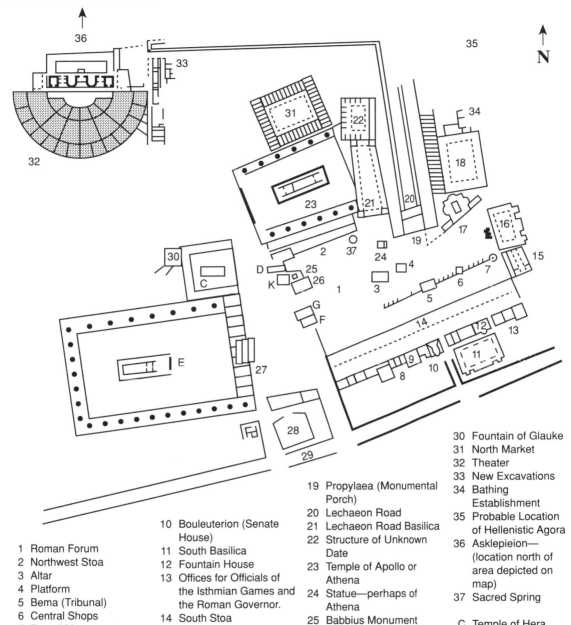

1 Roman Forum
2 Northwest Stoa
3 Altar
4 Platform
5 Bema (Tribunal)
6 Central Shops
7 Round Monument
8 South Shops
9 Douvir's Office (later a bathhouse)
10 Bouleuterion (Senate House)
11 South Basilica
12 Fountain House
13 Offices for Officials of the Isthmian Games and the Roman Governor.
14 South Stoa
15 Tabularium (Library)
16 Julian Basilica
17 Fountain of Peirene
18 Peribolos of Apollo
19 Propylaea (Monumental Porch)
20 Lechaeon Road
21 Lechaeon Road Basilica
22 Structure of Unknown Date
23 Temple of Apollo or Athena
24 Statue—perhaps of Athena
25 Babbius Monument
26 Fountain
27 Western Shops
28 Cellar Building
29 Decumanus
30 Fountain of Glauke
31 North Market
32 Theater
33 New Excavations
34 Bathing Establishment
35 Probable Location of Hellenistic Agora
36 Asklepieion— (location north of area depicted on map)
37 Sacred Spring

C Temple of Hera
D Temple of Tyche
E Corinthian Temple (Tiberius or earlier)
F Temple of Venus
G Temple of Clarion Apollo
K Identification of Building Unknown (perhaps a temple)

huge Lechaion Road Basilica, sixteen shops, vaulted and constructed of masonry with dirt floors, opened onto the road. A long row of Central Shops was built at the point where the Upper Forum dropped to the Lower Forum. And on the western terrace of the Temple Hill, behind the Roman temples, a series of West Shops and the Northwest Stoa (two groups of six each) were built in the reign of Augustus.[76]

Another strip of shops along the Northwest Stoa end of the Forum resemble the West Shops, but they are of later construction. The West Shops and the Northwest Stoa are from the reign of Augustus, but a careful look at the construction of the Northwest Shops, reveals that they were built over the eastern part of what had been the Northwest Stoa, after the Stoa was no longer used. This apparently dates them to the second century.[77] One of those shops still stands and is the most conspicuous structure in the Forum. Therefore, it has a certain appeal to visitors who would like to think that Paul might have worked there. Unfortunately, it dates from much later. Many similar shops are well preserved in the forum of Ephesus. It was in shops like these that Paul worked in Corinth, making tents or tapestries, perhaps for spectators to the Isthmian Games.[78]

Among other commercial interests of Corinth are three bronze-working establishments found near the gymnasium,[79] north of the Temple of Clarion Apollo (Temple G),[80] and east of the Lechaion Road below the Peribolos of Apollo.[81] All three of these complexes seem to date to the first century A.D. and immediately make us think of Paul's well-known reference to "sounding brass and clanging cymbals" in 1 Corinthians 13:1. Bronze mirrors found in the city call to mind his reference in verse 12 to seeing "in a mirror dimly."

In 1 Corinthians 10:25 Paul mentions a meat market (μάκελλον) in Corinth, so the location of this business has received much attention among scholars. F. J. DeWaele placed it in the North Market.[82] Henry J. Cadbury discussed the background and use of

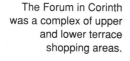

The Forum in Corinth was a complex of upper and lower terrace shopping areas.

West shops in the Corinthian forum stood along the base of Temple Hill.

the Greek and Latin terms, without solving the archaeological problem.[83] Broneer, pointing out that it was customary among Greek and Roman merchants to group themselves according to product, tried to locate the meat (or "food")[84] market district in the South Shops. He based his theory on an inscription found incised in the front wall of one of the South Shops. Although incomplete, it might have read "Λουκιος λαν[ι]ος." If the last word is correctly restored and if it represents a transliteration of the Latin word *lanius* ("butcher"), then the sign may be translated "Lucius butcher," and evidence of a butcher's shop may have been found.[85] A positive sign that this was the butchers' district is that thirty-one of the thirty-three shops uncovered here had wells that were not used for drawing of water, since no rope marks were found on the rims. Broneer says they were used as "coolers" for perishable goods such as meat. He concludes that these shops were "unquestionably" markets.[86]

However, since Broneer's theory was published, further excavation of the site has determined that "before the end of the reign of Augustus the shops on the ground floor [of the South Shop area] began to be converted into administrative offices and most of the wells of the former shops or taverns became dumps for the rubbish that accumulated during the remodellings."[87]

After the 1985 excavations east of the theater, Williams added an interesting chapter to the whole discussion of Corinthian meat markets. Close to the theater he found buildings with two or more stories. The upper floors were residential apartments, but whose lower floors had ovens and windows for street selling. Williams thinks these functioned as combination tavern and butcher shops. These were unlike Italian *tabernae* in that they did not have wine counters, and they had ovens. His observations provide new and fascinating possibilities for archaeologists to consider:

> Buildings 1 and 3 appear to have been equipped for commercial rather than domestic use, as indicated by wide entrances and cooking facilities rather more elaborate than anything needed in a private house. Large quantities of discarded bones, mostly from skulls and lower legs, were found piled in the southwest corner of the southwest room of Building 3, as well as around the ovens in the kitchen of that building. . . . Ribs and other meaty parts of slaughtered beasts . . . were carried away and consumed elsewhere. Perhaps the ribs, thighs and other meaty portions were hawked along with their attached bones at the time of performances in the theater.[88]

So, there we have it—evidence for ancient fast-food dining by the theater. Though the possibility is exciting, these places are dated between two earthquakes, one that shook Corinth in 77 and another during the reign of Hadrian. They thus appear to be too late for background to Paul's correspondence.[89] (We might note in passing that several years after Broneer identified the market with the South Stoa, he wrote another article which suggested that a commercial building north of the Lechaion Road Basilica might have been the meat market.)[90]

Civic Architecture in Corinth

Upon entering Corinth Paul would have seen evidence of an active and cultured populace. Like modern Rome, ancient Corinth was adorned with beautiful water fountains. The large Lower Fountain of Peirene at the east side of the entrance to the Forum provided the major water supply for the city[91] and predated the Roman invasion of 146. It had not been destroyed, since the water was needed by the conquerors. The source for this fountain and its recessed pool were renovated in the time of Augustus. Six arched openings or chambers were constructed in the facade on the south end of the fountain. Behind these six chambers were four reservoirs fed through supply tunnels from the slopes of the Acrocorinth. The four reservoirs were connected by a transverse supply tunnel. Water could be drawn from fifteen spouts along this channel. A two-story wall, the lower one Doric and the upper Ionic, was built around the fountain.[92]

Reservoirs behind the arches of the Lower Fountain of Peirene provided much of Corinth's water.

The Fountain of Glauce, just west of Temple Hill and adjacent to the west side of the so-called "Temple of Hera," was repaired, and the Upper Fountain of Peirene on the Acrocorinth was reopened with a new concrete vault above the stairs descending to the previously vaulted spring during a building program which began in 44 B.C. and lasted for many years.[93] Another fountain stood at the west end of the Forum near the Babbius monument.[94] The Fountain of Lerna at the Asklepieion was repaired,[95] and the bath and fountain to the west of the Asklepieion temple complex were remodeled. A swimming pool and a chamber with six water basins in it were installed at this bath during the time of Tiberius. Water for the fountains and the bath were supplied from the same source.[96] Shortly after this time, another large bath complex was built.[97] The most elaborate structure in the South Stoa was another fountain house, this one covered with marble of various colors and entered through a *distyle-in-antis* (two columns between antae) facade. Since there was no local quarry, marble was rare in Corinth in the Greek period, but the Roman rebuilders transported much of it in from quarries around Athens near which both Pentelic and Hymettian (so-called "Kara") marble were quarried.

A beautifully constructed monumental porch (*propylaea*), with a large central arch and smaller arches on either side, stood between the Forum and the Lechaion Road from the time of Augustus. Beside it, the Lechaion Road Basilica was probably used as a law court.[98] A building at the east end of the Forum, adjacent to the south side of the Julian Basilica, has been identified as possibly a *tabularium* (archives)[99] or a library.[100] It was built possibly during the reign of Augustus and probably destroyed in the reign of Tiberius; then it was rebuilt by Cnaeus Babbius Philinus, a Corinthian magistrate, with slight modification of the rooms and added grandeur. Philinus also erected a lovely circular monument among the Roman temples on the western side of the Forum. On the marble podium of the monument an inscription is still partially preserved (for a discussion of the inscription, see pp. 322–333).[101]

In the center of the South Stoa is a large room with elliptical walls that was built about A.D. 50. Identified as the Bouleuterion (βουλευτήριον—council chamber), this is where the legislative body of the city met. Most all of the thirty-three "wine shops and restaurants" in the South Stoa had been demolished and were in the process of being replaced by ten administrative buildings at the time Paul arrived in Corinth.[102] One of these, the third building from the east end, has been definitely identified as the office of the president of the Isthmian Games.[103] A floor mosaic in the office depicts a nude athlete, wearing a crown of withered celery and holding a palm branch, which symbolizes victory.[104] The athlete stands before Eutychia, the goddess of good fortune. The two buildings east of this one may have served as offices for other game officials, perhaps for the *Hellanodikai*, who judged and awarded the prizes.[105]

Pavement near the theater contained the Erastus inscription.

One of the most imposing structures in Corinth, as in many other ancient cities, was the theater, which was used for theatrical

performances and for large civic meetings. Built as a Greek theater in the fifth century B.C., it was situated northwest of the
forum and faced the north, with a view of the slopes leading to
the Gulf of Corinth. The theater would seat about fourteen thousand spectators in fifty-five rows of seats.[106] The Romans rebuilt
it, retaining its seating capacity, and erecting a typical *scaenae
frons*, which enclosed the seating area and restricted the view to
the interior.[107] The first Roman renovation is dated by Williams
"probably soon after A.D. 44,"[108] with repairs made again after the
earthquake in 77.[109]

Erastus Inscription

Before A.D. 50, a 62-square-foot area was paved with stone near
the northeast corner of the theater.[110] In April 1929, a slab of gray
Acrocorinthian limestone was found *in situ* during excavation of
this pavement. The original height of the stone was 2.1 feet and
its width was 7.4 feet. On it was part of a Latin inscription in letters 7 inches high. Two other pieces, containing most of the rest
of the inscription, were found in 1928 and 1947 in other parts of
the theater. The inscription reads:

ERASTVS–PRO–AEDILIT[at]E S–P–STRAVIT

In full: *Erastus pro aedilitate sua pecunia stravit*.[111]

The translation thus would be, "Erastus in return for his aedile-
ship laid (the pavement) at his own expense." From other evidence found in the excavation this Erastus was identified as none
other than the "the city treasurer" mentioned by Paul in Romans
16:23, a letter written from Corinth. Three primary reasons favor
this identification. First, the pavement was laid around A.D. 50,

the time when Erastus would likely have been converted; second, the name *Erastus* is uncommon and is not found in Corinth other than in this inscription. Third, the particular Greek word used by Paul for "treasurer" (οἰκονόμος) describes the work of a Corinthian *aedile*.[112] The editor's description of the office sheds light on the position of this prominent citizen of Corinth, who is mentioned twice elsewhere in the New Testament.

> In addition to duoviri, the *only regularly elected officials* in a Roman colony were the aediles. These were also chosen annually and in pairs, and in many colonies (though not at Corinth) the four annual magistrates were known collectively as the quattuorviri. The triple functions of a colonial aedile are discussed in detail by Kubitschek [*PW* 1.458–63]. Aediles were primarily city business managers, being responsible for the upkeep and welfare of city property such as *streets, public buildings, and especially the marketplaces* (hence their Greek title ἀγορανόμοι), as well as the *public revenue* therefrom. They also served as judges, and it is probable that *most of a colony's commercial and financial litigation was decided by them* rather than by the duoviri. The third responsibility of colonial aediles was for public games, but in this respect the Corinthian aediles were singularly fortunate. Corinth was a unique colony in that the city controlled the management of games which were internationally famous. It therefore administered the Isthmian festivals by means of a completely separate set of officials. Therefore, the Corinthian aediles, thus relieved of all responsibility for public entertainment, were, in effect, confined in their activities to local economic matters. It is possibly for this reason that Paul does not use the customary word ἀγορανόμος to describe a Corinthian aedile, but calls him οἰκονόμος (Romans 16:23) [emphasis added].[113]

The importance and influence of an aedile, who was subject to public election, is self-evident. It is interesting that a similar inscription appears on both the pedestal and the epistyle of the Babbius Monument in the western section of the forum. It reads:

[C]N–BABBIVS–PHILINUS–AED[ILIS]–PONTIF[EX]
D[E]–S[VA]–P[ECVNIA]–F[ACIENDVM]–C[VRAVIT]–IDEMQVE–I
IIVIR–P[ROBAVIT].[114]

This inscription may be translated, "Cnaeus Babbius Philinus, aedile and pontifex, had this monument erected *at his own expense*, and he approved it in his official capacity as duovir." The language, then, is from one who held the same office as Erastus and made a similar gift to the city. Babbius is known to have served under Augustus and Erastus was aedile under Nero. Eleven aediles have now been identified, whose tenures ranged

The Babbius Monument in the Forum was a gift to the public from a thankful aedile.

from the reigns of Augustus to Marcus Aurelius. At least five others received honorary aedileships.[115]

The extent to which the rebuilt Greek city of Corinth adopted Roman ways after colonization is indicated by the predominance of Latin inscriptions. Of 104 inscriptions dating from colonization in 44 B.C. to the reign of Hadrian in the early second century, 101 are in Latin and only three in Greek.[116] Yet the Romanization may have been in the administrative and official, rather than the everyday, spheres. Paul wrote to the church there in Greek. By the reign of Hadrian Greek had reestablished itself once again as the official language.

The Tribunal (Bema)

One of the most important discoveries at Corinth relating to the New Testament is the bema, the speaker's platform, where proclamations were read and citizens appeared before appropriate officials. At the tribunal in Corinth, probably in the summer of 51, Paul stood before Gallio (Acts 18:12–17; see pp. 225–227 for a discussion of Pauline chronology). Situated in the center of the row of Central Shops, the platform was close to the Bouleuterion. The platform on which the speakers stood was at the elevation of the South Stoa terrace behind it, while the spectators stood about 7.5 feet below on a stone pavement. This pavement, which was at the level of the Lower Forum, was built onto the north side of the platform.

The bema was discovered in 1935 and identified by Broneer in 1937.[117] It is described in detail and carefully analyzed in the later excavation reports.[118] The restoration is "fairly certain in all details, except those of the crowning elements."[119] The place where Paul stood before Gallio,[120] may be described with some confidence of accuracy:

Figure 30
Tribunal (Bema) in Corinth

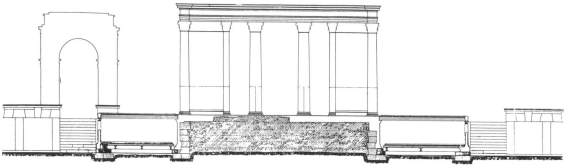

Courtesy of the American School of Classical Studies at Athens.

This was the Corinthian version of the Imperial Rostra at Rome, in many details a conscious reproduction, in a more formal design, of the Rostra and some of its adjacent structures, built as a unity with architectural details inspired by the Erechtheum in Athens. In the center was a high, broad platform rising on two blue marble steps and an elaborate base molding, probably with imitation beaks of ships attached to white marble orthostates surmounted by a crown molding and a blue marble paving. Above this rose a superstructure enclosing a platform on the back and part way along the sides. It consisted of white marble piers with three doors or openings in the rear facade, and L-shaped wings around the ends of the rear facade, and along the sides. Benches of blue marble ran along the inner edge of the L-shaped wings, and above the benches rose a wall of blue marble. . . . On either side of this central structure, but at the level of the Lower Agora, was an open rectangular exedra or schola reflecting the architecture of the L-shaped wings of the central part, with blue marble benches along the back and outer side. Above these, again, rose a wall of blue marble. At the back, the wall rose to the height of the Upper Agora.[121]

Steps on both sides of the bema led to the higher level in back (south) so the platform was entered from the rear. Also on the south side, a monumental marble wall with a pier on each side rose imposingly behind the speakers, majestically framing anyone on the bema and screening out distractions in the background.[122]

The identity of the bema is so certain partly because of seven pieces to an inscription which have been found in the vicinity of the stand. John Kent has reconstructed the inscription's text to read:

A[ ]SA[ ]ROST[RA-] IN[CRU]STA–MAR[MORAQU]E–O[MNIA–S–P]–F–C–[EX] TEST[AMENTO]

One of the clearest links between Corinth's archaeology and Scripture is the bema where Paul stood before Gallio.

("He revetted the Bema and paid personally the expense of making all its marble").[123]

The official name of the structure is *Rostra* in the Latin inscription, but to the Greek-speaking populace it was the βῆμα. The similarity, of course, to the Erastus pavement and Babbius monument are unmistakable. According to Wiseman, the bema inscription may be dated to the reign of either Augustus or Claudius.[124] Kent places the bema's construction between 25 and 50 on the basis of the style in which the letters are formed.

The Roads

The road system of Corinth is better understood because of recent excavations. A major east-west street (*decumanus*) of the Roman city was found about 50 meters south of the podium of the Corinthian Temple (Temple E); from the temple it ran along the south side of the South Basilica. The street was about 3.80 meters wide and had a sidewalk along its north edge of about 1.76 meters wide.[125] Another decumanus was found to end at the court which stood northeast of the theater. The Lechaion Road would have served as the *cardo maximus*. These roads clearly indicate a Roman grid system was used in the reconstruction of Greek Corinth.[126]

The Lechaion Harbor

The Lechaion Road ran north to the seaport city of Lechaion, from which ships sailed into the Corinthian Gulf and on to Europe. Lechaion's harbor was the most convenient for Corinth, and since at least 394 B.C. low defensive walls stretched along the sides of this road. Strabo referred to it in the first century A.D. in connection with Corinth and Cenchreae.[127]

From 1956 a series of excavations by Dhimitrios Pallas uncovered a fifth-century Christian basilica west of the harbor; at 223.7 meters long, it is the largest church yet found in Greece.[128] A Roman nympheum (from between the third and sixth centuries) was found southeast of the harbor. Inner harbors, whose dates of construction remain unknown, were connected to the outer harbor waterways by a narrow channel which still carries water. A number of the outer harbor's poros walls and quays now lie in the water. Roman walls protrude from the fields nearby, and much of the surface pottery dates to the first and second centuries A.D.[129] In 1972 part of an early Roman stoa was found at nearby Tagara between the old main road and the railway, lying largely under the railway and facing the harbor.[130] A stoa with workshops from the first or second century A.D. was found nearby in 1976.[131]

The Harbor at Cenchreae

The other harbor of Corinth, with access to eastern Mediterranean ports and to Asia, was Cenchreae, located about 6.5 miles east of Corinth and about 2.5 miles south of Isthmia.[132] From Cenchreae Paul sailed to Syria at the end of his third missionary journey (Acts 18:18), and in Romans 16:1 Paul commended Phoebe, who was a deacon or servant of the church in Cenchreae. Located in a quiet alluvial triangle, the city was connected to Corinth's Cenchrean Gate by a road which ran northwest-southeast through Examilia.[133]

Virtually nothing has been found of the main city of Cenchreae, which lay northwest of the harbor, because during five seasons of excavation from 1963 to 1968 the government restricted work to the harbor except in 1966. One limiting factor

Archaeological investigation has been restricted to Cenchrea's harbor.

may be modern security concerns, since a military installation lies nearby.[134] Excavation by Indiana University and the University of Chicago, under the auspices of the American School of Classical Studies in Athens,[135] were restricted to a small strip of the coast between Isthmia and the spa of the Bath of Helen, near the modern village of Kechries.[136] The picturesque harbor thus far excavated, dates to the Roman period. The earlier Greek harbor is nearby to the west since the Romans decided to build a new one in 44 B.C. The Roman harbor originally contained about 1600 feet of shoreline and was 98,000 square feet. In comparison with other Greek and Roman harbors, this one was rather small: The harbor at Piraeus (Kantharos) was 2.46 million square feet; at Piraeus (Zea), 738,000 square feet; at Caesarea Maritima, 656,000 square feet; at Lechaion (Inner), 328,000 square feet, and at Piraeus (Munychia), 229,000 square feet.[137] Cenchreae Harbor remains free of silt, even today, unlike the Greek harbor. One reason is that there is no major river near Cenchreae to cause river silting and coastal drift.[138] Two large breakwaters, were constructed around a natural bay. The modern shore is about 7.5 feet lower than during New Testament times, due to seismic activity. The harbor's breakwaters or moles are completely submerged.[139] Pottery and coins give evidence to a city whose commercial life, prosperity, and general status was inextricably tied to Corinth's.[140] Almost all the coins uncovered have been of Greek mintage or from the eastern Mediterranean, confirming that Cenchrea's commercial significance was the link it provided between Corinth and the east.

The Roman harbor's southwest mole extended 295 feet southeastward from an artificial pier, which itself extended almost 500 feet from the shore. This pier contained many warehouses, a large system of *piscinae* (fish tanks) which postdate the warehouses, numerous small shops and religious shrines. The Temple of Isis, mentioned by Pausanias, has possibly been identified in this area on the south side of the warehouses.[141] On the mosaic floor of this apsidal structure were found more than one hundred plaster panels overlayed with glass *opus sectile* depicting a variety of scenes and people, including Plato and Homer.[142] These decorations made of shaped tiles date to about 370. Plaster panels, found still in their shipping crates, contained scenes of Egypt and the Nile, indicating the influence of the Egyptian cult of Isis. The mosaic floor of this temple today is approximately at sea level and is submerged at high tide. Originally it must have stood considerably higher.

Extending along the western side of the harbor were a number of irregularly-shaped commercial structures.[143] On the promontory north of the eastern mole a series of buildings, perhaps residential, have been discovered. They include, possibly, the Temple of Aphrodite.[144] The 40-foot-wide end of the mole is almost rectangular, and the excavators suggest a bronze statue of Poseidon seen by Pausanius may have stood there.[145] A Roman tomb, probably from the first century A.D., was found about .5 mile northeast of the harbor.[146] Moldings on the partially preserved limestone tomb resemble those on the base molding of the bema and the Temple of Tyche at Corinth,[147] both of which date to the reign of Tiberius.[148] Attempts made to restore the tomb's inscription indicate that it may belong to L. Castricius Regulus, one of the most prosperous and generous Corinthians. Scranton relates that Regulus was *duovir quinquennalis* at Corinth during the reign of Tiberius (A.D. 14–37) and the first Corinthian to become president (ἀγωνοθέτης) over the Isthmian Games in the Roman era.[149]

Nicopolis

Paul tells Titus (3:12), probably in 64, of his intention to spend the winter at Nicopolis in the Epirus district of northwestern Greece. Possibly he even wrote 1 Timothy and Titus from here, as subscriptions on some ancient manuscripts indicate, (e.g., "πρὸς Τίτον ἐγράφη ἀπὸ Νικοπόλεως").[150] At some point in his ministry, Paul made a preaching trip as far as Illyricum, which was near the western end of the Via Egnatia in Dyrrhachium.[151]

Nicopolis was a relatively new city when Paul may have wintered there. It was founded by Augustus Caesar after 31 B.C. on

The author stands alongside the once impressive victory monument to Augustus.

the site occupied by his troops during the battle of Actium.[152] Josephus wrote that "most of their public buildings" were built for the people of Nicopolis by Herod the Great,[153] for it was Herod's intent to ingratiate himself with Augustus, by whose grace he was allowed to rule the Jews. Helping construct a new city in honor of Augustus's victory over Mark Antony and Cleopatra (whom Herod feared) was an impressive way to curry the emperor's favor.

On a high hill north of the ancient city, just above the site of the modern village of Smyrtoula, Augustus erected a monument to his victory which could be seen for miles around.[154] The spot offers a magnificent view of the Gulf of Ambracia. Dio Cassius reported that "On the spot where he had his tent, he made a platform of squared masonry and adorned it with the rams of ships he had captured, and consecrated there a kind of open-air shrine to Apollo."[155] Remains of this monument lie in disarray around the curved southern edge of the hill and contain many of the twenty-five known pieces of a huge Latin inscription that ran along the frieze of a Corinthian stoa.[156] This inscription may resolve a controversy concerning the dedication of the city of Nicopolis. Strabo and Dio Cassius ascribed the dedication to Apollo,[157] while Suetonius said the city was dedicated to Neptune.[158] Reexamination of the inscription, along with a newly-found segment, shows that it refers to Neptune and emphasizes the maritime nature of the victory at Actium.[159]

Strabo spoke of two harbors at Nicopolis, located on the eastern and western sides of the neck of the narrow peninsula; both sites are visible from the monument of Augustus. Clearly discernible, in the northern part of the city, are a stadium (in a poor state of preservation), a theater, and part of a bathhouse about .5 mile to the southwest. Greek archaeologists have excavated at Nicopolis since the early 1900s, and have published articles in several periodicals.[160] A small odeum built during the reign of Augustus in the center of the Augustan walls of the city is remarkably well preserved. Near the Odeum are remains of a bathhouse, some reservoirs, and an aqueduct that brought water to the city from the Louros River. These were all part of an impressive and beautiful city, which still may hold answers for students of the life and travels of the apostle Paul.

Dodona

During the winter of 64 as during his theorized stay in Nicopolis, or perhaps on another occasion, Paul would have surely visited Dodona, one of the most beautifully situated cities in all of Greece.[161] It is 40 miles north of Nicopolis at the foot of the towering (1974 feet), snowcapped Mount Tomaros. In the *Iliad* the city is cited as a sanctuary of Zeus who "ruled over wintry Dodona."[162] The *Odyssey* declared that Odysseus went "to Dodona, to hear the will of Zeus from the high-crested oak of the god."[163] Herodotus called it the most ancient oracle in Greece,[164] and among the oracles it was venerated even more highly than the oracle of Apollo at Delphi, which finally took its place.[165] Dodona's isolated location eventually contributed to its neglect by worshipers, travelers, and scholars. However, the experience of sitting at the top of the carefully restored cavea of the theater, beside beautifully snowcapped peaks and of feeling the stiff breeze the mountain valley funnels across the theater, is well worth the visit. Even in the spring one may share Homer's impression of "wintry Dodona"!

The third-century B.C. Greek theater, with a seating capacity comparable to that of the well-known theater in Epidaurus, is the most prominent feature of the site. Excavations were first conducted at the theater more than a century ago.[166] More recent excavations, which began again in 1944,[167] have been accompanied by the restoration of the theater with a cavea that measures 71.8 feet in diameter, a stone stage 102.3 feet wide and an orchestra which measures 62.3 feet in diameter. In the Augustan period the theater was converted into an arena, and the lowest seating was replaced by a protective wall. It is one of the most beautifully preserved and situated theaters in the whole of Greece. To the

Excavations at Dodona included restoration of the Greek theater.

theater's east was a partially preserved βουλευτήριον (council chamber), farther to the east was the Sanctuary of Zeus, consisting of three temples: Zeus Naios, Aphrodite, and Dione. Only the foundations of these temples remain.

Rome

The Heart of Rome

Rome was built on seven hills along the east bank of the Tiber River, about 15 miles from its mouth. At the city's center were the Palatine and Capitoline hills. Eastward from there, in an arc from the south to the north, lay the Aventine, Caelian, Esquiline, Viminal, and Quirinal hills. The heart of the city was the area between the Palatine and Esquiline hills; people gathered there in the Roman Forum and the imperial fora to conduct commercial, political, and religious affairs. By the first century B.C. the Palatine had become the choicest residential area in Rome with the homes of such notables as Cicero, Mark Antony, and Augustus Caesar. Augustus was born in this district.[168] Just to the south of the Palatine area was the Colosseum, and to the west, between the Palatine and Aventine hills, stood the Circus Maximus (see p. 60). Many Christians lost their lives in the arena of the Circus Maximus. Impressive temples and bathhouses surrounded

The Colosseum is the world's most famous Roman architecture.

this central area, including the Pantheon and the Baths of Agrippa to the northwest.

Rome under the Republic

During the period of the republic, many ancient buildings in Rome were restored or rebuilt. After Rome conquered Greece in 146 B.C., Roman architects were impressed with various forms of Greek art and utilized them in their reconstructions. The Temple of Saturn, the Temple of Concord, and the Temple of Castor and Pollux were all rebuilt in the Roman Forum in the second century B.C. The large warehouses on the west bank of the Tiber were built in 193 B.C. The Appian Way, dating from 312 B.C., was lined with tombs during this period. The Tabularium (state archives) was constructed on the Capitoline in 78 B.C. Two bridges were constructed between 80 and 50 B.C. to connect the Tiberine Island, the Theater of Pompey, and the Portico of the Hundred Columns in the Campus Martius (or Plain of Mars, which was the low-lying area in the bend of the Tiber just northwest of the city walls). At the close of this period, Julius Caesar reconstructed the

Figure 31
The Fora of Imperial Rome

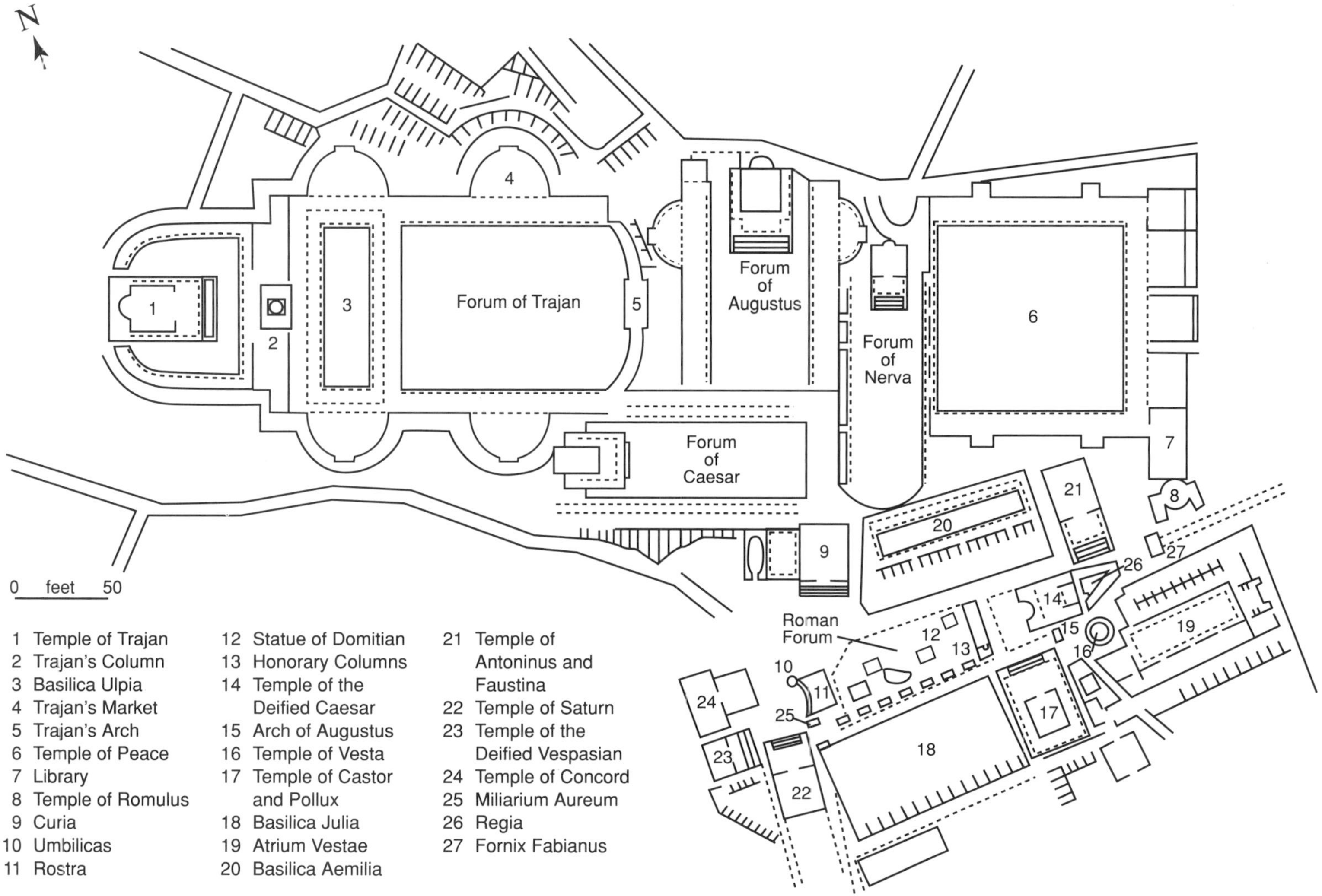
N
0 feet 50
Forum of Trajan
Forum of Augustus
Forum of Nerva
Forum of Caesar
Roman Forum
1 Temple of Trajan
2 Trajan's Column
3 Basilica Ulpia
4 Trajan's Market
5 Trajan's Arch
6 Temple of Peace
7 Library
8 Temple of Romulus
9 Curia
10 Umbilicas
11 Rostra
12 Statue of Domitian
13 Honorary Columns
14 Temple of the Deified Caesar
15 Arch of Augustus
16 Temple of Vesta
17 Temple of Castor and Pollux
18 Basilica Julia
19 Atrium Vestae
20 Basilica Aemilia
21 Temple of Antoninus and Faustina
22 Temple of Saturn
23 Temple of the Deified Vespasian
24 Temple of Concord
25 Miliarium Aureum
26 Regia
27 Fornix Fabianus

Roman Forum and in 54 B.C. added the Basilica Julia to its western end. It has been suggested that Paul heard his death sentence in this building, which was rebuilt on a larger scale by Augustus in A.D. 12.[169] Julius Caesar also built the first of the imperial fora, the Forum of Caesar, with the Temple of Venus at its western end. This forum lay adjacent to the eastern side of the Roman Forum.

Imperial Rome under the Julio-Claudians

Beginning with the work of Augustus, under whose reign Christ was born, Rome was greatly expanded during the period of the empire. Augustus completed Julius Caesar's building program, transforming the southeast corner of the Roman Forum into a vast memorial to Caesar which included the Temple of Julius Caesar. In 29 B.C., the same year the Temple of Julius Caesar was dedicated, Augustus also dedicated a triumphal arch at the east end of the Roman Forum in honor of his victory at Actium. It was replaced by a triple arch commissioned in 19 B.C. On the northeast side of Caesar's Forum, he built the Forum of Augustus, with a Temple of Mars at its northern end, and on the Palatine he constructed a massive imperial residence with the Temple of Apollo on its north side. In the Campus Martius, on the east bank of the Tiber, the Theater of Marcellus was built; today it is partially preserved. The Altar of Peace, decreed in 14 B.C. after Augustus returned from his victorious campaigns in Gaul and Spain, was completed and inaugurated in A.D. 9 in the Campus Martius. In this same area the Mausoleum of Augustus was also erected, as was the Pantheon, a temple dedicated to all the gods by Augustus's architect Agrippa between 27 and 25 B.C. This beautifully preserved structure was completely rebuilt by Hadrian between 120 and 125 and stands today as a model of the building activity of the emperor. Leonardo B. Dal Maso describes the construction as representing "the highest expression of the Romans' genius as architects and builders."[170]

In 20 B.C., Augustus erected the *Milliarium Aureum* ("Golden Milestone") at the west end of the Roman Forum. This stone was used to measure the distances to the main cities of the empire. Just north of it stood the Umbilicus Romae, which marked the center not only of Rome, but of the Roman world. The huge Rostra (speaker's platform) was relocated to a position adjacent to the east side of the Umbilicus, facing the open area to the east. The new curia ("senate chamber"), begun by Julius Caesar, was completed south of Caesar's Forum. Augustus built the magnificent porticos of Octavia, Vipsania, and Saepta Julia and rebuilt dozens of temples.[171] Augustus boasted that he found the city in stone and left it in marble.

Although Suetonius, the second-century biographer of the caesars, stated that, except for the erection of the Temple of Augustus and the restoration of Pompey's Theater, "no magnificent public works" marked the reign of Tiberius,[172] yet he restored the Temple of Castor and Pollux in the center of the Roman Forum, rebuilt the Temple of Concord at the west end of the Forum, and erected a triumphal triple arch between the Rostra and the huge Basilica Julia. The Basilica Aemilia, which was slightly smaller than the Basilica Julius, lay directly across the Roman Forum on its east side. Built in 179 B.C., it was restored under Augustus in 14 B.C. and under Tiberius in A.D. 22.

In A.D. 36 Caligula began an aqueduct, which was finished by Claudius in 52. By the time of Nerva there were nine aqueducts in Rome, according to Frontinus, who records their names. After the fire of A.D. 64, which Tacitus insisted was caused by Nero,[173] this depraved emperor rebuilt a considerable portion of the city including his 200-acre imperial palace, the "Golden House," which contained a 120-foot-high gilded bronze statue of himself as the sun. According to Suetonius, "parts of the house were overlaid with gold and studded with precious stones. . . . all the dining-rooms had ceilings of fretted ivory. . . . The main dining room was circular, and its roof slowly revolved in synchronization with the day and night sky."[174]

The Arch of Titus was built by Domitian as the south entrance to the Roman Forum.

A minora inside the Arch of Titus recalls the destruction of the Jewish temple.

Imperial Rome under the Flavians

Vespasian rebuilt the Temple of Claudius and in 72 began work on the Colosseum, which his sons Titus and Domitian completed. Dedicated in 80, the Colosseum was made of travertine stone, and its half columns embodied all three major Greek architectural orders (see pp. 61–63 for details of this structure). The Temple of Peace in the Forum of Peace on the south side of the Forum of Nerva was begun in 71 by Vespasian and completed in 75. Pliny regarded the Temple of Peace, the Basilica Aemilia and the Forum of Augustus as the three most beautiful buildings in the world.[175] Josephus was no less impressed:

> Vespasian decided to erect a temple of Peace. This was very speedily completed and in a style surpassing all human conception. For, besides having prodigious resources of wealth on which to draw he also embellished it with ancient masterpieces of painting and sculpture; indeed, into that shrine were accumulated and stored all objects for the sight of which men had once wandered over the whole world, eager to see them severally while they lay in various countries. Here, too, he laid up the vessels of gold from the temple of the Jews, on which he prided himself; but their Law and the purple hangings of the sanctuary he ordered to be deposited and kept in the palace.[176]

The Arch of Titus, the south gateway to the Roman Forum, was erected to honor Titus by Domitian and the senate in 81. Faced with Pentelic marble, its one arch depicts, among other things the spoiling of Jerusalem's temple. Jews to this day refuse to walk through the Arch of Titus, since it shows the menorah, the table of shewbread, the sacred trumpets, and tablets fastened on sticks being carried away. Domitian also built the Stadium of Domitian, now the Piazza Navona in 86. This stadium had originally been built of wood by Julius Caesar and Augustus and restored by Nero. Domitian's was finished of stone and brickwork to serve as a headquarters for the Capitoline Games. It would seat about twenty thousand. Next to the stadium he built an odeum.

Special Structures

Near Tivoli, about 15 miles southeast of Rome, Hadrian, the emperor who restored Athens and turned Jerusalem into a Gentile city named Aelia Capitolina, built the most magnificent palace in the Mediterranean world. Erected between 125 and 135, this vast complex of buildings covered more than 750 acres with the architecture of various places that had impressed him during his travels throughout the empire (see pp. 76–77). Its baths, pools, Temple of Venus, and lodging for soldiers, fit the mood of Hadrian's empire-wide building program.[177]

One intriguing structure in Rome is the Mamertine Prison, which is at the foot of Capitoline Hill near the Temple of Concord. Since the sixteenth century it has been called *San Pietro in Carcere*, preserving a tradition that Peter was imprisoned there. Either Peter or Paul or both could have been incarcerated in this two-level prison.[178] Paul spent two years in house arrest in Rome (Acts 28: 16, 30) but he was later imprisoned again (2 Tim 4:6–8), possibly as he awaited his final trial and execution.

Four churches in Rome have some claim to direct connections with the New Testament. The Church of Saint Peter in the Vatican, located across from the Campus Martius on the west side of the Tiber River, marks the traditional burial place of Simon Peter. Gaius, a presbyter in the church in Rome at the end of the second century, located the burial monuments (τροπαῖα, "trophies") of Peter at what is now the Vatican and of Paul on the Ostian Way.[179] In the fourth to sixth centuries a number of documents

The Canopus in Hadrian's Villa compound.

Mamertine Prison, where Paul may have awaited execution.

stated that Peter was buried in this location.[180] Excavations under Saint Peter's from the 1940s produced no conclusive evidence regarding the bones of Peter, although reports have circulated that they were found.[181] Portions of a church constructed by Constantine have been found beneath the Saint Peter Church. The apse of this former church was oriented precisely over a mid-second-century shrine (a two-story niche, or aedicula). This shrine was constructed over the first-century tomb thought to be that of Simon Peter.[182]

The Church of Saint Clement, located in the district of the Caelian Hill, east of the Colosseum, is built over a first-century house thought to have belonged to Clement of Rome. This Clement was the probable author of the epistle of 1 Clement (ca. A.D. 90) from the church in Rome to the church in Corinth[183] and the person Paul likely referred to in his letter from Rome to the Philippians (4:3). Irenaeus, in the late second century, wrote that Peter and Paul founded the church in Rome and were succeeded by Linus (2 Tim. 4:21), Anacletus, and Clement.[184] Jerome seems to refer to the Church of Saint Clement in his *Lives of Illustrious Men*.

The Church of Santa Pudenziana, located on the Via Urbana between the Viminal and the Esquiline hills may stand over the site of the house of Pudens, whose name was also mentioned in 2 Timothy 4:21 as a Roman Christian who sent greetings to Timothy via Paul's letter. A tradition suggests that he may have been a senator in whose home Christians met and that the church may preserve the name of his daughter. Fragments of a wall and a mosaic pavement from a house of the time of Augustus or earlier have been discovered beneath this church. Bricks stamped with the name of Pudens and dates equivalent to the years A.D. 127 to 129 have also been found among ruins from a second-century private bath. The church is known as early as the Byzantine period.[185]

The largest church in Rome, after Saint Peter's, is the Church of Saint Paul Outside the Walls. It is located on the Via Ostiense, about a mile from the Gate of Saint Paul. No real excavation has been done here, but the site is thought to be the location of the church built by Constantine to replace an oratory constructed over the place where Lucina, a Roman matron, had buried Paul in her vineyard.[186] When the present church was being built, a marble slab was uncovered under the altar. Inscribed in the slab with lettering from the time of Constantine were the words, "PAULO APOSTOLO MART[YRI]."[187] Jack Finegan points out that there was little reason for a church to be built in this area unless some special significance attached to it. For one thing, the site was in a pagan cemetery. It also was in a constricted space between two roads and on swampy land prone to flooding from the Tiber River.[188]

The Church of St. Paul Outside the Walls reveres the spot where Paul may have been buried.

Paul approached Rome from Puteoli along the Appian Way—one of 29 consular roads eminating from Rome toward the provinces. The city he entered was crowded with arches, streets, aqueducts, and buildings constructed on Greek architectural orders and punctuated with Egyptian obelisks. Augustus had moved the great obelisk of Rameses II from Heliopolis in Egypt to Rome around 10 B.C. and put it on the *spina* ("dividing wall") of the Circus Maximus. It is now at the Piazza del Popolo. He brought two other Egyptian obelisks to stand at the sides of his mausoleum. They now stand respectively on the Esquiline Hill and on the fountain of the Quirinal Hill. Apparently, the obelisk in Saint Peter's Square originally stood on the spina of the Circus of Caligula and Nero. Other obelisks brought by subsequent emperors to adorn the capital may be seen throughout the city.

For students of the New Testament and archaeology, Rome should not be remembered so much for its ancient architecture as for its central role in providing the world with an empire of peace and prosperity, an era in which the message of Christianity was effectively disseminated through Greek-speaking Jewish emissaries working in a Greco-Roman culture. That such a cultural and linguistic melting pot might contribute to the spread of the Gospel was all part of what Paul means when he refers to God's plan "in the fullness of time" (Gal. 4:4)

The Discovery and Contributions of Ancient Documents

The Discovery of Ancient Papyri

Archaeology embraces more than excavation. Some of the most exciting contributions to the study of the New Testament and its milieu have come from the efforts of people who share an enthusiasm for antiquities but do not participate in field excavation. A major case in point is the discipline of papyrology. Because Greek papyri and inscriptions relating to the New Testament and early Christianity continue to be discovered, the Ancient History Documentary Research Centre at Macquarie University under the directorship of E. A. Judge is publishing a series of volumes entitled *New Documents Illustrating Early Christianity*.[1] This publication makes new discoveries accessible to students of the New Testament and related fields. The discovery and handling of papyri are ably described by Eric Turner, professor of papyrology at University College in London, in a volume entitled *Greek Papyri: An Introduction*.[2] The ancient process of making writing material from the papyrus plant is outlined by the first-century geographer and historian Pliny the Elder.[3] It is noteworthy that the city of Gebal in Phoenicia imported so much Egyptian papyrus for manufacturing scrolls that its name was changed to Byblos ("book" or "scroll"). A similar occurrence happened in the Roman province of Asia, where the city of Pergamum, under King Eumenes II, gave its name to another writing material: the animal skins that were used as a substitute for papyrus. These skins were called *pergamēnē* (περγαμηνή, "parchment") in Greek. In the ancient world the library at Pergamum was second only to the library of Alexandria, Egypt.

The Codex Sinaiticus

The land of Egypt has yielded an abundance of papyri significant for the study of the New Testament. Some of them have been found purely by chance. In 1844, for example, Konstantin von Tischendorf, while visiting Saint Catherine's Monastery at the foot of Mount Sinai, found forty-three leaves of a fourth-century copy of the Old Testament in Greek lying in a wastebasket. Unfortunately, according to one of the monks, two similar basketsful had already been burned. In 1859 Tischendorf returned to the monastery and made a discovery whose importance surpassed the publication that same year of Charles Darwin's *Origin of Species*. A monk showed Tischendorf a fourth-century manuscript containing most of the Old Testament and all of the New Testament.[4] This manuscript, which has been dubbed the Codex Sinaiticus, is now in the British Museum.

The dramatic story of the acquisition of the manuscript from the monks has long been filled with enthralling questions of enchantment and intrigue, with differing viewpoints being expressed by Tischendorf and the monks. Interest in the Codex Sinaiticus was revived by the sensational announcement that during repairs to the monastery in 1975 eight more pages of the manuscript were found inside one of the walls. These pages match the Codex Sinaiticus exactly and contain passages from the Book of Genesis which are missing from the document in the British Museum. Since the number of significant items— manuscripts, pieces of manuscripts, and icons—found during the repairs may run as high as three to four thousand, a lid was understandably put on the story. News, however, leaked out in 1977, and the facts are now beginning to be pieced together.[5] We are reminded of what happened when interpretations of the Ebla tablets began to have adverse political ramifications for the nation of Syria.[6] Neither the ecclesiastical nor the political pow-

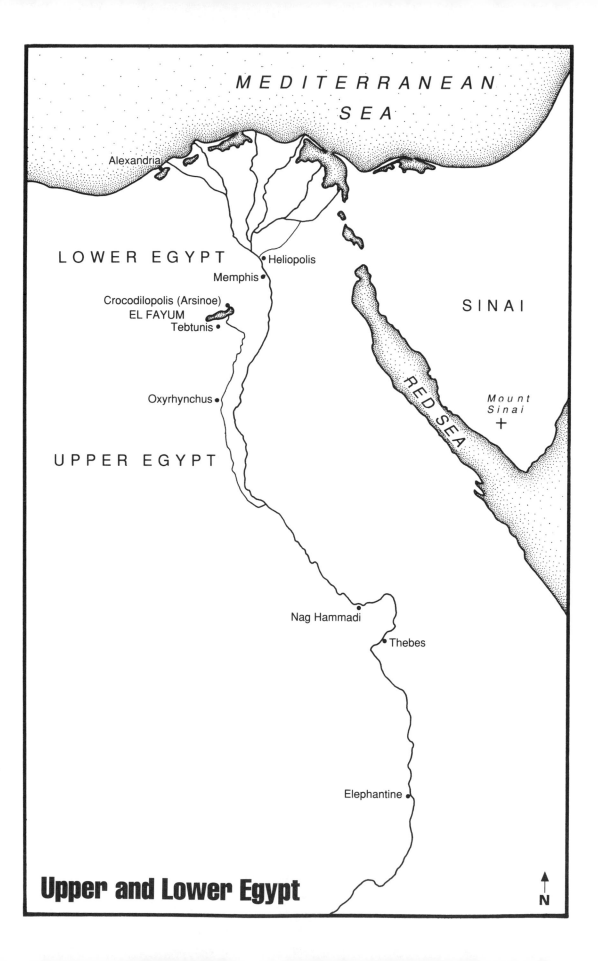

MEDITERRANEAN SEA

Alexandria

LOWER EGYPT

Heliopolis

Memphis

Crocodilopolis (Arsinoe)
EL FAYUM
Tebtunis

SINAI

RED SEA

Mount Sinai

Oxyrhynchus

UPPER EGYPT

Nag Hammadi

Thebes

Elephantine

Upper and Lower Egypt

N

ers in Egypt have forgotten the loss of their precious Sinaiticus manuscript, however it may have happened; and it could be a long time before the scholarly world will benefit from the latest accidental discoveries at the desert monastery.

The Oxyrhynchus Papyri

Actually, Greek papyri in Egypt were first discovered in the year 1778, when some Arabs who were digging for their own purposes in the Fayum district[7] (or was it at Gizeh?)[8] found about fifty rolls in an earthen pot. Unable to find a purchaser, they burned their discovery because of the smell it exuded! Only one roll survived; it is housed today in the National Museum at Naples.[9]

Some papyri had been found earlier, in 1752 and following years, at Herculaneum in southern Italy—one of those extremely rare examples of papyri being discovered outside the dry climate of Egypt.[10] In fact, of all known New Testament manuscripts, parchment or papyri, dating before the fourth century, only one has been found outside Egypt: a small portion on parchment of Tatian's *Diatessaron* ("Harmony of the Four Gospels") found at Dura-Europos in Syria.[11] Somewhat similar climatic conditions in Israel around the Dead Sea allowed the preservation of both the papyrus and parchment documents (Dead Sea Scrolls) that were discovered at Qumran, Khirbet Mird, and Wadi Murabba'at in 1947 and the years thereafter.

In Egypt further accidental discoveries of nonbiblical papyri were made in 1820 and 1847 near Memphis and Thebes as well as in 1877 at Crocodilopolis (modern Arsinoe). The impetus to acquire papyrus manuscripts did not come until later. Sir Flinders Petrie, the grand old British archaeologist who later laid the foundations for stratigraphical dating of ancient mounds in the Holy Land, was digging in Hawara, in the Fayum district of Egypt, in 1888, when he found a beautifully written roll of Homer. The next year, while digging in an unplundered Ptolemaic cemetery in Gurob, he found a large number of papyri[12] used as stuffing and wrapping in mummy cases.[13]

In 1897 the papyrologists B. P. Grenfell, A. S. Hunt and D. G. Hogarth were commissioned by the newly formed Graeco-Roman Branch of the Egypt Exploration Fund in London to concentrate on discovering ancient papyri in Egypt.[14] (Regrettably, since the outbreak of World War I in 1914, "the Graeco-Roman Branch of the Society has sponsored no excavation specifically to search for papyri.")[15] They began work in Tebtunis (in the southern Fayum) with some success, finding discarded papyri wrapped around sacred mummified crocodiles.[16.] They then moved to Oxyrhynchus (modern Behnesa in Middle Egypt), where thirteen seasons of digging (1897–1909) produced thousands of texts including several fragments of the Gospels, Acts, the Pauline Epistles, the General Epistles, and Revelation.

While Grenfell and his colleagues are models to the academic community of the way scholars should work together to achieve common goals ("such harmonious collaboration is rare among front-ranking scholars"),[17] the kind of digging these men did would not meet modern scientific standards. They began their search in cemeteries, believing papyri would have been buried with the dead and be best preserved there. It turned out, however, that rubbish heaps were the places to look; from village dumps they harvested Greek papyri "by the basketful."[18]

> The great mass of papyri come from the rubbish heaps, rising sometimes to a height of twenty to thirty feet, on the outskirts of old Egyptian towns and villages. Possibly out of a feeling of reverence for the written word, the inhabitants did not as a rule burn their old papers, but threw them out on these heaps. There they were quickly covered over with the fine desert sand, and, so long as they were above the damp level of the Nile, have remained practically uninjured down to the present day.[19]

Thus far 3875 documents have been published in the continuing series of *Oxyrhynchus Papyri*.[20] Equally amazing is that twenty-five of the seventy-three papyri enumerated in the appendices of the latest edition of *Novum Testamentum Graece* are from Oxyrhynchus.[21] Table 5 in the appendix is a sequential list of these papyri and the number assigned to each by the Institute for New Testament Textual Research in Münster, Germany. Their significance for New Testament studies lies in their antiquity: three of these papyri (Oxyrhynchus 657, 1009, 1079) have been dated to the third or fourth century; fourteen (2, 208, 402, 1008, 1171, 1228, 1229, 1355, 1596, 1597, 1598, 1780, 2383, 2384) to the third century; and one (2683) to the second or third century.[22]

The John Rylands Papyrus

The oldest New Testament fragment yet found is also a piece of papyrus; the John Rylands Papyrus Greek 457 equals **p**[52]) was acquired in 1920 by Grenfell, either in the Fayum or at Oxyrhynchus. It was placed in the John Rylands Library in Manchester, England, and published later by Colin Roberts.[23] The sheet has John 18:31–33 on the *recto* side (the side with the papyrus fibers running horizontally) and 18:37–38 on the *verso* (where the fibers run vertically). It was part of a codex rather than a scroll and has been dated by leading papyrologists to about A.D. 125.[24] It is of greater value for determining the date of the composition of the Gospel than it is for the type of text it rep-

The John Rylands Papyrus is the oldest extant fragment of the New Testament.

resents. For the autograph F. F. Bruce suggests a date of about A.D. 100.[25] This is certainly a valid conjecture for the exemplar of **p**[52], but the Gospel itself may have been written earlier. Since the discovery of the Dead Sea Scrolls there have been suggestions that the autograph of the Gospel may have been written as early as the forties!

The Chester Beatty Papyri

The "sensation of the 1930s" was the purchase of some papyri in Egypt by Chester Beatty, a well-known collector.[26] These documents were probably found in a cemetery or the ruins of a church in the neighborhood of Aphroditopolis,[27] and "reached him through the hands of natives and dealers."[28] Portions of these Chester Beatty Papyri, as they have now become known, were also purchased by the University of Michigan. The story of their acquisition can be reconstructed out of the five volumes published from 1933 to 1936 by Sir Frederick Kenyon, the director and principal librarian of the British Museum, and a volume by Henry Sanders of the University of Michigan.[29]

In 1930–31, Beatty purchased some papyri consisting of parts of the Old Testament, the New Testament, the apocalyptic book of Enoch, and a homily by Melito of Sardis, who lived in the second century.[30] At almost the same time, the University of Michigan purchased some fragments of Mark, Luke, and John matching the papyri purchased by Beatty and, in a rare display of generosity in matters of this kind, gave them to the collector. Kenyon published these documents in 1933 as fasciculus 1 which contained twelve plates. In 1933 he also published fasciculus 2, which contained the text of the Gospels and Acts which we now call **p**[45]. The next year fasciculus 2 was republished with plates.

That same year saw the publication of fasciculus 3, which included Pauline Epistles ($\mathbf{p}^{46}$) and Revelation ($\mathbf{p}^{47}$) with the apologetic note that the Paulines were "unfortunately sadly imperfect," omitting the text between Romans 11:36 and Philippians 4:14.

Providence smiled on the project, however; ten of the missing leaves containing these texts were found among twenty-four others which had been purchased by the University of Michigan in 1932–33. These ten were published by Sanders in 1935 along with what Kenyon had published shortly before; this volume thus contained "the whole of the extant portion of the Pauline Epistles."[31] It had hardly come from the press when Beatty purchased forty-six more leaves of the codex, which were then given to Kenyon to publish. In an example of the continuing cooperation and unselfishness that should characterize all such enterprises, the University of Michigan "spontaneously gave [Kenyon] permission for their leaves to be reprinted, and supplied photographs of them."[32] Thus Kenyon was able to publish "an almost complete copy of the Epistles of Paul,"[33] which is now dated to about A.D. 200.[34]

The Nag Hammadi Papyri

Another example of historically important New Testament manuscripts that were purchased from antiquities dealers or private individuals are the Nag Hammadi Papyri.[35] Their history contains all the ingredients of a first-rate novel that could have been penned by Sir Arthur Conan Doyle. In 1945 two brothers from the modern Egyptian village of al-Qasr (the site of ancient Chenoboskeion on the huge bend of the Upper Nile just north of Luxor) unearthed a large pottery jar containing thirteen codices which embrace sixty-one tractates or fragments thereof. The practice of storing precious documents in earthen jars can be traced to at least the sixth century B.C. when Jeremiah instructed that a deed be placed in a clay vessel for long-term preservation (Jer. 32:14). The reader may recall that some of the Dead Sea Scrolls were found in earthenware jars and that the museum where they are displayed in Jerusalem is built in the shape of a lid to such a jar.

A month after finding the books, the two men joined their five brothers and widowed mother in an act of blood revenge. They killed the young man who had killed their father six months earlier.[36] The village where their victim had lived was located adjacent to the spot where the two brothers had found the codices. Because of their fear of blood revenge being taken upon them in turn, they would later prove unwilling to return there to point out the location of their discovery. Indeed, two of their clan were subsequently killed by the brother of the young man they had killed.

The two brothers, fearing that the police investigating the young man's murder would search their house and confiscate the newly discovered documents, entrusted the papyri to the Coptic village priest, who kept them in his home. The priest's brother, who was a traveling teacher, saw the documents, assumed them to be valuable, and persuaded the priest to give him one. The brother then took the book to a Coptic physician in Cairo who was interested in the Coptic language, the language in which the codices were written. The physician called in the Department of Antiquities, which took control of the book and paid the priest's brother the nominal sum of two hundred fifty Egyptian pounds. The book was then placed in the Coptic Museum on October 4, 1946.

Meanwhile, the mother of the seven brothers repossessed the other books from the priest. She burned one of them (probably Codex XII, which consists of only a few fragmentary leaves), thinking it to be worthless and probably a source of bad luck. Muslim neighbors from the village and nearby Nag Hammadi took the rest. Since they had no interest in Coptic Christianity and were illiterate, all the codices eventually ended up in the hands of antiquities dealers. A gold merchant in Nag Hammadi took one to Cairo and sold it. In course of time the Egyptian Department of Antiquities gained control of all the documents, some of which had been taken out of the country by a Belgian dealer named Albert Eid. In May of 1952, his widow sold most of Codex I to the Jung Institute of Zurich, Switzerland, for more than ten thousand dollars.[37] Named the Jung Codex, it was returned to Cairo after publication.[38] Now all thirteen documents are together in the Coptic Museum in Old Cairo.[39]

The documents are generally referred to as the Nag Hammadi Papyri, probably because they were early on associated with Nag Hammadi.[40] They have been published in English translation under the editorship of James Robinson,[41] who was appointed to lead a committee of UNESCO scholars in studying and publishing the documents, a task that was inhibited for a time by the Suez Crisis of 1956. Among the important contributions these documents make to New Testament studies is the inclusion of the Gospel of Thomas, a collection of 114 purported sayings of Jesus (not to be confused with the Syriac narrative of Jesus' infancy that goes by the same name). Some of these sayings were previously known; others are new. Whether they are authentic is incapable of being demonstrated.

Scholarly articles and books on the sixty-one tractates included in Robinson's publication[42] have been voluminous, numbering more than five thousand to date. David Scholer provides an annual index of these works in the periodical *Novum Testamen-*

tum.[43] The Coptic texts were published gradually in a facsimile edition.[44] An excavation at Nag Hammadi, conducted by Robinson and Bastiaan Van Elderen, failed to produce any germane information about the specific community that produced the documents, although evidence of Christian monastic communities in the vicinity was found. The excavation of the Qumran community that produced the Dead Sea Scrolls, which were found in 1947, little more than a year later than the Nag Hammadi codices, was much more successful.

Papyrus Fragments among the Dead Sea Scrolls

A scholarly debate was ignited in 1972 when José O'Callaghan identified as pieces of the New Testament (from Mark, Acts, Romans, 1 Timothy, James and 2 Peter) several scraps of papyri found among the Dead Sea Scrolls in cave 7 at Qumran. He dated them before the John Rylands Papyrus, the oldest New Testament fragment yet discovered.[45] However, as Joseph Fitzmyer has remarked, "favorable reactions to the claims have only come from uncritical sources."[46] Containing only scattered words, the fragments are much too scanty for positive identification. In this respect, like so many of the papyrus and parchment fragments which contain numerous lacunae, they resemble the Irishman's coat "of which it was said that it consisted mostly of fresh air."[47]

A brief word about the Dead Sea Scrolls is in order here.[48] In spite of recent challenges to the contrary by Norman Golb,[49] there is now almost universal agreement that the little community at Qumran [50] that produced the scrolls was composed of Essenes, one of the three Jewish sects discussed by Josephus.[51] Looking back over three decades of debate, Frank Cross has concluded:

> The scholar who would "exercise caution" in identifying the sect of Qumran with the Essenes places himself in an astonishing position: he must suggest seriously that two major parties formed communistic religious communities in the same district of the desert of the Dead Sea and lived together in effect for two centuries, holding similar bizarre views, performing similar or rather identical lustrations, ritual meals, and ceremonies. He must suppose that one, carefully described by classical authors, disappeared without leaving building remains or even potsherds behind; the other, systematically ignored by the classical sources, left extensive ruins, and indeed a great library. I prefer to be reckless and flatly identify the men of Qumran with their perennial houseguests, the Essenes.[52]

Unfortunately, while the scrolls do provide us with important background material on the nature of sectarian Judaism in the time of Jesus, and on the possible relation of John the Baptist with the Essene sect (see pp. 160–161), they have not proven to be of any real significance for the study of the text of the New Testament.[53]

The Bodmer Papyri

If the Chester Beatty Papyri were the sensation of the thirties, the discovery of the Bodmer Papyri in the fifties was even more significant for the study of the New Testament: "The Bodmer papyri surpass the Chester Beatty papyri in the quality of their preservation, in the length of their texts, and in their textual significance."[54] Procured by Martin Bodmer in Egypt, these twenty-two papyri include segments of the New Testament along with passages from the Old Testament, early Christian literature, and Homer.[55] The most important for New Testament studies are Bodmer II ($\mathbf{p}^{66}$, John), Bodmer VII–VIII ($\mathbf{p}^{72}$, portions of 1 and 2 Peter and Jude), Bodmer XIV–XV ($\mathbf{p}^{75}$, portions of Luke and John), and Bodmer XVII ($\mathbf{p}^{74}$, portions of Acts and the General Epistles). When publication began in 1956, their importance was immediately recognized, and the appetite of archaeologists and New Testament scholars whetted.[56]

Current scholarship assigns $\mathbf{p}^{74}$ to the seventh century, $\mathbf{p}^{72}$ to the third or fourth, $\mathbf{p}^{75}$ to the third, and $\mathbf{p}^{66}$ to about A.D. 200.[57] However, Herbert Hunger, director of the papyrological collections in the National Library at Vienna, thinks $\mathbf{p}^{66}$ should be dated as early as the first half of the second century![58] Like the Beatty Papyri these major discoveries have had an impact on efforts to reconstruct the New Testament text (see pp. 356–57).

The Contributions of the Papyri

Fresh Perspectives on the New Testament Canon

The John Rylands Papyrus and such others as $\mathbf{p}^{46}$, the earliest known copy of the Pauline Letters (about A.D. 200), are causing a reevaluation of earlier studies that placed the composition of John and some of the Pauline corpus (e.g., pastorals, Ephesians, Colossians) in the second century. Clearly, an earlier date is now demanded for John, and questions must be raised not only about the late dates assigned to certain other books, but also about authorship and canonical position. Hebrews is not only included in the Pauline corpus of $\mathbf{p}^{46}$, but stands in second position behind Romans.[59] Furthermore, from the paragraph-numbering system employed in Vaticanus, one of our oldest and best codices, it is clear that in the exemplar used in copying, Hebrews was placed among the Pauline Letters. Galatians ends with paragraph 58;

Ephesians begins with 70. Hebrews, which follows 2 Thessalonians, begins with paragraph 59. It is obvious that in an ancestor of Vaticanus the Epistle to the Hebrews was positioned between Galatians and Ephesians.[60]

Furthermore, the papyri have supplied us with an enriched perspective of our canon. It is, helpful to be reminded that for centuries our New Testament was not a single printed volume supplied with all sorts of helps (maps, dictionaries, concordances, indexes, etc.). The individual books and letters were circulated separately. Earlier opinions to the contrary notwithstanding,[61] these documents were probably written on codices rather than scrolls from the beginning.[62] Pagan documents were written on papyrus scrolls, while Jewish literature was produced on leather scrolls. The reason why Christians chose to use papyrus codices is not known, but it may have been partially economical (the book form allowed writing on both sides of the sheet). The use of codices may also have been part of the ongoing religious and cultural separation between the Christian community and the Jewish community in the second century—a separation seen also in the church's use of the Greek translation of the Old Testament (the Septuagint) while the Jews used the Hebrew original and the church's use of the term *ecclēsia* (ἐκκλησία) for their assemblies while the Jews used the term *synagōgē* (συναγωγή).[63] The Christians may only have been following the trend of the times, as Kurt and Barbara Aland suggest,[64] but it is more feasible to believe that pragmatic reasons dictated the use of the codex. For example, the codex form greatly simplified the procedure of finding specific texts, an extremely difficult task for anyone working with large scrolls.[65]

Of all known New Testament papyri, only four ($\mathbf{p}^{12}$, $\mathbf{p}^{13}$, $\mathbf{p}^{18}$, $\mathbf{p}^{22}$) are from scrolls; the remainder are codices.[66] The sheer bulk of the New Testament books, if written in scroll form, would have made their use burdensome. Kenyon estimated that on scrolls 15 inches in height, the letter of Paul to the Romans would be 11 1/2 feet in length; Mark's Gospel, the shortest, 19 feet, and Luke, the longest, 32 feet long. The entire New Testament, if written on a single scroll, would have been more than 200 feet in length.[67] The early church never produced such a document, not only because it would have been impossible to use, but also because the New Testament canon was not agreed upon until considerably later than the first century. Some books were not universally accepted until the fourth century; indeed, the Syrian Church today still accepts only twenty-two of the twenty-seven books in the Western canon, excluding 2 Peter, 2 and 3 John, Jude, and Revelation.[68]

Since one scroll could not contain all four Gospels, the desire of the church to treat them as a unit, as evidenced in Tatian's second-century harmony (the *Diatessaron*), would inevitably have led the church to use codices, if it had not already been using them. Such would have been the effect of the very process of canonization. We now have examples of single codices from the third and fourth centuries that include the Gospels and Acts together.[69] As early as the second century the notion of an authoritative and exclusive canon was a major point of contention between gnostics and orthodox Christians in Egypt.[70] The gnostics, who were given to esoteric and charismatic approaches to religious authority, were confronted by orthodox church leaders who used traditional arguments based on books that were acceptable to the mainline church. The Gnostics countered by creating their own religious library, which set forth teachings of Jesus that they considered both legitimate and authoritative.[71] Almost all of the manuscripts and manuscript fragments of noncanonical Gospels from the first and second centuries emanate from these gnostic circles.[72] In the midst of such controversy, the necessity of establishing limits on a canon was thus felt as early as the second century. The discovery of the papyri have contributed greatly to our understanding of the larger corpus of books out of which our canon was eventually drawn.

Study of the papyri led to indefensible assertions that fragments of a fifth Gospel had been found,[73] assertions somewhat reminiscent of the claims that the Temple Scroll may represent a sixth book of the Pentateuch.[74] Papyrus Egerton 2, which was purchased from a dealer in the summer of 1934 by the British Museum, was published the next year by the manuscript keepers of that museum, H. Idris Bell and T. C. Skeat.[75] What they called "An Unknown Gospel" was labeled "A New Gospel" by C. H. Dodd in a major article written in 1936,[76] and was included by Edgar Hennecke and Wilhelm Schneemelcher among the "Apocryphal Gospel Fragments."[77] Strictly on the basis of its script, Bell and Skeat date Egerton 2 to the middle of the second century A.D.[78] While admitting that this is precarious, they feel confident that they are correct. Dodd dates the document earlier, placing it in the period between the fall of the temple and the revolt against Hadrian (A.D. 70–135).[79]

The fragment consists of brief stories about Jesus taken from the four canonical Gospels.[80] If it is to be considered New Testament text, it is, along with the John Rylands Papyrus of John 18, one of the two oldest pieces in existence. In any event it clearly establishes, along with the Rylands fragment, a very early date for the text of John's Gospel,[81] and gives strong indication of an early date for the literary form of Mark 1:40–44. The Greek text is accessible,[82] and English translations are abundant.[83]

Another document hailed by some as a fifth Gospel[84] is the Gospel of Thomas that was found among the Nag Hammadi codices (see p. 358).[85] It can scarcely be considered a true Gospel, however, for it is not a history of Jesus' ministry, but a collection of sayings attributed to him.

Knowledge of the Basic Format of Ancient Letters

One of the valuable byproducts of the papyrological discoveries is new knowledge of the form in which letters were written in New Testament times. We now have more than nine thousand ancient letters that are Christian in character; in addition there are innumerable pieces of everyday nonreligious correspondence.[86] Since twenty-one of the twenty-seven documents in the New Testament are letters (the exceptions are the four Gospels, Acts, and Revelation, though the last two do contain letters),[87] the importance of this genre in our canon is self-evident.

Studying the papyri, Adolf Deissmann drew a distinction between letters and epistles.[88] Letters are the ordinary correspondence of families and businesses. Being occasional in nature and lacking literary intent, they are written merely to convey information. Epistles, on the other hand, are literary in nature and intended for publication. Examples are the correspondence of Pliny the Younger and Seneca. The New Testament documents, Deissmann argued, are letters rather than epistles; they were written by and for common people, and reflected a Christian movement that was fundamentally made up of the lower classes. This would also suggest that the letters were not meant for publication and is pertinent to the question of whether the authors were aware that they were writing Scripture.

Although Deissmann's differentiation between letters and epistles has not found wide acceptance, his observation that the New Testament was not written as a second Torah is worth noting. Even though it is called the New Testament, it contains none of the genres of the Old Testament, with the possible exception of Acts and Revelation. The letters, being only occasional correspondence written to meet specific needs of the growing young church in particular sociological settings, have no counterpart in the Old Testament.

Deissmann also made an original and important contribution when he showed that the New Testament letters employed a form which was commonly used in Paul's day. This form has been explored in numerous recent scholarly contributions.[89] From study of the papyri John White, for example, has concluded that most ancient letters followed a basic pattern:

Salutation—sender, addressee, greeting
Thanksgiving

> *Body*—formal opening, basic content, connective and transitional for-
> mulae, (and in Christian letters, concluding eschatological climax,
> apostolic parousia)
> *Ethical Exhortation and Instructions* (paraenesis)
> *Closing*—greetings (in Christian letters, doxology, benediction)[90]

Figure 32 illustrates how this pattern was followed by both the Book of Philemon and a typical letter of the second or third century A.D. Calvin Roetzel finds this format as well in Romans, 1 Corinthians, 2 Corinthians, Galatians, Philippians and 1 Thessalonians.[91]

Proceeding unnecessarily from the presupposition that the Pauline Letters were written as literature,[92] White has also argued that the bodies of Paul's letters are, unexpectedly, in the basic style of the nonliterary papyri.[93] White's position, unfortunately, injects further confusion into the differentiation Deissmann tried to make between letters and epistles, and hence into our understanding of the nature of the New Testament documents.

Clarification of the Nature of New Testament Greek

One of the most important contributions of the ancient papyri is the clarification they have provided about the nature of the language in which the New Testament text was written. Before their discovery we had little external information about the kind of Greek used in its composition. The language was so unlike classical Greek that it was considered to be unique. Edwin Hatch, a well-known authority in Greek, wrote in 1889: "Biblical Greek is thus a language which stands by itself."[94] And Friedrich Blass, who wrote the authoritative *Grammatik des neutestamentlichen Griechisch* in 1896,[95] commented once in a review that New Testament Greek was "to be recognized as something peculiar, obeying its own laws."[96] In 1863 Richard Rothe had gone so far as to describe it in these terms: "We can indeed with good right speak of a language of the Holy Ghost. . . . The Divine Spirit . . . takes the language . . . and makes of it a characteristic religious variety."[97] The noted lexicographer, Hermann Cremer, concurred with Rothe: "We have a very clear and striking proof of this in New Testament Greek."[98]

But then Deissmann wrote the first of three enlightening volumes which proved to be landmark studies demonstrating convincingly that the New Testament was written in a kind of Greek closer to the newly discovered papyri than to Plato.[99] It was written not in a "Holy Spirit language," but in a common (κοινή) dialect which was used in everyday correspondence. However, Bruce has cautioned that "we should not . . . exaggerate this similarity between New Testament Greek and the ver-

Figure 32
The Basic Format of Ancient Letters

	Nonreligious Papyrus	Philemon (RSV)
Salutation		
Sender	Irenaeus	Paul, a prisoner for Christ Jesus, and Timothy our brother (v. 1)
Recipient	Apollinarius his dearest brother	Philemon our beloved fellow worker and Apphia our sister and Archippus our fellow soldier, and the church in your house (vv. 1–2)
Greeting	Many greetings	Grace to you and peace from God our Father and the Lord Jesus Christ (v. 3)
Thanksgiving (prayer)	I pray continually for your health, and I myself am well	I thank my God always when I remember you in my prayers (v.4)
Body	(Information about his arrival on a grain boat from Egypt to Rome)	(Discussion of the return of Onesimus the slave [vv. 8–16])
Ethical Exhortation	(Absent)	Receive him . . . charge to my account . . . refresh my heart in Christ . . . prepare a guest room for me (vv. 17–22)
Closing Peace Wish	(Absent)	(Absent from Philemon but present elsewhere in Paul's letters)
Greetings	Many salutations to your wife and to Serenus and to all who love you, each by name	Epaphras, my fellow prisoner in Christ Jesus, sends greetings to you, and so do Mark, Aristarchus, Demas, and Luke, my fellow workers (vv. 23–24)
Kiss	(Absent)	(Absent from Philemon but present elsewhere)
Close (Grace and Benediction)	Goodbye	The grace of the Lord Jesus Christ be with your spirit (v. 25)

The secular letter, which is taken from C. K. Barrett, ed., The New Testament Background: Selected Documents (London: SPCK, 1957), 29, reads in full:

Irenaeus to Apollinarius his dearest brother many greetings. I pray continually for your health, and I myself am well. I wish you to know that I reached land on the sixth of the month Epeiph and we unloaded our cargo on the eighteenth of the same month. I went up to Rome, on the twenty-fifth of the same month and the place welcomed us as the god willed, and we are daily expecting our discharge, it so being that up till today nobody in the corn fleet has been released. Many salutations to your wife and to Serenus and to all who love you, each by name. Goodbye. Mesore 9. (Addressed) To Apollinarius from his brother Irenaeus.

The letter was originally published in Ägyptische Urkunden aus den königlichen Museen zu Berlin: Griechische Urkunden 1 (Berlin: 1895), #27. The comparison with Philemon is drawn from Calvin J. Roetzel, The Letters of Paul: Conversations in Context, 2d ed. (Atlanta: John Knox, 1982), 30–31.

nacular of the papyri,"[100] a point made also by A. D. Nock.[101] In 1930, James Moulton and George Milligan produced an extensive one-volume dictionary of New Testament Greek "illustrated from the papyri and other non-literary sources."[102] It needs to be updated now because of the vast amount of material that has been discovered in the past sixty years. As a result of a meeting of scholars in 1985 to consider the feasibility, an Australian team is currently at work on that project. In a related effort to move in a somewhat different direction, a group of international scholars under the direction of F. W. Danker formed a team to produce an epigraphically oriented lexicon of the New Testament. Danker writes that this work will "incorporate epigraphical data along some of the lines that Moulton-Milligan did with papyri, but with the advantage of a more methodical approach."[103]

Impact on Textual Criticism

One of the most significant contributions which archaeology has made to New Testament studies is, and surely for a long time will be, the impact it is making on theories of how the Greek text was transmitted and is to be reconstructed. A general reexamination of prevailing views is taking place in the science of textual criticism at this writing; this is due specifically to the contribution of the papyrological discoveries. In a word, views previously held by the majority of textual critics about the New Testament text in the first three centuries have been seriously challenged if not completely discredited. A bit of background will be helpful at this point.

Until the great manuscript discoveries made by Tischendorf and others, the text of the New Testament that was predominantly used throughout the Christian world was the Byzantine text, which was imposed upon Christendom in an effort to unify the church.[104] Before the fifth century, the Alexandrian type of text (represented generally in Codex Vaticanus and Codex Sinaiticus) had been the most widely distributed form. By A.D. 450, however, it was already being greatly influenced by the Byzantine text; it then gradually diminished in importance until it virtually disappeared.

So pervasive was the Byzantine influence that approximately 95 percent of the more than five thousand manuscripts extant today are of the Byzantine type.[105] Several factors account for this development: (1) the decline of the patriarchate in Alexandria along with the rise in importance of the one in Byzantium; (2) the spread of Islam after the sixth century, and (3) the emergence of Latin as the predominant language of the Western church by the third century,[106] which meant that Greek manuscripts were not needed there as much as they were in the East, where Greek was still the lingua franca and the Greek text was paramount.[107] It is primarily to the Eastern churches that the credit goes for the preservation and distribution of the Greek text of the New Testament.

Such was the situation when the great manuscript discoveries were made in the nineteenth century. Until then almost all known manuscripts were of the Byzantine type and had been produced after the eighth century. The Greek text published by Erasmus in 1516 from these types of manuscripts dominated scholarly use. The third edition of his text became the basis of the *Textus Receptus* ("accepted text"), which was used for most subsequent translations. So the discovery of early Alexandrian-type manuscripts (Sinaiticus and Vaticanus) prompted B. F. Westcott and F. J. A. Hort of Cambridge to publish a new Greek text based on them (1881). So impressive was the quality of the new discoveries that Westcott and Hort labeled them "neutral" texts, believing they were closer to the originals than anything yet known. In reality there is, of course, no such thing as a neutral text.[108]

Shortly before, Tischendorf had published his monumental edition of the Greek New Testament, the *Editio octava critica maior* (1872), which was based on Sinaiticus. And in 1898 Eberhard Nestle, having compared the texts of Westcott-Hort and Tischendorf, published his *Novum Testamentum Graece*. The fate of the Textus Receptus was sealed, and textual criticism proceeded henceforth from the premises laid down by Westcott and Hort on the basis of the new manuscript discoveries.

But a weakness in the work of nineteenth-century New Testament scholars was that they did not have any manuscript that originated prior to the fourth century, although what they did have was significantly older than the very late manuscripts on which the Textus Receptus was based. Beginning essentially in the 1930s, the discovery of New Testament papyri dating from the second century filled this gap. The impact of the discovery of these papyri has been phenomenal. As the introduction to the most recent edition of the *Novum Testamentum Graece* states: "Neither Codex Vaticanus nor Codex Sinaiticus (nor even **p**[75] of two hundred years earlier) can provide a guideline we can normally depend on for determining the text. The age of Westcott-Hort and of Tischendorf is definitely over!"[109]

The current status of the Greek text is apparent in the fact that this latest edition contains "more than five hundred changes" from the previous edition.[110] This means that the Greek Testament is still in the process of change! On the other hand, the extent of agreement among the several editions of the Greek Testament over the past one hundred years is impressive and encouraging. Indeed, among seven of the leading editions of the Greek Testament (Tischendorf, Westcott-Hort, von Soden, Vogels, Merk,

Bover, and the twenty-fifth of Nestle-Aland) there is "complete accord . . . apart from orthographical differences."[111]

The papyri have revolutionized our understanding of the text in the first three centuries, though perhaps not as definitively as we might wish or as the Alands might like us to believe.[112] When the Chester Beatty Papyri were found in the 1930s, it was determined that **p**[45] and **p**[46] contained such an irregular text that pre-fourth century texts could no longer be regarded as homogeneous. The inconsistencies indicated that second- and third-century texts were probably eclectic and differed extensively from each other. Thus Westcott and Hort were shown to be wrong in assuming that only one type of text was transmitted through these early centuries, namely, the type witnessed to by the fourth-century "neutral" manuscripts of the Alexandrian family.

The discovery of the Bodmer Papyri in the 1950s further clouded the issue. The quality of **p**[66] (the Gospel of John) surpassed anything in the Chester Beatty Papyri and seemed to confirm the theory of early textual heterogeneity. However, **p**[75] (the Gospels of Luke and John) in the Bodmer collection "proved this [theory] to be wrong because its text was so close to that of Codex Vaticanus that it could even be suspected of being its exemplar."[113] On the basis of a fresh collation of the papyri, the Alands now think there were three kinds of text in the first three centuries:[114]

1. *Normal texts* (e.g., **p**[52]) which transmitted the original with a limited amount of variation.[115] A manuscript in this category represents a "relatively faithful tradition which departs from its exemplar only occasionally, as do New Testament manuscripts of every century."[116]
2. *Free texts* (e.g., **p**[45], **p**[46], and **p**[66]),[117] which dealt with their exemplars "in a relatively free manner, with no suggestion of a program of standardization," and "exhibited the most diverse variants."[118] While this kind of text is not at all typical of the early period,[119] "it is their collations that have changed the picture so completely."[120]
3. *Strict texts* (e.g., **p**[75]), which "transmit the text of an exemplar with meticulous care . . . and depart from it only rarely."[121]

"Although many details are obviously still debatable, there can be no doubt," conclude the Alands, "that the earlier view of the textual situation before the rise of the major text types is now due for a radical and thorough review."[122]

Questions are already being raised as to whether the latest edition of *Novum Testamentum Graece* (the twenty-sixth) is becoming a new Textus Receptus,[123] and the Alands's confidence in the ability of the papyri to clarify the pre-fourth-century text is being challenged. In a recent article, J. H. Petzer argues that "instead of bringing greater clarity, [they] have brought greater confusion, because enough papyri have been discovered to prove the older theories, reconstructions of the history of the text, wrong, but there is still not enough evidence to supply new theories. . . . What is needed today is not so much a re-interpretation of the existing facts, but rather a new set of facts."[124] Nevertheless, Petzer feels that "currently [the Alands's] theory seems to explain the text of the papyri best,"[125] a position strongly opposed by Eldon J. Epp.[126] Fueling this discussion is the Alands's constant use of the term *Standard Text*,[127] for which they have been criticized; but Petzer points out that it is neither the Alands nor their publishers who have made the latest edition of *Novum Testamentum Graece* the "Standard Text" (as the Elzevirs had done when they published the Textus Receptus in the seventeenth century), but the fact that it has substantially outsold all other texts.[128] Furthermore, "it is clear that this text is probably the best and closest to the autographs that New Testament Textual Criticism can come today."[129] Whatever merit each side in this controversy may have, it is becoming increasingly clear that in reconstructing the text we must pay closer attention to internal evidence than has been done in the past.[130]

Insight into the Use of Divine Names in the New Testament Texts

One noteworthy contribution the papyri makes to our understanding of the text of the New Testament is the insight they give us into the aura of sanctity that attached to divine names.[131] We have long known that when Jewish scribes copied the name יהוה (*Yahweh*—"Jehovah" or "Lord"), which appears more than six thousand times in the Old Testament, they washed their hands both before and afterwards because it was "the name that defiles the hands." The name was so holy that it was, and still is, considered irreverent to pronounce it. Yigael Yadin says, "From the Second Temple period onwards it was never uttered by Jews, and the practice is followed to this day."[132] They used the term אֲדֹנָי (*Adonai*, "my Lord") instead, which the ancient scribes wrote in the margin of the Hebrew Bible wherever *Yahweh*, the divine Tetragram (or Tetragrammaton, i.e., "Four Letters"), occurred.

Yadin has argued that the scribal practice at Qumran, where the Dead Sea Scrolls were found, was to make a distinction between canonical and noncanonical texts by using two different kinds of script for the divine name. Although in the canonical books the scribes entered the divine name in the late Aramaic script in which all their Hebrew texts were written, in the noncanonical books they used the old Hebrew script for the divine name.[133] However, Harmut Stegemann has produced several examples of biblical as well as nonbiblical texts from Qumran in which the Tetragram is written in both kinds of script.[134] The reason for the fluctuation in scripts for the divine name is an enigma. George Howard has shown that Greek translations made by Jewish scribes contain the Tetragram in Hebrew, while copies made later by Christian scribes replace the Hebrew *Yahweh* with the Greek κύριος ("Lord").[135] This suggests that the presentation of the divine name in a distinctive way—whether preserving it in old Hebrew in the texts employing the Aramaic script of Hebrew or preserving it in the Aramaic script in the texts employing Greek—was a uniquely Jewish practice in the beginning.

The point of all this in connection with New Testament manuscripts is that a related but somewhat different phenomenon occurs in some of our very early texts. The mid-second-century Papyrus Egerton 2 employs abbreviations for various divine names, including God, Lord, Father, and Jesus.[136] A third-century manuscript of the *Shepherd of Hermas* similarly uses abbreviations for Lord, God, Spirit, and Son,[137] so the practice was not limited to Scripture. These abbreviations normally consist of the first and last letters of the divine name, although sometimes the first and second are used, or even three letters as in the case of Spirit (ΠΝΑ, ΠΝΙ, etc.). A horizontal line is placed above the letters to show that they form a contraction for a divine name.

At times the use of an abbreviation gives us an insight into the early church's interpretation of a text. For example, in John 3:6 Jesus said to Nicodemus, "That which is born of the spirit is spirit." Should either of the words for "spirit" be understood as referring to the Holy Spirit? In **p**[66], which dates to about A.D. 200, the scribe wrote out the second word for "spirit" normally (πνεῦμα, *pneuma*), but abbreviated the first as a *nomen sacrum* (ΠΝΣ), thus indicating his belief that the Holy Spirit is meant by the first term. That the two words stand side by side serves to highlight the contrast (ἐκ τοῦ πνς πνεῦμά ἐστιν, *ek tou pns pneuma estin*).[138] Sacred abbreviations are found consistently in early New Testament manuscripts.[139] Thus, the uniquely Jewish practice of occasionally writing the covenant name of God in different script is matched by the equally unique Christian practice of using abbreviations for sacred names. The Alands assert that "manuscripts of the Septuagint, the Greek version of the Old Testament, can be assigned with confidence to a Christian or Jewish origin on the basis of their use or non-use of the *nomina sacra* forms."[140] Whether the Christian practice arose directly from the Jewish one, as Ludwig Traube suggested long ago,[141] is uncertain. Howard thinks it arose among Gentile Christians who, having nothing comparable to the distinctive treatment that Jews gave to the name *Yahweh*, invented the abbbreviations to compensate for this deficiency.[142]

Another fact worth noting is that as late as the third century some scribes who copied the Greek manuscripts did not use the Greek word κύριος for the Tetragram, but transcribed the Aramaic characters יהוה (*Yahweh*) into Greek as ΠΙΠΙ (*PIPI*).[143] It is possible that they did not recognize the peculiar-looking Aramaic letters in the Old Testament exemplar they were using. For at the beginning of the fifth century Jerome tells us that "certain ignorant ones, because of the similarity of the [Aramaic and Greek] characters, when they would find [יהוה] in Greek books, were accustomed to pronounce PIPI."[144] On the other hand, this could have been a means of simply assigning these unique Aramaic characters a special Greek form in order to perpetuate their distinctiveness for Christians. It has been suggested that Origen in the third century or Eusebius in the fourth may have made the change into Greek.[145]

This whole issue becomes even more intriguing when we consider the possibility that the New Testament autographs, written almost entirely by Jewish Christians (the possible exception being Luke-Acts), may have preserved the Jewish custom and retained the divine name in Aramaic script in quotations from the Old Testament. Thus they may have followed the lead of some Jewish authors who used one script for the divine name when they quoted Scripture and another when they themselves referred to God. Similarly, it was customary at Qumran to use the Tetragram freely when one was either copying or introducing Scripture quotations into a commentary, but to use *El* ("God") in original material written for a commentary.[146]

Having references to Yahweh clearly indicated would be of enormous help, for any verses that refer to "the Lord" are unclear as to whether Christ or God (Yahweh) is meant. For example, Peter's quotation (in Acts 2:34) of David, "The Lord said to my Lord," is unclear until the Hebrew original (Ps. 110:1) is read: "Yahweh says to my Adonai." Such verses that quote the Old Testament would be clearer if YHWH (the Tetragram) were used in the New Testament.

Another case in point is Romans 10:16, which quotes Isaiah 53:1, "Lord, who has believed our report?" "Lord" would seem to refer to Christ, for "the word of Christ" is a reading which appears in the most recent New Testament texts of verse 17, even though many of the ancient witnesses have "the word of God."[147] Actually, the word *Lord* does not appear in the Hebrew text of Isaiah 53:1, although it does appear in the Greek text, which Paul quotes, as Κύριε. Since this word became a surrogate in Christian copies of the Septuagint for YHWH, it is natural to assume that κύριε in the Septuagint of Isaiah 53:1 refers to YHWH. It undoubtedly slipped into the Septuagint from an early Hebrew lemma (in commentaries, the setting forth of a text prior to its discussion) which led to the inference that the YHWH mentioned in the second part of Isaiah 53:1 is the person being addressed in the first part of that verse. Since this verse is Scripture rather than commentary, Jewish scribal practice would have dictated the use of "Yahweh" rather than "Adonai." The verse would then have read, "Yahweh, who has believed our report?"[148] This is the way Paul would have understood the Septuagint. Contrary to current textual criticism, then, the reading in Romans 10:17 should probably be "the word of God" rather than "the word of Christ." Rudolf Bultmann's argument that "the unmodified expression 'the Lord' is unthinkable (*nicht denkbar*)" in Jewish usage (and thus unthinkable in Isa. 53:1a)[149] is now rebutted by several Palestinian Aramaic texts which have the word *Mare* or *Marya* ("Lord") as a title for God. Thus, pre-Christian Jews did refer to God in an absolute sense as "the Lord."[150]

New Light on Ancient Words

Occasionally the discovery of a new papyrus or (more frequently) an unearthed inscription greatly improves understanding of the meaning of particular Greek words. For example, the word νεανίσκος (*neaniskos*, "youth"), which appears several times in the New Testament (Matt. 19:20, 22; Mark 14:51; Luke 7:14; Acts 2:17; 5:10; 1 John 2:13–14), has been found in an inscription recording the Gymnasiarchal Law of Beroea. This lengthy inscription sets up a threefold classification: παῖδες (*paides*), children up to age fifteen; ἔφηβοι (*epheboi*), ages fifteen to seventeen; and νεανίσκοι (*neaniskoi* or νέοι, *neoi*), ages eighteen to twenty-two.[151] This same inscription contains one of our earliest references to πολιτάρχαι (politarchs), Roman officials in Greece whose existence had been denied for some time (see pp. 294–295). Similarly, the use of πρώτη in the enigmatic reference

Inscriptional evidence was the first non-New Testament contact with the Roman politarchs.

The longer version of Romans 13:3, found at Caesarea Maritima.

to Philippi as the "chief city" of Macedonia (Acts 16:12) is affirmed by its use on ancient coins (see p. 284).

Names which appear in the New Testament have been found in tomb inscriptions in Jerusalem: (1) from the Talpiot suburb we have the name *Jesus* in Greek;[152] (2) from the Givat ha-Mivtar suburb we have the Hebrew names *Simon, Martha, Saul,* and *Salome* inscribed on ossuaries;[153] and (3) the name *Sapphira* has been found in Talpiot, both in Greek and in Hebrew.[154] In addition, the Aramaic name *Cephas* (Gk. Peter) has turned up in the pre-Christian Elephantine Papyri in a reference to a Semite (probably a Jew) named "Aqab, son of Cephas."[155]

Two mosaics of the text of Romans 13:3 have been found in Caesarea Maritima, on the coast of Israel. We discovered the longer one during our excavation in 1972.[156] The shorter one had previously been found by Abraham Negev in 1960. The two texts, dating no later than the fifth century, are located on the floor of a large public building (perhaps a praetorium or archives), and are identical to our Greek text of that passage except for a linguistic peculiarity prevalent in modern Greece today: in the phrase "If you would not *fear* the authorities, do that which is good," one text has φοβεισθαι and the other φοβισθαι, the two being pronounced the same.[157] These inscriptions are as old as some of our oldest manuscripts of the New Testament and are obviously important for purposes of comparison.

Excavations in the Judean desert of Israel, conducted by Yizhar Hirschfeld and Rivka Birger from 1981 till 1988, have produced a mosaic of a part of 1 Corinthians 15:52–53. It was laid in front of a burial cave near the Khirbet ed-Deir monastery, east of Hebron and south of Tekoa. A photograph graciously sent to me

The shorter mosaic version of Romans 13:3.

by Professor Hirschfeld shows that the inscription, which speaks of the resurrection of the body, was situated so that it was read as one faced the tomb.[158] The text reads:

> δει το φθαρτον τουτο ενδυσασθαι αφθαρσιαν και το θνητον τουτο ενδυσασθαι αθανασιαν. σαλπισει γαρ και οι νεκροι αναστησονται ["This perishable nature must put on the imperishable, and this mortal nature must put on immortality. For the trumpet will sound, and the dead will be raised" (RSV).]

The inscription, which dates from the fifth or sixth century,[159] places verse 53 before the portion from verse 52. The word γαρ ("for") is omitted from the beginning of the quote, and the last word—αναστησονται ("will be raised")—represents the Byzantine type of text (Codices A, D, F, G, and P) rather than the earlier Alexandrian texts (**p**[46] and the Codices א, B, and C), which have εγερθησονται (also meaning "will be raised"). The value of such discoveries for the history of the New Testament text is obvious.

Palestinian Aramaic texts discovered in the last quarter century have also contributed to our knowledge of New Testament words.[160] In a text from the second century B.C. the Aramaic expression "our Lord" has been found in the form *marana*, which enables us to read the Pauline expression in 1 Corinthians 16:22 as μαρανα θα rather than μαραν αθα. The translation should be, "Our Lord, come."[161] Similarly, another debate should now be ended with the discovery that some Aramaic texts used the word *El* for God. This means that the words *Ēli Ēli lema sabachthani* which Jesus spoke on the cross (Matt. 27:46), were not part Hebrew and part Aramaic, but all Aramaic.[162]

These examples are only a few representatives of the contribution which archaeology is making to the study of the New Testament text.[163] To list more would be to go beyond the scope of this volume. It is hoped that our brief summary of the fresh insights that new discoveries of ancient documents are bringing to the study of the canon, genres, language, and individual words of the New Testament will encourage some readers to explore further.

Endnotes

Introduction

1. James Robinson, ed., *The Nag Hammadi Library* (San Francisco: Harper and Row, 1977).

2. The inscription was discovered by the Italian Archaeological Mission, 1959–63. See *EAEHL*, 1.272, 277.

3. *Teaching of Addai* 7b–11a; see the new translation of the Syriac text by George Howard, *The Teaching of Addai*, Society of Biblical Literature Texts and Translations: Early Christian Literature Series 4, ed. R. L. Wilken et al., (Chico, Calif.: Scholar's, 1981), 33.

4. Orosius, *Seven Books of History Against the Pagans*, 7.6, 15–16.

5. "Life of Claudius" 25, in Suetonius, *The Twelve Caesars*, trans. Robert Graves (Baltimore: Penguin, 1957), 197.

6. See Jack Finegan, *Archaeology of the New Testament: The Mediterranean World of the Early Christian Apostles* (Boulder, Colo.: Westview, 1981), 5.

7. Van A. Harvey, *The Historian and the Believer* (New York: Macmillan, 1966).

8. Robert Guelich, "The Gospels: Portraits of Jesus and His Ministry," *JETS* 24 (June 1981): 117–126; I. Howard Marshall, *I Believe in the Historical Jesus* (Grand Rapids: Eerdmans, 1977).

9. I. Howard Marshall, *Luke: Historian and Theologian* (Grand Rapids: Zondervan, 1970); Martin Hengel, *Acts and the History of Earliest Christianity* (Philadelphia: Fortress, 1979); Charles Talbert, ed., *Perspectives on Luke-Acts* (Edinburgh: T and T Clark, 1978); Leander E. Keck and J. Louis Martyn, eds., *Studies in Luke-Acts* (Nashville: Abingdon, 1966).

10. William Ramsay, *St. Paul the Traveller and the Roman Citizen* (London: Hodder and Stoughton, 1908); *The Bearing of Recent Discovery on the Trustworthiness of the New Testament* (Grand Rapids: Baker, 1953); *The Cities of St. Paul* (London: Hodder and Stoughton, 1907); *Was Christ Born at Bethlehem?* (London: Hodder and Stoughton, 1898).

11. See Henry O. Thompson, ed., *The Answers Lie Below* (Lanham, Md.: University Press of America, 1984), 1–185. For a brief overview see John McRay, "Archaeology and the Bible," in Tim Dowley, ed., *Discovering the Bible* (Grand Rapids: Eerdmans, 1986), 7–26.

12. *ASOR Newsletter* 39.3 (April, 1988): 10; Dan Cole, "Ground Penetrating Radar—New Technology Won't Make the Pick and Trowel Obsolete," *BAR* 14 (Jan.–Feb. 1988): 38–40.

13. James F. Strange, "Computers and Archaeological Research," in Joel Drinkard, et.al. eds., *Benchmarks in Time and Culture* (Atlanta: Scholar's Press, 1988): 307–24.

14. Darrell Lance, "American Biblical Archaeology in Perspective," *BA* 36 (Spring 1982): 100; Mortimer Wheeler, *Archaeology from the Earth* (Baltimore: Penguin, 1956), 109–10; Roger Moorey, *Excavation in Palestine* (Grand Rapids: Eerdmans, 1981), 18.

15. Paul Lapp, "Palestine: Known but Mostly Unknown," *BA* 26 (Dec. 1963): 123ff. *Oxford Bible Atlas* (ed. Herbert G. May, 3d ed. [New York: Oxford University Press, 1985]), 94–95, lists 210 sites excavated, but does not include Tell Miqne (Ekron) or Kursi (Gergesa). The official list of excavations for 1990 includes descriptions of only twenty-two projects (Caren Green-berg, comp., *Archaeological Excavations in Israel 1990* [Jerusalem: Israel Department of Antiquities and Museums, Ministry of Education and Culture, 1990]).

16. At the time of the publishing of M. A. Beek's *Atlas of Mesopotamia* (Camden, N.J.: Nelson, 1962), fewer than thirty of the more than five thousand identified mounds of ancient Mesopotamia had been the subject of major excavations.

17. R. Cohen and W. G. Dever, "Preliminary Report of the Pilot Season of the 'Central Negev Highlands Project,'" *BASOR* 232:29–46 (1978); Preliminary Report of the Second Season of the 'Central Negev Highlands Project,'" Ibid. 236:41–60 (1979); "Preliminary Report of the Third and Final Season of the 'Central Negev Highlands Project,'" Ibid. 243:57–77 (1981).

18. See Richard Hope, "The Limitation of Surface Surveys," in D. R. Keller and D. W. Rupp, *Archaeological Survey in the Mediterranean Area*, BAR International Series 155 (Oxford: Biblical Archaeology Reader, 1983), 45ff.

19. P. R. S. Moorey, "Kathleen Kenyon and Palestinian Archaeology," *PEQ* (Jan.–June 1979): 3–9.

20. Gus Van Beek, "Excavation of Palestinian Tells," in Drinkard, *Benchmarks in Time and Culture*, 131–68; see also Arlene M. Rosen, *Cities of Clay: The Geoarchaeology of Tells* (Chicago: University of Chicago Press, 1986).

21. John McRay, "Excavation of Low-Level Settlement Sites," in Drinkard, *Benchmarks in Time and Culture*, 169–78.

22. Henry O. Thompson, "Thoughts on Archaeological Method," *BAR* 3 (Sept. 1977): 25–33; note Magen Broshi's comments about Kenyon's methodology

in *Biblical Archaeology Today* (Jerusalem: Israel Exploration Society, 1985), 478.

23. John J. Davis, "Excavation of Burials," in Drinkard, *Benchmarks in Time and Culture*, 179–208; see also D. Glenn Rose, "The Bible and Archaeology: The State of the Art," in L. G. Perdue, L. E. Toombs, and G. L. Johnson, eds., *Archaeology and Biblical Interpretation* (Atlanta: John Knox, 1987), 53–64.

24. Richard Saley, "Report on the ASOR Photogrammetric Workshop," *ASOR Newsletter* 37.2 (Oct. 1985): 14.

25. D. R. Brothwell, *Digging Up Bones*, 3d. rev. ed. (Ithaca, N.Y.: Cornell University Press, 1981).

26. Joel Drinkard, Jr., "Epigraphy as a Dating Method," in Drinkard, *Benchmarks in Time and Culture*, 417–40.

27. Oded Borowski, "Ceramic Dating," in Drinkard, *Benchmarks in Time and Culture*, 223–50.

28. William F. Albright, *The Excavation of Tell Beit Mirsim in Palestine*, vol. 1, *The Pottery of the First Three Campaigns*, AASOR 12 (1932).

29. Paul Lapp, *Palestinian Ceramic Chronology: 200 B.C.–A.D. 70* (New Haven, Conn.: American Schools of Oriental Research, 1961); Ruth Amiran, Ancient Pottery of the Holy Land (Jerusalem: Masada, 1969); John W. Hayes, Late Roman Pottery (London: British School at Rome, 1972); Varda Sussman, *Ornamented Jewish Oil Lamps* (Jerusalem: Israel Exploration Society, 1982); Nabil Khairy, "Technical Aspects of Fine Nabatean Pottery," *BASOR* 250 (1983): 17–40.

30. Robert H. Smith, "Household Lamps in Palestine in Old Testament Times," *BA* 27 (Feb. 1964): 2ff.; idem, "Household Lamps in Palestine in Intertestamental Times," *BA* 27 (Dec. 1964): 101ff.; idem, "Household Lamps in Palestine in New Testament Times," *BA* 29 (Feb. 1966): 2ff.; Paul Lapp, "The Importance of Dating," *BAR* 3 (March 1977): 13–22.

31. Nahman Avigad, *Discovering Jerusalem* (Nashville: Nelson, 1983), 88. For a recent assessment of the "New Archaeology," see Lawrence E. Toombs, "A Perspective on the New Archaeology," in Perdue et al., *Archaeology and Biblical Interpretation*, 41–52.

32. For a study of the cultural implications of pottery making see Dean Arnold, *Ceramic Theory and Cultural Process*, New Studies in Archaeology (Cambridge: Cambridge University Press, 1985).

33. Examples of other types of pottery and their variations of style in the New Testament period may be seen in Lapp, *Palestinian Ceramic Chronology*.

34. Herbert Hamburger, "Money, Coins," in *IDB* 3.423–35; Baruch Kanael, "Ancient Jewish Coins and Their Importance," *BA* 26 (May 1963): 38–62; Harold Mattingly, *Coins of the Roman Empire in the British Museum*, 4 vols. (London: Trustees of the British Museum, 1965–68); idem, *Roman Coins* (London: Methuen, 1967); A. R. Reifenberg, *Ancient Jewish Coins* (Jerusalem: Rubin Mass, 1969); Ya'akov Meshorer, *Jewish Coins of the Second Temple Period* (Tel Aviv: Am Hassefer, 1967); H. A. Seaby, *Greek Coins and Their Value* (London: B. A. Seaby, 1966); Hugh Goodacre, *A Handbook of the Coinage of the Byzantine Empire* (London: Spink, 1967).

35. John W. Betylon, "Numismatics and Archaeology," *BA* 48 (Sept. 1985): 162-65.

36. A hoard of gold coins from the Arabic period was recently found in the Greek Orthodox excavations at Capernaum. Thousands of bronze coins were previously found at Capernaum in the Franciscan excavations of the synagogue.

37. James M. Weinstein, "Radiocarbon Dating," in Drinkard, *Benchmarks in Time and Culture*, 235–60; R. E. Taylor, *Radiocarbon Dating: An Archaeological Perspective* (San Diego: Academic, 1987).

38. J. Callaway and James M. Weinstein, "Radiocarbon Dating of Palestine in the Early Bronze Age," *BASOR* 225 (1977): 1–16; Fekri Hassan, "Radiocarbon Chronology of Archaic Egypt," *JNES* 39 (July 1980): 203–7.

39. Brian M. Fagan, *In the Beginning: An Introduction to Archaeology*, 5th ed. (Boston: Little, Brown, 1985), chap. 7; Michael B. Schiffer, ed., *Advances in Archaeological Method and Theory*, vol. 9 (San Diego: Academic, 1986).

40. M. J. Aitken, *Thermoluminescence Dating* (San Diego: Academic, 1985).

41. Avraham Horowitz, "Palynology," in Drinkard, *Benchmarks in Time and Culture*, 261–78.

42. David Grose, "The Formation of the Roman Glass Industry," *Archaeology* 36 (July–Aug. 1983): 38–45.

43. See also Paul Lapp, "Importance of Dating," *BAR* 3 (March 1977): 13–22; idem, *The Tale of the Tell*, ed. Nancy Lapp (Pittsburgh: Pickwick, 1975), 31–49.

44. Roger Boraas, "Publication of Archaeological Reports," in Drinkard, *Benchmarks in Time and Culture*, 325–36.

Chapter 1

1. J. B. Ward-Perkins, *Cities of Ancient Greece and Italy: Planning in Classical Antiquity* (New York: Braziller, 1974), 29.

2. William Stephens, *The New Testament World in Pictures* (Nashville: Broadman, 1987), 80.

3. Plutarch *Parallel Lives*, "Alexander" 1.5.

4. For a description of the religious ritual involved, see Pierre Grimal, *Roman Cities*, trans. and ed. G. Michael Woloch (Madison: University of Wisconsin Press, 1983), 12ff.

5. O. A. W. Dilke, *The Roman Land Surveyors* (New York: Barnes and Noble, 1971).

6. Polybius *Histories* 4.31.10.

7. See Ferdinando Castagnoli, *Orthogonal Town Planning in Antiquity* (Cambridge, Mass.: MIT Press, 1972).

8. Vitruvius *On Architecture* 1.6.1. For the methods used to determine directions see 1.6.6–7; Pliny the Elder *Natural History* 18.76–77.

9. Magen Broshi, "Standards of Street Widths in the Roman-Byzantine Period," *IEJ* 27.4 (1977): 232–35.

10. D. S. Robertson, *Greek and Roman Architecture*, 2d ed. (Cambridge: Cambridge University Press, 1974), 193.

11. Whether Herod built a colonnaded street or just a portico on one side is disputed; see p. 230.

12. George M. A. Hanfmann and William E. Mierse, *Sardis from Prehistoric to Roman Times: Results of the Archaeological Exploration of Sardis 1958–1975* (Cambridge, Mass.: Harvard University Press, 1983), 142, esp. nn. 28 and 29.

13. A. R. Seager, "The Synagogue at Sardis," in Lee Levine, ed., *Ancient Synagogues Revealed* (Jerusalem: Israel Exploration Society, 1981), 179.

14. For brief discussions see J. B. Ward-Perkins, *Roman Architecture* (New York: Abrams, 1977), 120ff.; idem, *Roman Imperial Architecture* (New York: Penguin, 1983), 233ff.; Grimal, *Roman Cities*, 68ff.; Jerome Carcopino, *Daily Life in Ancient Rome* (New Haven, Conn.: Yale University Press, 1940), 254ff.; Robertson, *Greek and Roman Architecture*, 243.

15. Homer *Odyssey* 8.249.

16. See illustrations in Harry T. Peck, ed., *Harper's Dictionary of Classical Literature and Antiquities* (New York: Harper, 1898), 186.

17. Pliny *Natural History* 36.121.

18. According to the *Regionaries*, two descriptions of Rome written in the fourth century, there were either 856

(Carcopino, *Daily Life*, 287ff., 314 n. 40) or 952 baths (Peck, *Harper's Dictionary*, 187).

19. Juvenal *Satires* 7.233.

20. Carcopino, *Daily Life*, 256.

21. Vitruvius *On Architecture* 5.10.

22. Mixed bathing is first mentioned by Pliny the Elder (*Natural History* 23.153). It was condemned by respectable citizens (Quintilian *Institutio oratoria* 5.9.14).

23. Vitruvius *On Architecture* 5.10.1.

24. B. Brodribb, *Roman Brick and Tile* (Glouster, England: Alan Sutton, 1987), 91.

25. Vitruvius *On Architecture* 5.10.5.

26. Pliny *Natural History* 33.152.

27. Vitruvius *On Architecture* 5.10.1.

28. Alberto Carpiceci, *Pompeii Two Thousand Years Ago* (Florence: Bonechi, n.d.), 26; Peck, *Harper's Dictionary*, 192.

29. David Small, "Late Hellenistic Baths in Palestine," *BASOR* 266 (May 1987): 59–74, esp. pp. 65ff.

30. Pliny *Natural History* 28.55.

31. Ibid., 33.153.

32. Carcopino, *Daily Life*, 258–60.

33. Small, "Hellenistic Baths," 59.

34. Mordechai Gichon, "The Roman Bath at Emmaus: Excavations in 1977," *IEJ* 29.2 (1979): 101.

35. Small, "Hellenistic Baths," 65. Ehud Netzer points out that "most of [Herod's] buildings were executed according to the traditional, local building technology. Only in those buildings which incorporated the Roman technique of concrete faced with *opus reticulatum* and *opus quadratum* (mainly at Jericho) was there any echo of the new Roman imperial technology and architecture" ("In Reply," in Lee Levine, ed., *The Jerusalem Cathedra* [Jerusalem: Yad Izhak Ben-Zvi Institute, 1981], 77).

36. *The Mishnah*, trans. and ed. by Herbert Danby, ed., (Oxford: Oxford University Press, 1954), 732–45 ("Mikwaoth").

37. *Didache* 7, in *The Apostolic Fathers*, trans. Kirsopp Lake, 2 vols. (Cambridge, Mass.: Harvard University Press, 1952), 1.319ff.—" . . . "Baptize . . . in running (ζῶντι, 'living') water . . . [or] cold water. . . . If you have neither, pour water three times on the head." The intent is to thereby produce running water, a symbol of purity. See William S. LaSor, "Discovering What Jewish Miqva'ot Can Tell Us about Christian Baptism," *BAR* 13 (Jan.–Feb. 1987): 58.

38. Nahman Avigad, *Discovering Jerusalem* (Nashville, Nelson, 1983), 139–43.

39. Herodotus *History* 3.60.1. The translation is by Aubrey de Selincourt (Baltimore: Penguin, 1954), 199–200.

40. Frontinus *De aquis urbis Romae* 4. Frontinus was appointed superintendent of the aqueducts in A.D. 96 and died in 106.

41. Peck, *Harper's Dictionary*, 106. A smaller amount, 222,237,060 gallons a day, is given by Carcopino (*Daily Life*, 38 n. 68, citing Frontinus *De aquaeductibus* 65–73), but some aqueducts, such as the Traiana, which did not open until A.D. 109, were not included in the estimate.

42. Pliny *Natural History* 36.122.

43. Peck, *Harper's Dictionary*, 105–6.

44. Harry B. Evans, "Nero's *Arcus Caelimontani*," *AJA* 87.3 (July 1983): 392–99.

45. George Hauck and Richard Novak, "Water Flow in the Castellum at Nîmes," *AJA* 92.3 (July 1988): 393.

46. Ward-Perkins, *Cities*, 34.

47. For the renovations made in the Theater of Dionysus at Athens see James H. Butler, *The Theatre and Drama of Greece and Rome* (New York: Chandler, 1972), 34.

48. A. Pickard-Cambridge, *The Dramatic Festivals of Athens*, 2d ed. (Oxford: Oxford University Press, 1968).

49. Vitruvius *On Architecture* 5.6.9.

50. For a detailed look at the history of the development of ancient theater see Margarete Bieber, *The History of the Greek and Roman Theater*, rev. ed. (Princeton, N.J.: Princeton University Press, 1961); T. B. L. Webster, *Greek Theatre Production*, 2d ed. (London: Methuen, 1970). On the three basic parts of the theater see William Smith, *A Dictionary of Greek and Roman Antiquities* (London: John Murray, 1878), 1121–24; and Peck, *Harper's Dictionary*, 1551ff.

51. Aristotle *Poetics* 1449a.

52. Erika Simon, *The Ancient Theatre*, trans. C. E. Vafopoulou-Richardson (New York: Methuen, 1982), 5.

53. Peter D. Arnott, *An Introduction to the Greek Theatre* (New York: St. Martin's, 1959), 36.

54. Simon Tidworth, *Theatres: An Architectural and Cultural History* (New York: Praeger, 1973), 18.

55. Vitruvius *On Architecture* 5.3.8; 5.5.1–7. Regarding the acoustics of natural theaters in Palestine see B. Cobbey Crisler, "The Acoustics and Crowd Capacity of Natural Theaters in Palestine," *BA* 39 (Dec. 1976): 128–42.

56. For a general description of the nature and function of Roman theaters see Mary Boatwright, "Theaters in the Roman Empire," *BA* 53 (December 1990): 184–92.

57. Butler, *Theatre and Drama*, 109–10.

58. Livy *History of Rome* 48.

59. Suetonius *Lives of the Caesars*, "Augustus" 45. Good examples of Roman theaters built under the empire are to be found in Italy (Ostia, Verona, Benevento, Minturno, and Fiesole), France (Orange, Lyon, Arles, and Vaison), North Africa (Sabratha, Timgad, Dougga, and Leptis Magna), Turkey (Aspendos), Israel (Caesarea Maritima), and Greece (Nicopolis).

60. Ward-Perkins, *Roman Imperial Architecture*, 259ff.

61. See the description of Roman theater construction in Vitruvius *On Architecture* 5.6.1–9. David Small, "Studies in Roman Theater Design," *AJA* 87.1 (Jan. 1983): 55–68, has argued that Vitruvius was not used as exclusively as has been thought. In most theaters studied construction of the stairways for the stages followed Vitruvius, but a different method was widely used in designing the stages.

62. Josephus *Antiquities of the Jews* 14.8.5 (150) speaks of a meeting (ἐκκλησία) of the presiding officers of Athens in the theater.

63. See A. Ovadiah and C. Gomez de Silva, "Some Notes on the Roman Theatre of Beth Shean (Scythopolis)," *SCI* 6 (1981–82): 84–94.

64. Robert Montilla, "The Awnings of Roman Theatres and Amphitheatres," *Theatre Survey* 10 (1969): 75–88.

65. Pliny *Natural History* 19.23.

66. Lucretius *De rerum natura* 4.75ff.

67. Gilbert Bilezikian, *The Liberated Gospel: A Comparison of the Gospel of Mark and Greek Tragedy* (Grand Rapids: Baker, 1977); James Blevins, "The Genre of Revelation," *Review and Expositor* 77 (1980): 393–408.

68. Ward-Perkins, *Roman Imperial Architecture*, 262.

69. Butler, *Theatre and Drama*, 128; John Humphrey, *Roman Circuses: Arena for Chariot Racing* (London: Batsford, 1986).

70. Butler, *Theatre and Drama*, 132.

71. Robertson, *Greek and Roman Architecture*, 283.

72. Ibid., 283–88; Ward-Perkins, *Roman Imperial Architecture*, 67–71.

73. Pliny *Natural History* 19.24.

74. Carcopino's superlative *Daily Life in Ancient Rome* chronicles from literary records the many and varied types of these atrocities.

75. Seneca *Epistle* 7.

76. Carcopino, *Daily Life*, 243.

77. J. G. Davies, *Daily Life of Early Christians* (New York: Duell, Sloan and Pearce, 1953), 76–116; see also W. H. C. Frend, *Martyrdom and Persecution in the Early Church* (New York: Doubleday, 1967); Herbert B. Workman, *Persecution in the Early Church* (New York: Abingdon, 1960); Henri Daniel-Rops, *The Church of Apostles and Martyrs* (New York: Doubleday, 1962); Butler, *Theatre and Drama*, 126–43.

Chapter 2

1. Amos Kloner, "Ancient Synagogues in Israel: An Archaeological Survey," in Lee Levine, ed., *Ancient Synagogues Revealed* (Jerusalem: Israel Exploration Society, 1981), 11; Eric M. Meyers, "Early Judaism and Christianity in the Light of Archaeology," *BA* 51 (June 1988): 69–79; Dennis E. Groh, "Jews and Christians in Late Roman Palestine: Towards a New Chronology," *BA* 51 (June 1988): 80–96; Eric M. Meyers and L. Michael White, "Jews and Christians in a Roman World," *Archaeology* 42 (March–April 1989): 26–33.

2. A. T. Kraabel, "Unity and Diversity among Diaspora Synagogues," in Lee Levine, ed., *The Synagogue in Late Antiquity* (Philadelphia: American Schools of Oriental Research, 1987), 49–60; idem, "The Diaspora Synagogue: Archaeological and Epigraphic Evidence since Sukenik," in *Aufstieg und Niedergang der römischen Welt*, ed. Hildegard Temporini and Wolfgang Haase, sec. 2, vol. 19, pt. 1 (Hawthorne, N.Y.: Walter de Gruyter, 1979), 477–510; G. Foerster, "A Survey of Ancient Diaspora Synagogues," in Levine, *Ancient Synagogues Revealed* (hereafter *ASR*), 164–71; Eric M. Meyers, "The Cultural Setting of Galilee: The Case of Regionalism and Early Judaism," in *Aufstieg und Niedergang*, ed. Temporini and Haase, sec. 2, vol. 19, pt. 1, pp. 686–702. See also articles on individual synagogues of the Diaspora in *ASR*; Geoffrey Wigoder, *The Story of the Synagogue: A Diaspora Museum Book* (San Francisco: Harper and Row, 1986).

3. Jerusalem *Megilla* 3:1, 73d.

4. John Wilkinson, "Christian Pilgrims in Jerusalem during the Byzantine Period," *PEQ* 108 (1976): 76–77.

5. Lee Levine, "Ancient Synagogues—A Historical Introduction," in *ASR*, 4.

6. Lee Levine, "The Second Temple Synagogue: The Formative Years," in Levine, *Synagogue in Late Antiquity*, 9.

7. Yigael Yadin, "The Synagogue at Masada," in *ASR*, 19–23; G. Foerster, "The Synagogues at Masada and Herodium," in *ASR*, 24–29; Doron Chen, "The Design of the Ancient Synagogues in Judea: Masada and Herodium," *BASOR* 239 (1980): 37–40.

8. Adolf Deissmann, *Light from the Ancient East*, trans. Lionel R. M. Strachan (New York: George H. Doran, 1927), 439–41; Kloner, "Ancient Synagogues," 11.

9. Zvi Uri Maoz, "The Synagogue of Gamla and the Typology of Second-Temple Synagogues," in *ASR*, 35.

10. S. Gutman, "The Synagogue at Gamla," in *ASR*, 33.

11. See Groh, "Jews and Christians," 80–96.

12. See the articles on various Galilean synagogues in *ASR*; Hershel Shanks, *Judaism in Stone: The Archaeology of Ancient Synagogues* (San Francisco: Harper and Row, 1979).

13. We now have about 125 Greek inscriptions from synagogues in the Mediterranean area, approximately 50 of which are from Palestine. About 110 Aramaic and Hebrew inscriptions have also been found in synagogues from Upper Galilee and the Golan Heights in the north to Beersheba in the south (J. Naveh, "Ancient Synagogue Inscriptions," in *ASR*, 133). Some synagogues have inscriptions in more than one language. In Lower Galilee, Greek writing was found in about 40 percent of the synagogues where inscriptions have been discovered, Hebrew in 40 percent, and Aramaic in 50 percent. In Upper Galilee only a few inscriptions in Greek have been found; Hebrew writings have been found in about 40 percent of the inscription-yielding synagogues, and Aramaic in 66 percent (Eric M. Meyers, "Galilean Regionalism as a Factor in Historical Reconstruction," *BASOR* 221 [1976]: 97).

14. Examples include synagogues at Beth Shearim, Capernaum, and Chorazin.

15. Examples include synagogues at Beth Shan, Beth Alfa, Hammath-Tiberias, Eshtemoa, Susiya, and Gaza.

16. Meyers, "Galilean Regionalism," 99. On synagogue decoration see Edwin R. Goodenough, *Jewish Symbols in the Greco-Roman Period*, abr. ed., ed. Jacob Neusner (Princeton, N.J.: Princeton University Press, 1988).

17. See especially Levine, "Second Temple Synagogue," 7–32; idem, "Ancient Synagogues," 1–10; Kloner, "Ancient Synagogues," 11–18; Moshe Dothan, "Research on Ancient Synagogues in the Land of Israel," in *Recent Archaeology in the Land of Israel*, ed. Hershel Shanks (Washington, D.C.: Biblical Archaeology Society, 1981); Eric M. Meyers, "Synagogue Architecture," in *IDB* supp., 842; idem, "The Current State of Galilean Synagogue Studies," in *ASR*, 127–37; idem, "Ancient Synagogues in Galilee: Their Religious and Cultural Setting," *BA* 43 (Spring 1980): 97–108; Zvi Uri Maoz, "Ancient Synagogues of the Golan," *BA* 51 (June 1988): 116–28.

18. Stanislao Loffreda, "The Late Chronology of the Synagogue of Capernaum," in *ASR*, 52–56; but see also G. Foerster, "Notes on Recent Excavations at Capernaum," in *ASR*, 57–59; and Michael Avi-Yonah, "Some Comments on the Capernaum Excavations," in *ASR*, 60–62; "Meiron," *EAEHL* 3.856.

19. Eric M. Meyers, "The Synagogue at Horvat Shema," in *ASR*, 70–74; idem, "Synagogues of Galilee," *Archaeology* 35 (May–June 1982): 51–58.

20. D. Barag et al., "The Synagogue at En-Gedi," in *ASR*, 116–19; Z. Yeivin, "The Synagogue of Eshtemoa," in *ASR*, 120–22; S. Gutman et al., "Excavations in the Synagogue at Horvat Susiya," in *ASR*, 123–28.

21. Moshe Dothan, "The Synagogue at Hammath Tiberias," in *ASR*, 63–69.

22. Maoz, "Ancient Synagogues," 116–28.

23. Eric M. Meyers and Carol Meyers, "American Archaeologists Find Remains of Ancient Synagogue Ark in Galilee," *BAR* 7 (Nov.–Dec. 1981): 24–39; idem, "The Ark of Nabratein—A First Glance," *BA* 44 (Fall 1981): 237–43; "Excavations at En-Nabratein, Upper Galilee: The 1980 Season," *ASOR Newsletter* 2 (Sept. 1980): 3–7, 10–11; "Kefar Neburaya," in *EAEHL* 3.710–11.

24. A. R. Seager, "The Synagogue at Sardis," in *ASR*, 178–84.

25. Yadin, "Masada," 19–23; Foerster, "Masada and Herodium," 24–29; Gutman, "Gamla," 30–34; Maoz, "Gamla," 35–41.

26. Meyers, "Galilean Regionalism," 99. Kloner ("Ancient Synagogues," 18) agrees: "There is no chronological distinction between the various regional types."

27. In addition to the previously mentioned articles see also "Gamla: The Masada of the North," *BAR* 5 (Jan.–Feb. 1979): 12–19.

28. Maoz ("Gamla," 40–41) thinks these three earliest types were patterned after the Hellenistic secular halls of assembly (ἐκκλησιαστήρια or βουλευτήρια); Yadin ("Masada," 20 n. 1) shared that view about Masada.

Foerster agrees and looks also at Nabatean temples as possible models ("Architectural Models of the Greco-Roman Period and the Origin of the 'Galilean' Synagogue," in *ASR*, 47). Ehud Netzer argues that the basilical type may have been modeled after the Roman triclinium (dining room) ("The Herodian Triclinia: A Prototype for the 'Galilean-Type' Synagogue," in *ASR*, 49–51). Nahman Avigad regards Masada as the prototype ("The 'Galilean' Synagogue and Its Predecessors," in *ASR*, 42–44).

29. Levine, "Second Temple Synagogue," 10ff.

30. James F. Strange and Hershel Shanks, "Synagogue Where Jesus Preached Found at Capernaum," *BAR* 9 (Nov.–Dec. 1983): 24–31. See also pp. 000–000.

31. E. W. Saunders, "Christian Synagogues and Jewish Christianity in Galilee," *Explor* 3 (1977): 70–78.

32. Wayne A. Meeks, *The First Urban Christians: The Social World of the Apostle Paul* (New Haven, Conn.: Yale University Press, 1983), 75–77.

33. Saunders, "Christian Synagogues," 70–78; Bellarmino Bagatti, "Christian Synagogues and Sacred Grottos," chap. 5 in *The Church from the Circumcision* (Jerusalem: Franciscan, 1971), 112–36.

34. Max Cary, *A History of Rome*, 2d ed. (New York: Macmillan, 1962), 732.

35. Asher Ovadiah, *Corpus of the Byzantine Churches in the Holy Land* (Bonn: Peter Hanstein, 1970), 15.

36. Eusebius *Life of Constantine* 3.43 (written about A.D. 338); *NPNF*, 1.530-31. See pp. 214–216.

37. D. S. Robertson, *Greek and Roman Architecture*, 2d ed. (Cambridge: Cambridge University Press, 1974), 213. See the entire chapter, "Temple Architecture of the Roman Empire."

38. See especially A. G. McKay, *Houses, Villas and Palaces in the Roman World* (London: Thames and Hudson, 1975); Robertson, *Greek and Roman Architecture*, chap. 17; Nahman Avigad, *Discovering Jerusalem* (Nashville: Nelson, 1983), chap. 3; H. Keith Beebe, "Domestic Architecture and the New Testament," *BA* 38 (Sept., Dec. 1975): 89–104. Excellent drawings are to be found in J. Robert Teringo's *Land and People Jesus Knew* (Minneapolis: Bethany House, 1985).

39. A list is contained in Rodolfo Lanciani, *The Ruins and Excavations of Ancient Rome* (Boston: Houghton Mifflin, 1897; New York: Bell, 1979 reprint), 597–98.

40. Avigad, *Discovering Jerusalem*, 83ff.

41. Ibid.

42. Ibid.

43. Ibid., 106.

44. Ibid., 95.

45. Ibid., 120–38; see also Nahman Avigad, "The Burnt House Captures a Moment in Time," *BAR* 9 (Nov.–Dec. 1983), 66–72.

46. See Jerome Carcopino, *Daily Life in Ancient Rome* (New Haven, Conn.: Yale University Press, 1940), 41.

47. For a description of the insulae see Carcopino, *Daily Life*, 22–51; McKay, *Houses*, 81ff.; Robertson, *Greek and Roman Architecture*, 307ff.

48. As listed in the *Regionaries* and the *Notitia*, catalogs of the fourteen regions of Rome. See McKay, *Houses*, 83; Carcopino, *Daily Life*, 23.

49. Strabo *Geography* 5.3.7.

50. Aurelius Victor *Epitome de Caesaribus* 13.13; cf. *Digest* 39.l.l.17 (cited in Carcopino, *Daily Life*, 25 n. 19).

51. Charles Williams, "Corinth, 1985: East of the Theater," *Hesperia* 55 (1986): 146. See pp. 000–000.

52. J. B. Ward-Perkins, *Roman Architecture* (New York: Abrams, 1977), 97–104.

53. Vitruvius *On Architecture* 2.8.17.

54. Strabo *Geography* 16.2.23.

55. At Pompeii and Herculaneum, for example (Robertson, *Greek and Roman Architecture*, 307). Some houses in Rome and Ostia give no indication of mica or glass near the windows (Carcopino, *Daily Life*, 35).

56. Pliny the Younger *Epistles* 7.21.2; 9.36.1.

57. Juvenal *Satires* 6.333.

58. Suetonius *Lives of the Caesars*, "Vespasian" 23.

59. See further in Carcopino, *Daily Life*, 42ff.

60. Juvenal *Satires* 3.236–59; cf. Martial *Epigrams* 12.57.

61. Pliny the Younger *Epistles* 9.36.1.

62. McKay, *Houses*, 83f.

63. For a fuller description of these insulae see McKay, *Houses*, 212–17.

Chapter 3

1. Y. Meshorer, "A Stone Weight from the Reign of Herod," *IEJ* 20.1–2 (1970): 97–98.

2. Josephus *Jewish War* 1.21.11 (425).

3. IG2², 3440. See also Pittakes, *AE* 42 (1860), p. 1798, Inscrip. #3442.

4. IG2², 3441. See also Pittakes, *AE* 53 (1860), p. 1935, Inscrip. #3768.

5. Agora Inventory 1.2658. See *SEG* 12 (1955), p. 48, #150, and the comments of B. D. Meritt, *Hesperia* 12 (1952), p. 370, #14. The inscription reads as follows: [ο δημος βασιλεα Ηρωδην Ευ]σεβη και [φιλοκαισαρα αρετης] ενεκα [και ευεργεσι]ας.

6. Ehud Netzer, "Herod's Building Projects: State Necessity or Personal Need?" in Lee Levine, ed., *The Jerusalem Cathedra* (Detroit: Wayne State University Press, 1981), 48ff.

7. Josephus *Jewish War* 1.21.11 (422–25).

8. Netzer, "Herod's Building Projects," 48.

9. See J. B. Ward-Perkins, *Roman Imperial Architecture*, "The Pelican History of Art," (New York: Penguin, 1983), 310, 313.

10. Especially, Josephus *Jewish War* 1, 2, and 5, and *Antiquities of the Jews* 15–17; Netzer, "Herod's Building Projects," 48.

11. Josephus *Antiquities* 15.11.2 (390).

12. Ibid., 15.11.5 (420).

13. Netzer, "Herod's Building Projects," 58.

14. Michael Zimmerman, "Tunnel Exposes New Areas of Temple Mount," *BAR* 7 (May–June 1981): 41.

15. Murray Stein, "How Herod Moved Gigantic Blocks to Construct Temple Mount," *BAR* 7 (May–June 1981): 42–46.

16. Ibid.

17. Ehud Netzer and Sara Ben-Arieh, "Remains of an Opus Reticulatum Building in Jerusalem," *IEJ* 33.3–4 (1983): 163–75; Ehud Netzer, "Herod's Family Tomb in Jerusalem," *BAR* 9 (May–June 1983): 52–59.

18. See my chapter on the "Church in Greece" for more on this temple. See also, John Travlos, *Pictorial Dictionary of Ancient Athens* (New York: Praeger, 1971), 494–96.

19. J. B. Ward-Perkins, *Roman Architecture* (New York: H. N. Abrams, 1977), 20 (plate 13), 48, 55 (plates 61–63).

20. Josephus *Antiquities* 15.11.3 (391).

21. Josephus *Jewish War* 6.9.1 (409–13).

22. Hillel Geva, "The 'Tower of David' —Phasael or Hippicus?" *IEJ* 31.1–2 (1981): 57–65.

23. Josephus *Antiquities* 15.11.5 (412).

24. Pliny the Elder *Natural History* 5.15.70.

25. Sukkah 51b.

26. Josephus *Antiquities* 15.11.5 (414).

27. Mark Twain, *Innocents Abroad* (New York: Harper, 1911), 358–59.

28. Kathleen and Leen Ritmeyer, "Reconstructing Herod's Temple Mount in Jerusalem," *BAR* 15 (Nov.–Dec. 1989): 23–42.

29. For a description of the temple of New Testament times see Joseph Patrich, "The *Mesibbah* of the Temple According to the Tractate *Middot*," *IEJ* 36:3–4 (1986): 215–33.

30. Josephus *Jewish War* 1.21.1 (401); see also Benjamin Mazar, "The Temple Mount," in Israel Exploration Society, *Biblical Archaeology Today*, ed. Janet Amitai (Jerusalem: Israel Exploration Society, 1985), 468.

31. "The whole circumference of the city was thirty-three furlongs" (Josephus *Jewish War* 5.4.3 [159]).

32. Josephus *Jewish War* 1.21.1 (401).

33. Benjamin Isaac, "A Donation for Herod's Temple in Jerusalem," *IEJ* 33.1–2 (1983): 86–92. On Herodian chronology see O. Edwards, "Herodian Chronology," *PEQ* 114 (1982): 129–42.

34. Benjamin Mazar, *The Mountain of the Lord* (Garden City: N.Y.: Doubleday, 1975), 276.

35. Ibid., 274–75.

36. Josephus *Antiquities* 15.11.5 (412).

37. Stewart Perowne, *The Life and Times of Herod the Great* (Nashville: Abingdon, 1959), 133.

38. See Mazar, *Mountain of the Lord*, 143ff., and Kathleen and Leen Ritmeyer, "Reconstructing the Triple Gate," *BAR* 15 (Nov.–Dec. 1989): 49–53.

39. Kathleen Kenyon, *Jerusalem: Excavating 3000 Years of History* (London: Thames and Hudson, 1967), 142.

40. John Wilkinson thinks that "for the whole late Roman and Byzantine period, the masonry at this corner stood like the ruin of a great tower" (*Jerusalem as Jesus Knew It* [London: Thames and Hudson, 1978], 92).

41. *Middoth* 1:3.

42. Spencer Corbett, "Some Observations on the Gateways to the Herodian Temple in Jerusalem," *PEQ* 84 (1952): 7–14. He feels that "the Western Hulda Gate vaults, with their plane-bedded pendentives, might really survive from the original Herodian building" (p. 14).

43. Mazar, *Mountain of the Lord*, 148.

44. Ibid., 143.

45. Ibid., 146.

46. Benjamin Mazar, "Herodian Jerusalem in the Light of the Excavations South and South-West of the Temple Mount," *IEJ* 28.4 (1978): 237.

See Hershel Shanks's critical evaluation of these excavations in his book review of "Excavating in the Shadow of the Temple Mount," *BAR* 12 (Nov.–Dec. 1986): 20–38.

47. *Middoth* 2:2.

48. Tosephta *Sanhedrin* 2:2.

49. *Middoth* 1:3. A parchment from Oxyrhynchus (#840, lines 25–28) tells about a Pharisee, a chief priest, who purified himself in the Pool of David (Bethesda? see pp. 186–88), exclaiming: "I went down into it by one stair and by the other I came up out, and I have put on white and clean clothes." (Jack Finegan, *Hidden Records of the Life of Jesus* [Philadelphia: Pilgrim, 1969], 229).

50. *Middoth* 1:9. See Mazar, "Herodian Jerusalem," 236.

51. Mazar, *Mountain of the Lord*, 127, 145.

52. Mazar, "Herodian Jerusalem," 236.

53. Mazar, *Mountain of the Lord*, 128.

54. Ibid., 135.

55. Lee Levine, "Archaeological Discoveries from the Greco-Roman Era," in *Recent Archaeology in the Land of Israel*, ed. Hershel Shanks and Benjamin Mazar (Washington, D.C.: Biblical Archaeology Society, 1984), 81.

56. See the diagram in Mazar, "Herodian Jerusalem," 235.

57. Mazar, *Mountain of the Lord*, 129, 135; idem, "Herodian Jerusalem," 234.

58. Carol Rosenberg, "Arabs Fear Tourist Attraction May Be an Underground Plot," *Chicago Tribune*, 14 Aug. 1988, sec. 1, p. 27.

59. Josephus *Antiquities* 15.11.5 (410).

60. Mazar has a brief discussion of the four gates (*Mountain of the Lord*, 133–34).

61. Ibid., 221–22.

62. Ibid., 132.

63. Josephus *Antiquities* 15.11.5 (412).

64. Ibid., 15.11.5 (414).

65. Babylonian, *'Aboda Zara* 8b; *Sanhedrin* 41a.

66. *Middoth* 5.3–4.

67. Wilkinson, *Jerusalem*, 142.

68. Levine, "Archaeological Discoveries," 82; Benjamin Mazar, "Archaeological Excavations near the Temple Mount," in *Jerusalem Revealed*, ed. Yigael Yadin (Jerusalem: Israel Exploration Society, 1975), 27, 35; idem, "Herodian Jerusalem," 234; idem, *Mountain of the Lord*, 138; *EAEHL*, 2.603.

69. Josephus *Jewish War* 4.9.12 (582).

70. Gaalyah Cornfeld, ed., *The Historical Jesus: A Scholarly View of the Man and His World* (New York: Macmillan, 1982), 120–57.

71. James Fleming, "The Undiscovered Gate Beneath Jerusalem's Golden Gate," *BAR* 9 (Jan.–Feb. 1983): 24–37. See the subsequent discussion of Fleming's article in *BAR* 9 (May–June 1983): 27–28. Fleming had published a brief note on his 1969 experience in the *Alumni News* (1971) of the Institute of Holy Land Studies (Jerusalem) and in the *Near East Archaeological Society Bulletin* (1974).

72. Josephus *Jewish War* 5.5.1 (184–89); *Antiquities* 15.11.2–7 (388–425).

73. Michael Avi-Yonah, "Jerusalem of the Second Temple Period," in *Jerusalem Revealed*, ed. Yadin, 13, 86.

74. Mazar, "Temple Mount," 466–67.

75. Y. Tsafrir, "The Location of the Seleucid Akra in Jerusalem," in *Jerusalem Revealed*, ed. Yadin, 86.

76. Josephus credits Solomon with the construction of the Eastern Wall (Josephus *Jewish War* 5.5.1 [185]).

77. Ernest-Marie Laperrousaz, "King Solomon's Wall Still Supports the Temple Mount," *BAR* 13 (May–June 1987): 36–37.

78. Fleming, "Undiscovered Gate," 24ff.

79. Asher Kaufman, "Where the Ancient Temple of Jerusalem Stood," *BAR* 9 (March–April 1983): 40–59.

80. Ibid., 54.

81. Lawrence Sporty supports this position by arguing that the Church of the Holy Sepulchre also lay in the same axis with the Golden Gate and the temple foundations. It was built over the ruins of the Hadrianic Temple of Aphrodite precisely because that temple had been built on the same axis as the Jewish temple and elevated above it in order symbolically to express Roman dominance over Judea. "The Location of the Holy House of Herod's Temple," *BAR* 54:1 (March 1991): 28–35.

82. Dio Cassius *Roman History* 69.12.1.

83. Lawrence Sporty, "The Location of the Holy House of Herod's Temple," *BA* 53 (December 1990): 194–204.

84. David M. Jacobson, "Ideas Concerning the Plan of Herod's Temple," *PEQ* 112 (1980): 33–40.

85. Josephus *Antiquities* 15.11.4 (409).

86. L. H. Vincent, Jérusalem de l'Ancien Testament, recherches d'archéologie ed d'histoire, (Paris: Librarie Lecoffre, 1954), 1.193–221; idem, "Le Lithostrotos évangélique," Revue

Biblique 59 (1952): 513–30; idem, "L'Antonia, palais primitif d'Hérode," Revue Biblique 61 (1954): 87–101.

87. Jack Finegan, *Archaeology of the New Testament: The Life of Jesus and the Beginning of the Early Church* (Princeton, N.J.: Princeton University Press, 1970), 158.

88. Père Benoit, "The Archaeological Reconstruction of the Antonia Fortress," in *Jerusalem Revealed*, ed. Yadin, 87–89; idem, "L'Antonia d'Hérode le Grand et le Forum Oriental d'Aelia Capitolina," *HTR* 64 (1971): 158–61.

89. Josephus *Jewish War* 5.11.4 (467).

90. In an interview with Hershel Shanks ("The Religious Message of the Bible," *BAR* 12 [March–April 1986]: 66) Benoit refers to this study but does not give its title.

91. Josephus *Jewish War* 5.5.8 (242).

92. Dan Bahat and Magen Broshi, "Excavations in the Armenian Garden," in *Jerusalem Revealed*, ed. Yadin, 55–57; Ruth Amiran and A. Eitan, "Excavations in the Jerusalem Citadel," in *Jerusalem Revealed*, 52–54; idem, "Excavations in the Courtyard of the Citadel, Jerusalem, 1968–1969 (Preliminary Report)," *IEJ* 20.1–2 (1970): 9–17; Hillel Geva, "Excavations in the Citadel of Jerusalem, 1979–1980 (Preliminary Report)," *IEJ* 33.1–2 (1983): 55–71; Mazar, *Mountain of the Lord*, 39

93. Josephus *Jewish War* 5.4.3 (156–71).

94. Ibid., 6.9.1 (409–13).

95. Ibid., 5.4.3 (166).

96. Bahat and Broshi, "Excavations in the Armenian Garden," 55–57.

97. Josephus *Jewish War* 5.5.8 (241).

98. Ibid., 5.4.4 (176).

99. Philo *Delegation to Gaius* 38.

100. See John F. Wilson, "Archaeology and the Origins of the Fourth Gospel: Gabbatha," in *Johannine Studies: Essays in Honor of Frank Pack* (Malibu, Calif.: Pepperdine University Press, 1989), 221–30.

101. Josephus *Jewish War* 2.9.4 (175).

102. Ibid., 2.9.3 (172). Mention is made of a hippodrome (ἱπποδρομόν) in *Jewish War* 2.3.1 (44) and *Antiquities* 17.10.2 (255). This is probably a different structure whose exact location is not known.

103. For a summation and correlation of informed archaeologists' opinions on the nature and extent of the Northern Wall, see Hershel Shanks, "The Jerusalem Wall That Shouldn't Be There," *BAR* 13 (May–June 1987): 47–57.

104. Josephus *Jewish War* 5.4.2 (142–46); 5.7.2 (301); 5.8.2 (342).

105. Menahem Magen, "Recovering Roman Jerusalem—The Entryway Beneath Damascus Gate," *BAR* 14 (May–June 1988): 48–56.

106. Bruce Schein, "The Second Wall of Jerusalem," *BA* 44 (Winter 1981): 21–26.

107. Josephus *Jewish War* 5.4.2 (146).

108. Joachim Jeremias, *Jerusalem in the Time of Jesus* (Philadelphia: Fortress, 1969), 27, 83–84—he puts the population of the entire land of Israel at this time at half a million; John Wilkinson, *Jerusalem*, 66; see also idem, "Ancient Jerusalem: Its Water Supply and Population," *PEQ* 106 (1974): 33–51, esp. 46–51; Anthony Byatt, "Josephus and Population Numbers in First Century Palestine," *PEQ* 105 (1973): 51–60; Harold W. Hoehner, *Herod Antipas*, Society for New Testament Studies Monograph 17 (Cambridge: Cambridge University Press, 1972), 52–53, 291–95.

109. Magen Broshi, "Estimating the Population of Ancient Jerusalem," *BAR* 4 (June 1978): 10–15, esp. 13; idem, "La population de l'ancienne Jérusalem," *RB* 82 (1975): 5–14.

110. Michael Avi-Yonah, "Survey of the Density and Numbers of the Population in Ancient Eretz Israel," in *Essays and Studies in the Lore of the Holy Land* (Jerusalem: Neumann, 1964), 114–24 (in Hebrew). See also Richard M. Mackowski, *Jerusalem, City of Jesus* (Grand Rapids: Eerdmans, 1980), 184 n. 1.

111. Josephus *Against Apion* 1.22 (197); see Mackowski, *Jerusalem*, 184 n. 1.

112. Josephus *Against Apion* 1.22 (183, 186, 190, 205).

113. For a summary of these estimates suggested by eighteen scholars see Byatt, "Josephus and Population Numbers in First Century Palestine," *PEQ* 105 (1973): 51–60; see also Magen Broshi, "The Population of Western Palestine in the Roman-Byzantine Period," *BASOR* 236 (1979): 1–10. Yigal Shiloh critically reviews several of the data used in computing the population of ancient Israel: tax lists, seating capacity of local theaters, agricultural potential and population, water resources, daily water consumption, enclosed and roofed living space, and the number of residential units in towns (Rome and Ostia used here) ("The Population of Iron Age Palestine," *BASOR* 239 [1980]: 25–35). See also the discussion by Michael Avi-

Yonah, *The Holy Land: From the Persian to the Arab Conquest* (Grand Rapids: Baker, 1966), 220–21.

114. See also the diagram of the Temple Mount in Mazar, *Mountain of the Lord*, 129.

115. Gaalyah Cornfeld, *The Mystery of the Temple Mount: New Guidebook to Discovery* (Tel Aviv: Bazak Israel Guidebook, 1972), 36.

116. Rivka Gonen, "Was the Site of the Jerusalem Temple Originally a Cemetery?" *BAR* 11 (May–June, 1985): 44–55.

117. Mazar, *Mountain of the Lord*, 210–12.

118. Ibid., 210.

119. Josephus *Jewish War* 5.3.2 (108).

120 See the extensive discussion of Jerusalem's water supply in Hershel Shanks's interview of Amihai Mazar, "A New Generation of Israeli Archaeologists Comes of Age," *BAR* 10 (May–June 1984): 46–61. See also Mazar's article "The Aqueducts of Jerusalem," in *Jerusalem Revealed*, ed. Yadin, 79–84.

121. Josephus *Jewish War* 2.9.4 (175); *Antiquities* 18.3.2 (60).

122. Josephus *Antiquities* 15.8.1 (268).

123. George Adam Smith, Jerusalem: *The Topography, Economics and History from the Earliest Times to* A.D. 70, 2 vols. (London: Hodder and Stoughton, 1908), 2.493.

124. Conrad Schick, "Herod's Amphitheatre," *Palestine Exploration Fund Quarterly Statement* (July 1887): 161–67 (map on 150); see also A. Schalit, "König Herodes: Der Mann und sein Werk" (Berlin: W. De Gruyter, 1969), 370–71.

125. Emil Schürer, *History of the Jewish People in the Time of Jesus Christ*, rev. and trans. Geza Vermes et al., 2d rev. ed., 4 vols. (Edinburgh: T. and T. Clark, 1973–87), 1.304–5 n. 56.

126. See n. 97.

127. Josephus *Antiquities* 15.8.1 (268).

128. Netzer and Ben-Arieh, "Remains," 163–75; Netzer, "Herod's Family Tomb," 52–59.

129. Josephus *Jewish War* 1.33.9 (673); *Antiquities* 17.8.3 (199).

Chapter 4

1. Josephus *Jewish War* 1.33.9 (670–73); *Antiquities of the Jews* 17.8.3 (196-99).

2. Netzer, "Searching for Herod's Tomb," *BAR* 9 (May–June, 1983): 41.

3. Ibid., 30–51.

4. Josephus *Antiquities* 15.9.4 (323–25).

5. Ehud Netzer, Jewish Rebels Dig Strategic Tunnel System," *BAR* 14 (July-August 1988): 18–33.

6. See the map of aqueducts in Hershel Shank's interview of Amihai Mazar, "A New Generation of Israeli Archaeologists Comes of Age," *BAR* 10 (May–June 1984): 49.

7. Oded Borowski, "The 1987 Lahav Excavations," in *ASOR Newsletter* 39.3 (April 1988): 10. See the picture there.

8. Josephus *Jewish War* 1.33.9 (670–73) (Trans. G. A. Williamson, rev. ed. [New York: Penguin, 1980]).

9. James L. Kelso, "The First Campaign of Excavation in New Testament Jericho," *BASOR* 120 (1950): 11–22; idem, "New Testament Jericho," *BA* 14 (May 1951): 34–43; James L. Kelso and D. C. Baramki, *Excavations at New Testament Jericho and Khirbet en-Nitla*, AASOR 29–30 (1955); James L. Kelso, "Jericho (New Testament)," in Charles F. Pfeiffer, ed., *The Biblical World* (Grand Rapids: Baker, 1966), 303–5; James L. Kelso, "The Ghosts of Jericho," *National Geographic* 100.6 (Dec. 1951): 825–44.

10. James B. Pritchard, "The 1951 Campaign at Herodian Jericho," *BASOR* 123 (1951): 8–17; idem, *The Excavations at Herodian Jericho 1951*, AASOR 32–33 (1958).

11. Ehud Netzer, "The Hasmonean and Herodian Winter Palaces at Jericho," *IEJ* 25.2–3 (1975): 89–100; idem, "The Winter Palaces of the Judean Kings at Jericho at the End of the Second Temple Period," *BASOR* 228 (1977): 1–13; Ehud Netzer and Eric M. Meyers, "Preliminary Report on the Joint Jericho Excavation Project," *BASOR* 228 (1977): 15–27; Ehud Netzer, "Herodian Jericho," *BAR* 4 (Nov.–Dec. 1978): 10–14; Suzanne Singer, "The Winter Palaces of Jericho," *BAR* 3 (June 1977): 1–17. See the sections on Herodian Jericho by Netzer, G. Foerster, and G. Bacchi in *EAEHL* 2.552, 564–70.

12. Josephus *Jewish War* 1.21.4 (407).

13. Ehud Netzer, "Miqvaot (Ritual Baths) of the Second Temple Period at Jericho," *Qad.* 11.2–3 (1978): 54–59 (in Hebrew).

14. Josephus *Jewish War* 1.22.2 (437).

15. Kelso, "First Campaign," 11–22.

16. Ehud Netzer, "The Hippodrome That Herod Built at Jericho," *Qad.* 13.3–4 (1980): 104–7.

17. Yigael Yadin, "The Excavation of Masada—1963/64. Preliminary Report," *IEJ* 15.1–2 (1965): 1–120; idem, *Masada: Herod's Fortress and the Zealot's Last Stand* (New York: Random House, 1966); idem, "Masada: A Zealot Fortress," in *Archaeological Discoveries in the Holy Land* (New York: Thomas Y. Crowell, 1967), 168–74; idem, "Masada," in *IDB* supp., 577–80; "Masada," in *EAEHL* 3.793–816.

18. Josephus *Jewish War* 7.8.4 (295–96).

19. Yadin, *Masada: Herod's Fortress*, 31.

20. Yigael Yadin, "The Synagogue at Masada," in Lee Levine, ed., *Ancient Synagogues Revealed* (Jerusalem: Israel Exploration Society, 1981), 19–23.

21. G. Foerster, "The Synagogues at Masada and Herodium," in Levine, *Ancient Synagogues Revealed* (hereafter *ASR*), 24–29.

22. S. Gutman, "The Synagogue at Gamla," in *ASR*, 30–34; Zvi Uri Maoz, "The Synagogue of Gamla and the Typology of Second-Temple Synagogues," in *ASR*, 35–41.

23. For studies on the history of Caesarea see Charles Fritsch et al., eds., *Studies in the History of Caesarea Maritima*, vol. 1, *The Joint Expedition to Caesarea Maritima*, BASOR 219 (1975).

24. Josephus *Jewish War* 1.21.5 (408).

25. Netzer suggests that this palace was subsequently converted into a praetorium ("The Promontory Palace," in *Excavations at Caesarea Maritima 1975, 1976, 1979—Final Report*, ed. Lee Levine and Ehud Netzer, *Qedem* 21 [1986]: 149–59).

26. Josephus *Antiquities* 16.5.4 (150–53).

27. Ibid., 16.5.1 (136).

28. Ibid., 15.9.6 (341).

29. Ibid., 16.5.1 (136–41).

30. The official report is being published by Edwin Mellen Press in fourteen volumes under the general title *The Joint Expedition to Caesarea Maritima: Excavation Reports*, and is being edited by Robert J. Bull (director), Edgar Krentz, and Olin Storvick (field supervisors). See also Robert J. Bull, "Caesarea Maritima: The Search for Herod's City," *BAR* 8 (May–June 1982): 24–40; idem, "Caesarea," *IDB* supp., 120; idem, *The Joint Expedition to Caesarea Maritima: Preliminary Reports in Microfiche* (Madison, N.J.: Drew University Institute for Archaeological Research, 1982).

31. The best available book on the site is the beautifully done volume by K. G. Holum, Robert L. Hohlfelder, Robert J. Bull, and Avner Raban, *King Herod's Dream: Caesarea on the Sea* (New York: Norton, 1988).

32. Josephus *Jewish War* 1.21.5 (410).

33. Vitruvius, *On Architecture* 2.61.

34. Lindley Vann, "Herod's Harbor Construction Recovered Underwater," *BAR* 9 (May–June 1983) 14.

35. Avner Raban and Robert L. Hohlfelder, "The Ancient Harbors of Caesarea Maritima," *Archaeology* 34 (March–April 1981): 56–60; Avner Raban and E. Linder, "Caesarea, the Herodian Harbour," *International Journal of Nautical Archaeology* 7 (1978): 238–43; Avner Raban, "Discovery of a Round Tower in Caesarea Harbor Disclosed," *Center for Maritime Studies News* 2 (1979); Robert L. Hohlfelder, "Caesarea Beneath the Sea," *BAR* 8 (May–June 1982), 42–47, 56; Vann, "Herod's Harbor," 10–14; Robert L. Hohlfelder et al., "Sebastos, Herod's Harbor at Caesarea Maritima," *BA* 46 (Summer 1983): 133–43; Avner Raban, ed., "Proceedings of the First International Workshop on Ancient Mediterranean Harbors: Caesarea Maritima," June 24–28, 1983, *Harbour Archaeology* (Haifa: Center for Maritime Studies, Haifa University, 1985); for an interpretative history of the harbor see H. Keith Beebe, "Caesarea Maritima: Its Strategic and Political Significance to Rome," *JNES* 42 (July 1983): 195ff.

36. Charles Fritsch and I. Ben-Dor, "The Link Expedition to Israel, 1960" *BA* 24 (Feb. 1961): 50–56.

37. The harbor is described in Josephus *Jewish War* 1.21.5–7 (408–14); *Antiquities* 15.9.6 (331–41).

38. L. M. Hopfe and G. Lease, "The Caesarea Mithraeum: A Preliminary Report," *BA* 38 (March 1975): 1–10.

39. Philip Mayerson, "Choricius of Gaza on the Watersupply System of Caesarea," *IEJ* 36.3–4 (1986): 269–72; Y. Olami and Y. Peleg, "The Water Supply System of Caesarea Maritima," *IEJ* 27.2–3 (1977): 126–37.

40. See the discussions in Herbert Hamburger, "A New Inscription from the Caesarea Aqueduct," *IEJ* 9.3 (1959): 188–90; Abraham Negev, "The High Level Aqueduct at Caesarea," *IEJ* 14.4 (1964): 237–49; D. Barag, "An Inscription from the High Level Aqueduct of Caesarea—Reconsidered," *IEJ* 14.4 (1964): 250–52; Abraham Negev, "A New Inscription from the High Level Aqueduct at Caesarea," *IEJ* 22.1 (1972): 52–53; Y. Olami and J. Ringel, "New Inscriptions of the Tenth Legion Fretensis from the High Level Aqueduct at Caesarea," *IEJ* 25.2–3 (1975): 148–50.

41. Josephus *Jewish War* 1.21.7 (414).

42. Jeffrey Blakely, "A Stratigraphically Determined Date for the Inner Fortification Wall at Caesarea Maritima," in Henry O. Thompson, ed., *The Answers Lie Below: Essays in Honor of Lawrence Edmund Toombs* (Lanham, Md.: University Press of America, 1984), 3–38.

43. Further excavation in the harbor area and the vaults inside the Crusader Fort have provided the data tending to confirm this pre-Herodian date for these walls (Avner Raban, "The City Walls of Straton's Tower: Some New Archaeological Data," *BASOR* 268 [1987]: 71–88).

44. Josephus *Jewish War* 1.21.8 (415); *Antiquities* 15.9.6 (341).

45. Josephus *Antiquities* 15.9.6 (341).

46. Ibid., 18.3.1 (57); *Jewish War* 2.9.3 (172).

47. Gustaf Dalman, *Sacred Sites and Ways* (London: SPCK., 1935), 278 n. 2.

48. Josephus *Antiquities* 19.8.2 (343–50); Acts 12:21–23.

49. Antonio Frova et al., *Scavi di Caesarea Maritima* (Rome: Bretschneider, 1966).

50. Abraham Negev, *Caesarea* (Tel Aviv: E. Lewin-Epstein, 1967), 34. For more information on Israeli work at Caesarea see Lee Levine, *Roman Caesarea: An Archaeological-Topographical Study*, Qedem 2 (1975); "Caesarea," in *EAEHL* 1.270–85.

51. See the forthcoming *Greek and Latin Inscriptions of Caesarea Maritima, Joint Expedition to Caesarea Maritima: Excavation Reports*, ed. Robert Bull et al.; Bull, "Caesarea Maritima," *BAR* (1982): 33; Frova, *Scavi*.

52. Josephus *Jewish War* 1.21.7 (414).

53. Josephus *Antiquities* 15.8.5 (297–98).

54. G. A. Reisner, C. S. Fisher, and D. G. Lyon, *Harvard Excavations at Samaria: 1908–1910* (Cambridge, Mass.: Harvard University Press, 1924), 1.199; Nahman Avigad, "Samaria," in *EAEHL* 4.1034, 1047–50.

55. Reisner et al., *Samaria*, 1.198ff.

56. Ibid., 1.199; 2, plan 10.

57. Ibid., 1. 208–9.

58. J. W. Crowfoot, Kathleen M. Kenyon, and E. L. Sukenik, *The Buildings at Samaria* (London: Palestine Exploration Fund, 1942), 37.

59. Ibid., 51.

60. Fred Albertson has recently argued that a temple represented on a relief fragment in the Vatican-Museo Nazionale Romano shares architectural features with Augustan and early

Tiberian monuments. It may give some idea of how this temple in Samaria looked before its destruction ("An Augustan Temple Represented on an Historical Relief Dating to the Time of Claudius," *AJA* 91.3 [July 1987]: 441–58).

61. Josephus *Antiquities* 15.8.5 (298).

62. Reisner et al., *Samaria*, 1.213ff.

63. Ibid., 1.211.

64. Ibid., 1.219.

65. André Parrot, *Samaria: The Capital of the Kingdom of Israel* (London: SCM, 1958), 103.

66. Josephus *Antiquities* 15.8.5 (298).

67. See Dan Bahat, "Does the Holy Sepulchre Church Mark the Burial of Jesus?" *BAR* 12 (May–June 1986): 34.

Chapter 5

1. Josephus *Antiquities of the Jews* 18.3.3 (63–64).

2. Shlomo Pines, *An Arabic Version of the Testimonium Flavianum and Its Implications* (Jerusalem: Israel Academy of Sciences and Humanities, 1971). For an evaluation of this book and a discussion of the entire question see Zvi Baras, "Testimonium Flavianum: The State of Recent Scholarship," in *World History of the Jewish People*, vol. 8, *Society and Religion in the Second Temple Period*, eds. Michael Avi-Yonah and Zvi Baras (Jerusalem: Masada, 1977), 303–13.

3. Josephus *Antiquities* 20.9.1 (200).

4. Suetonius *Lives of the Caesars*, "Claudius" 25.

5. Tacitus *Annals* 15.44.

6. *Sanhedrin* 43a.

7. Lucian *Death of Peregrine* 11–13.

8. Josephus *Antiquities* 18.2.1 (26).

9. Vardaman sent me his unpublished manuscript affirming this date. The manuscript is entitled *The Year of the Nativity: Was Jesus Born in 12 B.C.? A New Examination of Quirinius (Luke 2:2) and Related Problems of New Testament Chronology*.

10. *INik* 2.2.1594; see G. H. R. Horsley, *New Documents Illustrating Early Christianity*, 5 vols. (Sydney: Macquarie University Press, 1981–87), 4.182.

11. *INik*. 2.2.1336; Horsley, *New Documents*, 4.182. Variants for the name appear in the Greek text of Luke 2:2 as κυρινίου and κυρ(ε)ινίου.

12. British Museum P Lond 904—Frederick G. Kenyon and H. Idris Bell, *Greek Papyri in the British Museum* (London: British Museum,

1907), 3.125, plate 30; George Milligan, *Greek Papyri* (Cambridge: Cambridge University Press, 1910), 72–73; Adolf Deissmann, *Light from the Ancient East*, trans. Lionel R. M. Strachan (New York: George H. Doran, 1927), 270 n.7.

13. B. P. Grenfell, A. S. Hunt, et al., *Oxyrhynchus Papyri* (London: Egypt Exploration Fund, 1898–), 2.207.

14. Ibid., 2.255; Milligan, *Greek Papyri*, 44.

15. James H. Moulton and George Milligan, *The Vocabulary of the Greek Testament* (London: Hodder and Stoughton, 1952), 59–60.

16. Grenfell et al., *Oxyrhynchus Papyri*, 2.254; Moulton and Milligan, *Vocabulary*, 60.

17. Josephus *Antiquities* 18.2.1 (26).

18. Moulton and Milligan, *Vocabulary*, 60.

19. Tertullian *Adversus Marcionem* 4.19.

20. See n. 12.

21. See n. 14.

22. Jerome, Letter 58 "To Paulinus" in *NPNF* 6.120: "Even my own Bethlehem, as it now is, that most venerable spot in the whole world of which the psalmist sings: 'The truth hath sprung out of the earth' (Ps. 85:11), was overshadowed by a grove of Tammuz, that is, of Adonis; and in the very cave where the infant Christ had uttered his earliest cry, lamentation was made for the paramour of Venus."

23. Paulinus of Nola *Epistle* 31.3 in *CSEL* 29–30.270: "For the emperor Hadrian, in the belief that he could destroy the Christian faith by the dishonoring of a place, dedicated a statue of Jupiter on the place of the passion, and Bethlehem was profaned by a grove of Adonis."

24. Justin Martyr *Dialogue with Trypho* 78.

25. Protevangelium of James 18:1–2—referred to by Origen in the early third century.

26. Origen *Contra Celsum* 1.51.

27. Eusebius *Life of Constantine* 3.41.

28. Ibid., 3.43.

29. Sozomen *Ecclesiastical History* 2.2.1.

30. Sulpicius Severus *Sacred History* 2.33.

31. Epiphanius *Panarion* 30.4ff.

32. Bellarmino Bagatti, *The Church from the Circumcision* (Jerusalem: Franciscan, 1971), 126.

33. This date is affirmed in correspondence received from Vardaman on Jan. 4, 1988, which contained a brief unpublished article entitled "When Did Jesus' Ministry Begin, and

When Was Paul in Damascus? An Unrecognized Coin of Aretas IV, Struck in Damascus." For a defense of the date see Jerry Vardaman, "Jesus' Life: A New Chronology," in Jerry Vardaman and Edwin Yamauchi, eds., *Chronos, Kairos, Christos: Nativity and Chronological Studies Presented to Jack Finegan* (Winona Lake, Ind.: Eisenbrauns, 1989), 55–82. Vardaman here modifies his previously held date of A.D. 17, which appeared in "Jesus' Life: A New Chronology," *Biblical Illustrator* 11:2 (Winter 1985): 12–18.

34. *CIG* 3, #4521; see reports of ongoing excavations at Abila in the Decapolis by Harold W. Mare in *Near East Archaeological Society Bulletin*.

35. Communication received from William F. Albright, dated 23 Dec. 1959.

36. Rainer Riesner, "Bethany Beyond the Jordan (John 1:28). Topography, Theology and History in the Fourth Gospel," *Tyndale Bulletin* 38 (1987): 29–64.

37. John McRay, "John the Baptist and the Dead Sea Scrolls," *RQ* 4 (1960): 80–88. For an opposing view see William S. LaSor, *The Dead Sea Scrolls and the New Testament* (Grand Rapids: Eerdmans, 1972), 142–53.

38. Manual of Discipline 8.14.

39. William S. LaSor, "Discovering What Jewish Miqva'ot Can Tell Us about Christian Baptism," *BAR* 13 (Jan.–Feb. 1987): 58.

40. Cairo Damascus Document 12.14f.

41. LaSor, *Dead Sea Scrolls*, 152.

42. Josephus *Antiquities* 15.11.5 (412).

43. Baruch Sapir and Dov Neeman, *Capernaum* (Tel Aviv: Interfaith Survey of the Holy Land, 1967).

44. See the valuable review and evaluation of their publications by James F. Strange in "The Capernaum and Herodium Publications," *BASOR* 226 (1977): 65–73; *BASOR* 233 (1979): 63–69.

45. Virgilio Corbo et al., *La sinagoga di Cafarnao dopo gli scavi del 1969* (Jerusalem: Franciscan, 1970); Virgilio Corbo, *Cafarnao I: Edifici della città* (Jerusalem: Franciscan, 1975); Stanislao Loffreda, *Cafarnao II: La ceramica* (Jerusalem: Franciscan, 1974).

46. G. Foerster, "Notes on Recent Excavations at Capernaum," *IEJ* 21.4 (1971): 207–11; the article may also be seen in Lee Levine, ed., *Ancient Synagogues Revealed* (hereafter *ASR*) (Jerusalem: Israel Exploration Society, 1981), 57–59.

47. Stanislao Loffreda, "The Synagogue of Capernaum: Archaeological Evidence for Its Late Chronology," *LA* 22 (1972): 5–29. His viewpoints were also published in "The Late Chronology of the Synagogue of Capernaum," *IEJ* 23.1 (1973): 37–42; and in *ASR*, 52–56.

48. Michael Avi-Yonah, "Editor's Note," *IEJ* 23.1 (1973): 43–45; or see *ASR*, 60–62.

49. Stanislao Loffreda, "A Reply to the Editor," *IEJ* 23.3 (1973): 184.

50. A. Spijkerman, "Moneta della sinagoga di Cafarnao," *LA* 20 (1970): 7–52.

51. James F. Strange and Hershel Shanks, "Synagogue Where Jesus Preached Found at Capernaum," *BAR* 9 (Nov.–Dec. 1983): 24–31.

52. Stanislao Loffreda, "Ceramica ellenistico–romana nel sottosuolo della sinagoga di Cafarnao," *Studia Hierosolymitana* 3 (1982): 273–312; Virgilio Corbo, "Resti della sinagoga del primo sècolo a Cafarnao," *Studia Hierosolymitana* 3 (1982): 313–57.

53. Virgilio Corbo, "La casa di S. Pietro a Cafarnao," *LA* 18 (1968): 5–54; idem, "St. Peter's House in Capernaum Rediscovered," *CNI* 20.1–2 (1969): 39–50; idem, *The House of Saint Peter at Capharnaum: A Preliminary Report of the First Two Campaigns of Excavations, April 16–June 19, Sept. 12–Nov. 26, 1968*, trans. S. Saller (Jerusalem: Franciscan, 1969); idem and Stanislao Loffreda, *New Memoirs of Saint Peter by the Sea: Excavations Conducted by the Custody of the Holy Land, 1968* (Jerusalem: Franciscan, n.d.); Stanislao Loffreda, *Capharnaum: The Town of Jesus* (Jerusalem: Franciscan, 1985); James F. Strange and Hershel Shanks, "Has the House Where Jesus Stayed in Capernaum Been Found?" *BAR* 8 (Nov.–Dec. 1982): 26–37.

54. James Charlesworth, *Jesus Within Judaism: New Light from Exciting Archaeological Discoveries* (New York: Doubleday, 1988), 112.

55. Emmanuele Testa, Cafarnao IV: *Graffiti della casa de S. Pietro* (Jerusalem: Franciscan, 1972); Strange, "Capernaum and Herodium Publications," *BASOR* 233 (1979): 64–69; Strange and Shanks, "Has the House," 35–37.

56. H. Keith Beebe disputes this, claiming the roof would not have been substantial enough to support the men ("Domestic Architecture and the New Testament," *BA* 38 (Sept., Dec. 1975): 102–4). The examples of "arch-and-slab" architecture he posits for this story, however, are from several centuries later.

57. Corbo and Loffreda, *New Memoirs*, 26; Strange, "Capernaum and Herodium Publications" *BASOR* 233 (1979): 63–69.

58. Testa, *Cafarnao IV*.

59. Strange, "Capernaum and Herodium Publications," *BASOR* 233 (1979): 63–69.

60. J. E. Sanderson, "Capernaum," in R. K. Harrison, ed., *Major Cities of the Biblical World* (Nashville: Nelson, 1985), 80–81.

61. Vasillios Tzaferis et al., *Excavations at Capernaum, vol. 1: 1978–82* (Winona Lake, Ind.: Eisenbrauns, 1989); Vasillios Tzaferis and M. Peleg, "Kefar Nahum," in Ayala Sussman and R. Greenberg, eds., *Excavations and Surveys in Israel—1984*, 6 vols. (Jerusalem: Israel Department of Antiquities and Museums, 1981–1988), 3.64, 4.59.

62. Vasillios Tzaferis, "New Archaeological Evidence on Ancient Capernaum," *BA* 46 (Dec. 1983): 201.

63. Gaalyah Cornfeld, ed., Josephus: *The Jewish War* (Grand Rapids: Zondervan, 1982), 250 n. 519c.

64. Josephus *Jewish War* 3.10.8 (519).

65. Vasillios Tzaferis, "A Pilgrimage to the Site of the Swine Miracle," *BAR* 15.2 (March–April 1989): 45–51; idem, "El–Koursi," *IEJ* 22.2–3 (1972): 176–77.

66. Asher Ovadiah, "Two Notes on the Early Byzantine Complex at Kursi," *PEQ* 109.2 (1977): 123–24; idem and C. Gomez de Silva, "Supplementum to the Corpus of the Byzantine Churches in the Holy Land," *Levant* 13 (1981): 200–61. I had the opportunity of photographing many of these mosaics in 1970 just after they were discovered. They have since been removed from the site.

67. "Gergesa," in *Archaeological Encyclopedia of the Holy Land*, ed. Abraham Negev, rev. ed. (Nashville: Nelson, 1986).

68. Eusebius, *Das Onomastikon der biblischen Ortsnamen*, ed. Erich Klostermann (Hildesheim: Georg Olms, 1966), 74, line 13 (author's translation).

69. Cited in Tzaferis, "El–Koursi," 177.

70. J. Soutar, "Gerasenes, Gergesenes," in *A Dictionary of Christ and the Gospels*, ed. James Hastings (Edinburgh: T. and T. Clark, 1906).

71. Tzaferis, "Pilgrimage," 51.

72. William Sanday, *Sacred Sites of the Gospels* (Oxford: Clarendon, 1903), 27.

73. The words resemble each other in Greek and may have been miscopied in the various manuscripts.

74. Eutychius of Alexandria *Book of the Demonstration* 310ff.

75. Bargil Pixner, "The Miracle Church of Tabgha on the Sea of Galilee," *BA* 48 (Dec. 1985: 196–206.

76. Andreas E. Mader, *Die Ausgrabungen auf dem deutschen Besitz et–Tabgha am See Genesareth, Das Heilige Land* 78 (1934): 1–15, 41–66, 89–103, 129–49; Alfons Schneider, *Die Brotvermehrungskirche von et–Tabgha am Genesarethsee und ihre Mosaiken*, Collectanea Hierosolymitana 4 (Paderborn: F. Schoeningh, 1934), 8ff.

77. Bernhard Gauer, "Werkbericht über die Instandsetzung der Boden Mosaiken von Heptapegon am See Tiberias," *Journal of the Palestine Oriental Society* 18 (1938): 233–53.

78. Stanislao Loffreda, "Sondaggio nella chiesa della moltiplicazione dei pani a Tabgha," *LA* 20 (1970): 370–80. Idem, "The Rock of the Primacy at Tabgha," in Corbo and Loffreda, *New Memoirs*, 42–70.

79. Renate Rosenthal and Malka Hershkovitz, "Tabgha," *IEJ* 30.3–4 (1980): 207.

80. For further bibliography on Tabgha see Eleanor Vogel and Brooks Holtzclaw, *Bibliography of Holy Land Sites* (Cincinnati: Hebrew Union College–Jewish Institute of Religion, 1982), 1.6, 2.84.

81. Josephus *Antiquities* 18.2.1 (28).

82. Josephus *Life* 399.

83. Ibid., 406.

84. Josephus *Jewish War* 3.10.7 (515).

85. Ibid., 2.6.3 (93–100).

86. Shelley Wachsmann, Kurt Raveh, and Orna Cohen, "The Kinneret Boat Project: The Excavation and Conservation of the Kinneret Boat," *International Journal of Nautical Archaeology* 16 (Aug. 1987): 243. For a full report on the excavation see *The Excavation of an Ancient Boat in the Sea of Galilee*, Atiqot 19, English series (Jerusalem: Israel Department of Antiquities, 1990).

87. Matt. 8:18, 23–27; 9:1; 14:13–14, 22–33; 15:39; 16:5; Mark 4:35–41; 5:18, 21; 6:32–34, 45–51; 8:9–10, 13–14; Luke 5:2; 8:22–25, 37; John 6:16–24; 21:3–8.

88. Magdala was the birthplace of Mary Magdalene (Matt. 27:56, 61). Jesus may have visited here, for the area or site called Dalmanutha in some texts of Mark 8:10 is also called Magadan, Magedan, and Magdala. The parallel in Matt. 15:39 has Magadan or Magedan.

89. For a picture of both the Galilee boat and the mosaic boat see Shelley Wachsmann, "The Galilee Boat—2,000-Year-Old Hull Recovered Intact," *BAR* 14 (Sept.–Oct. 1988): 19–33.

90. Bargil Pixner, "Searching for the New Testament Site of Bethsaida," *BA* 48 (Dec. 1985): 212.

91. Eusebius *Onomastikon*, 174, line 23 (Klostermann edition).

92. Zeev Yeivin, "Chorazin," *IEJ* 12.2 (1962): 152–53; idem, "Excavations at Khorazin 1962–1964," *EI* 11 (1971): 141–57 (in Hebrew); idem, "Ancient Chorazin Comes Back to Life," *BAR* 13 (Sept.–Oct. 1987): 22–39; idem and Nahman Avigad, "Chorozain," in *EAEHL* 1.299–303; see further relevant bibliography in Vogel and Holtzclaw, *Bibliography*, 1.25, 2.23.

93. Zeev Yeivin, "Korazim—1983/84," in *Excavations and Surveys*, 3.66–71; idem, "Ancient Chorazin," 22–39.

94. Josephus *Jewish War* 3.9.7 (443); 7.2.1 (23).

95. Ibid., 2.9.1 (168).

96. Josephus *Antiquities* 18.2.1 (28).

97. Josephus *Jewish War* 3.10.7 (514); *Antiquities* 15.10.3 (363).

98. The texts of the Greek inscriptions are collected, though not translated, in C. R. Conder and H. H. Kitchener, *Survey of Western Palestine* 6 vols. (Jerusalem: Kedem, 1970), 1.112–113.

99. Ibid., 1.111.

100. Josephus *Jewish War* 3.10.7 (514).

101. Josephus *Antiquities* 20.9.4 (211). For Roman names of the city see Michael Avi-Yonah, *Gazetteer of Roman Palestine*, Qedem 5 (1976): 44–45.

102. Josephus *Antiquities* 15.10.3 (361).

103. For a picture and discussion of the map see *Atlas of Israel* (Jerusalem: Survey of Israel, Ministry of Labour, 1970), 1/2 ("Cartography," ed. Joseph Elster).

104. Israel Finkelstein, "The Holy Land in the Tabula Peutingeriana: A Historical—Geographical Approach," *PEQ* 111 (1979): 29.

105. M. Hartal, "Banias," in *Excavations and Surveys*, 4.7–8.

106. Ibid., 9.

107. "News in Brief: Banias, Nature Reserve," in *Excavations and Surveys*, 4.119.

108. Josephus *Antiquities* 15.10.3 (363); *Jewish War* 1.21.3 (404).

109. A. R. Reifenberg, "Unpublished and Unusual Jewish Coins," *IEJ* 1 (1950–51): 176.

110. Ya'akov Meshorer, *Jewish Coins of the Second Temple Period* (Tel Aviv, Am Hassefer, 1967), plate 10, no. 76; see the discussion on pp. 76–77.

111. A. Kindler, "A Coin of Herod Philip—the Earliest Portrait of a Herodian Ruler," *IEJ* 21.2–3 (1971): 161.

112. F. de Saulcy, *Numismatique de la Terre Sainte* (Paris: Rothchild, 1874), 315–16, plate xviii; see the discussion by George Adam Smith, *The Historical Geography of the Holy Land*, 4th ed. (London: Hodder and Stoughton, 1896), 473–76.

113. Zev Vilnay, *The Guide to Israel* (Jerusalem: Hamakor, 1972), 473.

114. Josephus *Life* 86.

115. Gustaf Dalman, *Sacred Sites and Ways* (London: SPCK, 1935), 101–6.

116. Josephus *Antiquities* 18.2.1 (27).

117. Ibid., 14.5.4 (91); *Jewish War* 1.8.5 (170).

118. Josephus *Antiquities* 14.15.4 (414).

119. Ibid., 17.10.9 (289).

120. Josephus *Life* 37.

121. Josephus *Antiquities* 18.2.3 (36).

122. Josephus *Life* 376–77; *Jewish War* 3.2.4 (32).

123. Josephus *Life* 38.

124. Frederick G. Kenyon, ed., *Chester Beatty Biblical Papyri* (London: Emery Walker, 1933), fasc. 2, *The Gospels and Acts*, "Text," 4.; "Plates," f.4.v.

125. Richard Batey, "Is Not This the Carpenter?" *NTS* 30 (1984): 249–58.

126. Shirley Jackson Case, "Jesus and Sepphoris," *JBL* 45 (1926): 14–22. The idea was repeated in his book *Jesus: A New Biography* (Chicago: University of Chicago Press, 1927), 199–212.

127. Sepphoris is spelled in a number of ways: Σεπφωρις (Sepphōris) (The earliest use is in Josephus *Antiquities* 13.12.5 [338]); Σεπφōυριν (Sepphōrin) (Epiphanius *Panarion* 30.11); Σαπφουρει (Sapphourei) (Ptolemy *Geography* 5.16.4); Σεπφωρηνων (Sepphōrēnōn, the genitive of Σεπφωρηνοι Sepphōrēnoi) (on a coin of Trajan [A.D. 98–117]). See Michael Avi Yonah and E. Stern, "Sepphoris," in *EAEHL* 4.1051. The city's name was changed to Διοκαισαρεια ("City of Zeus and Caesar"), probably beginning with Hadrian (A.D. 117–138). The name does not occur in the New Testament, unless the variant reading Σαμφουριν (Samphourin) in Codex D (Bezae) of John 11:54 refers to Sepphoris, which is not likely.

128. Leroy Waterman, *Preliminary Report of the University of Michigan Excavations at Sepphoris, Palestine, in 1931* (Ann Arbor: University of Michigan Press, 1937).

129. James F. Strange and R. W. Longstaff, "Sippori—1985," in *Excavations and Surveys*, 4.100–2, 6.98.

130. Eric M. Meyers, Ehud Netzer, and Carol Meyers, "Sepphoris, 'Ornament of All Galilee,'" *BA* 49 (March 1986): 4–19.

131. Strange and Longstaff, "Sippori—1985," in *Excavations and Surveys*, 6.97

132. Richard Batey, "Jesus and the Theatre," *NTS* 30 (1984): 563–74.

133. Strange and Longstaff, "Sippori—1985," in *Excavations and Surveys*, 6.97

134. Private conversation, 19 Dec. 1988.

135. Telephone call from Jerusalem, 1 Dec. 1988.

136. For a survey of some of the rabbinic traditions and insights into selected aspects of the city's history see Stuart S. Miller, *Studies in the History of Traditions of Sepphoris*, Studies in Judaism in Late Antiquity 37 (Leiden: E. J. Brill, 1984).

137. Eric M. Meyers, Ehud Netzer, and Carol Meyers, "Artistry in Stone: The Mosaics of Ancient Sepphoris," *BA* 50 (Dec. 1987): 223–31; Carol Meyers, "Excavations at Sepphoris, 1987," *ASOR Newsletter* 39.2 (Jan. 1988): 1–2; Hershel Shanks, "Prize Find: Mosaic Masterpiece Dazzles Sepphoris Volunteers," *BAR* 14 (Jan.–Feb. 1988): 30–33.

138. Talmud *Megilla* 2:2.

139. Tosephta *'Erubin* 7.2.146.

140. For A.D. 18 see Michael Avi-Yonah, "The Foundation of Tiberias," *IEJ* 1 (1950–51): 160–69; for A.D. 23 see Harold W. Hoehner, *Herod Antipas* (Grand Rapids: Zondervan, 1980), 93–95.

141. Josephus *Life* 37.

142. Josephus *Jewish War* 3.2.4 (34); *Life* 232.

143. The excavations were conducted by N. Slousch in 1921 and Moshe Dothan in 1961; see Vogel and Holtzclaw, *Bibliography*, 1.34.

144. G. Foerster, "Tiberias," in *EAEHL* 4.1171–76.

145. "Tiberias: Preview of Coming Attractions," in *BAR* 17 (March-April 1991): 44–51.

146. Reported in Ayala Sussman and R. Greenberg, eds., *Excavations and Surveys in Israel: 1988-89* Vol. 6 (Jerusalem: Israel Antiquities Authority, 1990), 7–45.

147. Sussman, *Excavations and Surveys*, vols. 7, 8 (1990), 15–32. See also "Glorious Beth Shean," *BAR* 16 (July-Aug. 1990): 17–31.

148. *BAR* 16 (July-Aug. 1990): 31.

149. *Excavations and Surveys*, 6.42.

150. Eusebius *Onomastikon* 164, line 3 (Klostermann edition).

151. In Jerome's translation, #154.

152. *SWP* 2.172ff.

153. *LPPTS* 3.41–42; *CCSL* 175.216. See the description in Adamnan's account of Arculf's travels, *Adamnai de locis sanctis libri tres*, in P. Geyer, ed., *Itinera Hierosolymitana saeculi IIII–VIII*. CSEL 39.270.

154. *SWP* 2.176.

155. Edward Robinson and E. Smith, *Biblical Researches in Palestine, Mount Sinai and Arabia Petraea*, 3 vols. (Boston: Crocker and Brewster, 1841), 3.108.

156. *SWP* 2.176.

157. Ibid., 177.

158. Ibid.

159. E. Damati, "'Askar," *IEJ* 22 (1972): 174.

160. R. W. Dajani, "Nablus—A Roman Cemetery Discovered," *ADAJ* 11 (1966): 103.

161. Josephus *Antiquities* 11.8.2 (310); 11.8.7 (346–47); 12.5.5 (257–64); 13.9.1 (254–58).

162. Robert J. Bull excavated the site until the 1967 Israeli-Arab war erupted and the dig closed down according to the rules of the Geneva convention governing occupied territory. For a brief discussion see Robert J. Bull, "Gerizim," in *IDB* supp., 361, and the attached bibliography.

Chapter 6

1. There is a slight variation between the NASB and RSV. The RSV and the New Revised Standard Version capitalize *Sheep Gate*, regarding it as a proper place name. The NASB does not.

2. John Wilkinson, *Jerusalem as Jesus Knew It* (London: Thames and Hudson, 1978), 96.

3. 3Q15—M. Baillet, J. T. Milik, and Roland de Vaux, *Discoveries in the Judean Desert*, vol. 3. *Les "Petites Grottes" de Qumran* (Oxford: Clarendon, 1962), pt. 1, pp. 271–72, 297; J. M. Allegro, *The Treasure of the Copper Scroll*, 2d ed. (Garden City, N.Y.: Doubleday, 1964), 84.

4. Frank Moore Cross, Jr., in Baillet et al., *Les "Petites Grottes,"* pt. 1, pp. 217–19.

5. Col. XI, lines 12–13 (translation from Jack Finegan, *Archaeology of the New Testament: The Life of Jesus and the Beginning of the Early Church* [Princeton, N.J.: Princeton University Press, 1970], 143).

6. Finegan, *Archaeology of the New Testament*, 143.

7. The Greek text with English translation may be seen in Jack Finegan, *Hidden Records of the Life of Jesus* (Philadelphia: Pilgrim, 1969), 226–30, Section 282. See his bibliography for the parchment on p. 226.

8. Michael Avi-Yonah, "Jerusalem," in *EAEHL* 2.612. See also Joachim Jeremias, *The Rediscovery of Bethesda: John 5:2*, New Testament Archaeology 1, ed. Jerry Vardaman, (Göttingen: Vandenhoeck and Ruprecht, 1949).

9. Finegan, *Archaeology: Life of Jesus*, 146.

10. See the layout of Jerusalem in Wilkinson, *Jerusalem*, 62.

11. Y. Tsafrir, "When Was the Cardo of Jerusalem Built?" in *Eighth Archaeological Conference in Israel, Abstracts* (Jerusalem: 1981); see also Ronny Reich,"Four Notes on Jerusalem—4. The Date of Construction of the Jerusalem Cardo," *IEJ* 37.2–3 (1987): 164–67.

12. Nahman Avigad, *Discovering Jerusalem* (Nashville: Nelson, 1983), 213–29.

13. Eusebius *Onomastikon* 58, lines 21–26 (Klostermann edition).

14. *CCSL* 175.15.

15. Benjamin Mazar, *The Mountain of the Lord* (Garden City, N.Y.: Doubleday, 1975), 202.

16. *CCSL* 175.16.

17. Josephus *Jewish War* 5.4.1 (140); 5.4.2 (145); 5.6.1 (252).

18. Wilkinson, *Jerusalem*, 106.

19. Josephus *Jewish War* 5.4.2 (143—45)—Gaalyah Cornfeld, ed., *Josephus: The Jewish Jewish War* (Grand Rapids: Zondervan, 1982), 336; G. A. Williamson, *Josephus: The Jewish War*, rev. ed. (New York: Penguin, 1980), 287; H. St.J. Thackeray, Ralph Marcus, et al., *Josephus*, Loeb Classical Library, 9 vols. (Cambridge, Mass.: Harvard University Press, 1979), 3.243; William Whiston, *The Life and Works of Flavius Josephus* (Philadelphia: The John C. Winston, n.d.), 781 (The "New Updated Edition" of Whiston makes no changes in the translation—*The Works of Josephus*, [Peabody, Mass.: Hendrickson, 1987], 704.)

20. Wilkinson, *Jerusalem*, 63.

21. David Adan (Bayewitz), "The 'Fountain of Siloam' and 'Solomon's Pool' in First Century C. E. Jerusalem," *IEJ* 29.2 (1979): 92–100.

22. Josephus *Antiquities of the Jews* 7.3.1 (63–64).

23. Yigal Shiloh, *Excavations at the City of David*, vol. 1 (1978–82), *Qedem* 19 (1984): 21–24.

24. Ibid., 23; Hershel Shanks, "The City of David after Five Years of Digging," *BAR* 11 (Nov.–Dec. 1985): 37–38.

25. Josephus *Jewish War* 2.16.2 (340); 5.4.1 (140); 5.4.2 (145); 5.6.1 (252); 5.9.4 (410); 5.12.2 (505); 6.7.2 (363); 6.8.5 (401).

26. Initially reported in the *Chicago Tribune*, 22 April 1986.

27. This discovery was published by J. T. Milik in an article entitled "Trois tombeaux juifs récemment découverts au sud-est de Jérusalem," *LA* 7 (1956–57): 232–39.

28. Joseph A. Fitzmyer, "The Aramaic Qorban Inscription from Jebel Hallet et-Turi and Mark 7:11/Matthew 15:5," in *Essays on the Semitic Background of the New Testament* (Missoula, Mont.: Scholars, 1974), 96 (originally published in *JBL* 78 [1959]: 60–65).

29. Ibid.

30. Benjamin Mazar, *The Excavations in the Old City of Jerusalem: Preliminary Report of the First Season, 1968* (Jerusalem: Israel Exploration Society, 1969), 15; idem, "The Excavations South and West of the Temple Mount in Jerusalem: The Herodian Period," *BA* 33 (May 1970): 55 (this article contains an excellent photo of the inscription and the birds).

31. *Ma'aser Sheni* 4:10.

32. *Nedarim* 2:2.

33. Eusebius *Onomastikon* 58, lines 15–17.

34. Ibid.

35. Ibid., 59, line 17.

36. S. Saller, "Bethany," *ADAJ* 1 (1951), 44; idem, "Bethany," *ADAJ* 2 (1953); 82–83; idem, *Excavations at Bethany* (1949–53), PSBF 12 (Jerusalem: Franciscan, 1957), 9–33; Stanislao Loffreda, "Due tombe a Betania presso le Suore della Nigrizia," *LA* 19 (1969): 349–66; idem, "La tomba n. 3 presso le Suore della Nigrizia a Betania," *LA* 24 (1974): 142–69.

37. See the full discussion of the church and tomb with photos in Finegan, *Archaeology: Life of Jesus*, 91–95.

38. Bellarmino Bagatti and J. T. Milik, *Gli scavi del "Dominus Flevit" (Monte Oliveto-Gerusalèmme)*, vol. 1, *La necròpoli del periodo romano*, PSBF 13 (Jerusalem: Franciscan, 1958).

39. Finegan, *Archaeology: Life of Jesus*, 243–44.

40. Bellarmino Bagatti, *The Church from the Circumcision* (Jerusalem: Franciscan, 1971), 137–306.

41. Nahman Avigad, "The Tombs in Jerusalem," in *EAEHL* 2.636.

42. For the Hebrew and Greek forms as well as the numbers of the burials and ossuaries where these names occur, see Finegan, *Archaeology: Life of Jesus*, 246.

43. Benjamin Mazar, "Archaeological Excavations near the Temple Mount," in *Jerusalem Revealed*, ed. Yigael Yadin (Jerusalem: Israel Exploration Society, 1975), 33; idem, *Mountain of the Lord*, 233.

44. *CCSL* 135.17–18.

45. Eusebius *Onomastikon* 74, lines 18–18.

46. Ibid., 75, line 19.

47. See the diagram and discussion in Finegan, *Archaeology: Life of Jesus*, 104–8.

48. Josephus *Jewish War* 2.17.6 (426).

49. *CCSL* 175.16.

50. *CCSL* 135.118.

51. Michael Avi-Yonah, *The Madaba Mosaic Map* (Jerusalem: Israel Exploration Society, 1954), 16–18.

52. Avigad, *Discovering Jerusalem*, 229–46.

53. Magen Broshi, "Excavations in the House of Caiaphas, Mount Zion," in *Jerusalem Revealed*, ed. Yadin, 57–60.

54. See the discussions of the area in Mazar, *Mountain of the Lord*, 147–52; Wilkinson, *Jerusalem*, 166–72.

55. Magen Broshi, "Excavations on Mount Zion, 1971–72," *IEJ* 26.1 (1976): 81–88.

56. Ibid., 84.

57. Josephus *Jewish War* 2.17.6 (426).

58. *CCSL* 175.118.

59. *NPNF* 7.116.

60. *CCSL* 175.118.

61. Finegan, *Archaeology: Life of Jesus*, 148.

62. Bargil Pixner, "Church of the Apostles Found on Mt. Zion," *BAR* 16 (May–June, 1990): 16–35.

63. Antonio Frova, "L'Inscrizione di Ponzio Pilato a Cesarea," *Rendiconti* 95 (1961): 419–34.

64. Jerry Vardaman, "A New Inscription Which Mentions Pilate as 'Prefect,'" *JBL* 81 (1962): 70–71.

65. Alexander Jannaeus crucified eight hundred Jews in Jerusalem (Josephus *Antiquities* 13.14.2 [380]). The slave revolt against Rome, led by Spartacus in 73–71 B.C., ended in the crucifixion of six thousand slaves, whose crosses were "set up like telegraph posts along the whole length of the Via Appia" (Max Cary, *A History of Rome*, 2d ed. [New York: Macmillan, 1962], 365). Josephus saw "many" Jewish prisoners crucified in Tekoa at the end of the first revolt (*Life*, 420).

66. Vassilios Tzaferis, "Crucifixion—the Archeological Evidence," *BAR* 11 (Jan.–Feb. 1985): 44; Nico Haas, "Anthropological Observations on the Skeletal Remains from Givat ha-Mivtar," *IEJ* 20.1–2 (1970): 51.

67. Vassilios Tzaferis, "Jewish Tombs at and near Givat ha-Mivtar, Jerusalem," *IEJ* 20.1–2 (1970): 18–32. See the discussion of tombs on pp. 207–11. This man was found in Cave 1, Ossuary 4, Chamber B.

68. J. Naveh, "The Ossuary Inscriptions from Givat ha-Mivtar," *IEJ* 20.1–2 (1970): 35; Tzaferis, "Crucifixion," 53.

69. Yigael Yadin, "Epigraphy and Crucifixion" in *IEJ* 23.1 (1973): 18–19.

70. Haas, "Anthropological Observations" in *IEJ* 20:1–2 (1970): 38–59, plate 24.B.

71. Tzaferis, "Crucifixion," 52.

72. Joseph Zias and Eliezer Sekeles, "The Crucified Man from Givat ha–Mivtar: A Reappraisal," *IEJ* 35.1 (1985): 22–27; idem, "The Crucified Man from Givat ha–Mivtar: A Reappraisal," *BA* 48 (Sept. 1985): 190–91.

73. This is based on the assumption that a Hebrew letter *heth* rather than a *he*, stood in the inscription. Yigael Yadin, "Epigraphy and Crucifixion," *IEJ* 23·1(1973): 19.

74. Ibid. , 20–21.

75. *Acts of Peter* 37.

76. S. Lieberman, "Sin and Its Punishments," in *Louis Ginzberg Jubilee Volume* (New York: American Academy for Jewish Research, 1946), 302.

77. William Edwards et. al. , "On the Physical Death of Jesus Christ," *Journal of the American Medical Association* 255.11 (21 March 1986): 1461.

78. W. S. McBirnie, *The Search for the Authentic Tomb of Jesus* (Montrose, Calif.: Acclaimed, 1975); Gabriel Barkay, "The Garden Tomb: Was Jesus Buried Here?" *BAR* 12 (March–April 1986): 49.

79. Benjamin Mazar, "Iron Age Burial Caves North of the Damascus Gate, Jerusalem," *IEJ* 26.1 (1976): 1–8.

80. Stanislao Loffreda, "Typological Sequence of Iron Age Rock-Cut Tombs in Palestine," *LA* 18 (1968): 244–78; idem, "The Late Chronology of Some Rock-Cut Tombs of the Selwan Necropolis, Jerusalem," *LA* 23 (1973): 7–36; Mazar, "Iron Age Burial Caves," 1–8; Gabriel Barkay and Amos Kloner, "Jerusalem Tombs from the Days of the First Temple," *BAR* 12 (March–April 1986): 23–39; L. Y. Rahmani, "Ancient Jerusalem's Funerary Customs and Tombs," pt. 2, *BA* 44 (Fall 1981): 229–35.

81. Othmar Keel, "The Peculiar Headrests for the Dead in First Temple Times," *BAR* 13 (July-Aug. 1987): 50–53; Gabriel Barkay, "Burial Headrests as a Return to the Womb—A

Reevaluation," *BAR* 14 (March–April 1988): 48–50.

82. Barkay, "Garden Tomb," 56; pottery and inscriptions have substantiated the date (51, 54).

83. See the following for a comprehensive look at tombs of this period: *Archaeological Encyclopedia of the Holy Land*, ed. Abraham Negev, rev. ed. (Nashville: Nelson, 1986), 203; L. Y. Rahmani, "Ancient Jerusalem's Funerary Customs and Tombs," a four-part series in *BA* 44 (Summer 1981): 171–77 (personal, social, and theological dimensions of Jewish burials), 44 (Fall 1981): 229–35 (Israel burials until the exile), 45 (Winter 1982): 43–53, (second-temple tombs in Jerusalem), 45 (Spring 1982): 109–19, (sarcophagi used in burials); *idem*, "Jason's Tomb," *IEJ* 17.2 (1967): 61–100; Nahman Avigad, "Jerusalem: The Tombs in Jerusalem. The Second Temple Period," in *EAEHL* 2.628–41; Finegan, *Archaeology: Life of Jesus*, 202–57 (extensive material); Rachel Hachlili, "A Second Temple Period Jewish Necropolis in Jericho," *BA* 43 (Fall 1980): 235–41; idem, "Ancient Burial Customs Preserved in Jericho Hills," *BAR* 5 (July–Aug. 1979): 28–35; idem, "A Jewish Family in Jericho," *BASOR* 230 (1978): 45–56; idem and Ann Killebrew, "The Saga of the Goliath Family—As Revealed in Their Newly Discovered 2000-Year-Old Tomb," *BAR* 9 (Jan.–Feb. 1983): 44–53; Eric M. Meyers, "Secondary Burials in Palestine," *BA* 33 (Feb. 1970): 2–29.

84. On the *kôkh*-type tombs (singular of *kôkhîm*) see: S. Saller and E. Testa, *The Archaeological Setting of the Shrine of Bethphage* (Jerusalem: Franciscan, 1961): 47–64; Finegan, *Archaeology: Life of Jesus*, 185ff.; Tzaferis, "Jewish Tombs," 18–27.

85. Rahmani, "Ancient Jerusalem's Funerary Customs and Tombs," *BA* 45 (Spring 1982): 109–19; Meyers, "Secondary Burials," 2–29; Tzaferis, "Jewish Tombs," 27–32.

86. Finegan, *Archaeology: Life of Jesus*, 189.

87. Tzaferis, "Jewish Tombs," 30.

88. *Sanhedrin* 6:6; cf. *Pesahim* 8:8.

89. Joseph Kohlbeck and Eugenia Nitowski, "New Evidence May Explain Image on Shroud of Turin," *BAR* 12 (July–Aug. 1986): 22. See further the study of tomb types in Finegan, *Archaeology: Life of Jesus*, 181–219.

90. The RSV renders it "Mount Zion, in the far north," and the NIV gives "Like the utmost heights of Zaphon is Mount Zion. " The Hebrew word may refer to either the direction north or

the sacred mountain Zaphon. Note again Gordon's arbitrariness.

91. See the article and further bibliography by Jerome Murphy-O'Connor, "The Garden Tomb and the Misfortunes of an Inscription," *BAR* 12 (March–April 1986): 54–55.

92. For example, Gabriel was "both priest of the Holy Resurrection and superior [of the monastery] of St. Stephen," according to the sixth-century historian Cyril of Scythopolis in his *Life of St. Euthymius*, n. 39; see Murphy-O'Connor, "Garden Tomb," 54.

93. Dan Bahat, "Does the Holy Sepulcher Church Mark the Burial of Jesus?" *BAR* 12 (May–June 1986): 26–45; Charles CoBasnon, "The Jesus of History," in *The Church of the Holy Sepulchre in Jerusalem*, trans. J.-P. B. Ross and C. Ross (London: Oxford University Press, 1974), chap. 5; Finegan, *Archaeology: Life of Jesus*, 163ff.; André Parrot, *Golgotha and the Church of the Holy Sepulchre* (London: SCM, 1957); J.-P. B. Ross, "The Evolution of a Church—Jerusalem's Holy Sepulchre," *BAR* 2 (Sept. 1976): 3–11. See also Lawrence Sporty, "The Location of the Holy House of Herod's Temple" in *BA* 53.4 (Dec. 1990): 194–204.

94. See my discussion of the Northern Wall on pp. 189–90. Note also Bruce Schein, "The Second Wall of Jerusalem," *BA* 44 (Winter 1981): 21–26; Kathleen Kenyon, *Jerusalem: Excavating 3000 Years of History* (London: Thames and Hudson, 1967), 153–54.

95. Vergilio Corbo, *Il Santo Sepolcro di Gerusalèmme: Aspetti archeològici dalle origini al periodo crociato*, pts. 1–3 (Jerusalem: Franciscan, 1981–82).

96. See Magen Broshi and Gabriel Barkay, "Excavations in the Chapel of St. Vartan in the Holy Sepulchre," *IEJ* 35.2–3 (1985): 108ff.

97. These include (1) the tomb traditionally attributed to Nicodemus and Joseph of Arimathea (#28 in Corbo's list—a heretofore unknown passage to this tomb was found in Corbo's excavation beneath the rotunda of the church); (2) the so-called tomb of Jesus (#1 and #2 in Corbo's plates); (3) a large tomb in front of the church, probably originally containing kôkhîm; and (4) a kôkh-type tomb found in the nineteenth century under the Coptic convent (see Bahat, "Holy Sepulchre Church," 31–32).

98. Eusebius *Life of Constantine* 3.26.

99. Ibid., 3.33.

100. Found during the removal of a burial, probably that of Licinius, who

died in A.D. 326 and was disinterred (ibid., 3.30).

101. Jerome *Letter 58* ("To Paulinus"), in *NPNF* 6.120.

102. Eusebius *Life of Constantine* 3.26, 30.

103. Eusebius *Ecclesiastical History* 5.5.2. Eusebius's list includes James, who was called the Lord's brother, Simeon, Justus, Zacchaeus, Tobias, Benjamin, John, Matthias, Philip, Seneca, Justus, Levi, Ephres, Joseph, and Judas. He writes that "such were the bishops in the city of Jerusalem, from the Apostles down to the time mentioned, and they were all Jews."

104. Eusebius, *Life of Constantine*, 3. 25–26.

105. Ibid., 3.43.

106. Sozomen *Ecclesiastical History* 2.2.1 (*PG* 67.929).

107. Sulpicius Severus *Sacred History* 2.33 (*PG* 20.148); Socrates Scholasticus *Church History* 1.17 (*PG* 67.118).

108. See Bahat's comparison ("Holy Sepulchre Church," 40ff.) of the differences between Vergilio Corbo and Charles Couasnon, two of the leading authorities on the excavations. And see J.-P. B. Ross's discussion ("Evolution of a Church," 3–8) of Couasnon's book, *The Church of the Holy Sepulchre in Jerusalem* (London: Oxford University Press, 1974).

109. Eusebius *Life of Constantine* 3.33–34.

110. Ibid., 3.35.

111. Ibid., 3.36.

112. Shulamit Eisenstadt, "Jesus' Tomb Depicted on a Byzantine Gold Ring from Jerusalem," *BAR* 13 (March–April 1987): 46–49.

113. Ya'akov Meshorer, "Ancient Gold Ring Depicts the Holy Sepulchre," *BAR* 12 (May–June 1986): 46–48.

114. Avi-Yonah, *Madaba Mosaic Map*, 54.

115. Mark Twain, *Innocents Abroad* (New York: Harper, 1911): 315–16.

116. Lazarus was further described as bound hand and foot with κειρίαι (bandages, swaddlings, or graveclothes).

117. As D. Moody Smith suggests— "Mark 15:46: The Shroud of Turin as a Problem of History and Faith," *BA* 46 (Dec. 1983): 252–53.

118. Kenneth R. Clark, "Shroud of Turin Controversy Resumes," *Chicago Tribune*, 17 January 1988, p. 1.

119. Ian Wilson, *The Shroud of Turin: The Burial Cloth of Jesus Christ?* (Garden City, N.Y.: Doubleday, 1978).

120. Their names and institutions are listed in Kenneth Weaver, "The

Mystery of the Shroud," *National Geographic* 157.6 (June 1980): 751.

121. Ibid., 750.

122. Kohlbeck and Nitowski, "New Evidence," 23.

123. Weaver, "Mystery of the Shroud," 747–48.

124. Private conversation, 27 September 1988.

125. Kenneth Stevenson and Gary Habermas, *The Shroud and the Controversy* (Nashville: Nelson, 1990), 44–60.

126. Kohlbeck and Nitowski, "New Evidence," 23–29.

127. Ibid., 28. It is, however, difficult to see how body heat could be a factor since Jesus died before being taken down from the cross, and his body would have cooled quickly.

128. Produced by Q.E.D. and the British Broadcasting Company, 1987. Syndicated to the Discovery Channel in the USA and aired 31 July 1987.

129. See discussions in L. Y.Rahmani, "Shroud of Turin," *BA* 43 (Fall 1980): 197; Francis L. Filas, "The Shroud of Turin: Roman Coins and Funerary Customs," *BA* 44 (Summer 1981): 135–37; William Meacham, "On the Archaeological Evidence for a Coin-on-Eye Jewish Burial Custom in the First Century A.D.," *BA* 49 (March 1986): 56–59; Rachel Hachlili and Ann Killebrew, "The Coin-in-Skull Affair: A Rejoinder," *BA* 49 (March 1986): 59–60; L. Y. Rahmani, "Whose Likeness and Image is This? (Mark 12:16)," *BA* 49 (March 1986): 60–61.

130. This identification is made in *Archaeological Encyclopedia of the Holy Land*, 130–31, and Finegan, *Archaeology: Life of Jesus*, 178.

131. Josephus *Jewish War* 2.5.1 (71)—Ἀμμαοῦς; *Antiquities* 17.10.7 (282)— Ἐμμαοῦς.

132. Sozomen *Ecclesiastical History* 5.21.

133. Eusebius *Onomastikon* 90, lines 15–17—Ἐμμαοῦς (Luke 24:13). "ὄθεν ἦν Κλεώπας ὁ ἐν τῷ κατὰ Λουκᾶν Εὐαγγελίῳ. αὔτη ἐστὶν ἡ νῦ'ν Νικόπολις τῆς Παλαιστίνης ἐπίσημος πόλις"

134. *LPPTS* 1.28; *CCSL* 225.20); P. Geyer, ed., *Itinera Hierosolymitana Saeculi IIII–VIII*, CSEL 39.25.

135. Bruce M. Metzger, *A Textual Commentary on the Greek New Testament* (New York: United Bible Societies, 1971), 184–85.

136. Wilkinson, *Jerusalem*, 163.

137. Josephus *Jewish War* 7.6.6 (217)— Ἀμμαοῦς in the Greek text.

138. Wilkinson, *Jerusalem*, 164. Motza is referred to in Joshua 18:26 as belonging to the tribe of Benjamin, and the Mishnah locates it "below Jerusalem" (*Sukkah* 4:5). It is now generally identified with the modern Jewish site of Mevasseret Ziyyon (the Arabic name is Qalunyah), located 4 miles northwest of Jerusalem on the road to Tel Aviv—see Yohanan Aharoni, *The Land of the Bible*, rev. ed. (Philadelphia: Westminster, 1979), 440; Yohanan Aharoni and Michael Avi-Yonah, *The Macmillan Bible Atlas* (New York: Macmillan, 1977), 82; *Atlas of Israel* (Jerusalem: Survey of Israel, 1970), 1/11 ("Cartography," ed. Joseph Elster). For a full discussion see Emil Schürer, *The Jewish People in the Time of Jesus Christ*, trans. John MacPherson, pt. 1, vol. 2 (New York: Scribner, n.d.), 253–55 n. 138.

139. Thackeray, Marcus et al., *Josephus*, 3.567 note d.

Chapter 7

1. John Knox, *Chapters in a Life of Paul* (New York: Abingdon-Cokesbury, 1950).

2. Gerd Luedemann, *Paul, Apostle to the Gentiles: Studies in Chronology*, trans. Stanley F. Jones (Philadelphia: Fortress, 1984)—the German original was published in 1980.

3. Robert Jewett, *A Chronology of Paul's Life* (Philadelphia: Fortress, 1979).

4. Jack Finegan, *Archaeology of the New Testament: The Mediterranean World of the Early Christian Apostles* (Boulder, Colo.: Westview, 1981), 9–49.

5. Orosius *Seven Books of History Against the Pagans*, 7.6.15–16 dated it to the ninth year of Claudius's reign, which Jack Finegan places at A.D. 49 (*Handbook of Biblical Chronology* [Princeton, N.J.: Princeton University Press, 1964], 319). See also Vincent Scramuzza, "The Policy of the Early Roman Emperors toward Judaism," in Frederick J. Foakes-Jackson and Kirsopp Lake, eds., *The Beginnings of Christianity*, 5 vols. (Grand Rapids: Baker, 1966), 5.295–96; Suetonius *Lives of the Caesars*, "Claudius" 25; *Teaching of Addai* 7b–11a (George Howard, *The Teaching of Addai* [Chico, Calif.: Scholars, 1981], 33).

6. She is not identified with any of Claudius's four known wives: Plautia Urgulanilla, Aelia Paetina, Valeria Messalina, and Agrippina, which may or may not be due to the Syriac text in which the document is written.

7. Howard, *Teaching of Addai*, 33 (10b). See the discussion in George Howard, "The Beginnings of Christianity in Rome: A Note on Suetonius, Life of Claudius XXV.4," *RQ* 24.3 (1981): 175–77.

8. On the vowel change see J. H. Moulton and W. F. Howard, *A Grammar of New Testament Greek* (Edinburgh: T. and T. Clark, 1929), 72; Friedrich Blass and A. Debrunner, *A Greek Grammar of the New Testament and Other Early Christian Literature*, ed. and trans. by Robert Funk (Chicago: University of Chicago Press, 1961), 24. *Chrestus* may be a modified form for *Christ*. See also Scramuzza, "The Policy of the Early Roman Emperors," 295–96, and William M. Ramsay, *St. Paul the Traveller and the Roman Citizen* (New York: Putnam's Sons, 1896), 48.

9. Josephus *Antiquities of the Jews* 19.5.2–3 (280–91); George Howard, "The Beginnings of Christianity in Rome: A Note on Suetonius, Life of Claudius XXV.4," *RQ* 24.3 (1981): 175–77.

10. Another Theodotus, a priest and synagogue president whose name was found on a pre–A.D. 70 inscription from a synagogue in Jerusalem, is called "son of Vettenus" and thus may have been a slave who had been freed by the prominent Roman family of the Vetteni, taking their name as was the custom. See Adolf Deissmann, *Light from the Ancient East*, trans. Lionel R. M. Strachan (New York: George H. Doran, 1927), 439–41; Jack Finegan, *Light from the Ancient Past*, 2d ed. (Princeton, N. J.: Princeton University Press, 1959), 306. William F. Albright felt that this synagogue of Theodotus may be connected with the "Synagogue of Freedmen" in Acts 6:9 (*The Archaeology of Palestine* [Baltimore: Penguin, 1960], 172).

11. Rachel Hachlili and Ann Killebrew, "The Saga of the Goliath Family—As Revealed in Their Newly Discovered 2,000-Year-Old Tomb," *BAR* 9 (Jan.–Feb. 1983): 52–53.

12. Adolf Deissmann, *St. Paul: A Study in Social and Religious Roman History* (New York: Hodder and Stoughton, 1912), app. I.

13. See the full Greek text in Deissmann, *St. Paul*, 246–47.

14. Finegan, *Handbook of Biblical Chronology*, 316–22.

15. For discussion of the Claudian inscription in relation to the dates for Paul, see Finegan, *Archaeology: Mediterranean World*, 12–13.

16. In addition to the chronologies already mentioned see, for A.D. 59, F. F. Bruce, *Paul: Apostle of the Heart Set Free* (Grand Rapids, Eerdmans, 1977), 475; for A.D. 61–62, George Ogg, *The*

Chronology of the Life of Paul (London: Epworth, 1968), 200.

17. The same information was given to Finegan, who has incorporated the date into his chronology (*Archaeology: Mediterranean World*, 14).

18. Ibid.

19. He would probably have left Caesarea in the fall since he spent three months shipwrecked on Malta during the winter non-sailing season (Acts 28:1, 11).

20. Strabo, *Geography* 16.2.5 calls it the metropolis of Syria and says it was not much smaller than Alexandria, Egypt, which Diodorus Siculus (*Bibliotheca* 17.52) says contained more than 300,000 ἐλεύθεροι ("free inhabitants"). See "The Size of the Population of Antioch," *Transactions of the American Philological Association* 89 (1958): 84–91. For aspects of Antioch's later history see J. H. W. G. Liebeschuetz, *Antioch: City and Imperial Administration in the Later Roman Empire* (Oxford: Clarendon, 1972).

21. Josephus *Jewish War* 7.3.3 (43): "The Jewish race, densely interspersed among the native populations of every portion of the world, is particularly numerous in Syria, where intermingling is due to the proximity of the two countries. But it was at Antioch that they especially congregated." See also C. H. Kraeling, "The Jewish Community at Antioch," *JBL* 51 (1932): 130–60.

22. Josephus *Jewish War* 7.3.3 (45).

23. For a history of the beginnings of Christianity in Antioch see Wayne A. Meeks and Robert L. Wilken, *Jews and Christians in Antiquities of Antioch in the First Four Centuries of the Common Era*, SBL Sources for Biblical Study 13 (Missoula, Mont.: Scholars, 1978), 1–52.

24. Eusebius *Ecclesiastical History* 3.36.2.

25. Ibid., 3.32. The *Chronicon* (see text in *GCS*) of Eusebius places the death of Ignatius of Antioch in the tenth year of Trajan (98–117), thus in 108.

26. Antioch is mentioned by Strabo, Evagrius, Procopius, Libanius, the emperor Julian, and John Chrysostom. Of especial value is the *Chronicle* of John Malalas, a Byzantine monk (A.D. 491–578). For publication of the text see Glanville Downey, *A History of Antioch in Syria: From Seleucus to the Arab Conquest* (Princeton, N. J.: Princeton University Press, 1961), 706. Books 8–18 were translated into English from Slavonic by M. Spinka in collaboration with G. Downey, under the title *Chronicle of John Malalas*

(Chicago: University of Chicago Press, 1940).

27. For overviews see Glanville Downey, *History of Antioch*; idem, *Ancient Antioch* (Princeton, N. J.: Princeton University Press, 1963); Fatih Cimok, *Antioch on the Orontes* (Istanbul: Us Tan Tma Merkezi, 1980). The reports of the "Committee for the Excavation of Antioch and Its Vicinity" were published under the title *Antioch-on-the-Orontes* (Princeton, N. J.: Princeton University Press, 1934–70). Five volumes have appeared, number 4 containing two parts.

28. Downey, *History of Antioch*, 70.

29. Ibid., 176–77.

30. Ibid., 154–57; Downey, *Ancient Antioch*, 75; J. B. Ward-Perkins, *Roman Imperial Architecture* (New York: Penguin, 1983), 325.

31. Downey, *History of Antioch*, 73, 141.

32. On the cult of the deified Julius, established by Augustus along with the cult of Rome, see Dio Cassius *Roman History* 51.20.6ff.

33. Downey, *Ancient Antioch*, 75; *History of Antioch*, 155.

34. Josephus *Jewish War* 1.21.11 (425).

35. D. S. Robertson, *Greek and Roman Architecture*, 2d ed. (Cambridge: Cambridge University Press, 1974), 291.

36. Ward-Perkins, *Roman Imperial Architecture*, 313 n. 15.

37. G.A. Williamson, rev. ed. (New York: Penguin, 1980); cf. H. St. J. Thackeray in the Loeb Classical Library, William Whiston (Peabody, Mass.: Hendrickson, 1987), and Gaalyah Cornfeld (Grand Rapids: Zondervan, 1982).

38. Josephus *Antiquities of the Jews* 16.5.3 (148)—trans. Ralph Marcus, Loeb Classical Library.

39. See the discussion in Downey, *History of Antioch*, 173–74, n. 46; idem, *Ancient Antioch*, 83; idem, "Building Records in Malalas," *Byzantinische Zeitschrift* 38 (1938): 300–311.

40. Josephus *Jewish War*, 1.21.11 (425); Downey, *History of Antioch*, 179.

41. Downey, *History of Antioch*, 84–85; Jean Lassus, "Antioch on the Orontes," in *Princeton Encyclopedia of Classical Sites*, ed. Richard Stillwell et al. (Princeton, N.J.: Princeton University Press, 1976), 62.

42. See the beautifully constructed diagram in Downey, *Ancient Antioch*, illus. 24; and in Ward-Perkins, *Roman Imperial Architecture*, 345, illus. 224.

43. Downey, *History of Antioch*, 169ff.

44. Ibid., 190ff.

45. The exact date is unrecorded (Downey, *History of Antioch*, 196).

46. Ibid.

47. Downey, *Ancient Antioch*, 90.

48. See E. J. Bickerman, "The Name of Christians," *HTR* 42 (1949): 71–124; Henry J. Cadbury, "Names for Christians and Christianity in Acts," in F. J. Foakes Jackson and Kirsopp Lake, eds., *The Beginnings of Christianity*, 5 vols. (Grand Rapids: Baker, 1966), 5.375–92.

49. Bruce M. Metzger, "Antioch-on-the-Orontes," *BA* 11 (Dec. 1948): 70.

50. G. A. Eisen, "The Great Chalice of Antioch," *Biblical Review* 11 (Jan. 1926): 40–75.

51. Downey, *History of Antioch*, 274.

52. H. H. Arnason, "The History of the Chalice of Antioch," *BA* 4 (Dec. 1941): 50–64; *BA* 5 (Feb. 1942): 10–16; Floyd V. Filson, "Who Are the Figures on the Chalice of Antioch?" *BA* 5 (Feb. 1942): 1–10; J. Rorimer, "The Authenticity of the Chalice of Antioch," in *Studies in Art and Literature for Belle da Costa Greene*, ed. Dorothy E. Miner (Princeton, N. J.: Princeton University Press, 1954), 161–68.

53. Roman coins from Damascus date until A.D. 34 in the reign of Tiberius, skip a number of years, and then resume in A.D. 62, during the reign of Nero. In the interim, Rome apparently did not exercise direct control over the area, Caligula allowing Aretas IV, king of the Nabateans, to govern Damascus (Aretas had experienced problems with the former emperor, Tiberius, who had sent Vitellius against him in 36/37). Caligula felt that he needed the Nabateans as a buffer against Parthia. In fact Aretas seems to have controlled the east side of the Jordan from Arabia in the south to Damascus in the north. Aretas died in 39 or 40.

54. Josephus *Antiquities of the Jews* 14.2.3 (29). Mark Antony later gave the city to Cleopatra, who held it until Octavian captured it again (*Antiquities* 15.3.8 [79]; 15.4.1 [88–93]).

55. Evidence of this affiliation is the Damascus Rule or the Cairo Damascus Document as it is also known, which was found in 1896 in a synagogue in Cairo, and fragments of which were also found in the Dead Sea Scrolls; see Geza Vermes, *The Dead Sea Scrolls: Qumran in Perspective* (Cleveland: Collins and World, 1978), 48ff. The Hebrew text and German translation are found in Eduard Loshe, *Die Texte aus Qumran* (Darmstadt: Wissenschaftliche, 1964), 66ff. An English translation is found in Geza Vermes,

The Dead Sea Scrolls in English (Baltimore: Penguin, 1966), 95ff.

56. Josephus *Jewish War* 2.20.2 (561).

57. These are the two "rivers of Damascus" to which Naaman of Syria compared to the Jordan (2 Kings 5:12).

58. Philip K. Hitti, *Roman History of Syria* (New York: Macmillan, 1951), 472.

59. Finegan, *Archaeology: Mediterranean World*, 61.

60. Terence B. Mitford, "Roman Rough Cilicia," in *Aufstieg und Niedergang der römischen Welt*, ed. Hildegard Temporini and Wolfgang Haase, sec. 2, vol. 7, pt. 2 (Hawthorne, N.Y.: Walter de Gruyter, 1980), 1238.

61. Strabo *Geography* 14.5.12.

62. In one of his two orations given in Tarsus around A.D. 110. *Oration* 33.34. See T. Callander on these two Tarsian orations in *JHS* (1904): 62.

63. Strabo *Geography* 14.5.10.

64. Ibid.

65. Jerome *Illustrious Men* 5. Gischala, or Gush Halav, has been explored and two synagogues excavated by Eric M. Meyers; see "Excavations at Gush Halav in Upper Galilee," in Lee Levine, ed., *Ancient Synagogues Revealed* (Jerusalem: Israel Exploration Society, 1981), 75ff.

66. Strabo *Geography* 14.5.13.

67. His biographer, Philostratus, gives a less glowing view of Tarsus than does Strabo; but Philostratus is considerably later (ca. A.D. 200) and is probably influenced by Dio Chrysostom's negative views (Philostratus *Life of Apollonius* 1.7; cf. 6.34).

68. Hetty Goldman, *Excavations at Gözlü Kule, Tarsus*, 3 vols. (Princeton, N. J.: Princeton University Press, 1950–63), esp. vol. 1, *The Hellenistic and Roman Periods*.

69. William Ramsay, *The Cities of St. Paul* (London: Hodder and Stoughton, 1907), 85–246.

70. Mitford, "Roman Rough Cilicia," 1230 ff.

71. See Robert Sherk, "Roman Galatia: The Governors from 25 B.C. to A.D. 114," in *Aufstieg und Niedergang der römischen Welt*, ed. Hildegard Temporini and Wolfgang Haase, sec. 2, vol. 7, pt. 2 (Hawthorne, N. Y.: Walter de Gruyter, 1980), 954ff.; Anthony D. Macro, "The Cities of Asia Minor under the Roman Imperium," in *Aufstieg und Niedergang*, sec. 2, vol. 7, pt. 2, p. 666; F. F. Bruce, *The Epistle to the Galatians: A Commentary on the Greek Text*, NIGTC (Grand Rapids: Eerdmans, 1982), 3–18; William Ramsay, *A Historical Commentary on St. Paul's Epistle to the Galatians* (New York:

Putnam, 1899); idem, "Galatia," in *Dictionary of the Bible*, ed. James Hastings, 5 vols. (New York: Scribner, 1900), 2.81–91; idem, "Galatia," in *International Standard Bible Encyclopedia* 4 vols. (Grand Rapids: Eerdmans, 1979–88), 2.1154–55.

72. Strabo says this was because the Roman prefects might not always be present to administer justice or to have armed forces with them (*Geography* 14.5.6).

73. On client kings see Percy C. Sands, *The Client Princes of the Roman Empire under the Republic* (Cambridge: Cambridge University Press, 1908), and David Magie, *Roman Rule in Asia Minor to the End of the Third Century after Christ*, 2 vols. (Princeton, N. J.: Princeton University Press, 1950)—under Pompey, 1.371–78; under Mark Antony, 1.433–36; under Augustus, 1.442–45, 475–76, and under Augustus and Tiberius, 1.494–96.

74. Strabo specifically mentions Cilicia Tracheia (*Geography* 14.6.1). The others are discussed by Barbara Levick, *Roman Colonies in Southern Asia Minor* (Oxford: Clarendon, 1967), 27–28.

75. Strabo *Geography* 12.5.1; 12.6.5. The date may be discerned from Dio Cassius *Roman History* 53.26.3, who, while describing events in the year 25 B.C., affirms that Augustus made Galatia a province at the time of the death of Amyntas. For Augustus's ideas of governing this part of the world see Glen W. Bowersock, *Augustus and the Greek World* (Oxford: Clarendon, 1965), 42–61.

76. The Tolistobogii (around Pessinus and Gordium), the Tectosages (around Ancyra) and the Trocmi (on the right bank of the Halys)—Strabo *Geography* 12.5.1–2.

77. On the question of Pamphylia see Sherk, "Roman Galatia," 959.

78. Shortly after Paul left the area, Pontus was added to Galatia in A.D. 64, and Armenia Minor in 72 (Sherk, "Roman Galatia," 962–63). For the creation of the province see Levick, *Roman Colonies*, 29ff.

79. Ramsay, *Cities of St. Paul*; Macro, "Cities of Asia Minor," 658ff.; A. H. M. Jones, *The Greek City from Alexander to Justinian* (Oxford: Clarendon, 1940); idem, *Cities of the Eastern Roman Provinces* (Oxford: Clarendon, 1971); Magie, *Roman Rule*; George M. A. Hanfmann, *From Croesus to Constantine: The Cities of Western Asia Minor and Their Arts in Greek and Roman Times* (Ann Arbor: University of Michigan Press, 1975).

For a survey of western Asia Minor see J. M. Cook and D. J. Blackman, "Archaeology in Western Asia Minor," *ARep*. 17 (1970–71): 33–62; succeeding it are Stephen Mitchell and A. W. McNicoll, "Archaeology in Western and Southern Asia Minor, 1971–78," *ARep*. 25 (1978–79): 59–90; and Stephen Mitchell, "Archaeology in Asia Minor, 1979–84," *ARep*. 31 (1984–85): 70–105. Annual reports on most of the current excavations in Turkey appear in *Anatolian Studies: Recent Archaeological Research in Turkey*. Broader in scope but less detailed is Machteld Mellink's annual newsletter "Archaeology in Asia Minor" in *AJA*—see most recently "Archaeology in Anatolia," in *AJA* 93.1 (Jan. 1989): 105–33. Since 1979, the Turkish Department of Antiquities has published reports of the preceding year's excavations, which are read in an annual colloquium (*I–V Kazi Sonuclari Toplantisi [1979–84]*). Epigraphical studies are abundant—in addition to Louis Robert's *Bulletin épigraphique* we have the newly revived *Supplementum Epigraphicum Graecum*, as well as the Cologne series *Inschriften griechischer Städten aus Kleinasien* (now running to 28 vols.), and the RECAM and RECAM II projects of the British Institute of Archaeology at Ankara. For further publications in Turkish and other languages see *ARep*. articles cited above; see also Edwin Yamauchi, "Recent Work in the Cities of Western Anatolia," *NEASB*, n.s. 13 (1979): 37–116 and n.s. 14 (1979): 5–48; Bastiaan Van Elderen, "Some Archaeological Observations on Paul's First Missionary Journey," in W. Ward Gasque and R. P. Martin, eds., *Apostolic Roman History and the Gospel* (Exeter: Paternoster, 1970), 151–61.

80. Stephen Mitchell, "Population and the Land in Roman Galatia," in *Aufstieg und Niedergang: der römischen Welt*, ed. Hildegard Temporini and Wolfgang Haase, sec. 2, vol. 7, pt. 2 (Hawthorne, N. Y.: Walter de Gruyler, 1980), 1058–59. Epigraphic indices for central Anatolia, compiled by Mitchell, show that 4.6 percent of the personal names found in the area are Celtic. Celtic place names presumably also replaced old Phrygian forms.

81. Ibid.

82. Strabo *Geography* 13.4.13; he describes central Anatolia as having a heterogeneous population consisting of Paphlagonians, Galatians, Phrygians, Lycaonians, Isaurians, and Pisidians, but does not try to clearly delineate their respective boundaries (12.4.4; 13.4.12; 14.5.7).

83. Magie, *Roman Rule*, 1.460.

84. William Ramsay, *St. Paul the Traveller and the Roman Citizen* (London: Hodder and Stoughton, 1908), 119; cf. 218.

85. Macro, "Cities of Asia Minor," 674–75.

86. Mitchell, "Population and the Land," 1063.

87. Strabo *Geography* 12.6.4—πρὸς with the dative case here probably means "near" (Magie, *Roman Rule*, 1.457) rather than "towards" (Barbara Levick, "Antioch," in *Princeton Encyclopedia of Classical Sites*, 60); see also Ramsay, *Cities of St. Paul*, 247–48; and Magie, *Roman Rule*, 2.1315 n. 21.

88. The modern name is not Turkish and probably preserves the original "Antioch" (Jones, *Cities of the Eastern Roman Provinces*, 128–29).

89. Besides Ramsay's well-known books referred to elsewhere in this chapter, see also "Some Inscriptions of Colonia Caesarea Antiochia," *JRS* 14 (1924): 172ff.; "Map of Yallowadj" and "Inscriptions of Antioch of Phrygia-towards-Pisidia," *JRS* 16 (1926): 107ff.; "Dedications at the Sanctuary of Colonia Caesarea," *JRS* 8 (1918): 107ff.

90. Ramsay published an unsatisfactory account of his work in *JRS* 8 (1918): 107–45. D. M. Robinson, who worked with him for a time, published a preliminary report of later excavations in *AJA* 28 (1924): 435–44, and an illustrated report of the sculptures in *Art Bulletin* 9 (1926): 5–69.

91. See the two reports by Stephen Mitchell, "Recent Archaeological Research in Turkey" in *AS* 33 (1983): 7–9 and *AS* 34 (1984): 8–10.

92. The *Res Gestae* is the "chronicle of Augustus' services, achievements and benefactions with an interpretation of his career which is not all the truth, for truth is not all its purpose" (F. E. Adcock, "The Achievement of Augustus," in *Cambridge Ancient History*, vol. 10, *The Augustan Empire*, ed. S. A. Cook et al. (Cambridge: Cambridge University Press, 1971), 593. A copy of the *Res Gestae* was left in the temple of the Vestal Virgins in Rome, copied on bronze tablets before Augustus's mausoleum in Rome, and chiseled in stone on the walls of many temples throughout Asia Minor. It is rather well preserved on the walls of the Temple of Rome and Augustus in Ancyra, Asia Minor. See *Res Gestae Divi Augusti*, trans. F. W. Shipley, Loeb Classical Library (New York: Putnam, 1924), 332ff.; Magie, *Roman Rule*, 1.459–60, 470, 476; Ward-Perkins, *Roman Imperial Architecture*, 21, 25, 279.

93. Mitchell, "Recent Archaeological Research," *AS* 33 (1983): 8.

94. That the temple was dedicated to Augustus is probable, though not unequivocally attested (Mitchell, "Recent Archaeological Research," *AS* 34 [1984]: 9).

95. Ward-Perkins, *Roman Imperial Architecture*, 280; Robertson, *Greek and Roman Architecture*, 210–12.

96. Mitchell, "Recent Archaeological Research," *AS* 33 (1983): 8.

97. Mitchell, "Recent Archaeological Research," *AS* 34 (1984): 9.

98. Mitchell, "Archaeology in Asia Minor, 1979–84," 99; on the cult, see S. R. F. Price, *Rituals and Power: The Roman Imperial Cult in Asia Minor* (Cambridge: Cambridge University Press, 1983).

99. "Substantial domestic houses with colonnades, courtyards and often several internal rooms" were found around the Sanctuary of Men and "over many of the central areas of the site." Mitchell, "Recent Archaeological Research," *AS* 34 (1984): 10.

100. Ramsay, *Cities of St. Paul*, 385–404.

101. Michael Ballance, "Site of Derbe: A New Inscription," *AS* 7 (1957): 147–51. The stone is now in the new Museum for Classical Antiquities at Konya.

102. Bastiaan Van Elderen, "Further Confirmation of the New Site for Derbe" (paper delivered at the 1963 annual meeting of the Society of Biblical Literature, New York); idem, "Some Archaeological Observations," 158, n. 2.

103. Both inscriptions are published in Van Elderen, "Some Archaeological Observations," 157–58.

104. Michael Ballance, "The Site of Derbe," 147–51; idem, "Derbe and Faustinopolis," *AS* 14 (1964): 139–40.

105. F. F. Bruce, *New Testament Roman History* (London: Nelson, 1969), 259.

106. Van Elderen, "Some Archaeological Observations," 159.

107. Bruce, *Paul*, 171.

108. Levick, *Roman Colonies*, 43, n. 2.

109. See Ekrem Akurgal, *Ancient Civilizations and Ruins of Turkey*, 2d ed. (Istanbul: Mobil Oil Turk A.S., 1970), 331 (I have been unable to obtain later editions). See also George E. Bean, *Turkey's Southern Shore: An Archaeological Guide* (New York: Praeger, 1968), 45–58; A. M. Mansel and A. Akarca, *Excavations and Researches at Perga* (Ankara: 1949). Excavations since the death of Mansel,

Perga's excavator, have been published in *TAD* by J. Inan.

110. Mitchell and McNicoll, "Archaeology in Western and Southern Asia Minor, 1971–78," 88; Ward-Perkins, *Roman Imperial Architecture*, 301.

111. Ward-Perkins, *Roman Imperial Architecture*, 301. For remains from the late Roman and Byzantine periods see Akurgal, *Ancient Civilizations*, 329–33; George E. Bean, "Perge," in *Princeton Encyclopedia of Classical Sites*, 692–93.

112. Levick, *Roman Colonies*, 43 n. 2.

113. Ward-Perkins, *Roman Imperial Architecture*, 299.

114. Levick, *Roman Colonies*, 43 n. 2.

115. See A. M. Mansel, *Die Ruinen von Side* (Berlin: Walter de Gruyter, 1963); an overall view of Mansel's years of excavating the site is now published in his *Side (1947–66): Yıllari Kazilari ve Arastirmalari Sonuclari* (Ankara: 1978). See also Mitchell and McNicoll, "Archaeology in Western and Southern Asia Minor, 1971–78," 88; Mitchell, "Archaeology in Asia Minor, 1979–84," 103; Akurgal, *Ancient Civilizations*, 336–41.

116. Ward-Perkins, *Roman Imperial Architecture*, 300, illus. 194.

117. Ibid., 299.

118. Strabo *Geography* 14.3.2.

Chapter 8

1. David Magie, *Roman Rule in Asia Minor to the End of the Third Century after Christ*, 2 vols. (Princeton, N.J.: Princeton University Press, 1950), 1.154–55; A. H. M. Jones, *Cities of the Eastern Roman Provinces* (Oxford: Clarendon, 1971), 59ff.

2. Magie, *Roman Rule*, 1.39.

3. David French, *Roman Roads and Milestones of Asia Minor*, vol. 1, *The Pilgrim's Road*, and vol. 2, *An Interim Catalogue of Milestones*, British Archaeological Reports, International Series 105 and 392 (Oxford: BAR., 1981, 1988).

4. Chester Beatty, p^{46}; original copyists of codices Vaticanus and Sinaiticus.

5. *TAD* 17.2 (1968): 73–76; 20.2 (1973): 17–27. Colin J. Hemer's report in a 1985 article that "it has not been excavated" apparently is meant to say that little has been done ("Seven Cities of Asia Minor," in R. K. Harrison, ed., *Major Cities of the Biblical World* [Nashville: Nelson, 1985], 242).

6. G. Petzl, *ZPE* 23 (1976): 243–50; see also Stephen Mitchell and A. W. McNicoll, "Archaeology in Western and Southern Asia Minor, 1971–78," *ARep.* 25 (1978–79): 70.

7. Ümit Serdaroğlu, "Thyateira," in *Princeton Encyclopedia of Classical Sites*, ed. Richard Stillwell et al. (Princeton, N.J.: Princeton University Press, 1976), 919.

8. Magie, *Roman Rule*, 1.47–48; *IGR* 4.1252 (λαναριοι). See also Magie, *Roman Rule*, 2.812 n. 79.

9. *IGR* 5.1250, 1213, 1265; see others cited in Magie, *Roman Rule*, 2.812 n. 80.

10. Strabo *Geography* 13.4.10.

11. Hemer, "Seven Cities," 246.

12. "I might almost say that the whole of the territory in the neighborhood of the Meander is subject to earthquakes" (Strabo *Geography* 12.8.17).

13. Suetonius *Lives of the Caesars*, "Tiberius," 8; Strabo *Geography* 12.8.18.

14. Strabo *Geography* 12.8.18; Tacitus *Annals* 2.47.

15. In A.D. 26, Laodicea was denied the honor of erecting a temple to the emperor Tiberius, because it lacked sufficient resources. This must be understood in a comparative sense (George E. Bean, *Turkey beyond the Maeander: An Archaeological Guide* [London: Ernest Benn, 1971], 249). However, Strabo, who died ca. A.D. 21, said that the fertility of its territory and the prosperity of certain of its citizens made Laodicea great (*Geography* 12.8.16).

16. Strabo *Geography* 14.27.

17. For background material in ancient sources see Magie, *Roman Rule*, 2.986–87. Most of the important inscriptions relating to Laodicea and nearby Colossae are found in *MAMA*, vol. 6, *Monuments and Documents from Phrygia and Caria*, and William M. Ramsay, *The Cities and Bishoprics of Phrygia, Being an Essay of the Local Roman History of Phrygia from the Earliest Times to the Turkish Conquest* (Oxford: Clarendon, 1895), vol. 1.

18. Pliny the Elder *Natural History* 5.29 (105); Bean, *Turkey beyond the Maeander*, 249.

19. Cicero *Ad Atticum* 6.3.9; see D. R. S. Bailey, *Cicero's Letters to Atticus*, 6 vols. (Cambridge: Cambridge University Press, 1968), 3.120–21.

20. Bean, *Turkey beyond the Maeander*, 251.

21. Ibid., 254–55.

22. Ramsay, *Cities and Bishoprics*, 1.72.

23. John Knox argued a fascinating but unconvincing view that Philemon may have been the overseer of the churches in the Lycus Valley in succession to Epaphras, and that Onesimus may have been the slave of Archippus, to whom appeal is made via Philemon to free Onesimus for missionary duty. Knox would place Philemon in Laodicea rather than in Colossae, which Col. 4:9 implies was the home of Onesimus (*Philemon among the Letters of Paul* [Chicago: University of Chicago Press, 1935], 18ff, 49; *Marcion and the New Testament* [Chicago: University of Chicago Press, 1942], 33–76). C. F. D. Moule provides a condensed summary of the argument in *The Epistles of Paul the Apostle to the Colossians and to Philemon*, Cambridge Greek Testament Commentary (Cambridge: Cambridge University Press, 1958), 14–18.

24. *MAMA* 6.15.

25. William F. Arndt and F. Wilbur Gingrich, *A Greek-English Lexicon of the New Testament and Other Early Christian Literature* (Chicago: University of Chicago Press, 1957), 283.

26. F. Blass and A. Debrunner, *A Greek Grammar of the New Testament and Other Early Christian Literature*, trans. Robert W. Funk (Chicago: University of Chicago Press, 1961), 68.

27. Strabo has an interesting description of the water, the channels, and the springs from which it arises (*Geography* 13.4.14).

28. Interim reports appear in *TAD* and *AS*; see also Mitchell and McNicoll, "Archaeology in Western and Southern Asia Minor, 1971–78," 75; Stephen Mitchell, "Archaeology in Asia Minor, 1979–84," *ARep.* 31 (1984–85): 94–97.

29. William Ramsay, "Hierapolis," in *Dictionary of the Bible*, ed. James Hastings, 5 vols. (New York: Scribner, 1900), 2.380; George E. Bean, *Turkey beyond the Maeander*, 235; idem, "Hierapolis," in *Princeton Encyclopedia of Classical Sites*, 390.

30. Eusebius *Ecclesiastical History* 3.31.2–3. F. F. Bruce supports this view (*Paul: Apostle of the Heart Set Free* [Grand Rapids: Eerdmans, 1977], 343).

31. See the bibliography on the inscriptions in Sherman Johnson, "Laodicea and Its Neighbors," *BA* 13 (Feb. 1950): 14 nn. 26, 30.

32. Dio Cassius *Roman History* 68.27 compared the spring to a similar spring in Babylon. The one in Hierapolis was enclosed in a sort of cistern and had a theater built over it. See also Strabo *Geography* 13.4.14.

33. W. Harold Mare, "Archaeological Prospects at Colossae," *NEASB* 7 (1976): 42.

34. Some of these are conveniently documented by Edwin Yamauchi, *Archaeology of New Testament Cities in Western Asia Minor* (Grand Rapids: Baker, 1980), 160–61.

35. Bean, *Turkey beyond the Maeander*, 257–59.

36. Ibid., 258—not Bean himself, as Yamauchi erroneously reported (*New Testament Cities*, 159).

37. Strabo *Geography* 12.8.14. See the text in the Loeb Classical Library; see also Mare, "Archaeological Prospects."

38. Otto F. A. Meinardus, "Colossus, Colossae, Colossi: Confusio Colossaea," *BA* 36 (Feb. 1973): 33–36.

39. Eric M. Meyers and L. Michael White, "Jews and Christians in a Roman World," *Archaeology* 42 (March–April 1989): 31.

40. George M. A. Hanfmann, *From Croesus to Constantine: The Cities of Western Asia Minor and Their Arts in Greek and Roman Times* (Ann Arbor: University of Michigan Press, 1975), 48–49.

41. Hanfmann provides the following figures: Ephesus, the largest, had two hundred thousand; Pergamum and Sardis had one hundred twenty thousand; and Smyrna had one hundred thousand (*From Croesus to Constantine*, 49). C. P. Jones excludes Sardis from his list of the largest cities (*The Roman World of Dio Chrysostom* [Cambridge, Mass.: Harvard University Press, 1978], 69).

42. Jones, *Roman World*, 69.

43. Strabo *Geography* 14.1.21.

44. Ekrem Akurgal, *Ancient Civilizations and Ruins of Turkey*, 2d ed. (Istanbul: Mobil Oil Turk A. S., 1970), 169.

45. For text and bibliography see G. H. R. Horsley, *New Documents Illustrating Early Christianity*, 5 vols. (Sydney: Macquarie University Press, 1981–87), 4.74.

46. Strabo *Geography* 12.8.15; 14.1.24; see his description of Ephesus in 14.1.20–24.

47. A helpful tool in the study of Ephesus is Richard Oster, *A Bibliography of Ancient Ephesus*, American Theological Library Association Bibliography Series 19 (Metuchen, N.J.: Scarecrow, 1987).

48. Dio Chrysostom *Discourses* 31.54 says money was kept here for safekeeping because the Temple of Artemis seemed to successfully resist violation through the years.

49. Strabo *Geography* 14.1.24.

50. Machteld Mellink, "Archaeology in Anatolia," *AJA* 93.l (Jan. 1989): 125.

51. Mitchell, "Archaeology in Asia Minor, 1979–87," 83.

52. An inscription found in the excavation of the Magnesian Gate traces the processional route from the Artemision, through the Magnesian Gate, to the theater, through the Koressos Gate, and back to the Artemision (Akurgal, *Ancient Civilizations*, 169).

53. "Recent Archaeological Research in Turkey," in *AS* 36 (1986): 193. On the Hippodamian pattern see pp. 000–000.

54. Akurgal, *Ancient Civilizations*, 157.

55. The agora had been raised under Augustus to the level of the southeastern gate constructed at that time; see "Recent Archaeological Research in Turkey," in *AS* 35 (1985): 191.

56. Ibid.

57. Two inscriptions in Latin and Greek, written on the triple gateway, record that these two former slaves, who had been freed by Agrippa, built the gate in honor of the emperor Augustus and his wife Livia, and in honor of Agrippa and Julia (Augustus's son-in-law and daughter) (Akurgal, *Ancient Civilizations*, 161).

58. On the importance of this office see A. H. M. Jones, *The Greek City from Alexander to Justinian* (Oxford: Clarendon, 1940), 238–40; and Magie, *Roman Rule*, 1.60, and 2.848 n. 32.

59. E. L. Hicks, *The Collection of Ancient Greek Inscriptions in the British Museum* III.2 (Oxford: Clarendon, 1980), 482 (see also the addendum on 294). The inscription, which dates to the mid-second century A.D., is conveniently available in Horsley, *New Documents*, 4.49–51.

60. Aristio from A.D. 92 to 93 (*IEph* 2.461, 508), who appears in at least twenty-five inscriptions, and a contemporary T. Flavius Pythio (Horsley, *New Documents*, 4.49–51).

61. Other provinces had similar officials—Bithyniarch, Galatarch, Lyciarch, etc. (Lily Taylor, "The Asiarchs," in F. J. Foakes Jackson and Kirsopp Lake, eds., *The Beginnings of Christianity* [Grand Rapids: Baker, 1966], 4.256).

62. See G. Abbott-Smith, *A Manual Greek Lexicon of the New Testament* (Edinburgh: T and T Clark, 1950), 95.

63. Strabo *Geography* 14.1.42.

64. Dio Chrysostom *Discourses* 35.10. See the discussion in Taylor, "Asiarchs," 256ff., and more recently the discussion in Horsley, *New Documents*, 4.46–55.

65. *IEph*; newly discovered inscriptions are being published in *Österre-*

ichische Jahreshefte. See "Recent Archaeological Research in Turkey," in *AS* 35 (1985): 191.

66. See the texts and extensive comments in Horsley, *New Documents*, 4.46–55, where the careers of four Asiarchs are traced on 49ff.

67. The most recent publication of a list of the Asiarchs is by M. Rossner, *StudClas* 16 (1974): 101–42; see also Horsley, *New Documents*, 4.49ff.

68. R. A. Kearsley, "Some Asiarchs of Ephesos," in Horsley, *New Documents*, 4.46ff. Glen W. Bowersock assumes that the Asiarchs were also high priests (*Augustus and the Greek World* [Oxford: Clarendon, 1965], 117). Rossner agrees (*StudClas* 16 [1974]: 102).

69. F. F. Bruce, *The Book of Acts*, New International Commentary on the New Testament, rev. ed. (Grand Rapids: Eerdmans, 1988), 376–77.

70. Akurgal, *Ancient Civilizations*, 148. For measurements based on recent excavation see "Recent Archaeological Research in Turkey," in *AS* 37 (1987): 189.

71. Ibid.

72. Ibid.

73. Mitchell and McNicoll, "Archaeology in Western and Southern Asia Minor, 1971–78," 72; Mitchell, "Archaeology in Asia Minor, 1979–84," 84; a detailed report of recent excavations is given in Anton Bammer, "Forschungen im Artemision von Ephesos von 1976 bis 1981," in *AS* 32 (1982): 61–87.

74. Argued by W. Jobst, *Ist. Mitt.* 30 (1980): 241–60; and K. Tuchelt, *Ist. Mitt.* 31 (1981): 180–82; see also Mitchell, "Archaeology in Asia Minor, 1979–84," 84.

75. Mitchell and McNicoll, "Archaeology in Western and Southern Asia Minor, 1971–78," 71.

76. Mitchell and McNicoll, "Archaeology in Western and Southern Asia Minor, 1979–84," 83.

77. Ibid.; "Recent Archaeological Research in Turkey," in *AS* 37 (1987): 189.

78. An impressive photo may be seen in Paul MacKendrick, *The Greek Stones Speak: The Story of Archaeology in Greek Lands*, rev. ed. (New York: St. Martin's, 1962), 423.

79. Eusebius *Ecclesiastical History* 3.17.1; 3.18.1. Eusebius in the fourth century seems to be citing Irenaeus in the second century. Irenaeus does affirm that the apocalyptic vision of Revelation was received in the reign of Domitian (*Against Heresies* 5.30.3—see the Greek text in Irenaeus, *Libros quinque adversus haereses*, ed. W. W. Harvey, 2 vols. [Ridgewood, N.J.: Gregg, 1965], 2.410).

80. Eusebius *Ecclesiastical History* 3.20.8–9; 3.21.l; Irenaeus *Against Heresies* 2.22.5; 3.3.4.

81. Robert H. Charles identifies the John at Ephesus as "the Elder" rather than "the Apostle" (*The Revelation of St. John*, International Critical Commentary 44, 2 vols. [New York: Scribner, 1920], 1.29–56.

82. Akurgal, *Ancient Civilizations*, 145.

83. Max Cary, *A History of Rome*, 2d ed. (New York: Macmillan, 1962), 510.

84. Magie, *Roman Rule*, 1.501.

85. Ibid.; Tacitus *Annals* 4.37–55.

86. Magie, *Roman Rule*, 1.572; 2.1432; cf. 1.448.

87. Ibid., 1.637; 2.1433, 1451.

88. Ibid., 2.1433.

89. Ibid., 2.1432.

90. Horsley, *New Documents*, 4.74; see also J. T. Wood, "Inscriptions from the City and Suburbs," in *Discoveries at Ephesus* (London: Longmans, Green, 1877), #12 and 15.

91. Magie, *Roman Rule*, 1.594, 615, and 619 respectively.

92. Ibid., 1.637.

93. See Wood, "Inscriptions from the Temple of Diana," in *Discoveries at Ephesus*, #1 and 2. See also the extended discussion and references in Magie, *Roman Rule*, 2.847–48; and inscription #28 with discussion in Horsley, *New Documents*, 4.127.

94. *IEph* 8.1; see index. For νεōποιος see Horsley, *New Documents*, 4.7, 127 (#1 and 28); for νεωποιος see Wood, "Inscriptions from the Temple of Diana," in *Discoveries at Ephesus*, #1 (n. 5) and 2; for νεωποιης see *IG2²*, #1678b.

95. William M. Ramsay, *The Church in the Roman Empire before A.D. 170*, 7th ed. (London: Hodder and Stoughton, 1903), 112–45.

96. *IEph* 6.2212; Horsley, *New Documents*, 4.7 (#1).

97. MacKendrick, *Greek Stones Speak*, 422.

98. E.g., James H. Moulton and George Milligan, *The Vocabulary of the Greek Testament* (London: Hodder and Stoughton, 1952); Arndt and Gingrich, *Greek-English Lexicon*. For other inscriptions see Horsley, *New Documents*, 4.7.

99. James Blevins, "The Genre of Revelation," *Review and Expositor* 77 (1980): 393–408.

100. It was customary for public gatherings to meet in the theater (*IEph* 1.27).

101. Barbara Levick, "Two Inscriptions from Pisidian Antioch," *AS* 15 (1965): 58–59.

102. *IEph*, 2.554. The form χαρκ– is equivalent to χαλκ– (see Horsley, *New Documents*, 4.10). In Acts Alexander is called, more briefly, *chalkeus* (χαλκεύς).

103. On the several fountains, gymnasia, and baths, see Veronika Mitsopoulou-Leon, "Ephesus," in *Princeton Encyclopedia of Classical Sites*, 306–10; Akurgal, *Ancient Civilizations*, 142–71.

104. Mitchell and McNicoll, "Archaeology in Western and Southern Asia Minor, 1971–78," 72.

105. Archibald Robertson and Alfred Plummer, *A Critical and Exegetical Commentary on the First Epistle of St. Paul to the Corinthians*, 2d ed., International Critical Commentary (Edinburgh: T. and T. Clark, 1958), 362.

106. Akurgal, *Ancient Civilizations*, 159–61.

107. Mitchell and McNicoll, "Archaeology in Western and Southern Asia Minor, 1971–78," 71.

108. Akurgal, *Ancient Civilizations*, 161; the inscription is in J. Keil, *Ephesos: Ein Führer durch die Ruinenstätte und ihre Geschichte*, 5th ed. (Vienna: Österreichisches Archäologisches Institut, 1964), 109.

109. Colin J. Hemer, "Audeitorion," *Tyndale Bulletin* 24 (1973): 128.

110. *AS* 36 (1986): 193.

111. Akurgal, *Ancient Civilizations*, 161.

112. Hanfmann, *From Croesus to Constantine*, 49. Magie puts the population of Ephesus, Pergamum, and Smyrna at approximately 200,000 in the Flavian period (*Roman Rule*, 1.585).

113. Magie, *Roman Rule*, 1.121.

114. Strabo *Geography* 13.4.5; Herodotus *History* 1.93.

115. Pliny the Elder *Natural History* 5.30.

116. Magie, *Roman Rule*, 1.47, 49. Pliny the Elder asserted that the process of dyeing was invented in Sardis (*Natural History* 7.56).

117. For a collection of these sources in the original with English translation see John G. Pedley, *Ancient Literary Sources on Sardis* (Cambridge, Mass.: Harvard University Press, 1972), esp. 62–66.

118. Pliny the Elder *Natural History* 2.86.

119. Strabo *Geography* 12.8.18.

120. Tacitus *Annals* 2.47.

121. Ibid., and Strabo *Geography* 12.8.18.

122. George M. A. Hanfmann and William E. Mierse, *Sardis from Prehistoric to Roman Times: Results of the Archaeological Exploration of Sardis 1958–1975* (Cambridge, Mass.: Harvard University Press, 1983), 144.

123. Ibid., 142.

124. Ibid., 275 n. 29.

125. Ibid., 280 n. 17.

126. David Mitten, "A New Look at Ancient Sardis," *BA* 29 (May 1966): 63.

127. See fig. 1 in Hanfmann and Mierse, *Sardis*.

128. Ibid., 143.

129. A. R. Seager, "The Building History of the Sardis Synagogue," *AJA* 76.4 (Oct. 1972): 425–35; idem, "The Synagogue at Sardis," in Lee Levine, ed., *Ancient Synagogues Revealed* (Jerusalem: Israel Exploration Society, 1981), 178–84; idem and A. T. Kraabel, "The Synagogue and the Jewish Community," in Hanfmann and Mierse, *Sardis*, 168–90.

130. Hanfmann and Mierse, *Sardis*, 143.

131. Hanfmann and Mierse, *Sardis*, 118, 145 (and n. 73), 146 (and n. 96).

132. F. K. Yegul, "Roman Architecture at Sardis," in Eleanor Guralnick, ed., *Sardis: Twenty-Seven Years of Discovery* (Chicago: Archaeological Institute of America, 1987), 50–51.

133. See the diagram in Hanfmann and Mierse, *Sardis*, fig. 173. A description of the stadium will be found in R. L. Vann, *The Unexcavated Buildings of Sardis* (Oxford: B.A.R. 1989).

134. "The unusual tangential conjunction of theater and stadium may be Hellenistic; but the barrel–vaulted eastern slope of the stadium is . . . post-A.D. 17 Roman construction" (Hanfmann and Mierse, *Sardis*, 116).

135. Vann, *Unexcavated Buildings*.

136. Hanfmann and Mierse, *Sardis*, 119.

137. H. C. Butler, *Sardis*, Publications of the American Society for the Excavation of Sardis, 17 vols. (Cambridge, Mass.: Harvard University Press, 1922–). Volume 1 contains an account of the several seasons of excavation of the temple. A detailed recent discussion of the work on the temple may be found in Report 1 of the expedition by George M. A. Hanfmann and Jane C. Waldbaum, *A Survey of Sardis and the Major Monuments Outside the City Walls* (Cambridge, Mass.: Harvard University Press, 1975), chaps. 4–7.

138. Butler, *Sardis*, 2.61, 135–39, and illus. 66.

139. Hanfmann and Waldbaum, Report 1, *Survey of Sardis*, 26, 75. The 1979 discovery of a cylindrical statue base with a dedicatory inscription in honor of Tiberius has been referred to on p. 145.

140. C. Ratté, T. Howe, and C. Foss, "An Early Imperial Pseudodipteral Temple at Sardis," *AJA* 90.1 (Jan. 1986): 45–68; Mitchell, "Archaeology in Asia Minor, 1979–84," 81.

141. Yegul, "Roman Architecture at Sardis," 50–51.

142. Ibid., 63, 65.

143. See Dio Cassius *Roman History* 51.20; Suetonius *Lives of the Caesars*, "Augustus," 53; Magie, *Roman Rule*, 1.417, 447.

144. Cary, *History of Rome*, 510.

145. Pergamum already had theirs to Augustus, and Ephesus had the world-renowned Artemis Temple. Smyrna was chosen by the Roman senate over Sardis because of the antiquity of its relations with Rome and its special services to the late Republic (Tacitus *Annals* 4.37–55; Magie, *Roman Rule*, 1.447, 501).

146. Dio Cassius *Roman History* 59.28.1.

147. See the discussion in Ratté et al., "An Early Imperial Pseudodipteral Temple," 66–67.

148. Strabo *Geography* 13.67.

149. Tacitus *Annals* 2.47.

150. On the Trajaneum see Magie, *Roman Rule*, 2.1451 n. 7.

151. Dio Chrysostom *Discourses* 31.148.

152. See the discussion of neōkoroi in connection with Ephesus (pp. 257–58); Magie, *Roman Rule*, 2.1432 n. 18, 1451 n. 7.

153. *Catalogue of Coins in the British Museum: Mysia* (London: British Museum, Department of Coins and Medals), 142, nos. 262–63; Magie, *Roman Rule*, 2.1451 n. 7.

154. See the annual reports in *AS*—"Recent Archaeological Research in Turkey."

155. Elisabeth Rhode, *Pergamon: Burgberg und Altar* (Berlin: Henschel, 1961); Max Kunze, *The Altar of Pergamum* (Berlin: State Museums, Department of Greek and Roman Antiquities, 1986).

156. Tacitus *Annals* 4.37.

157. See the excellent article on Pergamum by William Ramsay in *Dictionary of the Bible*, ed. Hastings, 3.749ff.

158. C. H. V. Sutherland, *Coinage in Roman Imperial Policy* (London: Methuen, 1951), 43 (see plate II, coin 4); Harold Mattingly and E. A. Sydenham, *Roman Imperial Coinage* (London: Spink, 1923), 1.61, no. 15; Magie, *Roman Rule*, 2.1293 n. 52. Coins with Augustus's image and a temple front having sometimes six but usually four columns were minted under Augustus and his successors in the first century (*Catalogue of Coins in the British*

Museum: Mysia, 137–38, nos. 236–37 and 252–53).

159. Vitruvius *On Architecture* 7.4.

160. Strabo *Geography* 13.1.54.

161. Dio Cassius *Roman History* 42.38.2.

162. Plutarch *Parallel Lives*, "Antony" 58.5.

163. *Encyclopaedia Britannica*, 1970 ed., s.v. "Library," 13.1032.

164. Vitruvius *On Architecture* 7.4.

165. Dio Cassius *Roman History* 42.38.2. *The Encyclopaedia Britannica* minimizes the damage done at this time, affirming that the library was not destroyed until the third century A.D. ("Library," 1032).

166. Plutarch *Parallel Lives* "Antony" 58.5.

167. Pliny the elder *Natural History* 13.21.

168. For the latest (1986) survey of the lower part of the theater and some of the terrace see "Recent Archaeological Research in Turkey," in *AS* 37 (1987): 214.

169. Ibid., 211–14; Machteld Mellink, "Archaeology in Asia Minor," *AJA* 85.4 (Oct. 1981): 475.

170. J. B. Ward-Perkins, *Roman Imperial Architecture* (New York: Penguin, 1983), 296.

171. For the gymnasium in Beroea see p. 296. For more on the gymnasium in Pergamum see Akurgal, *Ancient Civilizations*, 95ff.

172. Adolf Deissmann, *St. Paul: A Study in Social and Religious History* (New York: Hodder and Stoughton, 1912), 262.

173. Akurgal, *Ancient Civilizations*, 104.

174. The Asklepieion was founded about 400 B.C. (J. Schafer, "Pergamon," in *Princeton Encyclopedia of Classical Sites*, 691.

175. Ibid.

176. Ward-Perkins, *Roman Imperial Architecture*, 277; Schafer, "Pergamon," 691.

177. Akurgal dates it to A.D. 150 (*Ancient Civilizations*, 110).

178. Ward-Perkins, *Roman Imperial Architecture*, 277; see also Akurgal, *Ancient Civilizations*, 105ff.

179. Strabo *Geography* 14.1.37.

180. Akurgal, *Ancient Civilizations*, 121–22.

181. Strabo, *Geography* 14.1.37.

182. "Smyrna," in *PW* 3.1.758.

183. Akurgal, *Ancient Civilizations*, 122; idem, "Smyrna," in *Princeton Encyclopedia of Classical Sites*, 848.

184. E.g., Akurgal, *Ancient Civilizations*, 121.

185. Magie, *Roman Rule*, 2.1446 n. 50.

186. Ibid., 1.585.

187. Strabo *Geography* 14.1.37.

188. Akurgal, "Smyrna," in *Princeton Encyclopedia of Classical Sites*, 847.

189. Ibid.

190. Tacitus enumerates these cities, which included Ephesus, Pergamum, Miletus, Sardis, and Smyrna (*Annals* 4.15.4, 37–55). On the process of selection see the discussion on Pergamum (pp. 257–58), and Magie, *Roman Rule*, 1.501.

191. *IGR* 4.1391.

192. *Catalogue of Coins in the British Museum: Ionia*, 268, nos. 266–67; see also Magie, *Roman Rule*, 2.1360 n. 26.

193. *IGR* 4.541 and 1482b equals *CIL* 3.471; see also Magie, *Roman Rule*, 2.1474 n. 15.

194. *IGR* 4.1431.

195. Ward-Perkins, *Roman Imperial Architecture*, 287.

196. Ibid., 366–67.

197. Akurgal, *Ancient Civilizations*, 123.

198. Ibid.; idem, "Smyrna," in *Princeton Encyclopedia of Classical Sites*, 848.

199. Eusebius *Ecclesiastical History* 3.18.1.

Chapter 9

1. F. F. Bruce, *Commentary on the Book of the Acts*, New International Commentary (Grand Rapids: Eerdmans, 1956), 327.

2. Otto F. A. Meinardus, *St. Paul in Greece*, 4th ed. (Athens: Lycabettus, 1984), 4.

3. There is no reason to assume with Meinardus (*St. Paul*, 5) that Luke may already have been a Christian practicing medicine in Philippi when he came to meet Paul in Troas.

4. Mary Renault, *The Nature of Alexander* (New York: Pantheon, 1976), 21.

5. Pliny the Elder *Natural History* 36.5.25.

6. Richard Stoneman, ed., *A Literary Companion to Travel in Greece* (New York: Penguin, 1984), 246.

7. The major publication of the site is *Samothrace*, ed. Karl and Phyllis W. Lehmann, Bollingen Series 60, 4 vols. (Princeton, N.J.: Princeton University Press, 1958–69). A detailed report of the older excavations can be found in A. Conze et. al., *Archäologische Untersuchungen auf Samothrake*, 2 vols. (Vienna: Gerold, 1875, 1880). A good English summary of the excavations may be found in Karl Lehmann, *Samothrace: A Guide to the Excava-*

tions and the Museum, 5th ed. (Locust Valley, N.Y.: J. J. Augustin, 1983). A selected bibliography may be found at the end of this volume as well as in Phyllis W. Lehmann, "Samothrace," in *Princeton Encyclopedia of Classical Sites*, ed. Richard Stillwell et al. (Princeton, N.J.: Princeton University Press, 1976), 805–6. Unfortunately, no guidebooks in any language are sold at the Samothrace museum.

8. H. W. Catling, "Archaeology in Greece, 1986–87," *ARep.* 33 (1986–87): 51.

9. Fanoula Papazoglou, "Macedonia under the Romans," in M. B. Sakellariou, ed., *Macedonia: 4000 Years of Greek History and Civilization* (Athens: Ekdotike Athenon S.A., 1983), 198.

10. Meinardus, *St. Paul*, 8.

11. Recent discoveries, though not early Roman, are reported in English in H. W. Catling, "Archaeology in Greece," *ARep.* 24 (1977–78): 48–50; 25 (1978–79): 32; 31 (1984–85): 49–50; 33 (1986–87): 44. Reports in modern Greek can be found in: *ADelt* (1960): 219ff.; (1961–62): 235ff.; (1963): 257; (1964): 370ff., and (1967): 417. Older excavations sponsored by the government are reported in modern Greek in *PAE* (1937): 59ff., and *AE* (1938): 106ff.

12. Jack Finegan assumes it is Roman in origin and was rebuilt in the sixteenth century (*Archaeology of the New Testament: The Mediterranean World of the Early Christian Apostles* [Boulder, Colo.: Westview, 1981], 100).

13. Dimitrios Lazarides, "Neapolis," in, *Princeton Encyclopedia of Classical Sites*, 614.

14. *Acropolis*, 10 Nov. 1986.

15. Finegan confuses this church with the Church of Saint Nicholas (*Archaeology: Mediterranean World*, 101).

16. Strabo *Geography* 7.7.4.

17. C. Romiopoulou, "Un nouveau milliaire de la Via Egnatia," *BCH* 98 (1974): 813–16.

18. The distance is given in Latin as CC↓X. Romiopoulou comments: "L'emploi de la lettre [↓] pour désigner le chiffre 50 (le X de l'alphabet [chalcidique]), mais surtout la forme des lettres du texte grec, autorisent à dater l'inscription de la seconde moitié du IIᵉ siècle av. J.–C" ("Un nouveau milliaire," 814). The distance in Greek is clear— ΣΞ equals 260.

19. Papazoglou, "Macedonia," 200.

20. Polybius *Histories* 34.12. See further N. G. L. Hammond, *A History of Macedonia*, 2 vols. (Oxford: Clarendon, 1972, 1979), 1.21 n. 2. There is a full discussion of the road on pp. 19–58. Further bibliography may be found in

Romiopoulou, "Un nouveau milliaire," 813 n. 2.

21. Papazoglou, "Macedonia," 196 n. 24.

22. Ibid., n. 23.

23. Ibid., n. 24.

24. Ibid., 199.

25. *Genio colo[niae] Iul[. Au]g. Phi[lipp] . . .*—Paul Collart, "Inscriptions de Philippes," *BCH* 57 (1933): 328.

26. *. . . colo[niae] Iul(iae) Aug(ustae) Philipp(iensium) . . .*—Paul Collart, "Inscriptions de Philippes," *BCH* 56 (1932): 317. The name *Philippi* appears on a number of other inscriptions from the city as well (315, 320, 342, 349; Collart, "Inscriptions": 192).

27. Papazoglou, "Macedonia," 197.

28. Ibid., 192, 198.

29. Pliny the Elder *Natural History* 4.38; see also Papazoglou, "Macedonia," 198; Dimitrios Lazarides, "Amphipolis," in *Princeton Encyclopedia of Classical Sites*, 52.

30. Robin Barber, *Greece*, Blue Guide, 5th ed. (New York: Norton, 1987), 546.

31. Lazarides, "Amphipolis," 52.

32. The French excavations were reported in *BCH* during the 1920s and 1930s. See also Paul Collart, *Philippes: Ville de Macédoine depuis ses origines jusqu'à la fin de l'époque romaine* (Paris: E. da Boccard, 1937), and Paul Lemerle, *Philippes et la Macédoine orientale à l'époque chrétienne et byzantine* (Paris: E. de Boccard, 1945). More recently Michel Sève has been digging for the French School here in the library at the east end of the forum and in the theater. His reports appear in *BCH* in the 1970s and 1980s.

The primary Greek excavations are those of S. Pelekanides for the Archaeological Society of Athens, begun in 1960 and continued for about twenty years until his death. His reports and those of A. K. Orlandos appeared in *PAE* and *Ergon* during those years. Pelekanides' work was completed after his death by Ch. Bakirtzis. Ch. Penna and Chaido Koukouli-Chrysanthaki have been working respectively in the cemeteries and theater of Philippi, their publications appearing in *ADelt/Ch*. See also Dimitrios Lazarides' work in modern Greek, Οἱ Φίλιπποι (Thessaloniki: 1956).

33. Catling, "Archaeology in Greece," *ARep.* 31 (1984–85): 49.

34. Catling, "Archaeology in Greece," *ARep.* 32 (1985–86): 69.

35. Catling, "Archaeology in Greece," *ARep.* 31 (1984–85): 49.

36. An altar stele from the first or second century A.D. reads: [I]OVI

[F]ULMIN[I] MVNVS OLVSIVS MODESTVS—Catling, "Archaeology in Greece," *ARep.* 30 (1983–84): 50.

37. Catling, "Archaeology in Greece," *ARep.* 28 (1981–82): 42; 30 (1983–84): 50; 32 (1985–86): 69.

38. Ibid. The name Cornelius Rufus has also been found in an unidentified building in Beroea dating between the late Hellenistic and Byzantine periods—Catling, "Archaeology in Greece," *ARep.* 32 (1985–86): 64.

39. Catling, "Archaeology in Greece," *ARep.* 24 (1977–78): 49–50. *Ergon* (1976): 54–63.

40. Collart discusses the possible confusion of πύλης with πόλεως (*Philippes*, 459 n. 1), but there is not sufficient textual evidence for Nestle's twenty-sixth edition of the Greek New Testament to mention a variant.

41. Appian *Roman History* 4.13.106.

42. Collart, *Philippes, fasc. 5, Planches*, plate xliii; see also *Philippes*, 321 n. 1, and the discussion on 319–22 and 458–60.

43. Lemerle, *Philippes*, 24–27, plate I.

44. Some claim that it is on the site of the house where Paul stayed (Meinardus, *St. Paul*, 14)!

45. Catling, "Archaeology in Greece," *ARep.* 27 (1980–81): 34; *Ergon* (1979): 11–12; (1982): 14.

46. Barber, *Greece*, 637.

47. Finegan, *Archaeology: Mediterranean World*, 104.

48. Vitruvius *On Architecture* 5.2.1.

49. Barber, *Greece*, 637.

50. *ADelt/Ch* 31 (1976): 299–301; see also Catling, "Archaeology in Greece," *ARep.* 31 (1984–85): 49.

51. Two ruined arches which belonged to the Roman alterations were found in 1986 (*Proti*, 7 Jan. 1987).

52. Papazoglou, "Macedonia," 200.

53. Meinardus asserts, without reference to sources, that there was no synagogue in Amphipolis or Apollonia at this time (*St. Paul*, 27).

54. Lazarides, "Amphipolis," in *Princeton Encyclopedia of Classical Sites*, 52.

55. His work during those years is published in *Ergon*. See especially 1985 and 1986 for photos of recent finds.

56. *Ergon* reported on his efforts in the area of the five basilicas during the 1970s and 1980s.

57. Catling, "Archaeology in Greece," *ARep.* 31 (1984–85): 47.

58. Catling, "Archaeology in Greece," *ARep.* 33 (1986–87): 41.

59. Catling, "Archaeology in Greece," *ARep.* 32 (1985–1986): 67.

60. *Ergon* (1978): 17–22; (1980): 14–15; Catling, "Archaeology in Greece," *ARep.* 26 (1979–80): 44; 28 (1981–82): 41.

61. Catling, "Archaeology in Greece," *ARep.* 30 (1983–84): 49.

62. Catling, "Archaeology in Greece," *ARep.* 31 (1984–85): 47.

63. Catling, "Archaeology in Greece," *ARep.* 29 (1982–83): 45.

64. Catling, "Archaeology in Greece," *ARep.* 33 (1986–87): 43; see also *Ergon* 1985 and 1986.

65. E.g., "registration of ephebes, provision of references, attendance, appointment of teachers, courses of instruction, application to their activities, clothing, equipment, decorum, procedure for announcing the games, administration of the oath to the competitors, the committee of judges, conditions of winning and crowning of victors, penalties, ceremonial, etc." (Catling, "Archaeology in Greece," *ARep.* 31 [1984–85]: 48).

66. Catling, "Archaeology in Greece," *ARep.* 32 (1985–86): 68.

67. Chaido Koukouli-Chrysanthaki, "Politarchs in a New Inscription from Amphipolis," in *Ancient Macedonian Studies in Honor of Charles F. Edson*, ed. H. J. Dell (Thessaloniki: Institute for Balkan Studies, 1981), 229–41.

68. Such is the view of K. Sismanides, who published the inscription but does not regard Mygdonian Apollonia as its source (*AE* [1983]: 75–84; see also Catling, "Archaeology in Greece," *ARep.* 32 [1985–86]: 58).

69. When my wife and I visited the site in 1988, a local resident took us to a fenced-in yard behind his small roadside store and showed us an inscription in stone, which he had found in a nearby field and which he insisted that we take with us. We put it in the trunk of our car and took it to authorities in Athens for proper handling. It is probably an Islamic mortuary stele written in stylized Arabic.

70. Papazoglou, "Macedonia," 192, 194.

71. Ibid., 197–98.

72. Ibid., 539 n. 43.

73. Ibid., 201.

74. Strabo *Geography* 7.21.

75. Papazoglou, "Macedonia," 203.

76. Ibid., 539 n. 50.

77. J. Touratsoglou, *ADelt/Ch* 24 (1969): 329, plate 334.

78. See Michael Vickers, "Towards a Reconstruction of the Town Planning of Roman Thessaloniki," *AM* 1 (1970): 239ff.

79. In addition to the reports in *ADelt* see also Ch. Bakirtzis, "Περι

τους συγκροτήματος τῆς Ἀγορᾶς τῆς Θεσσαλονίκης," *AM* 2 (1977): 257ff.

80. See *ADelt* during the 1960s and 1970s.

81. Michael Vickers, "Thessalonike," in *Princeton Encyclopedia of Classical Sites*, 912.

82. See especially Catling, "Archaeology in Greece," *ARep.* 28 (1981–82): 32–36; *Arch* 7 (1983), which was devoted to Thessalonica; A. Papayannopoulos, Ἱστορία τῆς Θεσσαλονίκης (Thessaloniki: 1982).

83. *IG* 10.2.31.

84. Papazoglou, "Macedonia," 207 n. 111.

85. Finegan, *Archaeology: Mediterranean World*, 108.

86. Carl Schuler, "The Macedonian Politarchs," *Classical Philology* 55 (1960): 90–100.

87. J. M. R. Cormack, "The Gymnasiarchal Law of Beroea," in *Ancient Macedonia* II, Second International Symposium of the Institute of Balkan Studies, 19–24 Aug. 1973 (Thessaloniki: Institute for Balkan Studies, 1977), 139–49; see also a response by Jeanne Robert and Louis Robert in *Bulletin épigraphique* 9 (1978): 431ff.

88. See p. 292 and n. 68.

89. James H. Oliver, "The Dedication to Claudius at Beroea," *ZPE* 30 (1978): 150; a reply was made by J. Touratsoglou in *ZPE* 34 (1979): 272ff.

90. J. Touratsoglou, "Πρακτικά Β: Διέθνους Συνεδρίου Ἀρχαίας Μακεδονίας," in *Ancient Macedonia* II, Second International Symposium of the Institute of Balkan Studies, 19–24 Aug. 1973 (Thessaloniki: Institute for Balkan Studies, 1977), 481ff.

91. Koukouli-Chrysanthaki, "Politarchs," 238–39.

92. For a survey of that question see M. B. Hatzopoulos, "Les politarques de Philippopolis. Un élément méconnu pour la datation d'une magistrature macédonienne" (paper read at the Third International Congress of Thracology, Vienna, June 1980). For bibliography previous to 1973 see Fritz Geschnitzer, "Politarchs," in *PW* supp. 13 (1973), 483–500; see also B. Helly, "Politarques, Poliarches, et Politophylaques," in *Ancient Macedonia* II, 531ff.

93. Barber, *Greece*, 584.

94. Catling, "Archaeology in Greece," *ARep.* 32 (1985–86): 63.

95. Reported throughout the 1970s and 1980s in *ADelt/Ch* and briefly in *ARep.*

96. Photius Petsas, "Beroia," in *Princeton Encyclopedia of Classical Sites*, 151.

97. Catling, "Archaeology in Greece," *ARep.* 28 (1981–82): 39–40; 32 (1985–86): 63–65.

98. Dr. Makaronas, *Mak.* 2 (1951); Χρονικα Αρκαιολογικα 629–30, no. 71; Cormack, "Gymnasiarchal Law," 139–49; Robert and Robert, *Bulletin épigraphique* 9 (1978): 430ff.

99. Barber, *Greece*, 584.

100. Finegan, *Archaeology: Mediterranean World*, 125.

101. The Greek construction of the sentence is like that of 16:6 and 8 where the same words are used for "forbid" (κωλύω) and "pass through" (παρέρχομαι). The Western text of 17:15 may well have been influenced at this point by chapter 16.

102. N. G. L. Hammond, ed., *Atlas of the Greek and Roman World in Antiquity* (Park Ridge, N.J.: Noyes, 1981), map 12.

103. M. B. Hatzopoulos, "Strepa: A Reconsideration of New Evidence on the Road System of Lower Macedonia," in M. B. Hatzopoulos and L. D. Loukopoulou, *Two Studies in Ancient Macedonian Topography* (Athens: American School and National Hellenic Research Foundation, 1987), 18–60.

104. Dimitrios Pantermalis's work is reported in *Ergon*, *ADelt/Ch*, and *Mak.*

105. Catling, "Archaeology in Greece," *ARep.* 30 (1983–84): 43.

106. One is late Hellenistic, (Catling, "Archaeology in Greece," *ARep.* 29 [1982–83]: 38; 32 [1985–86]: 56); the other is a Roman Odeum (*ARep.* 29 [1982–83]: 38; 31 [1984–85]: 40).

107. Catling, "Archaeology in Greece," *ARep.* 30 (1983–84): 43; Dimitrios Pantermalis, *Dion: The Sacred City of the Macedonians at the Foothills of Mt. Olympos* (Athens: Archaeological Receipts Fund, 1987), 6.

108. Pantermalis, *Dion*, 5.

109. Philostratus *Life of Apollonius* 4.17; Pausanias mentions Mounikhias as well as Phaleron (*Description of Greece* 1.2.2).

110. John M. Camp, *The Athenian Agora* (London: Thames and Hudson, 1986), 17. I am especially indebted to Camp and T. Leslie Shear, Jr., directors of the Agora excavations, and to Judith Binder of the American School of Classical Studies in Athens, for their time and help with my research during my 1988 sabbatical. Their work, which is published in *Hesperia*, will be reflected in the following discussion.

111. T. Leslie Shear, Jr., "Athens: From City State to Provincial Town," *Hesperia* 50 (1981): 372.

112. Ibid., 368.

113. See especially Daniel J. Geagan, "Roman Athens: Some Aspects of Life and Culture. I. 86 B.C.–A.D. 267," in *Aufstieg und Niedergang der römischen Welt*, ed. Hildegard Temporini and Wolfgang Haase, sec. 2, vol. 7, pt. 1 (Hawthorne, N.Y.: Walter de Gruyter, 1979), 371–437; Camp, *Athenian Agora*, 181–214.

114. John M. Camp, *Gods and Heroes in the Athenian Agora* (Athens: American School of Classical Studies, 1980), 22; Shear, "Athens," 374.

115. Shear, "Athens," 373; Geagan, "Roman Athens," 389.

116. *IG* 2², #3271, lines 4–5. A dedication to Claudius is probably associated with some imperial construction in that year (Shear, "Athens," 367).

117. Son-in-law of Augustus, who defeated Mark Antony at Actium in 31 B.C. The monument was probably reworked just after 27 B.C.

118. Propylaea (437–432 B.C.), Athena Nike (427–424), Parthenon (447–438), and Erechtheion (finished after 359). The old Temple of Athena was probably completed in 529 B.C., and the Sanctuary of Artemis Brauronia in the fourth century.

119. Shear, "Athens," 363; John Travlos, *Pictorial Dictionary of Ancient Athens* (New York: Praeger, 1971), 494. Judith Binder suggests a date of 18 B.C.; Geagan says "sometime between 27/26 and 18/17 B.C." ("Roman Athens," 382).

120. See *IG* 2², #3173. See p. 100 for a picture.

121. See A. S. Benjamin and A. E. Raubitschek, "Arae Augusti," *Hesperia* 28 (1959): 65–85.

122. Geagan, "Roman Athens," 386; Shear, "Athens," 363.

123. Geagan, "Roman Athens," 383.

124. Pausanias *Description of Greece* 10.27.3; Dio Cassius *History of Rome* 60.6.8.

125. Travlos, *Pictorial Dictionary*, 28.

126. W. B. Dinsmoor, *Excavations of the Athenian Agora Picture Books* (Princeton, N.J.: American School of Classical Studies in Athens, 1985).

127. *IG* 2², #3175.

128. *IG* 2², #3251.

129. W. B. Dinsmoor, "The Temple of Ares at Athens," *Hesperia* 9 (1940): 50 n. 14; James H. Oliver, *Hesperia* 11 (1942): 82.

130. Camp, *Athenian Agora*, 14.

131. Shear, "Athens," 361.

132. Ibid.

133. Homer A. Thompson, *The Athenian Agora: A Guide to the Excavation and Museum*, 3d rev. ed., (Athens: Ekdotike Hellados, 1976), 120. The

bema is identified by a statement from Athenaeus *Deipnosophists* 5.212ef.

134. Shear, "Athens," 365.

135. Ibid., 362.

136. Pausanias *Description of Greece* 1.2.4 (trans. Peter Levi, in the Penguin Classics Series [New York: Penguin, 1984]).

137. Ibid., 5.14.8.

138. Recorded in Philostratus *Life of Apollonius* 6.3 (trans. F. C. Conybeare, in the Loeb Classical Library [Cambridge, Mass.: Harvard University Press, 1912]).

139. Diogenes Laertius *Lives of Eminent Philosophers* 1.110.

140. Comments on Acts 17:23, in *PG* 118.238.

141. Published in *PL* 215, cols. 1559–61 (256): "*Palladis in sedem humiliavit gloriosissimae genitricis veri Dei nunc assecuta notitiam quae dudum ignoto exstruxerat Deo aram.*" The full text is easily accessible in John Travlos and Alison Frantz, "The Church of Saint Dionysios the Areopagite and the Palace of the Archbishop of Athens in the 16th Century," *Hesperia* 34 (1965): 194. For this reference I am grateful to Judith Binder, who excerpted it for me from materials in her forthcoming book on *The Topography of Athens: A Sourcebook.*

142. Hugo Hepding, "Report [of excavations at Pergamum]," in *Ath. Mitt.* 35 (1910): 454–57; Adolf Deissmann, *St. Paul: A Study in Social and Religious History* (New York: Hodder and Stoughton, 1912), 261ff.

143. Eduard Norden, *Agnostos Theos* (Stuttgart: Teubner, 1913), 121, thinks Paul changed the plural to the singular for monotheistic application in his sermon.

144. Aratus *Phaenomena* 5.

145. Camp, *Gods and Heroes*, 30; see also Kirsopp Lake, "The Unknown God," in F. J. Foakes Jackson and Kirsopp Lake, eds., *The Beginnings of Christianity*, 5 vols. (Grand Rapids: Baker, 1966), 5.240–46. On the question of "unknown" versus "unknowable" and the significance of the lack of a definite article with "God" see F. F. Bruce, *The Book of Acts*, New International Commentary on the New Testament, rev. ed. (Grand Rapids: Eerdmans, 1988), 335, and W. J. Woodhouse, "Unknown God, Altar to the," in *Encyclopaedia Biblica*, ed. Thomas K. Cheyne and J. Sutherland Black, 4 vols. (New York: Macmillan, 1899–1903), 4.5229–31.

146. Homer A. Thompson, "The Odeion in the Athenian Agora," *Hesperia* 19 (1950): 31–141; 21 (1952): 90. See the discussion of Agrippa as a builder in G. Downey, *A History of Antioch in Syria: From Seleucus to the Arab Conquest* (Princeton, N.J.: Princeton University Press, 1961), 170ff. See also F. W. Shipley, *Agrippa's Building Activities in Rome* (St. Louis: Washington University, 1933).

147. Camp, *Athenian Agora*, 184.

148. Philostratus *Lives of the Sophists* 2.5.4.; 2.8.3–4.

149. Shear, "Athens," 361.

150. Ibid., 362.

151. Geagan mistakenly has northwest temple ("Roman Athens," 381). This is obviously a typographical error (see 386).

152. An inscription on a white marble stele from the temple of Athena Polias in Priene accords her divine honors, using the genitive Θεου Σεβαστου (C. T. Newton, ed., *The Collection of Ancient Greek Inscriptions in the British Museum* [Oxford: Trustees of the British Museum, 1886], 49, #428).

153. Shear, "Athens," 368; Thompson, *Athenian Agora*, 95; Geagan attributes the first colonnaded streets in Athens to the reign of Augustus ("Roman Athens," 381).

154. Strabo *Geography* 10.447.

155. Travlos, *Pictorial Dictionary*, 28.

156. Appian *Roman History* 2.102.

157. Travlos, *Pictorial Dictionary*, 28. For a list of early publications see Henry Robinson, "The Tower of the Winds and the Roman Market Place," in *AJA* 47 (1943): 293 n. 3. More recent work here by Greek archaeologists is reported in the journals of the Greek Archaeological Service and the Archaeological Society of Athens.

158. Varro, *De re rustica* 3.5.17; *IG* 12.5.891.

159. Vitruvius said that originally a revolving bronze Triton holding a wand pointed out which of the eight sculptured faces corresponded to the prevailing wind (*On Architecture* 1.6.4).

160. John Travlos, "Athens," in *Princeton Encyclopedia of Classical Sites*, 109; W. B. Dinsmoor, "The Temple of Ares and the Roman Agora," *AJA* 47 (1943): 383–84.

161. Shear thinks it was a headquarters for the market police ("Athens," 384).

162. Travlos, *Pictorial Dictionary*, 37.

163. For documentation of the following discussion see Shear, "Athens," and Geagan, "Roman Athens."

164. On the dedicatory inscription see B. D. Meritt, *Hesperia* 15 (1946): 233, no. 64; on the date see Shear, "Athens," 370.

165. Geagan, "Roman Athens," 374, 388.

166. Ibid., 388.

167. Daniel J. Geagan, "The Athenian Constitution after Sulla," *Hesperia*, supp. 12 (1967): 32, 48ff.

168. Ibid., 50.

169. The Royal Stoa was on the right, adjacent to the Stoa of Zeus as one entered the agora on the Panathenaic Way from the north. See Camp, *Athenian Agora*, 183, diagram 153.

170. Pseudo-Demosthenes, 25.23.

171. *IG* 4², 1.83 equals *SIG*³, 796B, II.

172. Lucian *Bis accusatus* 4.12; see Geagan, "Athenian Constitution," 53; Oscar Broneer, "Athens: City of Idol Worship," *BA* 21 (Feb. 1958): 27 n.4.

173. Travlos and Frantz, "Church of St. Dionysios," 157–202, plates 41–55.

174. See the *Oxford Dictionary of the Christian Church*, ed. F. L. Cross (New York: Oxford University Press, 1957), for the confusing identities; see also *Oxford Dictionary of Saints*, ed. David H. Farmer, 2d rev. ed. (Oxford: Oxford University Press, 1987); *Encyclopaedia Britannica*, 1910–11 ed., s.v. "Dionysius Areopagiticus," 8.284–85.

175. Catling, "Archaeology in Greece," *ARep.* 29 (1982–83): 6–7.

176. Pausanias *Description of Greece* 1.14.7–15.1. However, he mistakenly places Nero's "liberation speech" at the bema in Corinth rather than the theater in Isthmia. See James Wiseman, "Corinth and Rome I: 228 B.C.–A.D. 267," in *Aufstieg und Niedergang der römischen Welt*, ed. Hildegard Temporini and Wolfgang Haase, sec. 2, vol. 7, pt. 1 (Hawthorne, N.Y.: Walter de Gruyter, 1979), 505 and n. 262.

Chapter 10

1. Corinth has been the subject of two popular treatments in archaeological journals recently: Victor P. Furnish, "Corinth in Paul's Time—What Can Archaeology Tell Us?" *BAR* 14 (May–June 1988): 14–27; Jerome Murphy-O'Connor, "The Corinth that Saint Paul Saw," *BA* 47 (Sept. 1984): 147–59.

2. Robin Barber, *Greece*, Blue Guide, 5th ed. (New York: Norton, 1987), 261. James Wiseman puts the population above 145,000 (*The Land of the Ancient Corinthians*, Studies in Mediterranean Archaeology 50 [Göteborg: Paul Astroms, 1978]: 12).

3. Wilhelm Dorpfeld worked in the archaic temple ("Der Tempel von Korinth," *Ath. Mitt.* 11 [1886]: 297–308).

4. James Wiseman, "Corinth and Rome I: 228 B.C.–A.D. 267," in *Aufstieg und Niedergang der römischen Welt*, ed. Hildegard Temporini and Wolfgang Haase, sec. 2, vol. 7, pt. 1 (Hawthorne, N.Y.: Walter de Gruyter, 1979), 494.

5. Strabo *Geography* 8.6.20; 10.5.3.

6. Ibid., 8.6.20.

7. Ibid., 8. 6.20, 23.

8. Plutarch *Quaestiones conviviales* 5.3.1–3; 8.4.1; Pausanias *Description of Greece* 2.2.

9. E.g. Strabo *Geography* 8.4, 22; 9.1.

10. N. M. Verdelis, "Der Diolkos am Isthmos von Korinth," *Ath. Mitt.* 71 (1956): 51–59; idem, "Die Ausgrabung des Diolkos während der Jahre 1957–1959," *Ath. Mitt.* 73 (1958): 140–145; "Συνέχισις τῆς ἀνασκαφῆς τοῦ Διόλκου," *AE* (1956): 1–3; idem, "How the Ancient Greeks Transported Ships over the Isthmus of Corinth: Uncovering the 2550-year-old *Diolcos* of Periander," *ILN* 231 (19 Oct. 1957): 649–51; idem, "Ἀνασκαφὴ Διόλκου" *ADelt/Ch* 16 (1960): 79; idem, "Ἀνασκαφὴ τοῦ Διόλκου" *PAE* (1960): 136–43; (1962): 48–50.

11. See J. B. Salmon's discussion in *Wealthy Corinth: A History of the City to 338 B.C.* (Oxford: Oxford University Press, 1984), 137–38.

12. Brian MacDonald, "The Diolkos," *JHS* 106 (1986): 191–95; see also Salmon, *Wealthy Corinth*, 136–39; Wiseman, *Land of the Ancient Corinthians*, 45–46. R. M. Cook, "Archaic Greek Grade: Three Conjectures," *JHS* 99 (1979): 152–53.

13. MacDonald, "The Diolkos," 191–95.

14. Wiseman, *Land of the Ancient Corinthians*, 45 n. 1.

15. Thucydides *History of the Peloponnesian War* 8.7–8; Polybius *Histories* 5.101.4.

16. MacDonald, "The Diolkos," 195.

17. Verdelis, "Ἀνασκαφὴ τοῦ Διόλκου," *PAE* (1960): 141.

18. Diogenes Laertius (*Lives of Eminent Philosophers* 1.99) says "he wanted to dig a canal through the Isthmus." For an excellent and thoroughly documented brief survey of the canal's history, see Wiseman, *Land of the Ancient Corinthians*, 48–50.

19. Philostratus *Lives of the Sophists* 2.1.10.

20. Suetonius, *Lives of the Caesars* "Julius" 44.3; "Caligula" 21; "Nero" 19.

21. Josephus *Jewish War* 3.10.10 (540). Vespasian had his Jewish captives put in the stadium in Tiberias, where he executed 1200 of the elderly as "useless," sent 6000 to work on the canal, and gave Agrippa 30,400, whom he sold into slavery.

22. Philostratus *Life of Apollonius* 4.24. See the section drawing of Nero's work in Steve Kasas, *Corinth and Its Environs in Antiquity* (Athens: Filmographiki , 1974); see also the diagram in Wiseman, *Land of the Ancient Corinthians*, 45.

23. Wiseman, *Land of the Ancient Corinthians*, 50.

24. Strabo *Geography* 8.6.20.

25. Ibid.

26. Murphy-O'Connor, *St. Paul's Corinth* (Wilmington, Del.: Michael Glazier, 1983), 55–57.

27. Helen Hill Miller, *Greece Through the Ages* (New York: Funk and Wagnalls, 1972), 195.

28. Carl Blegen, "Excavations at the Summit," in *Corinth: Results of Excavations*, vols. (Princeton, N.J.: American School of Classical Studies at Athens, 1929–), 3.1.20.

29. Wiseman, "Corinth and Rome I," 531. See the diagrams and mosaic floors in Robert Scranton et. al., *Kenchreai, Eastern Port of Corinth*, vol. 1, *Topography and Architecture* (Leiden: E. J. Brill, 1978), 91–106.

30. Nancy Bookidis and Ronald Stroud, *Demeter and Persephone in Ancient Corinth* (Athens: American School of Classical Studies, 1987), 11; see also Nancy Bookidis, "The Sanctuary of Demeter and Kore: An Archaeological Approach to Ancient Religion," *AJA* 91 (1987): 480–81. See the diagrams in Nancy Bookidis and J. E. Fisher, "The Sanctuary of Demeter and Kore in Corinth: Preliminary Report IV," *Hesperia* 43 (1974): 267–307.

31. Personal conversation at the American School in Athens, 11 April 1988.

32. Richard Stoneman, ed., *A Literary Companion to Travel in Greece* (New York: Penguin, 1984), 105; see also Pausanias *Description of Greece* 10.28.1; Barber, *Greece*, 213 ("the fundamental substance of the Mysteries . . . was never divulged").

33. "We have found no important inscriptions to help us reconstruct the history of the Sanctuary. Nor for these critical centuries have we any descriptions of the site in classical literature. . . . In the absence of written testimony we are left with only the excavated finds and buildings themselves as clues in seeking to reconstruct the religious life of the Sanctuary" (Bookidis and Stroud, *Demeter and Persephone*, 11–13).

34. See the numerous photos in John Boardman and Eugenio La Rocca, *Eros in Greece* (London: John Murray, 1978).

35. W. K. C. Guthrie, *The Greeks and Their Gods* (Boston: Beacon, 1955), 164.

36. Bookidis and Stroud, *Demeter and Persephone*, 27.

37. Guthrie, *Greeks and Their Gods*, 56; James Frazer, *The Golden Bough*, 12 vols. (New York: Macmillan, 1922), vol. 2, chap. 11 ("The Sexes and Vegetation"). This was still practiced in some parts of the world such as Java, according to Frazer, when he collected his research a century ago.

38. Wiseman, "Corinth and Rome I," 509.

39. The evidence is summarized by Oscar Broneer in *Isthmia*, vol. 2, *Topography and Architecture* (Princeton, N.J.: American School of Classical Studies, 1973), 67–68; see also Pausanias *Description of Greece*. 2.2, who writes that the games were under the control of Sikyon after 146 B.C.

40. Oscar Broneer dates the return to Isthmia in the *agonothesia* of L. Castricius Regulus, between 7 B.C. and A.D. 3 ("Paul and the Pagan Cults at Isthmia," *HTR* 64 [1971]: 169 n. 2). Wiseman dates it in either 6 or 2 B.C. ("Corinth and Rome I," 533). Both use inscription #153, published by John Kent in *Corinth*, 8.3.72. See also the discussion of the date under inscription #152.

41. See the year-by-year publications for that decade in Oscar Broneer, "The Apostle Paul and the Isthmian Games," *BA* 25 (Feb. 1962): 7 n. 6. The more recent publications will be found in the multi-volume *Isthmia* (Princeton, N.J.: American School of Classical Studies, 1971–).

42. Broneer, "Paul and the Pagan Cults," 169; idem, "Apostle Paul," 2, 5.

43. L. Rutilius was *agōnothetēs* in A.D. 51. See Kent, in *Corinth* 8.3.31; Allen West, in *Corinth*, 8.2.66–69, #82. See also Daniel J. Geagan, "Notes of the Agonistic Institutions of Roman Corinth," *GRBS* 9 (1968): 71–75; Broneer, "Paul and the Pagan Cults," 185 n. 42.

44. Wiseman, "Corinth and Rome I," 504.

45. Here Nero made his famous speech granting to the area the freedom it already possessed! The text of the speech may be conveniently found in Suetonius *Lives of the Caesars*, "Nero," 23–24. See also *IG* 7.2713.

46. On the building remains see Broneer, *Topography and Architecture*; on those of Paul's period, see idem, "Apostle Paul," 2–31.

47. Murphy-O'Connor, *St. Paul's Corinth*, 15.

48. West, in *Corinth*, 8.2.54.

49. Wiseman cites the huge crowds at the games as a motivating factor in Paul's decision ("Corinth and Rome I," 504).

50. Ibid. See further Wiseman's discussion as to whether Corinth was the capital city of Achaea (501).

51. Philo *Delegation to Gaius* 281.

52. Suetonius *Lives of the Caesars*, "Claudius" 25.4; Orosius *Seven Books of History Against the Pagans* 7.6.15.

53. D. I. Pallas and S. P. Dautis, "Ἐπιγραφὲς ἀπὸ τὴν Κόρινθον," *AE* (1977): 61–83. See the list of Hebrew inscriptions in *Corinth*, 8.1.111, 115; 8.3.214. Others are referred to by Pallas in footnotes on page 81.

54. Benjamin Powell, "Greek Inscriptions from Corinth," *AJA*, n.s. 7 (1903): 60–61.

55. Kent, in *Corinth*, 8.1.79.

56. J. Kaplan, "A Samaritan Amulet from Corinth," *IEJ* 30 (1980): 196–98.

57. William Haygarth, "Greece: A Poem," in Stoneman, ed., *Literary Companion*, 97.

58. Oscar Broneer, "Corinth: Center of Paul's Missionary Work in Greece," *BA* 14 (Dec. 1951): 94.

59. Not *Laus Julia Corinthus* as previously thought. See Oscar Broneer, "Colonia Laus Julia Corinthiensis," *Hesperia* 10 (1941): 388–90; and the inscription in Kent, *Corinth*, 8.3.60, #130. The name was changed under Vespasian to *Colonia Iulia Flavia Augusta Corinthiensis*, but the original name was restored after the death of Domitian (Wiseman, "Corinth and Rome I," 497).

60. It is published in Princeton, New Jersey by the American School in Athens. Various editors, as might be expected, have had a part in the publications.

61. The former at the Gymnasium area and the Fountain of the Lamps in the northern part of the city, and the latter on Temple Hill. Reports have appeared in *Hesperia* from 1967 to 1976. See specific bibliography in Wiseman, "Corinth and Rome I," 448 nn. 32–33.

62. Some refer to the road as paved; e.g., Henry S. Robinson, "Corinth," in *Princeton Encyclopedia of Classical Sites*, ed. Richard Stilwell et al. (Princeton, N.J.: Princeton University Press, 1976), 242; Barber, *Greece*, 272. Others disagree; e.g., Murphy-O'Connor states that it was unpaved (*St. Paul's Corinth*, 30), and Wiseman speaks of it as both unpaved and graveled at this time ("Corinth and Rome I," 517, 520).

63. Carl Roebuck, *The Asklepieion and Lerna* in *Corinth*, vol. 14 (1951), plan D.

64. Murphy-O'Connor probably squeezes more out of the dining experience as a background for Paul's discussion of eating meat offered to idols (1 Cor. 8) than the situation would allow (*St. Paul's Corinth*, 161ff.).

65. C. K. Williams, "The Refounding of Corinth: Some Roman Religious Attitudes," in S. Macready and F. H. Thompson, eds., *Roman Architecture in the Greek World* (London: Society of Antiquaries, 1987), 26–37. The Apollo identification is derived almost entirely from the imprecise account of Pausanias (*Description of Greece* 2.3.6). Fragments of an inscription found on Temple Hill suggest Athena as a better possibility. See the discussion in Wiseman, "Corinth and Rome I," 475, 530, and footnotes.

66. Williams, "Refounding of Corinth," 31.

67. Strabo *Geography* 8.6.21; Pausanias *Description of Greece* 2.5.1.

68. See the drawings in Blegen, "Excavations at the Summit," plates VI and VII.

69. The identification of some of these is not agreed upon by all—Charles Williams in *Hesperia* 44 (1975): 25–29.

70. Evidence for these identifications is discussed by Wiseman, "Corinth and Rome I," 529.

71. Wiseman, "Corinth and Rome I," 522, suggests that it may have been a temple, and then demurs: "Unfortunately we cannot even be sure that K is a temple" (529). There is no archaeological evidence for dating its foundation, but Wiseman suggests a date after the A.D. 77 earthquake as possible (522).

72. Williams, "Refounding of Corinth," 29.

73. Robert Scranton, in *Corinth*, 1.2.131–65; 1.6.149–65.

74. Wiseman, "Corinth and Rome I," 473 n. 132.

75. Wiseman gives four reasons for the relocation ("Corinth and Rome I," 512).

76. Charles Williams, *Hesperia* 38 (1969): 54–55. The stoa had formerly been dated to the second century B.C. (Richard Stillwell, in *Corinth*, 1.2.89–119, 128–30).

77. Stillwell, in *Corinth*, 1.2.120–26, 129.

78. Broneer, "Apostle Paul," 5. For a discussion of these shops and relevant bibliography see Wiseman, "Corinth and Rome I," 509–21.

79. James Wiseman, *Hesperia* 36 (1967): 413–16; 38 (1969): 67–69.

80. See Carol Mattusch, "Corinthian Metalworking: The Forum Area," *Hesperia* 46 (1977): 380–81.

81. Ibid., 382; Stillwell, in *Corinth* 1.2.273.

82. F. J. DeWaele, "A Roman Market at Corinth," *AJA* 34 (1930): 452–53.

83. Henry J. Cadbury, "The *Makellum* in Corinth," *JBL* 53 (1934): 134–41.

84. Both definitions are given in William F. Arndt and F. Wilbur Gingrich, *A Greek-English Lexicon of the New Testament and Other Early Christian Literature* (Chicago: University of Chicago Press, 1957).

85. Oscar Broneer, "Studies in the Topography of Corinth at the Time of Paul," *AE* (1937): 125–33.

86. Ibid., 133.

87. Wiseman, "Corinth and Rome I," 513.

88. Charles Williams and Orestes Zervos, "Corinth, 1985: East of the Theater," *Hesperia* 55 (1986): 146.

89. H. W. Catling, "Archaeology in Greece, 1985–86," *ARep*. 32 (1985–86): 23.

90. Broneer, "Corinth: Center," 89.

91. See the discussion on the hydraulic engineering at Corinth in Robinson, "Corinth," in *Princeton Encyclopedia of Classical Sites*, 242.

92. For the fountain a little later see G. P. Stevens, "The Fountain of Peirene in the time of Herodes Atticus," *AJA* 38 (1934): 55–58; plate 7 has a reconstruction.

93. Stillwell, *Corinth*, 2.49.

94. It may have been built by Cn. Babbius Philinus, for an inscription which contained his name was found on the base of one of the marble dolphins that adorned the fountain: "CN–BABBIVS–PHILINVS–NEPTUNO–SACR(VM)" (Scranton, in *Corinth*, 1.3.32–36, and plate 15.1). See p. 332.

95. Roebuck, *Corinth*, 4.65–110.

96. James Wiseman, *Hesperia* 41 (1972): 16–22.

97. Baths of Eurykles (late first or early second century), north of the Peribolos of Apollo.

98. H. S. Robinson also identifies the Basilica of Julian and the South Basilica as law courts (*The Urban Development of Ancient Corinth*, 27—cited in Wiseman, "Corinth and Rome I," 517 n. 316).

99. Wiseman, "Corinth and Rome I," 514; on the identification of the building see Oscar Broneer, "Investigations at Corinth, 1946–47," *Hesperia* 16

(1947): 237; idem, in *Corinth*, 1.5.27–28.

100. Saul Weinberg, in *Corinth*, 1.5.5–29.

101. For a reconstruction of this monument see the drawings in Scranton, *Corinth*, 1.3 (1951).

102. Broneer, "Corinth: Center," 92; idem, in *Corinth*, 1.4.100–159.

103. Broneer, "Corinth: Center," 93.

104. Oscar Broneer, "The Isthmian Victory Crown," *AJA* 66.3 (July 1962): 260–63.

105. Wiseman, "Corinth and Rome I," 499–500.

106. Ibid.," 487. On the excavation of the theater see Stillwell, in *Corinth*, vol. 2, *The Theater*.

107. Stillwell, in *Corinth*, II, p. 32.

108. Charles Williams and Orestes Zervos, "Corinth, 1986: Temple E and East of the Theater," *Hesperia* 56 (1987): 5.

109. Williams and Zervos, "Corinth, 1985," 159.

110. L. Shear, "Excavations and Tombs of Corinth," *AJA* 33 (1929): 525.

111. Kent, in *Corinth*, 8.3.99, #232 and plate 21.

112. Ibid., 100. See also the recent discussion of Erastus as both aedile and oikonomos at Corinth by David Gill, "Erastus the Aedile," *Tyndale Bulletin* 40:2 (1989): 293–302. Colin J. Hemer notes that the cognomen Erastus was not uncommon among prominent people in Ephesus (*The Book of Acts in the Setting of Hellenistic History* [Tübingen: J. C. B. Mohr, 1989], 235).

113. Kent, in *Corinth*, 8.3.27.

114. West, in *Corinth*, 8.2, illus. #132; see also Scranton, in *Corinth*, 1.3.17–32.

115. For the full list see Kent, in *Corinth*, 8.3.27.

116. Ibid., 19.

117. Morgan, *AJA* 40 (1936): 471–74; Broneer, "Studies in the Topography," 125–28. A church was built over the structure, perhaps in the Byzantine period.

118. Scranton, in *Corinth*, 1.3.91ff.

119. Ibid., 98; see plan E.

120. There is no compelling reason to assume that the expansion of the South Stoa, in which the bema was located, in the second century affected this huge structure, as is suggested by Eric M. Meyers and L. Michael White, "Jews and Christians in a Roman World," *Archaeology* 42 (March–April 1989): 31. Nor is there any real evidence to justify Furnish's assumption that Paul appeared before Gallio at the North Basilica rather than where Acts says he did, at the bema ("Corinth in Paul's Time," 23). The proceedings

probably were not of a formal nature; and even if they were, such matters were often dealt with at a bema. Jesus was condemned by Pilate on just such a structure (called both a bema and a *Gabbatha* ["elevated place"] in John 19:13).

121. Scranton, in *Corinth*, 1.3.91.

122. Wiseman, "Corinth and Rome I," 516.

123. Kent, in *Corinth*, 8.3.128–29, # 322.

124. Wiseman, "Corinth and Rome I," 516 n. 308.

125. Williams and Zervos, "Corinth, 1986: Temple E and East of the Theater," 1–3.

126. Charles Williams and Orestes Zervos, "Corinth, 1981: East of the Theater," *Hesperia* 51 (1982): 118.

127. Strabo *Geography* 8.6.20, 22.

128. *PAE* (1965): 137–66.

129. Wiseman, *Land of the Ancient Corinthians*, 87–88.

130. *ADelt/Ch* 28 (1972): 228–29; H. W. Catling, "Archaeology in Greece," *ARep*. 25 (1978–79): 11.

131. *ADelt/Ch* 31 (1975): 64; H. W. Catling, "Archaeology in Greece," *ARep*. 31 (1984–85): 19.

132. Strabo *Geography* 6.8.20, 22.

133. "Researches in the Topography of Ancient Corinth—I," *AJA* 33 (1929): 345.

134. Robert L. Hohlfelder, "Kenchreaion the Saronic Gulf: Aspects of Its Imperial History," *Classical Journal* 71 (1975– 76): 219.

135. The official publication of the dig is *Kenchreai, Eastern Port of Corinth*, 5 vols. (Leiden: E. J. Brill, 1976–81); especially relevant for our discussion are vol. 1, Robert Scranton et al., *Topography and Architecture* (1978), and vol. 3, Robert L. Hohlfelder, *The Coins* (1978).

136. Wiseman, *Land of the Ancient Corinthians*, 52.

137. Joseph Shaw, "The Harborage," in *Kenchreai*, 1.14.

138. Hohlfelder, "Kenchreai on the Saronic Gulf," 221; Robert Scranton, "Kenchreai," in *Princeton Encyclopedia of Classical Sites* 446.

139. Scranton et al., Appendix E, "Changes in Relative Sea Level," in *Kenchreai* 1.144.

140. Hohlfelder reports that 1315 coins survived cleaning and closely mirror the coins minted at Corinth (*Kenchreai* 3.2).

141. Pausanias *Description of Greece* 2.2.3.

142. Robert Scranton and Edwin Ramage, "Investigations at Corinthian Kenchreai," *Hesperia* 36 (1967): 141–46, figs. 7–9, plates 38–44; Robert

Scranton, "Glass Pictures from the Sea," *Archaeology* 20 (1967): 163–73.

143. Robert Scranton, "The Harborside Commercial Facilities," *Kenchreai*, 1.39ff.

144. See the discussion by Wiseman in *Land of the Ancient Corinthians*, 52 n. 46.

145. Pausanias *Description of Greece* 2.2.3; see John Hawthorne, "Cenchreae: Port of Corinth," *Archaeology* 18 (1965): 197.

146. W. Willson Cummer, "A Roman Tomb at Corinthian Kenchreai," *Hesperia* 40 (1971): 205–31.

147. Scranton, in *Corinth*, 1.3.98–99, fig. 55.

148. Ibid., 66.

149. Cummer, "A Roman Tomb," 224.

150. These may be seen in the footnotes at the ends of the letters in *Novum Testmentum Graece*, 26th ed., ed. Eberhard Nestle and Kurt Aland (Stuttgart: Deutsche Bibelstiftung, 1979).

151. See C. E. B. Cranfield, *The Epistle to the Romans*, 2 vols., International Critical Commentary (Edinburgh: T. and T. Clark, 1981), 2.760–62.

152. Josephus *Antiquities of the Jews* 16.5.3 (147).

153. Ibid.; Josephus *Jewish War* 1.21.11 (425).

154. See the photos and reconstruction in William Murray, "The Spoils of Actium," *Archaeology* 41 (Sept.–Oct. 1988): 28–35.

155. Dio Cassius *Roman History* 51.1.3.

156. See James H. Oliver, "Octavian's Inscription at Nicopolis," *AJPh* 90 (1969): 178–82; John Carter points out that no one person has examined all twenty-five blocks ("A New Fragment of Octavian's Inscription at Nicopolis," *ZPE* 24 [1977]: 228).

157. Strabo *Geography* 7.7.6; Dio Cassius *Roman History* 51.1.3.

158. Suetonius *Lives of the Caesars*, "Augustus" 18.

159. Carter, "A New Fragment," 229.

160. Photios Petsas, "Ἀνασκαφη Ῥωμαικῆς Νικοπόλεως," *PAE* (1974): 79–88. See excavation reports in *PAE* 1913–16, 1918, 1921–24, 1926, 1929–30, 1937–38, 1940, 1956, 1961; *AE* 1913–14, 1916–18, 1922, 1929, 1952 (and articles in 1964–65, 1967, 1970–71); *ADelt* 1960–65, 1968–69. See also scattered reports in *JHS* 1938 (p. 226), 1939 (p. 198), 1952 (p. 101), 1953 (p. 121); *AJA* 1939 (p. 329), 1940 (p. 246); *BCH* 1921–30.

161. Acts 20:2 might allow some time for a visit to this region.

162. Homer *Iliad* 16.232.

163. Homer *Odyssey* 14.327; 19.296.

164. Herodotus *History* 2.52–60.

165. Yves Béquignon, "Dodona," in *Princeton Encyclopedia of Classical Sites*, 279.

166. C. Carapanos, *Dodone et ses ruines*, 2 vols. (Paris: Hachette, 1878).

167. See S. I. Dakaris, *AE* 1959 (1964); *Ergon* (1954ff.); J. M. Cook, "Archaeology in Greece," *JHS* 73 (1953): 121; 74 (1954): 159; *BCH* 77 (1953): 223; Hans-Peter Drögemüller, "Bericht über neuere Ausgrabungen in Griechenland," *Gymnasium* 68 (1961): 222–26; N. G. L. Hammond, *Epirus* (Oxford: Oxford University Press, 1967).

168. Ernest Nash, "Roma," in *Princeton Encyclopedia of Classical Sites*, 765.

169. Jack Finegan, *Archaeology of the New Testament: The Mediterranean World of the Early Christian Apostles* (Boulder, Colo.: Westview, 1981), 223.

170. Leonardo B. Dal Maso, *Rome of the Caesars* (Florence: Il Turismo, 1981), 40.

171. See Dal Maso, *Rome of the Caesars*.

172. Suetonius *Lives of the Caesars*, "Tiberius" 47.

173. Tacitus *Annals* 15.44.

174. Suetonius *Lives of the Caesars*, "Nero" 31.

175. Pliny the Elder *Natural History* 36.102.

176. Josephus *Jewish War* 7.5.7 (158–62), trans. H. St.J. Thackeray, in the Loeb Classical Library (Cambridge, Mass.: Harvard University Press, 1979).

177. For an evaluation of its place in architectural history see J. B. Ward-Perkins, *Roman Architecture* (New York: Abrams, 1977), 174ff.

178. Finegan, *Archaeology: Mediterranean World*, 224; see the comprehensive discussion of the deaths of Paul and Peter in Rome (22ff.).

179. Eusebius *Ecclesiastical History* 2.25.7.

180. "Martyrdom of Peter," "Martyrdom of Peter and Paul," and the "Acts of Peter and Paul," in R. A. Lipsius and M. Bonnet, *Acta apostolorum apocrypha*, 3 vols. (Hildesheim: Georg Olms, 1959), 1.11–12, 172, 216; *Book of the Popes (Liber pontificalis)*, vol. 1, *To the Pontificate of Gregory I* (New York: Columbia University Press, 1916), 5.

181. Margherita Guarducci, *The Tomb of St. Peter*, trans. Joseph McLellan (New York: Hawthorn, 1960), 12–35. See the challenge to Guarducci by J. M. C. Toynbee and J. B. Ward-Perkins, *The Shrine of St. Peter and the Vatican Excavations* (New York: Longmans, Green, 1956); G. F. Snyder, "Survey and 'New' Thesis on the Bones of Peter," *BA* 32 (Feb. 1969): 2–24; and Timothy Barnes's scathing review (*JTS*, n.s. 21 [1970]: 175–79) of Guarducci as well as of D. W. O'Connor, *Peter in Rome: The Literary, Liturgical, and Archeological Evidence* (New York: Columbia University Press, 1969).

182. Finegan, *Archaeology: Mediterranean World*, 27–28.

183. See the letter in *Apostolic Fathers*, trans. Kirsopp Lake, 2 vols., Loeb Classical Library (Cambridge, Mass.: Harvard University Press, 1945–46), 1.9–121.

184. Irenaeus *Against Heresies* 3.3.

185. Finegan, *Archaeology: Mediterranean World*, 234.

186. See *Rome and Central Italy*, Blue Guide, 2d ed. (London: Ernest Benn, 1964), 61.

187. Finegan, *Archaeology: Mediterranean World*, 30.

188. Ibid.

Chapter 11

1. G. H. R. Horsley, *New Documents Illustrating Early Christianity*, 5 vols. (Sydney: Macquarie University Press, 1981–87), 1.iv. A similar work in one volume is M. David and B. A. van Groningen, *Papyrological Primer*, 4th ed. (Leiden: E. J. Brill, 1965).

2. Eric G. Turner, *Greek Papyri: An Introduction* (Princeton, N.J.: Princeton University Press, 1968).

3. Pliny the Elder *Natural History* 13.21–27, 68–83. See also *Encyclopaedia Britannica*, 1970 ed., s.v. "Papyrology," 17.293–96; Jack Finegan, *Encountering New Testament Manuscripts* (Grand Rapids: Eerdmans, 1974), 19ff., 27ff.; Bruce M. Metzger, *Manuscripts of the Greek Bible* (New York: Oxford University Press, 1981), 14–19; Kurt Aland and Barbara Aland, *The Text of the New Testament*, trans. Erroll F. Rhodes (Grand Rapids: Eerdmans, 1987), 75–77.

4. Bruce M. Metzger tells the exciting story in detail in *Text of the New Testament* (Oxford: Oxford University Press, 1964), 42–46.

5. See the summation of the current status of our knowledge in J. H. Charlesworth, *The New Discoveries in St. Catherine's Monastery: A Preliminary Report on the Manuscripts* (Cambridge, Mass.: American Schools of Oriental Research, 1981).

6. Giovanni Pettinato, "The Royal Archives of Tell Mardikh-Ebla," *BA* 39.2 (May 1976): 44ff.; the entire issue of *BA* 39.3 (Sept. 1976); Hershel Shanks, "The Promise of Ebla," *BAR* 2 (Dec. 1976): 41–42; David Noel Freedman, "Leading Scholar Calls for Prompt Publication," *BAR* 4 (March 1978): 2–3; P. Maloney, "Assessing Ebla," *BAR* 4 (March 1978): 4–10; A. Mikaya, "The Politics of Ebla," *BAR* 4 (Sept.–Oct. 1978): 2–6; David Noel Freedman, "The Real Story of the Ebla Tablets: Ebla and the Cities of the Plain," *BA* 41 (Dec. 1978), 143–64; Hershel Shanks, "Syria Tries to Influence Ebla Scholarship," *BAR* 5 (March–April 1979): 36–38; Giovanni Pettinato, "Declaration on Ebla," *BAR* 5 (March–April 1979): 38–48; "Syrian Interview with Chief Ebla Archaeologist Matthiae," *BAR* 5 (March–April 1979): 48–50; Howard Lafay, "Ancient Ebla Opens a New Chapter of History," *National Geographic* 154.6 (Dec. 1978): 730–59. Paolo Matthiae, *Ebla: An Empire Rediscovered* (Garden City, N.Y.: Doubleday, 1981); Giovanni Pettinato, *The Archives of Ebla: An Empire Inscribed in Clay* (Garden City, N.Y.: Doubleday, 1981); Richard Ostling, "New Grounding for the Bible," *Time*, 21 Sept., 1981, 76–77.

7. George Milligan, *Here and There among the Papyri* (London: Houghton and Mifflin, 1922), 10.

8. Henry Meecham, *Light from Ancient Letters* (London: Allen and Unwin., 1923), 31.

9. Ibid.

10. Milligan, *Here and There*, 7.

11. New Testament Uncial 0212; see Aland and Aland, *Text of the New Testament*, 59.

12. *Encyclopaedia Britannica*, 1970 ed., s.v. "Papyrology," 17.293.

13. Milligan, *Here and There*, 11.

14. The exciting story of their work is chronicled by Eric G. Turner, "The Graeco-Roman Branch," in *Excavating in Egypt: the Egypt Exploration Society, 1882–1982*, ed. T. G. H. James (Chicago: University of Chicago Press, 1982). 161–78.

15. Ibid., 172.

16. See the picture in Turner, "Graeco-Roman Branch," 170.

17. Ibid., 171.

18. Ibid., 162.

19. James H. Moulton and George Milligan, *The Vocabulary of the Greek Testament* (London: Hodder and Stoughton, 1952), ix; James H. Moulton, *From Egyptian Rubbish Heaps* (London: C. H. Kelly, 1917).

20. B. P. Grenfell and A. S. Hunt, et. al., eds., *The Oxyrhynchus Papyri*, (London: Egypt Exploration Fund, 1898–).

21. *Novum Testamentum Graece*, 26th ed., ed. Eberhard Nestle and Kurt Aland (Stuttgart: Deutsche Bibelstiftung, 1979), 684–89. Though ninety-two papyri are actually listed, only eighty-eight make up the "official list," and another fifteen "by strict definition do not belong there," leaving a total of seventy-three. And though Nestle-Aland lists twenty-seven Oxyrhynchus papyri, two are not New Testament papyri: OP 209 (**p**[10]) is a writing exercise, and OP 2684 (**p**[78]) is a talisman (Aland and Aland, *Text of the New Testament*, 85).

22. Aland and Aland, *Text of the New Testament*, 57.

23. Colin H. Roberts, *An Unpublished Fragment of the Fourth Gospel* (Manchester: Manchester University Press, 1935). It is now conveniently available for study in Metzger, *Manuscripts*, 62. where there is a good photographic reproduction along with transcription and discussion.

24. Aland and Aland, *Text of the New Testament*, 57.

25. F. F. Bruce, *The Books and the Parchments* (London: Pickering and Inglis, 1963), 181.

26. Aland and Aland, *Text of the New Testament*, 57.

27. Frederick G. Kenyon, *The Text of the Greek Bible* (London: Duckworth, 1949), 39.

28. Frederick G. Kenyon, ed., *Chester Beatty Biblical Papyri*, 8 fascs. (London: Emory Walker, 1933–41), 1.6.

29. Ibid., fascs. 1–5; Henry A. Sanders, ed., *A Third-Century Papyrus Codex of the Epistles of Paul* (Ann Arbor: University of Michigan Press, 1935).

30. This second-century sermon to believers was published from fourteen leaves of manuscript, eight of which belong to the Beatty Collection and the other six to the University of Michigan. In the magnanimous spirit of international scholarship that characterized the entire Chester Beatty venture, Campbell Bonner of the University of Michigan was allowed to publish all fourteen leaves as a complete manuscript (Melito, *The Homily on the Passion*, ed. Campbell Bonner, Studies and Documents 12, ed. Kirsopp Lake and Silva Lake [Philadelphia: University of Pennsylvania Press, 1940]). Kenyon published the text and plates in *Chester Beatty Biblical Papyri*, fasc. 8. A very small and convenient copy was subsequently made available in B. Lohse, ed., *Die Passa-Homilie des Bischofs Meliton von Sardes*, Textus Minores 24 (Leiden: E. J. Brill, 1958). All known fragments of the work have been restudied recently in Melito, *On Pascha and Fragments*, ed. S. G. Hall, Oxford Early Christian Texts (Oxford: Clarendon, 1979). The sermon has also been found among the Bodmer papyri and published in volume 13 of that collection (see n. 54).

31. Sanders, *Third-Century Papyrus Codex*, 1.

32. Kenyon, *The Chester Beatty Biblical Papyri*, fasc. 3, supp., *Pauline Epistles*, vii.

33. Ibid.

34. Aland and Aland, *Text of the New Testament*, 99.

35. R. McL. Wilson, "Nag Hammadi and the New Testament," *NTS* 28 (1982): 289–302; John Dart, *The Jesus of Heresy and History: The Discovery and Meaning of the Nag Hammadi Gnostic Library* (San Francisco: Harper and Row, 1988); Floyd V. Filson, "New Greek and Coptic Gospel Manuscripts," *BA* 24 (Feb. 1961): 2–18; W. C. van Unnik, *Newly Discovered Gnostic Writings*, Studies in Biblical Theology 30 (London: SCM, 1960).

36. They "hacked off his limbs bit by bit, ripped out his heart, and devoured it among them as the ultimate act of blood revenge." The gruesome story was recounted "with relish" by Muhammad Ali, one of the two brothers who found the codices (James M. Robinson, *The Nag Hammadi Codices* [Claremont, Calif.: Institute for Antiquity and Christianity, 1977], 2).

37. Robert M. Grant, *The Secret Sayings of Jesus* (Garden City, N.Y.: Doubleday, 1960), 19.

38. H. C. Puech, G. Quispel and W. C. van Unnik, *The Jung Codex: A Newly Recovered Gnostic Papyrus*, trans. and ed. F. L. Cross (London: Mowbray, 1955).

39. This paragraph is largely a summary of the fuller discussion in Robinson, *Nag Hammadi Codices*, 2–3.

40. Jack Finegan, *Hidden Records of the Life of Jesus* (Philadelphia: Pilgrim, 1969), 111.

41. James M. Robinson, ed., *The Nag Hammadi Library in English*, 3d rev. ed. (San Francisco: Harper and Row, 1988); there is also a multivolume critical edition being published under the editorship of Robinson: *The Coptic Gnostic Library* (Leiden: E. J. Brill, 1975–).

42. Although sixty-one are listed in the table of tractates on p. xiii (*Nag Hammadi Library in English*), only forty-seven are translated and evaluated in the volume. James Brashler, who worked on six of the documents in Robinson's book, says there are fifty-two tractates ("Nag Hammadi Codices Shed New Light on Early Christian History," *BAR* 10 [Jan.–Feb. 1984]: 54–63).

43. This began with his bibliographical publication *Nag Hammadi Library: 1948–1969* (Leiden: E. J. Brill, 1971).

44. *Facsimile Edition of the Nag Hammadi Codices*, 12 vols. (Leiden: E.J. Brill, 1972–84). This set, which was published under the auspices of the Department of Antiquities of the Arab Republic of Egypt in conjunction with UNESCO, includes a volume of *Introduction* (1984) dealing with the history of the discovery and the research involved.

45. José O'Callaghan, "Papiros neotestamentarios en la cueva 7 de Qumrān?" *Biblica* 53 (1972): 91–100; following O'Callaghan is a short note in Italian by Carlo Martini which seems to concur with the identification (101–4). These fragments were so widely discussed that an English translation was published in *JBL* 91, supp. (1972): 1–20. But the identification has attracted little scholarly support—see Colin H. Roberts, "On Some Presumed Papyrus Fragments of the New Testament from Qumran," *JTS*, n.s. 23 (1972): 446–47; Pierre Benoit, "Note sur les fragments Grecs de la grotte 7 de Qumran," *RB* 79 (1972): 321–24; Gordon D. Fee, "Some Dissenting Notes on 7Q5 equals Mark 6:52–53," *JBL* 92 (March 1973): 109–12; Kurt Aland, "Über die Möglichkeit der Identifikation kleiner Fragmente neutestamentlicher Handschriften mit Hilfe des Computers," in J. K. Elliott, ed., *Studies in New Testament Language and Text* (Leiden: E. J. Brill, 1976), 14–38.

46. Joseph A. Fitzmyer, *The Dead Sea Scrolls*, 2d ed. (Missoula, Mont.: Scholar's, 1975), 119.

47. James H. Moulton, *From Egyptian Rubbish-Heaps* (London: Charles H. Kelly, 1917), 14.

48. On the initial discovery and related scholarly controversies see the definitive work of Qumran's excavator, Roland de Vaux, *Archaeology and the Dead Sea Scrolls* (London: Oxford University Press, 1973), as well as J. A. Sanders, "The Dead Sea Scrolls—A Quarter Century of Study," *BA* 36 (Dec. 1973): 110–48; Joseph A. Fitzmyer, "The Dead Sea Scrolls and the New Testament after Thirty Years," *Theology Digest* 29 (1981): 351–67 (a summary can be found in "New Testament Illuminated by the Dead Sea Scrolls," *BAR* 8 [Sept.–Oct. 1982]: 6–8); Yigael Yadin, *The Message of the Scrolls* (New York: Simon and Schuster, 1957; Frank Moore Cross, Jr., *The Ancient Library of Qumran and Modern Biblical*

Studies, rev. ed. (Grand Rapids: Baker, 1980); idem, "The Dead Sea Scrolls and the People Who Wrote Them," *BAR* 3 (March 1977): 1, 23–32; John C. Trever, *The Untold Story of Qumran* (Westwood, N.J.: Revell, 1965); Matthew Black, *The Scrolls and Christian Origins* (New York: Scribner, 1961); Millar Burrows, *The Dead Sea Scrolls* (New York: Viking, 1955); idem, *More Light on the Dead Sea Scrolls* (New York: Viking, 1958).

49. Norman Golb, "Khirbet Qumran and the Manuscripts of the Judean Wilderness: Observations on the Logic of Their Investigation," *Journal of Near Eastern Studies* 49:2 (April 1990): 102–14.

50. Named after the Wadi Qumran, the dry watercourse beside which it was located. The site lay on the northwest side of the Dead Sea, south of Jericho.

51. Josephus *Jewish War* 2.8.2–13 (119–61).

52. Cross, "Dead Sea Scrolls," 29; Joseph A. Fitzmyer, "The Qumran Scrolls and the New Testament after Forty Years," *Revue de Qumran* 13.49–52 (Oct. 1988): 609–20.

53. Geza Vermes, *The Dead Sea Scrolls: Qumran in Perspective* (Philadelphia: Fortress, 1981), 211–21; idem, *The Dead Sea Scrolls in English* (Baltimore: Penguin, 1966); Neil S. Fujita, *A Crack in the Jar: What Ancient Jewish Documents Tell Us about the New Testament* (Mahwah, N.J.: Paulist, 1986), 109–59; Yigael Yadin, *The Temple Scroll: The Hidden Law of the Dead Sea Sect*, (New York: Random House, 1985), 239–54; Cross, "Dead Sea Scrolls," 1ff; Fitzmyer, "Dead Sea Scrolls and the New Testament," 351–67; idem, "The Qumran Scrolls and the New Testament after Forty Years."

54. Aland and Aland, *Text of the New Testament*, 57.

55. The papyri have been published in a series as *Bibliotheca Bodmeriana*, ed. Victor Martin et al., 5 vols. (Cologne and Geneva: Bibliothèque Bodmer, 1956–62).

56. Floyd V. Filson, "A New Papyrus Manuscript of the Gospel of John," *BA* 20 (Sept. 1957): 54–63; idem, "The Bodmer Papyri," *BA* 22 (May 1959): 48–51; idem, "More Bodmer Papyri," *BA* 25 (May 1962): 50–57; J. Neville Birdsall, *The Bodmer Papyrus of the Gospel of John* (London: Tyndale, 1958).

57. Aland and Aland, *Text of the New Testament*, 57.

58. Herbert Hunger, "Zur Datierung des Papyrus Bodmer II (P66)," *Anzeiger der österreichischen Akademie der Wissenschaften*, phil.-hist. Kl. 4 (1960): 12–33, cited in Metzger, *Text of the New Testament*, 40 n.1.

59. Kenyon, *Chester Beatty Biblical Papyri*, fasc. 3, supp., *Pauline Epistles*, 21.

60. Metzger, *Manuscripts*, 41.

61. Both Milligan and Kenyon assumed that the New Testament books were originally written on scrolls. They also assumed that papyrus was not used for codices, and that the book form came into use only with the introduction of parchment (Milligan, *Here and There*, 28–29; Frederick G. Kenyon, *Handbook to the Textual Criticism of the New Testament*, 2d ed. [Grand Rapids: Eerdmans, 1953], 33–35).

62. Aland and Aland, *Text of the New Testament*, 75.

63. Jewish Christians in the earliest years called their assemblies synagogues (James 2:2).

64. Aland and Aland, *Text of the New Testament*, 76.

65. Luke commended the Beroeans as "more noble" than the Thessalonians because they "searched the Scriptures daily" in an effort to determine whether what they were being taught was valid (Acts 17:11).

66. Aland and Aland, *Text of the New Testament*, 102.

67. Kenyon, *Handbook*, 35.

68. Bruce M. Metzger, *The Early Versions of the New Testament: Their Origin, Transmission, and Limitations* (Oxford: Clarendon, 1977), 48.

69. Chester Beatty **p**[45] and Codex Bezae Cantabrigiensis D 05, a fifth-century manuscript.

70. James Brashler, "Nag Hammadi Codices," 58.

71. Robinson, ed., *Nag Hammadi Library*.

72. Sixteen of the noncanonical Gospels have been published and analyzed by Ron Cameron, ed., *The Other Gospels: Non-Canonical Gospel Texts* (Philadelphia: Westminster, 1982). Joachim Jeremias has a helpful survey of noncanonical sayings attributed to Jesus which were known before the Gospel of Thomas was discovered (*Unknown Sayings of Jesus* [New York: Macmillan, 1957]).

73. See Bruce, *Books and the Parchments*, 181 n. 2.

74. Yadin, *Temple Scroll*, 78–83.

75. H. I. Bell and T. C. Skeat, *Fragments of an Unknown Gospel and Other Early Christian Papyri* (London: British Museum, 1935), v.

76. C. H. Dodd, "A New Gospel," in *New Testament Studies* (Manchester: Manchester University Press, 1954), 12–52.

77. Edgar Hennecke, *New Testament Apocrypha*, ed. W. Schneemelcher, trans. A. J. B. Higgins et al., 2 vols. (Philadelphia: Westminster, 1959), 1.94–97.

78. Bell and Skeat, *Fragments*, 1.

79. Dodd, "A New Gospel," 21.

80. Bruce says the chief importance of the fragment is that it was "obviously written by someone who had the four canonical gospels before him and was well acquainted with them" (*Books and Parchments*, 181 n. 2). Cameron is unconvincing when he says that the papyrus "displays no dependance upon the gospels of the New Testament" (*Other Gospels*, 73).

81. Dodd, "A New Gospel," 50.

82. Bell and Skeat, *Fragments*, plates I–II; idem, *The New Gospel Fragments* (London: British Museum, 1935); Goro Mayeda, *Das Leben-Jesu-Fragment Papyrus Egerton 2 und seine Stellung in der urchristlichen Literaturgeschichte* (Bern: Paul Haupt, 1946), 7–11; Finegan, *Hidden Records*, 178–86; Dodd, "A New Gospel," 13–15.

83. Cameron, *Other Gospels*, 74–75; Finegan, *Hidden Records*, 178–86; Grant, *Secret Sayings*, 54–57; Hennecke, *New Testament Apocrypha*, 1.94–97.

84. See Bruce, *Books and the Parchments*, 262.

85. In addition to the official publications of this document listed in notes 41 and 44, there are good discussions of the text and its traditions in James M. Robinson and Helmut Koester, *Trajectories Through Early Christianity* (Philadelphia: Fortress, 1971). The Coptic text with English translation is available in convenient size in Antoine Guillaumont et. al., *The Gospel According to Thomas* (New York: Harper, 1959); and the theological significance of the document is discussed at length by Bertil Gartner in *The Theology of the Gospel According to Thomas* (New York: Harper, 1961).

86. Stanley K. Stowers, *Letter Writing in Greco-Roman Antiquity* (Philadelphia: Westminster, 1986), 15.

87. Acts records the letter sent by the Jerusalem council to the churches of Antioch, Syria, and Cilicia (15:23–29) and a letter from a Roman tribune to the governor Felix (23:26–30). Revelation contains letters to the seven churches of Asia Minor (chaps. 2–3).

88. Deissmann, *Bible Studies*, trans. A. Grieve (Edinburgh: T. and T. Clark, 1909), 3–59; for a recent treatment of the difference between documentary

and literary letters see John L. White, "A Discussion of *Light from Ancient Letters*," *Biblical Research* 32 (1987): 42–53.

89. Stowers, *Letter Writing*; John L. White, *The Form and Function of the Body of the Greek Letter*, Society of Biblical Literature Dissertation Series 2 (Missoula, Mont.: Scholar's, 1972); idem, *Light from Ancient Letters* (Philadelphia: Fortress, 1986); idem, "New Testament Epistolary Literature in the Framework of Ancient Epistolography" (paper read at the 1979 Annual Meeting of the Society of Biblical Literature); Calvin J. Roetzel, *The Letters of Paul: Conversations in Context*, 2d ed. (Atlanta: John Knox, 1982); Gordon J. Bahr, "Paul and Letter Writing in the First Century," *CBQ* 28 (1966): 465–77; idem, "The Subscriptions in the Pauline Letters," *JBL* 87 (March 1968): 27–41; William G. Doty, *Letters in Primitive Christianity* (Philadelphia: Fortress, 1973).

90. White, *Body of the Greek Letter*, 45.

91. Roetzel, *Letters of Paul*, 40.

92. White, *Body of the Greek Letter*, 45.

93. Ibid., 93–100.

94. Edwin Hatch, *Essays in Biblical Greek* (Oxford: Clarendon, 1889), 11.

95. Translated into English in 1898 by H. St.J. Thackeray as *Grammar of New Testament Greek* (London: Macmillan, 1898).

96. Friedrich Blass, *Theologische Literaturzeitung* 19 (1894), column 338 (cited by Deissmann in *The Philology of the Greek Bible* [London: Hodder and Stoughton, 1908], 43). As Deissmann points out, however, Blass later "altered his theoretical views on this question."

97. Richard Rothe, *Zur Dogmatik* (Gotha: Perthes, 1863), 238 (cited in Hermann Cremer, *Biblico-Theological Lexicon of New Testament Greek*, trans. William Urwick, 2d ed. [Edinburgh: T. and T. Clark, 1878], iv).

98. Cremer, *Biblico-Theological Lexicon*, iv.

99. Adolph Deissmann, *Bible Studies* (published in German in 1895 as *Bibelstudien*); *Neue Bibelstudien* (Marburg: Elwert, 1897), and *Light from the Ancient East*, trans. Lionel R. M. Strachan (New York: George H. Doran, 1927; published in German in 1908 as *Licht vom Osten*). Also of importance is "The Problem of 'Biblical' Greek," chap. 2 in *Philology of the Greek Bible*.

100. F. F. Bruce, *Are the New Testament Documents Reliable?* 4th ed. (Grand Rapids: Eerdmans, 1954), 98 n.1.

101. A. D. Nock, "The Vocabulary of the New Testament," *JBL* 52 (1933): 138.

102. James H. Moulton and George Milligan, *Vocabulary of the Greek Testament* (London: Hodder and Stoughton, 1930).

103. F. W. Danker, letter to prospective members of the team, 20 Nov. 1987. For an evaluation of the current status of this approach see Colin J. Hemer, "Reflections on the Nature of New Testament Vocabulary," *Tyndale Bulletin* 38 (1987): 65–92. See also G. H. R. Horsley, "Divergent Views on the Nature of the Greek of the Bible," *Biblica* 65 (1984): 393–403.

104. Similar efforts in behalf of certain translations of Scripture were made during various periods in history, such as the imposition of the Latin Vulgate on the Roman Catholic Church, and the attempted imposition of the Bishops' Bible and the King James Version on the Church of England; see *Cambridge History of the Bible*, 3 vols. (Cambridge: Cambridge University Press, 1963–70), 2.27–53, 80–154; 3.141–74, 361–82; Geddes MacGregor, *The Bible in the Making* (Philadelphia: Lippincott, 1959), 126–93; Ira M. Price, *The Ancestry of Our English Bible*, 3d rev. ed., ed. William A. Irwin and Allen P. Wikgren (New York: Harper, 1956), 225–320.

105. Jacob H. Greenlee, *An Introduction to New Testament Textual Criticism* (Grand Rapids: Eerdmans, 1964), 62.

106. Tertullian, though fluent in Greek, wrote all of his extensive corpus in Latin just before A.D. 200 (*Tertulliani Opera*, CCSL 1–2). Of Irenaeus's Greek and Latin texts written during this period (about A.D. 180), it is principally the Latin ones that have survived (Irenaeus, *Libros quinque adversus haereses*, ed. W. W. Harvey, 2 vols. [Ridgewood, N.J.: Gregg, 1965]; W. Sanday and C. H. Turner, eds., *Novum Testamentum Sancti Irenaei Episcopi Lugdunensis*, Old-Latin Biblical Texts 7 [Oxford: Clarendon, 1923]).

107. Gordon D. Fee, "The Textual Criticism of the New Testament," in *The Expositor's Bible Commentary*, ed. Frank E. Gaebelein, 12 vols. (Grand Rapids: Zondervan, 1976–), 1.425.

108. Aland and Aland, *Text of the New Testament*, 14.

109. *Novum Testamentum Graece*, 26th ed., ed. Eberhard Nestle and Kurt Aland (Stuttgart: Deutsche Bibelstiftung, 1979), 43*. The wording of this edition is identical to that of the third edition of the *Greek New Testament* published by the United Bible Societies

in 1975. There are differences, however, in paragraphing, orthography, and punctuation.

110. *Novum Testamentum Graece*, 42*; the previous edition (the 25th) was issued in 1963. Another evidence of ongoing changes is the fact that the first edition of the United Bible Societies was published in 1966, the second in 1968, the third in 1975, the third revised in 1983, and the fourth is in preparation at the time of this writing.

111. Aland and Aland, *Text of the New Testament*, 29.

112. Ibid., 93–95.

113. Ibid., 57.

114. Ibid., 93.

115. The others in this category include $\mathbf{p}^4$, $\mathbf{p}^5$, $\mathbf{p}^{12}$(?), $\mathbf{p}^{16}$, $\mathbf{p}^{18}$, $\mathbf{p}^{20}$, $\mathbf{p}^{28}$, $\mathbf{p}^{47}$, and $\mathbf{p}^{87}$ (ibid., 95).

116. Ibid., 64.

117. This category also includes $\mathbf{p}^{37}$, $\mathbf{p}^{40}$, $\mathbf{p}^{78}$, and possibly $\mathbf{p}^9$ and $\mathbf{p}^{13}$ (ibid., 93).

118. Ibid., 59, 64.

119. Ibid., 59.

120. Ibid., 93.

121. Ibid., 64; other examples include: $\mathbf{p}^1$, $\mathbf{p}^{23}$, $\mathbf{p}^{27}$, $\mathbf{p}^{35}$, $\mathbf{p}^{39}$, $\mathbf{p}^{64}$, $\mathbf{p}^{65}$(?), $\mathbf{p}^{67}$, and $\mathbf{p}^{70}$ (p. 95).

122. Ibid., 95.

123. H.-W. Bartsch, "Ein neuer Textus Receptus für das griechische Neue Testament?" *NTS* 27:5 (1981), 585–92.

124. J. H. Petzer, "The Papyri and New Testament Textual Criticism: Clarity or Confusion?" In J. H. Petzer and P. J. Hartin, eds., *A South African Perspective on the New Testament* (Leiden: E. J. Brill, 1986), 29.

125. Ibid., 22.

126. Eldon J. Epp, "A Meta-analysis of the Past, Present, and Future of New Testament Textual Criticism as Portrayed in the Alands' *Text of the New Testament*" (paper read at the Annual Meeting of the Society of Biblical Literature, Chicago, 21 Nov. 1988).

127. Aland and Aland, *Text of the New Testament*, 30, 34–36, 252ff., etc. They do, with appropriate humility, place the designation in italics!

128. Petzer, "Papyri," 28. He notes that others are also using this designation: T. Baarda, "Auf dem Wege zu einem Standard-Text des Neuen-Testaments?" *GTT* 80 (1980): 83–137; R. L. Omanson, "A Perspective on the Study of the New Testament Text," *BT* 34 (1983): 107–22; Bartsch, "Ein neuer Textus Receptus," 585.

129. Petzer, "Papyri," 28.

130. *The Greek New Testament*, ed. R. V. G. Tasker (Oxford: Oxford University Press, 1964), viii; J. H. Petzer, "Internal Criticism: A Neglected Aspect of New Testament Textual Criticism" (paper

read at the Annual Meeting of the Society of Biblical Literature, Boston, 6 Dec. 1987).

131. A helpful source on how the use of the divine names in the papyri found particularly in Egypt has enhanced our understanding of early Christianity and New Testament interpretation is Colin H. Roberts, *Manuscript, Society, and Belief in Early Christian Egypt* (Oxford: Oxford University Press, 1979).

132. Yadin, *Temple Scroll*, 67.

133. In support of this thesis, plates of the Habakkuk Commentary and Temple Scroll are produced; the former uses Hebrew script for the divine name, the latter Aramaic. Yadin thought this indicated that the sect considered the Temple Scroll canonical (*Temple Scroll*, 67).

134. Harmut Stegemann, "Religionsgeschichtliche Erwägungen zu den Gottesbezeichnungen in den Qumrantexten," in *Qumran: Sa piété, sa théologie et son milieu*, ed. M. Delcor et al., Bibliotheca Ephemeridum Theologicarum Lovaniensium 46 (Paris: Gembloux, 1978), 195–218. These examples are conveniently available in Metzger, *Manuscripts*, 33 n. 59.

135. George Howard, "The Tetragram and the New Testament," *JBL* 96 (March 1977): 63–83; idem, "The Name of God in the New Testament," *BAR* 4 (March 1978): 12ff.

136. Bell and Skeat, *Fragments*, 2.

137. Campbell Bonner, *A Papyrus Codex of the Shepherd of Hermas* (Ann Arbor: University of Michigan Press, 1934), 18.

138. *Bibliotheca Bodmeriana*, ed. Martin, 5.48.

139. Metzger lists fifteen such abbreviations: the words for God, Lord, Jesus, Christ, Son, Spirit, David, Cross, Mother, Father, Israel, Savior, Man, Jerusalem, and Heaven (*Manuscripts*, 36). Other abbreviations were also employed in the early centuries; e.g., abbreviations for Moses, Isaiah, and

Prophet are to be found in Papyrus Egerton 2.

140. Aland and Aland, *Text of the New Testament*, 76.

141. Ludwig Traube, *Nomina Sacra: Versuch einer Geschichte der christlichen Kürzung* (Munich: C. H. Beck, 1907), 3.1.32.

142. Howard, "Tetragram and the New Testament," 76.

143. Ibid., 73 nn. 52, 56; Metzger, *Manuscripts*, 35. In the Temple Scroll the Tetragram is written יהוה rather than יהוה.

144. Jerome *Letter* 25 ("To Marcella"), cited in Metzger, *Manuscripts*, 35 n. 73.

145. Ibid., n. 69.

146. Howard ("Tetragram and the New Testament," 66–67) presents two illustrations: 1QpHab 10:6–7 (equals Hab. 2:13) and 1QpHab 11:10 (equals Hab. 2:16).

147. See the discussion in Bruce M. Metzger, *A Textual Commentary on the Greek New Testament* (New York: United Bible Societies, 1971), 525.

148. Other examples are discussed by Howard, "Tetragram and the New Testament," 76–83.

149. Rudolph Bultmann, *Theology of the New Testament*, 2 vols. (London: SCM, 1952), 1.51 equals *Theologie des Neuen Testaments* (Tübingen: Mohr, 1948), 52.

150. Joseph A. Fitzmyer, "The Aramaic Language and the Study of the New Testament," *JBL* 99 (1980): 13.

151. J. M. R. Cormack, "The Gymnasiarchal Law of Beroea," *Ancient Macedonia* II, Second International Symposium of the Institute of Balkan Studies, 19–24 Aug. 1973 (Thessaloniki: Institute for Balkan Studies, 1977), 139–49.

152. E. L. Sukenik, "The Earliest Records of Christianity," *AJA* 51.4 (Oct. 1947): 351–65.

153. J. Naveh, "The Ossuary Inscriptions from Givat ha-Mivtar," *IEJ* 20.1–2 (1970): 33–38.

154. Ignazio Mancini, *Archaeological Discoveries Relating to the Judaeo-Christians*, PSBF collectio minor 10 (Jerusalem: Franciscan, 1970), 21.

155. Joseph A. Fitzmyer, *To Advance the Gospel: New Testament Studies* (New York: Crossroad, 1981), 115–18.

156. Robert J. Bull, "Caesarea Maritima: The Search for Herod's City," *BAR* 8 (May–June 1982): 38–39.

157. The longer inscription adds the words "and you will be praised by it."

158. Yizhar Hirschfeld, letter to John McRay, 14 Dec. 1987. A brief report mentioning an inscription about resurrection, but not identifying or reproducing it, was made by Hirschfeld and Rivka Birger in "Hirbet ed- Deir: A Byzantine Monastery in the Judaean Desert," *Israel: Land and Nature*, 10 (Spring 1985): 110–14.

159. Hirschfeld and Birger, "Hirbet ed-Deir," 114.

160. Emil G. Kraeling, *The Brooklyn Museum Aramaic Papyri: New Documents of the Fifth Century B.C. from the Jewish Colony at Elephantine* (New York: Arno, 1969); G. R. Driver, *Aramaic Documents of the Fifth Century B.C.* (Oxford: Clarendon, 1954); Matthew Black, *An Aramaic Approach to the Gospels and Acts*, 2d ed. (Oxford: Clarendon, 1954). A list of many new publications of Aramaic documents can be found in Joseph A. Fitzmyer, "The Aramaic Language and the Study of the New Testament," *JBL* 99 (March 1980): 5–7; idem, "The Contribution of Qumran Aramaic to the Study of the New Testament," *NTS* 20 (1973–74): 382–407.

161. Joseph A. Fitzmyer, "Aramaic Language," 13; idem, "New Testament Kyrios and Maranatha and their Aramaic Background," in *To Advance the Gospel*, 218–35.

162. Ibid. Fitzmyer, "Aramaic Language," 15.

163. See Hemer, "Reflections," 75–76; Horsley, *New Documents*.

Tables

Table 1
Archaeological Periods

Persian	539–332 B.C.
Hellenistic	332–63 B.C.
Roman	
Early Roman	63 B.C.–A.D. 70
Middle Roman	60–180
Late Roman	180–325
Byzantine	325–640
Early Arab	640–1099
Cursader	1099–1291

Table 2
Greek and Roman Gods

Greek	Roman	Relationship or Characteristics	Attributes
Aphrodite	Venus	love, beauty	dove
Apollo	Phoebus	sun, music, poetry, art	bow, lyre
Ares	Mars	tumult, war	spear, helmet
Artemis	Diana	moon, chastity, hunting	stag
Athena	Minerva	wisdom	owl, olive
Demeter	Ceres	earth, fecundity	sheaf, sickle
(Hades)	Pluto	underworld	scepter, horses
Hephaestus	Vulcan	fire, industry, blacksmith of gods	hammer, anvil
Hera	Juno	sky queen, marriage, Zeus's wife	peacock
Hermes	Mercury	trade, eloquence, messenger of gods	caduceus, wings
Hestia	Vesta	hearth, domestic virtues, home	eternal life
Poseidon	Neptune	sea, earthquake	trident
Zeus	Jupiter	sky, supreme god, king of gods	scepter, thunder

Table 3
Nabatean Kings of the New Testament Period

Obodas I	95–87 B.C.
Rabbel I	88–86 B.C.
Aretas III Philhellene	86?–62
Obodas II	62–47
Malichus I	47–30
Obodas III	30–9
Aretas IV	9 B.C.–A.D. 40
Malichus II	40–70
Rabbel II	70–106

Table 4
Roman Emperors and Other Rulers

Selected Roman Emperors *

Augustus	27 B.C.–A.D. 14	Caracalla	211–217
Tiberius	14–37	Alexander Severus	222–235
Gaius Calgula	37–41	Gordian III	238–244
Claudius	41–54	Philip the Arab	244–249
Nero	54–68	Decius	249–251
Galba	68–69	Valerianus	253–260
Otho	69	Aurelian	270–275
Vitellius	69	Diocletian	284–305
Vespasian	69–79	Galerius	293–311
Titus	79–81	Constantine	306–337
Domitian	81–96	Constantius II	337–361
Nerva	96–98	Constans	337–350
Trajan	98–117	Julian the Apostate	361–363
Hadrian	117–138	Theodosius I	378–395
Antoninus Pius	138–161	Arcadius	395–408
Marcus Aurelius	161–180	Justinian I	483–565
Commodus	180–192	Heraclius	610–641
Septimus Severus	193–211		

The Procurators

Coponius	ca. A.D. 6–9	Tiberius Alexander	46–48
M. Ambibulus	9–12	Ventidius Cumanus	48–52
Annius Rufus	12–15	Antonius Felix	52–56(?)
Valerius Gratus	15–26	Porcius Festus	56(?)–62
Pontius Pilate	26–36	Albinus	62–64
Marcellus	36–37	Gessius Florus	64–66
Cuspius Fadus	41–46		

The Herodians

Herod the Great	37–4 B.C.	Philip the Tetrarch	4 B.C.–A.D. 34
Archelaus	4 B.C.–A.D. 6	Agrippa I	A.D. 37–44
Herod Antipas	4 B.C.–A.D. 39	Agrippa II	A.D. 50–100(?)

The Hasmoneans

Jonathan	160–143 B.C.	Salome Alesandra	76–67
Simon	143–135	Aristobulus II	67–63
John Hyrcanus	135–104	Hycranus II	63–40
Aristobulus I	104–103	Antigonus	40–37
Alexander Janneus	103–76		

*Some reigns overlap.

Table 5

New Testament Papyri from Oxyrhynchus

Oxyrhynchus	New Testament	Oxyrhynchus	New Testament
2	$\mathbf{p}^1$	1230	$\mathbf{p}^{24}$
208	$\mathbf{p}^5$	1354	$\mathbf{p}^{26}$
402	$\mathbf{p}^9$	1355	$\mathbf{p}^{27}$
657	$\mathbf{p}^{13}$	1596	$\mathbf{p}^{28}$
1008	$\mathbf{p}^{15}$	1597	$\mathbf{p}^{29}$
1009	$\mathbf{p}^{16}$	1598	$\mathbf{p}^{30}$
1078	$\mathbf{p}^{17}$	1780	$\mathbf{p}^{39}$
1079	$\mathbf{p}^{18}$	2157	$\mathbf{p}^{51}$
1170	$\mathbf{p}^{19}$	2383	$\mathbf{p}^{69}$
1171	$\mathbf{p}^{20}$	2384	$\mathbf{p}^{70}$
1227	$\mathbf{p}^{21}$	2385	$\mathbf{p}^{71}$
1228	$\mathbf{p}^{22}$	2683	$\mathbf{p}^{77}$
1229	$\mathbf{p}^{23}$		

Glossary of Technical Terms

abacus. The square slab at the top of a capital.

acropolis. Citadel or highest elevation of a city. Often the setting for the city's most striking temples and other public structures.

acroterium (-a). Ornamental projections from a pediment which serve as bases for sculpted figures.

adyton. Sanctuary of a Syrian temple.

agonothetes. President of the municipal organization sponsoring athletic games.

agora. In Greek cities, an open market or square for public affairs, corresponding to the Roman forum.

ambulatio. Promenade, walkway, or terrace for exercise.

amphitheater. Oval-shaped structure surrounding an arena for gladiatorial spectacles.

andesite. Igneous rock formed by the extrusion of lava flow at the earth's surface. It is extremely dark gray in color.

anta (-ae). Pier or pilaster made by thickening the end of a wall and providing it with a base and capital. On Greek temples the side walls of the inner sanctuary or cella often terminated in Antae to enclose porches. The facade was designed so that columns were set across the front of the porch. The columned porches were then said to be *in antis*.

apodyterium (-a). The changing room of a bathhouse.

apse. A semicircular section projecting from the side of a church or monumental building, often vaulted.

apsidal. Pertaining to an apse.

arch. A distinctly Roman architectural device in which wedge-shaped blocks were arranged in a semicircular covering for an opening so that pressure from a building's weight is exerted laterally instead of downward.

archaeomagnetism. Determination of the age of a ceramic vessel by measuring its magnetic field.

architrave. The horizontal beam which rests on columns or piers and which spans the space between them. It is the lowest or foundation level for the entablature and often decorated with sculpture.

arcosolium. A Hellenistic-to-Byzantine-period burial niche, designed to hold a sarcophagus. It was cut into the stone wall of a cave, with a ledge below and an arch above.

ashlar. Square or rectangular cut stones, uniform in size and shape and laid in horizontal courses.

astragal (roundel). A small convex molding with a rounded section, usually adorned with a carved or painted bead-and-reel.

atrium (-a). The central open area of a traditional Roman private house. It was entered through a vestibulum. As a roofless rectangular area, it was also known as a *compluvium*.

Attic base. Ionic or Corinthian column base consisting of an upper and lower torus which are separated by a scotia or trochilus.

autograph. The actual manuscript written by an individual.

balk (baulk). (1) The vertical face of the wall of soil left around a trench, or square; (2) the 3-foot-wide walkway left around the sides of a square.

balneum, balineum (-a). Public or private bathhouse of ordinary size, as distinct from the great public baths (thermae).

barrel vault. Semicylindrical ceiling based on the principle of the arch. This construction method is ideal for tunnels and is also called a *tunnel vault*.

basalt. Dense, dark gray or black, igneous volcanic rock.

basilica. An elongated rectangular building with a central nave and side aisles. Roman basilicas served as business and legal buildings.

bema. See **rostra**.

bipedalis (-es). Two feet thick, long, or high. See **tegula**.

boss. The untrimmed, projecting face of a stone after its edges or margins have been trimmed square or draft cut.

bouleuterion. Greek senate house, equivalent to a Roman curia.

broadhouse synagogue. Synagogue building with entrance and or bema for a Torah Ark on the long side of the rectangular meeting hall.

bucraneum (-a). Decorative motif in the form of an ox-skull or bull's head, shown frontally.

caementa. The irregular chunks of stone or brick used as aggregate in Roman concrete. See **opus caementicium**.

caldarium (-a). The hot room, or rooms, of a Roman bath.

canon. The authoritative list of books regarded as Scripture; in this text, primarily referring to the New Testament canon.

capital. The topmost section or member of a classical column or pilaster.

carbon 14. See **radiocarbon**.

cardo (-ines). Main street running north-south on a city grid.

caryatid. Sculptured female figure used instead of a column or pilaster to support an entablature.

casemate wall. A double wall with partitions

castellum aquae. The distribution point from which the water delivered by an aqueduct was dispatched to the various points of the town which it served.

cavea. (1) The auditorium of a theater; (2) the seating area of an amphitheater.

cella. The enclosed chamber or sanctuary of a Greek temple.

cenaculum (-i). (1) Dining room. (2) In later Roman architecture the upper story of a building.

ceramic typology. The observation of changing patterns or forms in ancient ceramic pottery, used to establish chronological sequence in dating.

chalcidicum. The porch in front of the narrow end of a basilica.

circus (Gk., **hippodrome**). Long, narrow arena for chariot racing. It was curved at one end and occasionally at both ends.

clerestory. A row of skylight windows which provided light for the nave of a basilica. They were set above the inner colonnades.

codex (**codices**). Ancient manuscript(s) bound in the form of a book rather than a scroll.

colonia. Originally a military colony of Roman or Latin citizens. Later the term was used to denote a privileged form of municipal status.

colonnade. A row of columns carrying an architrave.

columbarium (-a). (1) Pigeoncote or dovecote. (2) A sepulchral chamber with rows of small recesses to hold ash urns.

column. An isolated support or pier for a stone or masonry structure, composed of a base, a shaft, and a capital. It is distinct from antae and pilasters, which are attached to a wall, and from a post, which serves roughly the same function in a wooden building.

comitium. Enclosed place of political assembly.

compluvium. See **atrium**.

composite capital. A style of Roman architecture characterized by capitals that combine Ionic volutes with the bell shape of the Corinthian order.

corbel. A block embedded in a wall and partly projecting to support a weight. A stone bracket.

Corinthian order. A style of Greek architecture characterized by columns with capitals shaped as an inverted bell. Corinthian capitals are ornately decorated with scroll volutes and acanthus leaves. Invented in the late fifth century B.C. as a substitute for the Ionic, the Corinthian order was the most common in imperial Roman use.

cornice. The uppermost major division of classic entablature (above the frieze and architrave). It served the function of eaves, offering protection from rain next to the building.

course. Each horizontal row of bricks or stones.

crepidoma. The stepped platform of a Greek temple.

cruciform. In the form of a cross.

cryptoporticus. Underground vaulted corridor.

cuneus (-i). The wedge-shaped sections of seats in a theater or amphitheater.

curia. See **bouleuterion**.

decastyle. Consisting of ten columns.

decumanus. Main street running east and west on a city grid.

dendrochronology. Determination of a wooden object's age by examining the tree rings within the wood.

dentils. Decorative motif of rectangular blocks in the bed-mold of a cornice, occupying the space of a frieze. The pattern was derived from the appearance of ends of joists carrying a flat roof.

distyle. Consisting of two columns.

distyle in antis. Temple or porch front with two columns between antae.

diazoma. Horizontal walkway separating the rows of seats in a theater.

dipteral. (1) Having two rows of columns; (2) a double peristyle.

dipteros. A temple surrounded by two rows of columns.

domus. House. Dwelling of a well-to-do single family, as distinct from the taberna of the artisan and small tradesman and the apartment houses (insulae) of the middle-classes and the poor.

Doric Order. The oldest (seventh century B.C.) and simplest style of Greek architecture. Characterized by square capitals and a massive, tapered, fluted shaft. It was not widely used in monumental architecture of the Imperial age.

drum. One of the cylindrical sections of a column shaft.

echinus. (1) The convex moulding which supports the abacus of a Doric capital. The molding under an Ionic capital.

ekklesia (Lat., **ecclesia**). Greek word for assembly. It is usually translated "church" in New Testament usage.

engaged column. Column embedded in a wall, similar to a pilaster but rounded instead of squared. Engaged columns allow the strengthening of a wall while carrying forward the overall design.

entablature. In classic architecture the horizontal structure above the colonnade and below the roof or impediment. It is composed of the architrave or beam, the frieze, and the cornice on top. It also refers to these members when they appear at or near the top of a wall or over doors or windows.

ephebion (-eum). A spacious apartment in the Greek gymnasium where the youths between 18 and 20 years of age exercised.

ephoria. The office of a magistrate.

epistyle. An alternative term for architrave.

exedra (-ae). Semicircular or rectangular recess.

exemplar. An archetype from which another manuscript is copied.

facade. The vertical face of a building, usually its front.

fission-track dating. A method of determining age by measuring traces of split uranium-238 atoms present in obsidian and other glassy volcanic minerals.

flagstone. Flat, evenly shaped paving stone.

fluorine analysis. A method used to establish the relative dates of bones by measuring the amount of fluorine they have absorbed.

flutes. The vertical grooves cut into the shaft of a column.

forum (-a). In Roman cities, an open square for public affairs; marketplace. In Greek cities it was known as the agora.

fresco. Painting on plaster while it is still wet.

frieze. The middle member of an entablature, between the cornice and the architrave. Often enriched with relief carving.

frigidarium. The cold room of a Roman bath.

gymnasiarch. Superintendent of athletic training.

gymnasium (-a). A school for physical training which, by the first century A.D., was merging with the Roman bathhouse.

headers. Ashlar rectangular stones positioned in wall construction so that the ends, rather than the sides face outward. Headers and stretchers alternate in each course.

hemicycle. A curved or semicircular struture or arrangement.

herringbone pattern. V-shaped pattern.

heroon (heroum). Shrine dedicated to a deified or semideified dead person.

hetaira. A courtesan in ancient Greece.

hexastyle. Architectural style for a temple or porch front consisting of six columns.

hieron. Temple or sacred enclosure.

hippodrome. See **circus**.

Horizontal cornice. The cornice below the pediment.

horreum (-a). Storage building or granary.

Hymettos marble. Hard bluish marble from Mount Hymettus on the east side of Athens.

hypocaust. Ancient central heating system characterized by an airspace beneath the floor for the circulation of hot air.

impluvium. Shallow pool in the floor of an atrium for catching rain.

in situ. Literally "at the site"—used to designate the precise position in which artifacts and architectural fragments were originally found.

insula. (1) Tenement or apartment house for the middle classes and the poor, as distinct from a domus; (2) a city block.

Ionic order. A slender, ornate column developed in western Asia Minor. It was used throughout Greece from the fifth century B.C. It found limited use in the Roman West but was common in eastern provinces. From its base a shaft with 24 deep fluted rose to a volute-shaped capital. The architrave resting on the capitals was decorated by relief sculpture.

isodomic masonry. Ashlar masonry cut to standard sizes and laid in uniform courses.

ius italicum. A privilege granted in the imperial period under which provincial cities obtained the same rights as those commonly possessed by Italian cities, such as municipal self-government and exemption from poll and land taxes.

kôkh (-îm). Recessed niches for holding sarcophagai or bones in an ancient Roman tomb.

labrum. A basin, especially for bathing.

laconicum (-a). The dry hot-air room of a Roman bath.

lacuna. A gap in the text of a manuscript.

lectum (-î). Bed.

loculus (-i). Coffin or kokh niche for holding bones.

locus (-i). Any three-dimensional feature in a square, such as a layer of earth, a wall, pit, bin, etc.

macellum. Meat market.

magnetometer. A device used in subsurface detection to measure minor variations in the earth's magnetic field.

margin. Narrow, recessed border around the dressed, exposed surface of a stone.

matroneum. Section of a synagogue reserved for women and children.

meta. Turning point for the chariots in a Roman circus.

metope. In Doric architecture a thin, square panel, either plain or sculpted, between triglyphs in a frieze.

miqwaot. Facility for Jewish ritual bathing, either public or in a private home.

monopteros. A circular columned building that is roofed but contains no cella.

mosaic. A picture or inscription made by piecing small cut stones of different shapes and colors.

Munsell color chart. A diagram illustrating the various shades of soil color.

naiskos. Diminutive of naos. A small shrine.

naos. Shrine. In the Greek east the cella of a temple.

narthex. A vestibule leading to the nave of a church; the portico of an ancient church.

natatio. The swimming pool of a public bath.

nave. The central aisle of a building. or the central and side aisles of a cruciform church. The area designated for the laity in worship.

necropolis. Cemetery.

nitrogen dating. A method of determining the relative dates of bones on the basis of the amount of nitrogen and fibrous protein lost since death.

nomen sacrum. A sacred name; specifically, an abbreviation for a sacred name found in ancient manuscripts.

numismatics. The collection, study, and dating of coins.

nympheum (-a). Monumental public fountain-building, usually containing flowers and plants.

obelisk. Upright, four sided pillar (usually monolithic) that tapers toward the top to form a pyramid shape.

obsidian hydration dating. A method of determining age by measuring the thickness of water absorbed on the exposed surfaces of obsidian.

octastyle. Consisting of eight columns.

odeum (Gk., odeion). Small roofed theater, for concerts and lectures.

oecus. The principal living-room of a Greek house.

oikos. A Greek house.

opus caementicium. Roman concrete masonry of undressed stones (caementa) laid in a mortar of lime, sand, and the slow-hardening cement called pozzolana.

opus incertum. The facing of irregularly shaped small blocks used with opus caementicium.

opus quadratum. Ashlar masonry of large squared stones laid in horizontal courses.

opus reticulatum. The successor to opus incertum with a facing consisting of a network of small squared blocks laid in neat diagonal lines.

opus sectile. Paving or wall decoration made of shaped tiles of coloured stone of marble.

orchestra. Originally the circular dancing floor of a Greek theater; the semicircular space in front of the stage (proscaenium) of a Roman theater.

orders. Three distinctive styles of monumental buildings (Doric, Ionic, and Corinthian), most easily identified by the style of supporting columns. Mixed orders were already in widespread use in late Hellenistic times.

orthostat (orthostate). Upright slab of stone; particularly those used in Greek construction to form the lower part of a wall.

overburden. Accumulated debris.

paleoethnobotany. The study of plant life in ancient cultures.

palestra. Porticoed enclosure for sport and exercise; the exercise yard of a Roman bathhouse.

palynology. Pollen analysis.

papyri. Ancient writings on paper made from plants growing in the Nile River.

paraskenion (-a). Wings projecting from one of the two ends of the stage building of a Greek theater.

parchment. Ancient writing paper made from animal skins; vellum.

parousia. Theological term for the final coming of Christ.

parodos. Lateral entrance to the orchestra of a Greek theater.

pediment. The triangular gable at each end of a ridged roof, particularly on a classic temple, consisting of the tympanum, the raking cornice above it, and the horizontal cornice below it.

Pentelic marble. Excellent grade of white marble from Mount Pentelicus on the north side of Athens.

peribolos. An area, such as a temple precinct, enclosed by walls or columns.

peripteral. A structure, such as a temple, with an unbroken colonnade around all four sides.

peripteros. A temple surrounded by a row of columns.

peristasis. The row of columns surrounding a peripteral building.

peristyle. An open courtyard, or garden which is lined with, or surrounded by, porticos.

petrography. The description and systematic classification of rocks.

phase. A subdivision of a stratum.

photogrammetry. The science of measuring archaeological sites for maps or drawings by the use of aerial and surface photography.

photomicrography. Photography for the purpose of producing magnified images of small objects.

piazza. An open square.

pilaster. Vertical pier or support beam, usually rectangular in shape, which protrudes from a wall. Architecturally it is treated as a column.

piscina. Pool (lit. *fish-pool*); the plunge bath of a Roman bathhouse.

platea (Gk., plateia). Wide street or avenue.

plinth. A square block forming the bottom of an Ionic base.

podium. Platform or pedestal below a structure, especially in temples or columnar facades.

politarchs. Roman officials governing such Greek cities as Thessalonica and Beroea.

Pompeiian styles. Decorative schemes identified in the artwork of Pompeii which have been categorized into four sequential period styles: (1) imitation of colored marble on painted plaster or stucco (second century B.C.); (2) creation of the illusion of grand architecture (first century B.C.); (3) embellishment with delicate, irrational ornamentation (Augustan period–late first century B.C. and early first century A.D.); (4) fantasized renderings like those of (2) but more coarse and robust in color and composition (first century A.D.). It is now recognized that there was considerable time overlap in these styles.

portico. Colonnaded porch, particularly one at the front entrance to a building. Larger Greek temples had porticos on all four sides; a stoa.

potassium-argon dating. Determination of the age of an object on the basis of the half-life of the radioactive isotope of potassium as it decays to form argon.

potsherds. Broken pieces of ceramic pottery found in excavations.

pozzolana (Lat., pulvis puteolanus). The volcanic ash material which gave Roman concrete its strength and hydraulic properties.

Praetor (Propraetor). Rulers in a Roman province.

praetorium (praetorion). Official residence of the praetor.

probe trench. A small exploratory trench dug at an archaeological site to determine the extent or nature of a locus.

pronaus (Gk., pronaos). Porch in front of the cella of a temple.

propylaeum (-a; also propylon). One or more gate buildings at the entrance to the temenos or compound surrounding a temple or other monumental building.

proskenion. The stage of a Greek theater, corresponding to the pulpitum of a Roman theater.

prostyle. A temple with a columned porch or portico at one end only.

prytaneum (Gk., prytaneion). The administrative building or town hall of a Greek city.

pseudodipteros. A dipteral temple with the inner row of columns omitted.

pseudoisodomic. Appearing to be isodomic, that is, to be cut to a standard size and laid in uniform courses.

pseudoperipteral. A structure with a portico at one or both ends, but with some of the columns engaged instead of free-standing.

pulpitum. See **proskenion**.

quadrans. Roman coin of small value; the ordinary price of a bath.

quadrifrons (Gk., **tetrapylon**). Monumental arch with two intersecting passageways and four facades.

quadriporticus. Enclosed courtyard with porticos on all four sides.

radiocarbon dating. Radiometric dating method for determining the age of organic objects based on measuring the predictable rate of decay of the radioactive isotope of carbon 14 (C^{14}) in comparison to the rate ordinary isotope of carbon (C^{12}).

raking cornice. Sloping cornice which forms the upper surface of the classic pediment and follows the pitch of the roof. Moldings of this cornice match those of the horizontal cornice.

Res Gestae. A resume of the activities of Augustus Caesar, originally chiseled on bronze tablets and set up before his mausoleum in Rome. They are largely preserved on the walls of temples in Asia Minor, especially the Temple of Rome and Augustus in Ancyra in Asia Minor.

resistivity detector. Instrument used in subsurface detection. It measures slight variations in how objects below the ground level conduct electrical current.

revetment. Superficial facing (e.g. of terracotta or marble) applied to a wall built of some other material.

robbed seats. Theater or amphitheater seats which have been removed so the stone may be used in other projects.

Romanophile. One who loves Roman culture.

rosette. An ornament resembling a rose.

rostra. (also **rostrum** or **bema**) (1) The stage or "tribune" in the Forum at Rome. It was called the "rostra," the nautical designation for the curved prow of a ship, because it was ornamented with the prows of ships captured at Antium in 338 B.C.; (2) any speaker's platform.

roundel. See **astragal**.

row. The lines of stones laid to form the thickness of a wall.

sarcophagus. Stone coffin.

scaena frons. The backdrop of the stage in Roman theaters.

scotia (Gk., **trochilus**). A concave molding used in the Ionian column base. It separated two convex torus moldings.

section. (1) The two-dimensional face of a balk. (2) The balk drawing.

Septuagint. Third century B.C. Greek translation of the Hebrew Bible.

Serapion. A temple of the Egyptian goddess Serapis.

shaft. The body of a column between the base and the capital.

sima. The crowning moulding (originally the gutter) of a cornice.

skene. The wooden stage or scene building of a Greek theater.

skenographia. Paintings of architectural scenes attached to the stage building of a Greek theater.

slip. The clay coating on pottery formed by dipping the pot into clay-water of pea soup consistency, then firing it.

socle. The lower part of a wall. Originally a constructional feature, in Roman times it was commonly purely decorative.

soffit. The relatively small exposed undersurface of an architectural member, especially of an architrave or arch. The word would not be used to apply to a ceiling or vault.

spectrometer. An instrument used in determining the index of refraction of light waves.

spectroscope. Any instrument used to form and examine the light spectra.

spina. The long, narrow dividing wall down the center of a circus.

spira. Section of a column base between the upper torus and the plinth, sometimes having three astragal moldings and two scotia moldings.

square. A 25-foot-square excavation plot.

stade. Greek measure of distance; about 607 feet.

stadium. A course for foot racing.

stele. Upright stone slab used for inscriptions, reliefs, and tombstones.

stoa. A long, covered walk or hall with columns in front; a colonnade or portico.

stratification. The layers of a mound created by successive destructions.

stratigraphy. The process of observing, interpreting, and recording the layers of a mound created by successive destructions.

stratum (**strata**). A layer of soil containing artifacts and debris representing a particular time and culture at a site.

stretchers. Ashlar rectangular stones laid in wall construction so that the sides face outward. Headers and stretchers alternate in each course.

strigil. Iron tool used to scrape perspiration and oil from the body during bathing.

stylobate. The uppermost step of a temple platform forming on which stand the bases for columns.

subsurface interface radar. Instrument used to find tombs and buildings by measuring masses of density beneath the earth's surface.

sudatorium. The dry, hot-air room of a Roman bath.

suspensura. A support for the raised floor of a hypocaust.

taberna (**-ae**). Rectangular chamber opening directly off the street and used as shop, workshop, or habitation for shop keepers and artisans.

tablinum (**tabulinum**). (1) The central room at the far end of an atrium, originally the main bedroom; (2) archives or record room.

tabula ansata. Finished rectangular stone surface, with triangular shaped "ears" on the short sides, for inscriptions.

tabularum. Archive building.

tegula (**-ae**). Flat brick or tile.

419

tegulae bipedales. Tegulae measuring 2 feet square.

tell (tel). An unnatural mound created by the repeated destruction and rebuilding of ancient cities on the same site.

temenos. A sacred enclosure containing one or more temples.

templum. A consecrated place, sanctuary, or asylum.

tepidarium (-a). The warm room of a Roman bath.

terra sigallata. Top quality early Roman pottery. Its distinctive color is yellow with a red slip.

tessara (-ae). Small cube-shaped stones which are pieced together to form mosaics.

tetrapylon. Consisting of four columns.

te trastyle. See **quadrifrons**; **tetrapylon**

thermae. Large public bathing facility.

thermoluminescence dating. A method of determining the age of a ceramic vessel by measuring the amount of light energy emitted when it is reheated.

thermopolium. Shop which sold warm drinks.

tholos. Circular pavilion, often in the form of a monopteros.

top plan. The daily scale plan of a square.

torus. In Ionic and Corinthian columns a smooth, rounded molding which forms the very bottom level of the base. Sometimes there is also an upper torus, a higher convex molding which is separated from the lower torus by a concave molding called the scotia or trochilus.

trace-metal analysis. The study of ancient metal technology, including the procurement of materials and refinement of the final product.

travertine. Silvery grey calcareous building stone quarried near Tivoli.

tribunal. Raised platform for formal official use. See **rostra**.

triclinium (-a). A dining-room. The name arose from the Roman practice of installing three benches together in a "U" shape around a table.

triglyph. A vertical block supporting the cornice in Doric architecture. The Doric frieze alternated metopes and triglyphs. Each block was decorated by two vertical grooves cut into its front.

trireme. A Roman warship having three banks of oars.

trochilus. See **scotia**.

tufa. A concreted stone of volcanic dust; the principal local building stone of Latium and Campania.

tympanum (-on). The triangular wall-face of a pediment beneath the raking cornice.

variant. An alternative reading of a word or words in a document.

velum, velarium. The awning stretched above a forum, a theater, or an amphitheater to protect the public from the sun.

vestibulum. Vestibule, especially at the street entrance to a private house.

villa. (1) A country house, estate. (2) the home of a wealthy citizen.

volutes. Spiral scrolls decorating the angles of an Ionic or Corinthian capital.

vomitorium (-a). Entrance to a theater of amphitheater.

wadi. Arabic term for a watercourse which carries water only during the rainy season.

Wentworth scale. A system of measuring the size of stones and pebbles.

xystus. (1) Covered colonnade in a gymnasium; (2) enclosed garden.

Abbreviations

AASOR   *Annual of the American Schools of Oriental Research*

ADAJ   *Annual of the Department of Antiquities of Jordan*

ADelt   *Archaiologikon Deltion* [Ἀρχαιολογικὸν Δελτίον] (Published by the Archaeological Service of Greece)

ADelt/Ch   *Chronika of the ADelt*

AE   *Archaiologikē Ephēmeris* [Ἀρχαιολογικὴ Ἐφημερίς] (Published by the Archaeological Soceity of Athens)

AE/Ch   *Chronika of the AE*

AJA   *American Journal of Archaeology*

AJPh   *American Journal of Philology*

AM   *Archaia Makedonia* [Ἀρχαῖα Μακεδονία]

Arch   *Archaeologia* (Ἀρχαιολογία, semipopular quarterly in modern Greek, with very brief English summaries)

ARep.   *Archaeological Reports* (published by the Society for the Promotion of Hellenic Studies and the British School at Athens)

AS   *Anatolian Studies* (published by the British Institute of Archaeology at Ankara)

ASR   *Ancient Synagogues Revealed*, ed. Lee Levine, (Jerusalem: Israel Exploration Society, 1981)

Ath. Mitt.   *Mitteilungen des Deutschen Archäologischen Instituts, Athenische Abteilung)*

BA   *Biblical Archaeologist*

BAR   *Biblical Archaeology Review*

BASOR   *Bulletin of the American Schools of Oriental Research*

BCH   *Bulletin de Correspondance Hellenique*

BT   *Bible Translator*

CBQ   *Catholic Biblical Quarterly*

CCSL   *Corpus Christianorum Series Latina*

CIG   *Corpus Inscriptionum Graecarum*, Part II, *Inscriptiones Atticae (1828)*

CIL   *Corpus Inscriptionum latinarum*

CNI   *Christian News from Israel*

CSEL   *Corpus Scriptorum Ecclesiasticorum Latinorum*

EAEHL   *Encyclopedia of Archaeological Excavations in the Holy Land*, ed. Michael Avi-Yonah and Ephraim Stern (Jerusalem: Masada)

EI   *Eretz-Israel (in Hebrew)*

Ergon   Τὸ Ἔργον τῆς ἐν Ἀθήναις Ἀρχαιολογικῆς Ἑταιρεία" (published by the Archaeological Society of Athens)

GCS   *Die griechischen christlichen Schriftsteller der ersten drei Jahrhunderte* (published by the Kirchenväter-Commission der königliche preussischen Akademie der Wissenschaften)

GRBS   *Greek, Roman, and Byzantine Studies* (Duke University)

GTT   *Gereformeerd Theologisch Tijdschrift*

HTR   *Harvard Theological Review*

IDB   *Interpreter's Dictionary of the Bible*

IEJ   *Israel Exploration Journal*

IEph   *Inschriften griechischer Städte aus Kleinasien XI–XVII. Die Inschriften von Ephesos I–VIII*, ed. H. Wankel, et al. (Bonn: Habalt, 1979-84)

IG   *Inscriptiones Graecae: Inscriptiones Attica* (1935). Volumes II and III are now called IG2²

IGR   *Inscriptiones Graecae ad Res Romanas Pertinentes*

LN   *Illustrated London News*

INik   *Inschriften griechischer Städte aus Kleinasien IX–X.2. Katalog der antiken Inschriften des Museums von Iznik (Nikaia) I–II.2*, ed. S. Sahin, 3 vols. (Bonn: Habelt, 1979-82)

Ist. Mitt.   *Mitteilungen des deutschen archäologischen Instituts, Abteilung Istanbul*

JBL   *Journal of Biblical Literature*

JETS   *Journal of the Evangelical Theological Society*

JHS   *Journal of Hellenic Studies*

JNES   *Journal of Near Eastern Studies*

JRS   *Journal of Roman Studies*

LA   *Liber Annuus*

LPPTS   *Library of the Palestine Pilgrim's Text Society*

Mak	*Makedonika* (Μακεδονικά, published by the Society for Macedonian Studies)
MAMA	*Monumenta Asiae Minoris Antiqua*, ed. W. H. Buckler and W. M. Calder, 8 vols. (Manchester: American Society for Archaeological Research in Asia Minor, 1928–62)
NEASB	*Near East Archaeological Society Bulletin*
NIGTC	*New International Greek Testament Commentary*
NPNF	*Select Library of Nicene and Post-Nicene Fathers of the Christian Church*, 2d series, 14 vols. (New York: Scribner, 1890–1900)
NTS	*New Testament Studies*
PAE	*Praktika tēs Archaiologikēs Hetaireias* (Πρακ–τικὰ τῆς ᾿Αρχαιολογικῆς ῾Εταιρείας, published by the Archaeological Society of Athens)
PEQ	*Palestine Exploration Quarterly*
PG	*Patrologia Grecae*, ed. J. P. Migne
PL	*Patrologia Latina*, ed. J. P. Migne
PSBF	*Publications of the Studium Biblicum Franciscanum*

PW	A. Pauly and G. Wissowa, *Realencyclopädie der classischen Altertumswissenschaft*, 2d series
Qad.	*Qadmoniot* (in Hebrew)
Qedem	Monographs of the Institute of Archaeology, Hebrew University of Jerusalem
RB	*Revue Biblique*
RQ	*Restoration Quarterly*
SBL	*Society of Biblical Literature*
SCI	*Scripta Classica Israelica* (Yearbook of the Israel Society for the Promotion of Classical Studies)
SEG	*Supplementum Epigraphicum Graecum*
SIG³	*Sylloge Inscriptionum Graecarum*, ed. W. Dittenberger, 3d ed.
StudClas	*Studii Clasice* (published by the Society of Classical Studies in Romania)
SWP	C. Conder and H. Kitchener, *Survey of Western Palestine, 6 vols. (1872–78)*
TAD	*Turk Arkeoloji Dergisi*
TT	*Theology Today*
ZPE	*Zeitschrift für Papyrologie und Epigraphik*

Index